solutions@syngress.com

With over 1,000,000 copies of our MCSE, MCSD, CompTIA, and Cisco study guides in print, we have come to know many of you personally. By listening, we've learned what you like and dislike about typical computer books. The most requested item has been for a web-based service that keeps you current on the topic of the book and related technologies. In response, we have created solutions@syngress.com, a service that includes the following features:

- A one-year warranty against content obsolescence that occurs as the result of vendor product upgrades. We will provide regular web updates for affected chapters.

- Monthly mailings that respond to customer FAQs and provide detailed explanations of the most difficult topics, written by content experts exclusively for solutions@syngress.com.

- Regularly updated links to sites that our editors have determined offer valuable additional information on key topics.

- Access to "Ask the Author"™ customer query forms that allow readers to post questions to be addressed by our authors and editors.

Once you've purchased this book, browse to

www.syngress.com/solutions.

To register, you will need to have the book handy to verify your purchase.

Thank you for giving us the opportunity to serve you.

D1298188

SYNGRESS®

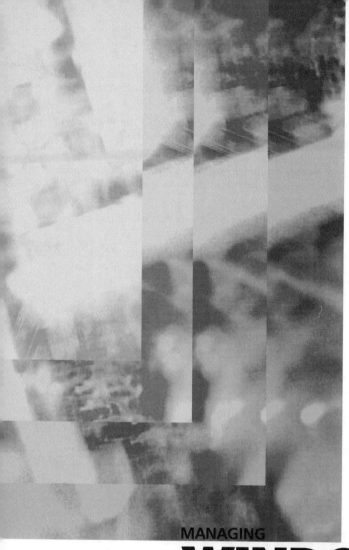

MANAGING
WINDOWS 2000
NETWORK SERVICES

SYNGRESS®

KEY	SERIAL NUMBER
001	9TRP52AXNJ
002	ZRX32G7TC4
003	CLNR528FV7
004	DC597PTRL6
005	K345Q81DBR
006	PF62NLA5MB
007	73DLA5ZX44
008	XRDF79CPW7
009	68BXM941DS
010	SMP4BPSMRN

PUBLISHED BY
Syngress Media, Inc.
800 Hingham Street
Rockland, MA 02370

Managing Windows 2000 Network Services

Printed in the United States of America

1 2 3 4 5 6 7 8 9 0

ISBN: 1-928994-06-7

Copy edit by: Barbara Rummler
Technical edit by: David Smith
Index by: Jennifer R. Coker
Project Editor: Mark A. Listewnik

Proofreading by: James Melkonian
Page Layout and Art by: Emily Eagar,
Vesna Williams, and Reuben Kantor
Co-Publisher: Richard Kristof

Acknowledgments

We would like to acknowledge the following people for their kindness and support in making this book possible.

Richard Kristof, Duncan Anderson, Jennifer Gould, Robert Woodruff, Kevin Murray, Dale Leatherwood, Shelley Everett, Laurie Hedrick, Rhonda Harmon, Lisa Lavallee, and Robert Sanregret of Global Knowledge, for their generous access to the IT industry's best courses, instructors and training facilities.

Ralph Troupe and the team at Rt. 1 Solutions for their invaluable insight into the challenges of designing, deploying and supporting world-class enterprise networks.

Karen Cross, Kim Wylie, Harry Kirchner, John Hays, Bill Richter, Michael Ruggiero, Kevin Votel, Brittin Clark, Sarah Schaffer, Luke Kreinberg, Ellen Lafferty and Sarah MacLachlan of Publishers Group West for sharing their incredible marketing experience and expertise.

Peter Hoenigsberg, Mary Ging, Caroline Hird, Simon Beale, Julia Oldknow, Kelly Burrows, Jonathan Bunkell, Catherine Anderson, Peet Kruger, Pia Rasmussen, Denelise L'Ecluse, Rosanna Ramacciotti, Marek Lewinson, Marc Appels, Paul Chrystal, Femi Otesanya, and Tracey Alcock of Harcourt International for making certain that our vision remains worldwide in scope.

Special thanks to the professionals at Osborne with whom we are proud to publish the best-selling Global Knowledge Certification Press series.

From Global Knowledge

At Global Knowledge we strive to support the multiplicity of learning styles required by our students to achieve success as technical professionals. As the world's largest IT training company, Global Knowledge is uniquely positioned to offer these books. The expertise gained each year from providing instructor-led training to hundreds of thousands of students worldwide has been captured in book form to enhance your learning experience. We hope that the quality of these books demonstrates our commitment to your lifelong learning success. Whether you choose to learn through the written word, computer based training, Web delivery, or instructor-led training, Global Knowledge is committed to providing you with the very best in each of these categories. For those of you who know Global Knowledge, or those of you who have just found us for the first time, our goal is to be your lifelong competency partner.

Thank your for the opportunity to serve you. We look forward to serving your needs again in the future.

Warmest regards,

Duncan Anderson
   President and Chief Executive Officer, Global Knowledge

Contributors

Debra Littlejohn Shinder (MCSE, MCP+I, MCT) is an instructor in the AATP program at Eastfield College, Dallas County Community College District, where she has taught since 1992. She is Webmaster for the cities of Seagoville and Sunnyvale, TX, as well as the family Web site at www.shinder.net. She and her husband, Dr. Thomas W. Shinder, provide consulting and technical support services to Dallas area organizations. She is also the proud mother of daughter, Kristen, who is currently serving in the U.S. Navy in Italy, and son, Kris, who is a high school chess champion. Deb has been a writer for most her life, and has published numerous articles in both technical and non-technical fields. She can be contacted at deb@shinder.net.

Thomas W. Shinder, M.D. (MCSE, MCP+I, MCT) is a technology trainer and consultant in the Dallas-Ft. Worth metroplex. Dr. Shinder has consulted with major firms including Xerox, Lucent Technologies and FINA Oil, assisting in the development and implementation of IP-based communications strategies. Dr. Shinder attended Medical School at the University of Illinois in Chicago, and trained in Neurology at the Oregon Health Sciences Center in Portland, Oregon. His fascination with interneuronal communication ultimately melded with his interest in internetworking and led him to focus on Systems Engineering. Tom works passionately with his beloved wife, Deb Shinder, to design elegant and cost-efficient solutions for small- and medium-sized businesses based on Windows NT/2000 platforms.

Tony Hinkle (MCSE+I, CNE, A+) is a systems consultant in Indianapolis, Indiana specializing in Microsoft Windows NT and BackOffice products. He has been a contributing author to a handful of technical books and has done some technical editing as well. In his spare time you, can find him exercising, cycling, playing frisbie, reading, or playing an addictive computer game.

Mark Larma (MCSE) is a Lead Systems Engineer for Nebraska Health System in Omaha, NE. He has an MCSE in both the 3.51 and 4.0 track, with an emphasis on messaging. He currently has certifications on Exchange, versions 4.0, 5.0, and 5.5. Mark has been using Windows NT since 1993 and Windows 2000 since mid-1998. He can be reached via email at mlarma@nhsnet.org.

Technical Editors

David Smith (MCSE + Internet) is a Windows 2000 Practice Leader who has been working with Windows 2000, Windows NT, SQL Server, Microsoft Exchange and Systems Management Server since their initial releases by Microsoft. An MCSE since 1994, David has worked for a number of organizations, including Bank of Bermuda, Microsoft Consulting Services, and various levels of government deploying NT infrastructure in 14 countries. He is currently working as a consultant for Exocom in Ottawa, Canada where he is helping large government and private industry customers migrate to Windows 2000.

Erik Sojka (MCSE) is a system administrator and trainer currently working for a major software company. He has a BS in Information Science and Technology from Drexel University.

Contents

Preface

It is hard to believe that less than 10 years ago, PC operating systems did not include networking software as a standard component, and certainly did not include TCP/IP. If you wanted to connect your PC to a network, you would load a DOS "TSR" program provided from your network operating system vendor. Once this was all done, you could save files and print using shared resources. This was not always such an easy task since Plug and Play hardware did not exist.

Nowadays, you can set up Windows 2000 Server or Professional as a gateway to the Internet using Internet Connection Sharing in less than a half an hour. From there, you simply configure workstations (either Windows 2000 Professional or Windows 98) to your network hub and, with only the most basic of network knowledge, you have connected several computers to the Internet and each other for file and printer sharing.

Networking Made Easier

Microsoft has worked very hard at making Windows 2000 much easier to use, to install, and to maintain. It is easy to say an operating system is "easier," but how is Windows 2000 "easier" than Windows 9x and Windows NT 4.0 when it comes to networking?

Installation and Plug and Play

The first thing you will notice with Windows 2000 is how much smoother the installation process goes than it does with either

Windows NT or Windows 95/98. This is especially true for those of us who are used to Windows 95 and NT 4.0, where "Plug and Play" was more of a concept than a reality. Windows 2000 does an excellent job of detecting new hardware, such as network cards, and loading the software to support them.

With Windows 2000, you will not spend as much time trying to get your Network Interface Card working properly as required with NT 4.0

Advanced Features Made Easy

Previously, setting up a Windows NT 4.0 Server to operate as a router to the Internet (using your modem) was a very tough challenge. You had two choices: install Routing and RAS Server from the NT 4.0 Option Pack, or install Shareware or other third-party software. In Windows 2000, all you need to do is connect to the Internet using your modem and turn on "Internet Connection Sharing." I admit this is a bit of oversimplification but if you read Chapter 8 you will see how simple this really is — and all without using any additional software.

Networking Made Better

Windows 2000 includes some new networking features that can make your network more secure and less expensive to operate. As you would expect, these new features are Internet-oriented, allowing you to take advantage of the vast resources that are now available. Before Windows 2000, most companies offering VPN solutions over the Internet required a dedicated "router" at each end to encrypt and decrypt your data. With Windows 2000's VPN solutions, you can simply set up your home workstation to encrypt your data as it travels over the Internet to your Windows 2000 Server at the office.

Virtual Private Networks

A couple of years ago, we were happy to connect to the office or the Internet using a 14.4 or a 28.8 modem and download our e-mail messages. Times have changed and our demands for remote networking have changed also. Virtual Private Networks (VPNs) allow you to use your existing Internet connection (be it a modem or a high-speed cable modem) to connect to your office. It is very simple to make such a connection and can save your company a considerable amount of money in long distance charges.

If you are able to get inexpensive high speed Internet access to your house, you can easily access your office network over a VPN.

IPSec

Of course, you know that much of the information traveling on your LAN is in "clear-text," but what can you do to secure critical data without spending a fortune on special network cards? Windows 2000 includes a new feature called IPSec that allows you to require encryption between two computers. While you may not require encryption among all computers, it might be the perfect addition to your new Human Resources server. In Chapter 6, you will see how to use IPSec (and other security measures) in less time than you can explain to your boss what a sniffer is.

Saving Money on Routers and Leased Lines

The router software that is part of Windows 2000 is excellent for small networks and branch offices. If your small network or branch offices already have a Windows 2000 Server, you can easily install Windows routing and save the cost of a dedicated router. To save even more money it is possible to use the Internet instead of a dedicated network as your network connection.

Organization Of This Book

If you are studying for one of the Windows 2000 MCSE exams, it is recommended that you work your way through each chapter of the book. Many of the chapters include walkthroughs that demonstrate of how to use the critical features being taught.

Chapter 10 of this book, "Fast Track," is an excellent review of the whole book and ideal to read the morning before your exams, or even before an interview for a new job.

If you want to perform a certain function, such as "connecting four computers to the Internet" or "set up a DHCP server," then it is recommended that you go directly to the relevant chapter, as outlined below.

Chapter 1: *New Features of Windows 2000* is a summary of "What Is New in Windows 2000." This chapter covers the most important feature of Windows 2000, Active Directory, and then moves on to cover the product line, upgrade strategy and coexistence with Windows 95/98 and NT 4.0.

Chapter 2: *Microsoft TCP/IP* is an overview of what TCP/IP is, and includes discussion of many of the new TCP/IP-related features of Windows 2000.

Chapter 3: *DHCP Server Management* provides details about not only what DHCP is, but also how it is implemented in Windows 2000. DHCP has been included in previous versions of Windows NT, but now it is a much more integrated component. It is critical that you assess current DHCP infrastructure before moving to Windows 2000.

Chapter 4: *Windows 2000 DNS* provides details about what DNS is and how it fits in with Windows 2000. Many organizations run their DNS Servers on UNIX; their Windows NT groups have very little to do with their configuration and support. With the introduction of Dynamic DNS, you will want to look carefully at integrating or replacing your current DNS servers with Windows 2000 DNS.

Chapter 5: *Developing a WINS Strategy* gives an overview of WINS and its upgrades in Windows 2000. You can run a Windows 2000 network without WINS, but it is still required for downlevel clients running Windows 95/98 and NT 4.0. The new features in Windows 2000 WINS are designed to make managing WINS a much less laborious process.

Chapter 6: *Secure TCP/IP Connections* covers the various methods of making a connection to your network securely using TCP/IP. This chapter delves into Secure Sockets Layer (SSL), Certificates, and Virtual Private Networks (VPN). VPNs are exciting because not only can they provide better service than traditional modems, they also offer large cost savings potential.

Chapter 7: *External Network Connections* shows you how to connect your Windows 2000 computer to a variety of external networks using systems such as modems and ISDN.

Chapter 8: *Connecting Small Offices and Home Offices to the Internet* is the chapter you should rush to if you have several computers at home or work and want to share one Internet connection. Using Internet Connection Sharing, you can quickly connect several computers on your LAN to the Internet using one connection such as a modem or DSL.

Chapter 9: *Creating a Routable Network Using Windows 2000* explains how you can join two or more LANS using Windows 2000 as your router. This is an ideal way to save money for small branch offices that may already have a Windows NT 4.0 server for file access. To save even more money, your connection could be a VPN tunnel over the Internet.

Chapter 10: *Administration and Ease of Use* focuses on the improved features for Plug and Play support and Point-to-Point Tunneling Protocol over the internet as well as coverage of automated connectivity with the Connection Manager.

Chapter 11: *Fast Track* is summary of the most important topics from the whole book. It is an excellent review for just before a meeting, interview or a Microsoft exam.

Other Windows 2000 Books By Syngress

In addition to this book, Syngress Media Inc. has already published two other books on Windows 2000 and is publishing two more in the spring of 2000. Please check our Web site at www.syngress.com for the latest announcements.

Windows 2000 Server System Administration Handbook

This book is an excellent resource to start learning about Windows 2000 from an administrator's point of view. It helps you obtain a better understanding of how to manage users and groups using Active Directory and how to use Microsoft Management Console (MMC). The following topics are covered in detail:

- Overview of Windows 2000 Administration
- Administration of Resources
- Managing Data Storage
- Monitoring Your Server
- Administering Active Directory
- Group Policy Objects
- Sharing File Resources by Using Dfs
- Implementing Disaster Protection

Configuring Windows 2000 Server Security

Windows 2000 includes a number of new security features; several of the network-related security features such as IPSec have been covered in this book. This book concentrates on many of the new Windows 2000 security features, including the following:

- Kerberos Server Authentication
- Security Configuration Tool Set
- Encrypting File System for Windows 2000
- Smart Cards
- Microsoft Windows 2000 Public Key Infrastructure

Managing Active Directory for Windows 2000 Server

Active Directory is the single most important change in Windows 2000 Server. As a replacement of Windows NT Domain structure, it is responsible for user authentication, but it is also used in many other areas of managing Windows 2000 including:

- User Information
- Security Policy (such as the user of IPSec)
- Workstation and Server Information — a.k.a. Dynamic DNS
- DHNP Server Authorization
- Shared Network Resources objects
- Printer information such as "color" and "double-sided" is stored in Active Directory for searching
- Remote Access Control

Available in Spring 2000

Syngress is releasing two new books in the spring of 2000 on Windows 2000:

- Windows 2000 Deployment Strategies
- Windows 2000 Configuration Wizards

Audience

This book is intended primarily for network managers and network administrators who are responsible for implementing Windows 2000 environments. This book goes into detail about not only how to use a given feature, but how the feature works. For example, the Chapter 4 on DNS gives you enough information so you can set up Windows 2000 DNS and integrate it into your existing DNS infrastructure.

Chapter 1

What Is New in Windows 2000

Solutions in this chapter:

- What Is New in Windows 2000

- Why You Should Upgrade to Windows 2000

- Windows 2000 Product Line

- How You Would Go About Upgrading

- Sample Upgrade Scenarios

Introduction

This book focuses primarily on the new and improved networking features in Windows 2000. If you are experienced with Windows NT 4.0 networking, then you will find this book an excellent method of learning what is new in Windows 2000 networking and how to design, plan, and implement these features in your organization.

This chapter outlines the major new networking features of Windows 2000, including Active Directory, and covers the upgrade process as well. Other topics covered include a brief discussion of what hasn't changed in Windows 2000, the Windows 2000 product family, and the system requirements for each version.

New Features of Windows 2000

Windows 2000 has dozens of new features, many of which are network-related. Microsoft includes a "partial list" of 36 new features in the Windows 2000 documentation, and many of these are new or improved networking features. Some of the new features, such as support for ATM, touch the network on the lower levels of the OSI model, while others reach into the upper layers to provide management of users, operating systems, applications, and network services. A big portion of this chapter will be devoted to Active Directory, the most substantial new feature of Windows 2000, and the upgrade process. So let's do a quick review of some of the more important new network features before we start into Active Directory territory. Remember, since this book focuses on networking, new features that are not related to networking have been omitted.

ATM

Asynchronous Transfer Mode is a data-link network protocol that possesses capabilities which make Ethernet and Token Ring obsolete. ATM is designed to deliver the multiple types of network traffic, including data, video, and voice, that meet the needs of a multipur-

For Managers

The OSI Model

The OSI model is a seven-layer logical structure that is used to help define network components. At the lowest layer you find the physical infrastructure (the cabling), and the highest layer contains network applications. The middle layers are composed of the protocols that are necessary for applications to communicate over the physical layer. The layers from top to bottom are: Application, Presentation, Session, Transport, Network, Data Link, and Physical. Many network components do not map precisely to one layer, and may overlap two or three layers. The OSI model is used primarily for explaining the role of a component or the relationship between different components in a network. See Chapter 2 for a diagram of the OSI model.

pose network. ATM devices can be configured to give priority to specific types of traffic and networks so quality guarantees can be enforced. ATM packets are a mere 53KB in size, 48KB data and 5KB header, which enables the architecture to enforce bandwidth priorities on a granular basis, enabling video and audio to travel in a more reliable stream rather than in big chunks.

Certificate Services

Several of the services available in the Windows NT 4.0 Option Pack are now included in Windows 2000 Server, including Certificate Services. Certificates are used most commonly to implement Secure Socket Layer communications on Web servers for the transmission of private information—your credit card number, for example. Certificate Services can also be used to make e-mail secure, provide digital signatures, and set up certification authorities that issue and revoke certificates.

DHCP

Dynamic Host Control Protocol (DHCP) is certainly not new, but it made the "What's New" list because it now interfaces with DNS and Active Directory. You'll be reading more about this in the next chapter, but it is included here to make a point—Active Directory integration is very pervasive in Windows 2000 and you'll likely find it in places you don't expect.

Disk Quotas

Many Windows administrators have been waiting for disk quotas to be integrated into the operating system. Until Windows 2000, enforcing disk quotas was only possible by installing a third-party application with that function. Disk quotas will be available in Windows 2000 on NTFS volumes, and will prevent users from using disk space that would exceed their quota, and will log an event when a user exceeds a warning level.

Group Policies

Another technology that Windows NT veterans will recognize is Group Policies, which made the list because this feature is now based on Active Directory. Group Policies in Windows 2000 will facilitate the installation of software, deliver user profiles, and enforce restrictions. Understanding and implementing group policies will be a top priority for networks that want to utilize the desktop management features of Windows 2000.

Indexing Service

It's often difficult for users to find documents on the network. The Indexing Service will help to restore some productivity for workers who spend time browsing in search of information. The Indexing Service, now bundled with Internet Information Server, will index documents of various types and languages so that users can easily find information for which they are looking. The Index Server is used in many Internet and Intranet applications, and ships with indexing filters for HTML and text files, Office 95, 97, and 2000 files, and Internet mail and news. Custom filters can be developed for other file types as well. The Indexing Service, a new feature in Windows 2000, allows you to easily find the occurrence of any string of text in documents. The utility to find files and folders (see Figure 1.1) uses the Indexing Service.

Figure 1.1 The indexing service is used when Search For Files or Folders is selected.

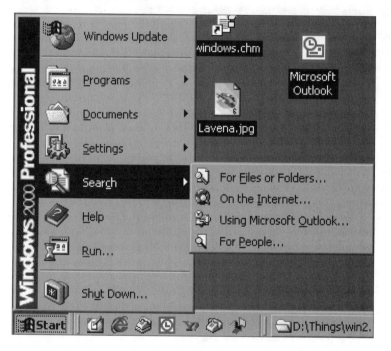

Intellimirror

Intellimirror replaces the Windows Briefcase, expands on roaming profiles, and adds software installation/maintenance and remote OS installation capabilities. Instead of adding files to the Briefcase for offline use, you can now configure any network files or folders for offline availability; they will appear just as if you were connected to the network. In other words, if you set a network drive, L: for example, to be mirrored, when you are offline the L: drive still appears under My Computer, although it has a red X to indicate that it isn't connected. Synchronized folders and files have a double arrow overlay in the lower left corner of the icon, indicating that the contents are available offline (see Figure 1.2).

Figure 1.2 Files and folders synchronized with Intellimirror appear with the blue arrows icon overlay indicating that they are synchronized items.

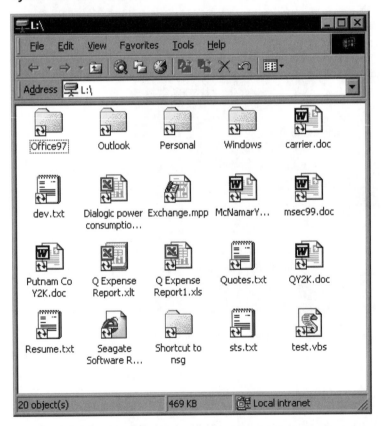

The software installation, user settings management, and remote OS installation functions of Intellimirror utilize Active Directory, Group Policies, Offline Files, Windows Installer, roaming user profiles, and Remote Installation Services to accomplish their tasks.

These features can be very powerful when combined with good network management practices. It should be obvious at this point that Active Directory is everywhere in Windows 2000, and that many Windows NT technologies have been extended and integrated with other components.

Internet Authentication Service

Internet Authentication Service (IAS) brings the ability to manage the authentication, accounting, authorization, and auditing of dial-up or Virtual Private Network (VPN) clients. IAS uses the Remote Authentication Dial-In User Service (RADIUS), which is covered in Chapter 7. Setting up a VPN will allow you to provide secure network connections to users over the Internet, and IAS is a service used to manage these types of connections.

Internet Connection Sharing

Many homes and small offices have a need for sharing an Internet connection, and there are a number of third-party products on the market that have filled this need. Windows 2000 can now share an Internet connection with a small network with a service that provides network address translation (NAT), addressing, and name resolution for other computers on the network. More information about this service is in Chapter 8. Microsoft has also included (NAT) in Windows 2000 Routing and Remote Access Services, which will be used in large networks.

Internet Information Server 5.0

The newest version of Microsoft's Web server is much like IIS 4.0 but has a truckload of new features. These include support for Web Distributed Authoring and Versioning (WebDAV), Web Folders, integrated FrontPage Server Extensions, support for some of the latest Internet standards, FTP Restart, Browser Capabilities Component, Self-Tuning ASP, encoded ASP scripts, process throttling, and the list goes on.

IPSec

Internet Protocol Security is an Internet Engineering Task Force (IETF) standard for encrypting IP traffic. IPSec can be used to secure your network and create a virtual private network (VPN) across the Internet for secure access to mobile or home-based workers.

Kerberos V5

Kerberos V5 is a network authentication protocol that can extend beyond the Windows network to other resources that support the protocol. Kerberos V5 includes mutual and delegated authentication support: mutual authentication, when both client and server provide authentication, and when delegated authentication user credentials are tracked end-to-end. For more information on Kerberos V5, see Chapter 6.

Layer 2 Tunneling Protocol

L2TP, a version of Point-to-Point Tunneling Protocol (PPTP) with enhanced security, is used for tunneling, address assignment, and authentication. PPTP depends on proprietary encryption technologies for implementing secure connections, whereas L2TP does not. It will likely become the standard for secure connections on the Internet since it does not rely on any vendors to provide additional encryption functionality. Windows 2000 IPSec and Routing and Remote Access support the L2TP protocol. See Chapter 6 for more information on Layer 2 Tunneling Protocol.

LDAP

Lightweight Directory Access Protocol is the main access protocol for Active Directory. Microsoft provided LDAP services with Internet Locator Server (ILS), which integrated with Microsoft NetMeeting. SiteServer 3.0 replaced ILS with the Membership Directory, but Windows 2000 Server negates the need for any additional products to provide these services.

Message Queuing

Another Option Pack service now in Windows 2000 is message queuing. Database and e-mail applications can use a message queuing service running on a server to deliver messages and database transactions. This service allows applications to continue running normally even if the delivery destination is temporarily unreachable. When it is once again available, the message queuing service will deliver the payloads. Developers can build applications to utilize message queuing for host-based and UNIX platforms as well.

Network Address Translation

Network Address Translation (NAT) is a feature that is used on many routers to connect networks using private IP address ranges to the Internet. NAT, as its name implies, translates addresses on IP packets so that devices on the Internet return all packets to the computer or router running NAT. The NAT device then forwards the data to the client that initiated the communication. This service also provides a layer of security because a device on the Internet can only initiate communications with a host that has a routable IP address. Computers communicating behind a NAT device are much safer from outside attack than systems that have Internet-routable IP addresses.

Quality of Service

Windows Quality of Service (QoS) allows you to tune how applications are allotted bandwidth. With the increased use of audio and video over networks it is necessary to ensure that enough bandwidth is available for these applications to deliver acceptable performance. QoS-based hardware and protocols, such as ATM, will enable multipurpose networks to meet the needs of voice and video applications in addition to the traditional uses of networks. See Chapter 2 for more information on QoS.

Routing and Remote Access

Routing and Remote Access, affectionately known as RRAS, was introduced for Windows NT 4.0 as an add-on. Remember that cool Steelhead code name? Just like all those Option Pack features, RRAS is now a service bundled with the OS. You can use RRAS to terminate dial-up or VPN clients, and provide IP, IPX, and AppleTalk routing. Windows 2000 can function as a remote access server, a VPN server, a gateway, or a router with the capabilities of RRAS. For more information on Routing and Remote Access, please refer to Chapter 9.

Terminal Services

Windows NT Server 4.0, Terminal Server Edition brought the technology pioneered by Citrix Systems into the Windows family; Microsoft has now integrated it further by making it a feature of Windows 2000 Server. Terminal Services allow thin clients and other devices running the appropriate client software to run terminal sessions on the server. This technology can be used to deploy applications remotely that were designed to run locally, to extend the useful life of client hardware, and, perhaps most importantly, to centralize computing resources to reduce the costs of infrastructure management. Additional licensing is necessary if you plan to use Terminal Services for user-run applications, although a two-user license is included with the operating system license for remote administration purposes.

Virtual Private Networking

Deploying a Virtual Private Network (VPN) enables users to access your network via the Internet with a secure, encrypted connection. Organizations can use L2TP and IPSec to create VPNs and reduce or eliminate the need to maintain dial-in services for remote users, who will simply use a national or global ISP. For more information on VPNs, see Chapter 6.

Active Directory

If you knew only one thing about the changes coming in Windows 2000 before you picked up this book, it would probably be this sea of change called Active Directory. If you plan to work with Windows 2000, then there's no question you will be learning about Active Directory. Because of Active Directory, Windows 2000 is being called the most significant piece of software that Microsoft has ever released. It is a fundamental change that affects the Windows operating system and Windows networking from top to bottom, and provides a structure for other applications to integrate more tightly into your Windows network than ever before.

Active Directory can be explained most simply as an information store and its supporting infrastructure. However, since the Windows domain structure, security, many services, and many applications use Active Directory, administrators who will be deploying, upgrading, and maintaining Windows 2000 can't consider it "just an information store." In the same way the Windows Registry contains information for the local operating system and applications, Active Directory is a repository of information for network objects—users, groups, computers, applications, security information, and more.

Understanding Active Directory terminology is necessary before planning or implementing a Windows 2000 network. If you read the Microsoft documentation without some fundamental understanding of the Active Directory language, you'll find it confusing at best.

Classes, Attributes, and Schema

An object within Active Directory belongs to a *class* of objects, which has any number of *attributes*. For example, a user object belongs to the User *class*, which is composed of *attributes* such as first name, last name, logon name, home directory, etc. A given attribute can belong to any number of classes. One of the most commonly used attributes is the Description attribute, which exists only once in the *schema* but is included in a number of classes.

The definition of the classes and attributes in a domain's Active Directory is called the *schema*, which is stored in the Active Directory. This means that the same tools used to manipulate Active Directory objects can be used to change the schema.

Applications and administrators can extend the schema by adding new classes of objects to Active Directory, as well as new attributes to classes. For example, if your workplace has a location system based on numbered columns in a building, you could add an attribute to user, computer, and printer classes to store this information. This information could be queried by any application to include the custom information on work orders and departmental delivery addresses. Many large organizations currently store much of the same data in a number of places—human resources databases, messaging server directories, IT support databases, production systems, etc. By integrating applications with Active Directory, the data can be kept in just one place.

Changing the schema is not something you'll want to do on a whim. Classes and attributes cannot be deleted, so you certainly don't want to create them without careful planning. They can, however, be deactivated, which is the next best thing to deletion—they can't be used, but they are still there. Large organizations will need to implement Active Directory change procedures to ensure that the integrity and stability of the directory remain intact whenever it is changed.

You have probably begun to realize the significant impact that Active Directory will have on organizations where it is utilized to its full extent. Managing Active Directory to make it usable, healthy, and secure will be an extremely high priority. As you have guessed, the scope of responsibility for administrators will broaden significantly when other applications begin to rely on Active Directory.

Organizational Units and Sites

If you have worked with other types of directory services, you are most likely familiar with *organizational units*. Organizational units are basically containers into which you put directory objects from your domain, such as users, groups, computers, or even other organizational units. Active Directory allows you to delegate administrative authority over organizational units to users and groups. The way you implement this distribution of authority is called the delegation model.

Within Active Directory you will also create *sites*. Sites are based on IP subnets, and a site should be created for each network with LAN speed bandwidth. A site can be composed of more than one subnet, so you will not necessarily create a separate site for each subnet. There is no direct correlation between sites and domains—a site can contain one or more domains, and a domain may contain one or more sites.

Site definitions enable Active Directory to determine how to use network resources most efficiently. Clients will use site information to determine from which domain controller to request services. This assures that the client will not try to authenticate to a domain controller across a WAN link if there is a domain controller in the local site. Site information is also used to control Active Directory replication traffic. Domain controllers in the same site will replicate more frequently than with domain controllers in other sites.

Domains, Trees, and Forests

Just as it was important to know the domain models for designing large Windows NT networks, you will need to know how Windows domains are best structured in Windows 2000 with Active Directory. Previously, with Windows NT, you needed to create a master domain, or multiple master domains, for large distributed Windows NT networks, as well as resource domains. User accounts were maintained on the master domain(s), which had one-way trusts established to each resource domain. This structure enabled a user to log on one domain, the master that held his or her user account, and access resources on both the master domain and the resource domains. In the case of multiple master domains, each resource domain had to create a one-way trust to each master domain since trusts were non-transitive. If complete centralized management was required, trusts had to be created between master domains as well.

Despite what you may have heard, Windows 2000 still has both domains and trusts. However, there are quite a few changes of which you might want to be aware.

Goodbye Domain SAM, Hello Active Directory

First off, once all of your Windows NT 3.x and 4.0 domain controllers are upgraded to Windows 2000, you can then say goodbye to the domain Security Accounts Manager (SAM), which has provided LAN Manager and Windows NT networks with a security infrastructure—until now. The domain SAM maintained domain user and computer accounts, which with Windows 2000 are objects in Active Directory. Windows 2000 can operate in "mixed mode" to maintain functionality with legacy domain controllers, but the full effect of Active Directory cannot be realized until the domain controllers are all Windows 2000 computers.

Domain Names

Windows 2000 domain names are structured according to DNS conventions as part of Microsoft's efforts to move the Windows platform away from NetBIOS. NetBIOS names can still be used to maintain compatibility with legacy Windows platforms; as you upgrade your domain, Windows 2000 will operate in mixed mode by default to support them. Eventually you will be able to disable NetBIOS on your Windows 2000 computers, and DNS will be the only method that computers use to resolve names. So you will configure a ".com" or ".edu" domain when you install a Windows 2000 domain controller, as well as a NetBIOS name. This is illustrated in Figure 1.3.

Trusts

Windows 2000 trusts are much like legacy Windows NT trusts. When a trust is established between domains, a user in one domain can be given permission to access resources in another domain. There are several differences, though, that are very important. For

Figure 1.3 When upgraded to Windows 2000, a Windows NT domain named EUROPE will become windows2000.com, and Active Directory will replace the SAM.

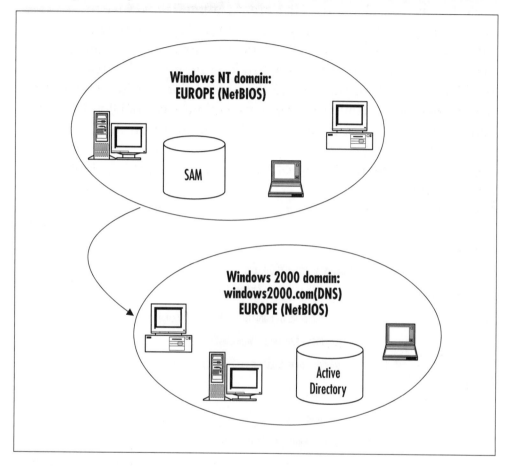

instance, Windows 2000 trusts can be transitive, meaning that when A trusts B and B trusts C, there will be an implied trust between A and C. Certain types of trusts are intransitive, though, and will be discussed later when we are discussing forests.

Trees

A Windows 2000 tree is a collection of trusting domains contained within a contiguous namespace. This simply means that a root domain (e.g., windows2000.com) and all of its subdomains (e.g., asia.windows2000.com, europe.windows2000.com) are considered a tree. The tree can extend as many layers deep as necessary to include every subdomain in the organization.

Whenever you install or upgrade to Windows 2000PDC, you must create a new Windows 2000 domain as a root domain or a subdomain. If you create it as a subdomain, a two-way transitive trust is automatically created to the parent domain (see Figure 1.4). If you upgrade a member server, you will have the opportunity to run DCpromo and make the system a Domain Controller.

Figure 1.4 A tree is a group of trusting Windows 2000 domains in a contiguous namespace.

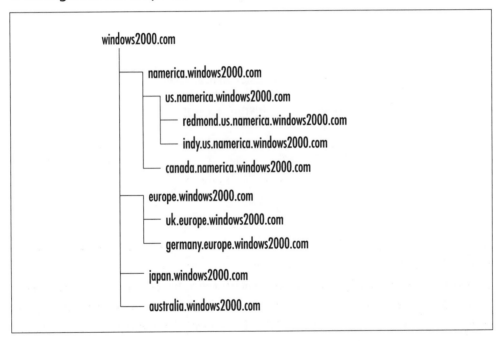

Forests

A Windows 2000 forest is, as you may have surmised, a collection of trees. When you have two separate root domains that need to be included in the same security structure, you create a two-way tran-

Figure 1.5 A forest is a collection of trusting trees that share a common Active Directory schema.

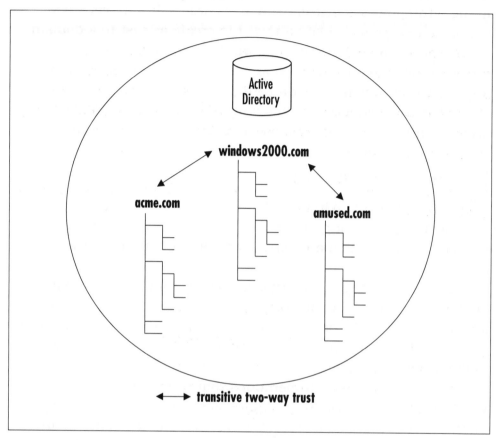

sitive trust between those two root domains, creating a forest. Since all of the trusts in the tree and forest are transitive, the root domains are the only ones that need to create the trust in order for any user in the forest to be able to access any resource in the forest given the proper permissions. The first domain created in the forest is considered the forest's root domain, and trees join the forest by establishing trusts to this root domain (see Figure 1.5).

The key to remembering what makes a tree and what makes a forest is the criteria of contiguous namespace. A tree is composed of trusting domains in a contiguous namespace, and establishing trusts between domains that do not have contiguous namespaces creates a forest. Tree and forest trusts are created automatically during the install process according to the answers you provide to the questions in the setup process regarding any trees or forests you wish to join.

So what happens when you need to create a trust to a domain outside of the forest? Just like in Windows NT, you can create a one-way non-transitive trust to any other domain. Creating a one-way trust each way makes it a two-way trust, but it's still not transitive. The tree and forest architecture should fill the organizational and administrative needs of most networks.

Domain Controllers

Unlike Windows NT, Windows 2000 Servers can be made domain controllers by installing Active Directory. If Active Directory is uninstalled from a domain controller, then it is no longer a domain controller.

Additionally, there is no primary domain controller in a Windows 2000 network. Any domain controller can service a request to create, delete, or change object attributes in the directory. The change is then replicated to all other domain controllers. This is known as a multimaster replication.

However, there are five operations that need to be filled on Windows 2000 networks that require single master functionality. These functions can be moved from one domain controller to another, and each function can exist on a different domain controller.

First, a schema master and a domain-naming master are required for each forest, and only one of each can exist in a given forest. Second, all modifications to the schema require access to the schema master, which then replicates the changes to the other domain controllers. The domain-naming master manages insertion and deletion of domains in the forest.

The remaining three operations require masters on the domain level. For the first, one domain controller for each domain is the relative ID master, which manages the distribution of sequences of relative IDs to the other domain controllers in its domain. The relative

ID is used to create security ID (SID) for a new object. Moving an object from one domain to another requires you to use the relative ID master to complete the process.

The second operation that requires a domain single master is PDC emulation. This is necessary for backward compatibility purposes, and it is also used to verify that a bad password attempt is indeed bad. In a Windows 2000 network, the PDC emulator gets preferential replication of password changes in the domain. When a domain controller receives a logon attempt with an incorrect password, it forwards the logon attempt to the PDC emulator. If the failed logon attempt was due to an unsynchronized recent password change, the PDC emulator will most likely have received the change and will process the logon accordingly.

Lastly, an infrastructure master is required for each Windows 2000 domain. Infrastructure masters update group-to-user references when members of a group are renamed or changed. When a group member that resides in a different domain is renamed or changed, it may appear that the member is no longer in the group for a short period of time. The infrastructure master of the group's domain updates the group to include the new name or location of the member, and then replicates the change just as it would any other change to the directory.

Global Catalogs

A global catalog is a full replica of all the objects in a given domain, and a partial replica of all objects in domains that are in the same forest. Global catalogs are maintained on domain controllers that are configured to host copies of the global catalog. By default, a global catalog is created on the first domain controller in a forest.

The global catalog provides group membership information to domain controllers during the log-on process. Therefore, if a global catalog is not available, log-on will fail since the domain controller cannot determine whether or not the user belongs to a group that has permission to log on. However, by some sleight of hand, Windows 2000 will allow members of the Domain Admins group to log on even if the global catalog is not available.

The global catalog makes it possible to find directory information for any object within the forest. The design goals for the global catalog queries were maximum speed and minimum network traffic. Since every copy of the global catalog contains information about every object in the forest, a query about an object in a different domain can often be satisfied by a catalog in the requestor's domain.

The Data Store

The Active Directory data store is replicated between all domain controllers and contains domain data, configuration data, and schema data. Domain data is comprised of user accounts, computer accounts, etc.—consider this to be where the information kept in the Windows NT SAM resides in Windows 2000.

The topology of the directory is contained in the configuration data. Here we have information about domains, trees, forests, domain controllers, and global catalogs. We defined the directory schema earlier, which is simply the defined classes and attributes.

A most important item to note is that all of the domains in a Windows 2000 forest share a common schema, configuration data, and global catalog. This makes it extremely important to plan changes to trees, forests, and the schema very carefully.

DNS and Active Directory

Active Directory relies on DNS very heavily. In fact, it won't even work without DNS. And it can't just be any old DNS; it has to comply with RFC 2052, *A DNS RR for specifying the location of services*. DNS running on Windows 2000 and Windows NT 4.0 SP4 satisfies this requirement, which is necessary for Active Directory to create Service Location (SRV) records in the DNS database. Older versions of DNS do *not* support these records, so they simply won't work for an Active Directory network. SRV records map services to servers, so Windows 2000 clients will use DNS to find domain controllers instead of WINS queries or network broadcasts. Microsoft also recommends that the DNS server supports dynamic updates (RFC 2136). This is not a requirement for Active Directory to function; nonetheless it is "highly recommended." It should also be noted that non-Microsoft servers are supported as long as they comply with the stated RFCs.

Real World Benefits of Windows 2000

Now that you have a good understanding of what Active Directory is and how it affects the Windows domain structure, you may be asking yourself what it does in practical terms for you and your network. The answer to that question depends on the present and future states of your network. Obviously, if you have a single domain with 20 computers, you are not going to benefit much from Active Directory. Small domains will most likely see more value in new services in Windows 2000, such as Internet connection sharing and RRAS. Additionally, a strong reason for upgrading to Windows 2000 is simply to stay with the technology mainstream. Many server applications will eventually require Windows 2000, and if you want to be able to upgrade to the latest versions, then it makes sense to plan ahead and install Windows 2000 sooner rather than later.

Large corporations deploying Windows 2000 will benefit in a number of ways. Windows NT domains were limited to about 30,000 user accounts per domain, which forced the implementation of master and multiple master domain structures for networks with more than 30,000 users. Active Directory, on the other hand, is designed to handle millions of objects, so some organizations will be able to consolidate their domains into one enterprise-wide domain. Obviously, managing one domain has numerous advantages over managing several domains. Not only will day-to-day support and management be easier, deploying new applications and services will be easier as well. Well-designed trees and forests will also make it easier for users to locate and use resources.

As we discussed earlier, Active Directory is designed so that other applications can integrate with it. The next release of Microsoft's messaging server, Exchange 2000, is tightly integrated with Active Directory and requires Windows 2000 as the operating system. Applications that utilize Active Directory will be easier to manage since they will be using Active Directory infrastructure and objects that already exist. Integration of applications with Active Directory can have a huge impact on a large organization that aggressively pursues the goal of eliminating redundant data across the enterprise.

More information on Active Directory can be obtained from Windows 2000 Help and the Microsoft Web site.

Windows 2000 Help on the Web:

http://windows.microsoft.com/windows2000/en/server/help/

Active Directory Overview:

http://www.microsoft.com/windows/server/Overview/exploring/directory.asp

Active Directory technical papers:

http://www.microsoft.com/windows/server/Technical/directory/default.asp

Active Directory deployment:

http://www.microsoft.com/windows/server/Deploy/directory/default.asp

Installing Active Directory

If you are upgrading or installing a new domain, you must install Active Directory on a server to make it a domain controller. Windows 2000 Server without Active Directory installed can function as a member server in a Windows NT or Windows 2000 domain, or as a standalone computer.

Before embarking on upgrading an existing domain or starting a new domain, there are several planning steps you need to take. Things you will need to plan in detail include:

- The Windows 2000 domain, tree, and forest architecture you will build
- Your DNS namespace
- The delegation model for your domains
- Organizational units
- The location of operations masters
- Site structure

Exercise 1.1 Installing Active Directory

This procedure follows the steps to create a new domain, tree, and forest. If you are adding to an existing Windows 2000 domain, tree, or forest, your experience will vary accordingly. A production environment is not a candidate for your first install—try it on a test server on an isolated test network first.

1. After Windows NT Server is installed, a page will appear after logon prompting you to complete the configuration of the server. This page can also be displayed by selecting Start | Programs | Administrative Tools | Configure Your Server. Click Active Directory and then Start to begin the installation. You can also start Active Directory installation by running dcpromo.exe from the Run dialog or command line.

2. The first dialog presented will give you the option to create a new domain or to add a domain controller to an existing domain. If you are adding a domain controller to an existing domain, you will skip to step 5 after completing this step.

3. Next, if you are creating a new domain, you will need to specify whether you are starting a new tree or creating a child domain in an existing tree, as shown in Figure 1.6.

Figure 1.6 Selecting the option to create a new domain tree or create a child domain in an existing tree.

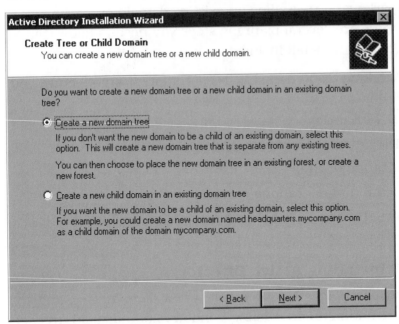

4. If you are creating a new tree, you are next given the option to create a new forest, or join one that already exists.

5. Now you will be prompted for the DNS name of the domain. In order to avoid problems later, it is best to have a DNS name that is registered with the organizations that manage the Internet's DNS namespace. If circumstances prevent you from obtaining one for the domain you are creating, you can just make one up. However, this can be a source of much aggravation later if the domain you are creating needs to join others and someone else has registered the name you used to set up the domain. The DNS name you use does not need to be similar to your Windows NT domain name. (see Figure 1.7)

6. The dialog to enter the NetBIOS domain name, for purposes of backward compatibility, is the next prompt you will see if you are installing Active Directory on a member server. This will be the domain name that Windows NT and Windows 9x clients use.

Figure 1.7 Specifying the DNS name for the Windows 2000 domain.

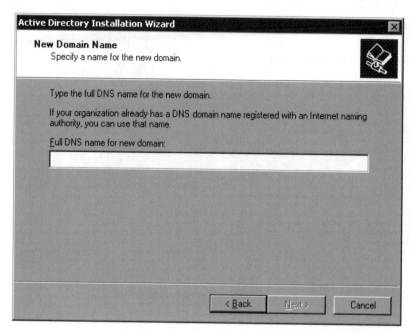

7. Next you will be given the opportunity to set the location of the Active Directory database and log files.

8. The location of the Sysvol folder is the next item. Active Directory creates a Sysvol folder to make the domain's public files available.

9. If the Active Directory setup process does not locate an authoritative DNS server for the domain name you specified, you will be prompted for the option to install DNS on the server.

10. Next is the option to set default permissions for backward compatibility with Windows NT or to use the defaults for pure Windows 2000 domains as shown in Figure 1.8.

11. If you ever need to restore Active Directory on the server, it needs to know what you would like the Administrator password to be. The next dialog will prompt you for the password assigned to the server's Administrator account when the computer is started in Restore Mode. Be sure to keep this password as long as this server is a domain controller!

Figure 1.8 Some applications require Active Directory permission to be set for backward compatibility.

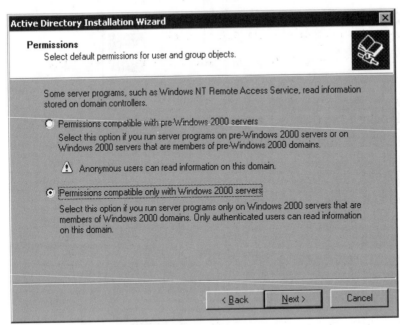

12. The next dialog will list all of the options you have to select. After clicking Next to accept, the system begins installing Active Directory. It keeps you informed of what it is doing during the process, and another dialogue is displayed when it is finished.

13. Reboot the server.

Product Line

Just as Windows NT had various versions of the operating system for different purposes, Windows 2000 comes in the flavor of your choice. Interestingly enough, of the versions that correlate to Windows NT 4.0 versions, one name is new, one is the same, and one uses a name revived from the Windows NT 3.x days.

Additionally, there is at least one other version that is planned for release a few months after the initial release of Windows 2000.

Windows 2000 Professional Edition

Windows 2000 Professional is designed for client PCs and is the upgrade to Windows NT Workstation. Clients running Windows 2000 Professional can participate in Windows NT domains just as Windows NT Workstation, but it also utilizes Active Directory services in a Windows 2000 domain. This version of Windows 2000 is tuned to provide maximum response to user applications, while other versions are configured to service network and server processes with the highest priority.

Of course there are numerous new features, but I will mention one of the most long-awaited—Plug and Play. This will make the tasks of support personnel responsible for installing new hardware much easier.

Windows 2000 Server Standard Edition

Yes, Microsoft has kept the Windows NT nomenclature on the front-line server version. Windows 2000 Server can participate in a Windows NT domain and also be a domain controller in a Windows 2000 network. Server Standard Edition includes Terminal Services and will meet the needs of small networks and many mid-size networks. It supports up to 4 CPUs and 4 GB of physical memory.

Windows 2000 Advanced Server Edition

This version hearkens back to the early days of Windows NT, when the Advanced Server name made its debut. Aside from its nostalgic name, Advanced Server maps to Windows NT Server, Enterprise Edition. Advanced Server provides support for up to 8 CPUs and 64 GB of memory, clustering, TCP/IP Network Load Balancing (NLB), and all the features of Standard Edition for power-hungry networks.

Windows 2000 Datacenter Edition

Speaking of power-hungry, Windows 2000 Datacenter is designed to run on systems with up to 32 CPUs and 64 GB of memory. It has all the features of Advanced Server as well. Systems running Windows 2000 Datacenter can support up to 10,000 simultaneous users for certain uses.

More information on the features of the Windows 2000 Server family can be found at http://www.microsoft.com/windows/server/ Overview/intro/introduce.asp.

What Has Not Changed

So far we've spent our time covering what's new. How about what *isn't* new? How much of your Windows NT knowledge will be useful for working with Windows 2000? Quite a lot, actually. A good understanding of Windows NT is really a necessary foundation for working with Windows 2000.

Core Architecture

Fortunately, the foundation of the operating system has remained intact. All of the things you learned about the Windows NT core architecture are still good to know—how it handles memory, interfaces with hardware, runs programs, etc. Despite the many changes that have been made, it is essentially the same operating system at its lowest layer. A good understanding and working knowledge of Windows NT will be a great foundation for working with Windows 2000.

Although the exact steps to configure many things have changed, you will find yourself swimming in well-known waters once you get started. For instance, the Windows NT Network Neighborhood icon on the desktop is named My Network Places in Windows 2000, and the familiar right-click and select Properties brings up the new Network and Dial-up Connections window, as shown in Figure 1.9.

Figure 1.9 Network and Dial-up Connections, a new window in Windows 2000, allows you to configure, connect, and check status of connections.

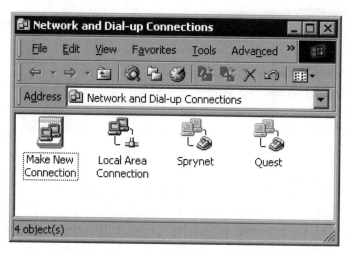

To install and configure clients, protocols, and services, you must view the properties of one of the connections. To install a new network adapter, however, you must use the Add/Remove Hardware Wizard in the Control Panel. Some things have been shuffled around a bit; you may spend a little time figuring out how to complete some operations the first time, but once you find out exactly where to do it, you'll have no problems if you are comfortable doing the same things in Windows NT.

Application Support

Since the core architecture has remained intact, Windows 2000 will still run most applications that run on Windows NT 4.0, including 16-bit programs. However, the more tightly an application was integrated with the Windows NT operating system, the more likely it is to have problems running on Windows 2000. You will certainly want to test every application thoroughly before upgrading any production computers. Even if you don't consider an application to be integrated with the operating system at all, it can still have problems. To create the line drawings in this chapter, I used a very popular business diagram application. Everything worked fine until I tried to save the file in a non-native format, and the conversion routine would cause that program to crash. This application is only one version old, and the newest version has just been released, so you will want to be certain that all software is tested regardless of its release date.

Check with the software publisher for information regarding Windows 2000 compatibility first, so you won't spend time rediscovering problems they've already uncovered, or be unaware of an issue they have discovered that your testing missed. It is often difficult to test every function of an application when you may not even be aware of all of its capabilities. In a large operating system upgrade project, one or more technical staff members are usually assigned to test applications. More often than not, they will be required to test software they have never even heard of before. To say the least, it is difficult for them to thoroughly test software about which they know nothing. Consequently, the tester will usually work with the users to boost the integrity of the test, but as we all know, users don't always know everything about the software they use either.

User Interface

The Graphical User Interface (GUI) that you've come to know and love in Windows NT 4.0 is for the most part intact, but many enhancements have been made. If you are familiar with the changes made by Active Desktop, you will find many of the same things in the Windows 2000 interface. Some of the improvements are merely aesthetic, such as the shadow behind the mouse cursor when running in high color or better video modes. You can also get more use out of your right mouse button, so be sure to try right-clicking for options where you tried with no success in Windows NT 4.0. One really great GUI enhancement is the drop-down list that appears when you are typing paths in Run or Open commands. As you begin typing a path, Windows 2000 moves ahead and displays folders and files that might complete or partially complete what you are typing. It even works when you are typing Universal Naming Convention

(UNC) names! This is a great feature for those of you who shun the mouse to gain the speed of typing. Now you don't have to remember the path exactly—you'll be getting some help.

Client Support

Windows 2000 will still offer file and print services for Windows, Windows NT, and Macintosh clients. An Active Directory client is available on the Windows 2000 Server CD for Windows 95, 98 and NT 4. This will allow Windows computers to take advantage of Active Directory services when possible, and will allow developers to write Active Directory-enabled applications for Windows 9x PCs.

Considerations Before Upgrading

Upgrading a network to Windows 2000 will require the time and effort of a small army on large networks. People who have never been involved in an enterprise-scale OS upgrade or migration effort often don't realize what a monumental task it can be. It really pays off to maintain a standard configuration on desktops and servers for these types of operations. The planning, preparation, and execution are much more difficult when the team responsible for the upgrade has to put in many hours of research and effort to deal with an unknown number of hardware and software configurations.

There are a number of steps that you need to take before you start to install the software. In fact, you may spend more time on planning, testing, and other preparation work than on the actual installation. The needs of your organization may require more items for preparation than are listed here, so be sure to give some thought to things that are unique in your environment and how upgrading to Windows 2000 will affect them.

System Requirements

The relatively simple task of buying or upgrading hardware to provide acceptable performance with the new operating system can be a nightmare. This is why it's always good to put the exact same hardware on every desk. If you know exactly what you have, you don't waste any time doing inventory. And even if you have a current inventory available, you will have to spend a lot of time analyzing it to determine what hardware you need to purchase if the PCs vary. Then you have to get the new hardware installed, which can be a project by itself! If every PC is the same, all you will need is a count. Then you know exactly what to order and it will be much easier to distribute and install since every PC gets the same thing.

So what about the hardware? What does Windows 2000 require? Table 1.1 shows the recommended CPU, RAM, and available disk space for Windows 2000 Professional, Server, and Advanced Server. Notice that Microsoft has been gracious enough to publish not only minimum RAM, but recommended RAM as well. Please make sure you are seated when you check out the available disk requirements.

Table 1.1 Hardware Specifications for Windows 2000 Systems

Version	CPU	RAM	Available Disk
Professional	133 MHz	32MB minimum 64MB recommended	650MB
Server Standard	133 MHz	64MB minimum 128MB recommended	850MB +100MB for each 64MB RAM
Advanced Server	133 MHz	64MB minimum 128MB recommended	850MB +100MB for each 64MB RAM

Upgrade Paths

If you thought you were going to upgrade your Windows 3.1 computers to Windows 2000, you might find this next section a reality check. However, as promised, Windows 2000 Professional can be installed as an upgrade from Windows 95 and Windows 98. Table 1.2 lists the available upgrade paths for Windows 2000 Professional, Server, and Advanced Server. Note that there is no upgrade path for Small Business Server or versions of Windows NT earlier than 3.51. Also, if you have Windows NT 4.0 Enterprise Edition, the only upgrade you can perform is to Windows 2000 Advanced Server. In order to upgrade to Advanced Server from any other version of Windows NT, you must purchase the full product, not the upgrade version.

Table 1.2 Upgrade Paths for the Windows 2000 Family

Upgrade To	From
Professional	Windows 95
	Windows 98
	Windows NT 3.51 Workstation
	Windows NT 4.0 Workstation
	Windows 2000 Professional Beta 3 and later
Server	Windows NT 3.51 Server
	Windows NT 4.0 Server
	Windows NT 4.0 Terminal Server
	Windows 2000 Server Beta 3 and later
Advanced Server	Windows NT 3.51 Server
	Windows NT 4.0 Server
	Windows NT 4.0 Terminal Server
	Windows 2000 Server Beta 3 and later
	Windows NT 4.0 Enterprise Edition
	Windows 2000 Advanced Server Beta 3 and later

Backups

Any system with critical data must be backed up before starting the installation process. Make sure that securing a good backup is part of your detailed upgrade plan. If you plan to start upgrading servers on Saturday morning, be sure that full backups are complete before the scheduled start time.

Most user workstations are not backed up on a daily basis; however, some migration projects will set aside disk space on a server so that workstation hard drives can be copied and put on a backup tape that is retained for a few months. This procedure is more common when a clean OS install is executed instead of an in-place upgrade. Most environments make an effort to train users to use network storage for items they can't afford to lose. However, if a file is lost that is critical, a company executive often won't side with the LAN policies and will hold you responsible even though it wasn't your fault.

Training

People who have been using Windows NT 4.0, Windows 95, and Windows 98 won't need any training to be able to use Windows 2000 and run applications. They will, however, need some training on how to use new features such as Intellimirror's file synchronization. It will be necessary for you to analyze how people use their computers and make sure they get trained on the new features of Windows 2000 that can make them more productive and efficient. For instance, desktop PC users may or may not need to know how to use file synchronization; so, if not, it would be a waste of time for everyone involved for them to learn it. If you need to have mobile and desktop users in the same training session, cover the mobile-specific issues last and allow the desktop users to leave early.

Network administrators, however, will likely need some Windows 2000 training to learn how to design and manage the new domain structure based on Active Directory, how to implement Group Policies and Intellimirror features, how to configure Windows 2000 for VPNs, managing Windows 2000 systems, etc. There is a lot to learn here. The move from Windows NT 4.0 to Windows 2000 is more substantial than from 3.51 to 4.0. It may not appear to be so on the surface, due to the GUI differences between 3.51 and 4.0, but Windows 2000 has a number of new features and capabilities that are going to require some training for Windows network administrators.

In addition to third-party books such as this one, administrators can attend Microsoft Official Curriculum classes. These courses are instructed by Microsoft Certified Trainers (MCT) and utilize course material developed by Microsoft. These classes are very good avenues to bring your IT staff up to speed on Microsoft products.

Domain Design

An important part of moving to Windows 2000 is to redesign your domain structure to best serve your network's needs. Some organizations have been working on this aspect of upgrading to Windows 2000 since the early beta versions were released. In addition to planning and designing, this effort has included restructuring DNS architecture and consolidating existing Windows NT domains.

You may find that your existing domain structure is exactly what you need for the best Windows 2000 environment. This will be most common for networks that have a single or small number of domains, but it is also possible that large companies with master domains will want to retain some or all of their current domain configuration.

Factors Affecting Design

Windows 2000 domains do not limit the number of user accounts that can be supported in a single domain. Large networks may find it best to consolidate the multiple Windows NT domains that were necessary due to the inability of Windows NT to scale beyond 30,000 users per domain. For example, domains that use the multiple master model may design their Windows 2000 model on a single master model if their requirements are to keep account management centralized.

Domain design can be affected by a number of items, and it will be necessary that the team responsible for the new domain design has a thorough technical and managerial understanding of all of these things:

Physical Structure of Network

The physical layout of your network will impact your Windows 2000 domain design less than it did in Windows NT. However, the location and number of domain controllers will be affected by this factor. One thing you want to keep in mind as you design your domain structure is any future plans for the physical network. You will want to make sure that your design will be appropriate six months from implementation, or at least you should know what resources you will need to add or reconfigure.

You can create sites, based on IP subnets, in Active Directory that help manage bandwidth between networks. This feature makes a single domain structure over a wide area network (WAN) more feasible than it was with Windows NT. Windows 2000 will replicate Active Directory information within a site more frequently than between sites. If an account or permissions change is made on a domain controller, other domain controllers in that site will receive the updated information before other domain controllers.

DNS Architecture

Organizations that have a good DNS design in place may want to model their Windows 2000 domain on it. This will require multiple domains, but with Windows 2000, system and account management can be centralized regardless of how many domains exist. It will make sense for many large organizations to follow this approach.

Current Windows NT Domain Structure

If you are pleased with your present Windows NT networking, then you may not see any real need to make significant changes to your domain structure. If your current domain structure is manageable and meets the needs of your environment, it may not be worth the effort involved to reorganize it.

Windows 2000 Upgrade Timeline

If the move to Windows 2000 is being driven by other factors, you may want to put domain design on the back burner. You can upgrade to Windows 2000 and retain your current domain structure, and then undertake a separate project later to restructure your domains. This approach will enable you to get Windows 2000 installed more quickly so that you can utilize its other capabilities sooner.

Flexibility of Windows 2000 Domains

With Windows NT, it is necessary to reinstall to change a computer from a member server to a domain controller, or to change the domain on a domain controller. These two limitations are not imposed in Windows 2000, so you can make more efficient use of resources. For instance, if a domain controller fails, you can install Active Directory on a member server, and after rebooting it will then be a domain controller. This capability means you can reduce the number of domain controllers even further, since you can quickly create a new one in an emergency.

Server Resources

Another consideration that may affect your domain design is the number of servers available to act as domain controllers. Some of your current domain controllers may not meet the system requirements to run Windows 2000, so consolidating domains and reducing the number of domain controllers you need may save the expense of upgrading or replacing some of your older hardware.

When to Restructure

Microsoft suggests that the actual restructuring of the domain will occur for most organizations after the upgrade to Windows 2000 is complete, as a second phase. This will enable the migration teams to focus on the Windows 2000 upgrade and get any associated issues resolved before tackling the task of restructuring the domain. The Microsoft white paper on domain migration does not give a scenario for a parallel upgrade and domain restructure.

One other possibility is to completely start over with a new domain structure. This will be the choice for networks that have an unmanageable Windows NT domain architecture in place and wish to get a clean start, or for a network that does not want to risk introducing instability into their current environment.

A third scenario is to upgrade leaving everything as it is and worry about the domain structure later. Since Windows 2000 domains can be restructured far more easily than Windows NT domains, organizations that want to quickly deploy Windows 2000 for reasons other than the domain architecture can delay the domain design process until after the computers have been upgraded.

Why to Restructure

There are several benefits that can be reaped from building a new domain design around Windows 2000. As you would expect, the larger, more complex networks see the most profits from the new domain capabilities, while smaller networks may not even be able to justify the expense of a domain overhaul.

Scalability

As mentioned earlier, Windows NT had a limitation of about 30,000 user accounts per domain, which forced the largest networks to use multiple master domain designs. Windows 2000 can accommodate millions of accounts, so the domain structure is no longer harnessed by this limitation. This may enable you to implement the domain structure you've really needed all along.

Administration

Using master and multiple master domains, Windows NT networks are able to provide somewhat centralized account management while still

Figure 1.10 Master and resource domains can be consolidated into one Windows 2000 domain with resource domains converted into organization units.

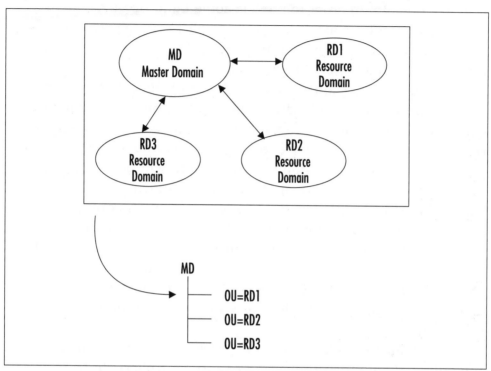

allowing various departments or sites to manage their own resource domains. The Windows 2000 architecture will enable you to have one domain and delegate administrative privileges to organization units, establishing the same security and administrative functions of a resource domain without the overhead of a separate domain. Servers in a given resource domain can be placed into an organizational unit, and the resource domain's administrator can be given administrative privileges to the organizational unit (see Figure 1.10).

Use of Hardware

If you have worked a WAN environment with multiple domains, you are probably aware of the additional hardware that is often necessary to support master and multiple master domain environments. In a master or multiple master domain network, each physical network must have a connection to one of the master domain's domain controllers in order to successfully utilize file servers and printers on the resource domain. In order to provide some fault tolerance, many organizations put a master domain controller on each resource domain network, or at least on the largest ones. This sometimes required a lot of additional hardware.

By eliminating resource domains and placing them in organizational units, you can reduce the overall number of domain controllers significantly. One server that is currently acting as a resource domain controller can become a Windows 2000 domain controller, and no other domain controllers will be necessary at that location. If that server is temporarily unavailable, clients will authenticate across the network to a domain controller somewhere else. Both the network link to other domain controllers and to the local domain controller must be unavailable at the same time for users to lose logon functionality. Even this contingency can be avoided if two of the previous resource domain controllers are made into Windows 2000 domain controllers.

Additionally, even if you retain the resource domain model, you can still eliminate the number of domain controllers. In this instance, you would most likely choose to place one or two domain controllers at the site, but you wouldn't need to have a domain controller for the parent domain since every domain controller in the tree can provide authentication services for any account (see Figure 1.11).

Business Justification

You may have already decided that you want to implement Windows 2000 on your network, but you probably don't control the organization's purse strings. So now you've got to come up with some numbers to prove that it makes financial sense to move to Windows 2000. Sometimes this can be the most difficult aspect of an upgrade project.

Figure 1.11 The number of domain controllers at a site with a resource domain can be reduced by consolidating the master and resource domains.

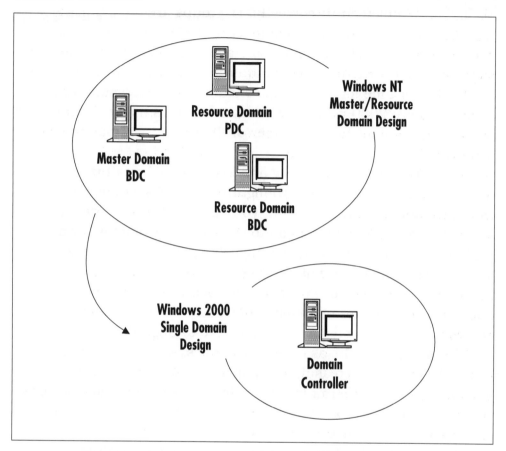

One of the things that might make this task more difficult is that you may not have firm numbers on how much staff time is spent installing software, managing security, administering user accounts, installing operating systems, etc. Even if you can make estimates on how much time Windows 2000 will save for a particular task, you don't have anything against which to compare—except a good estimate.

Windows 2000 has the potential to reduce staff time spent installing, upgrading, and repairing applications and operating systems, upgrading hardware, and managing systems and user accounts. Intellimirror has the potential to reduce software installation and configuration operations significantly if time is spent to design and implement it correctly. IT groups are sometimes not given adequate staff, time, or budget to design and test things appropriately. Shortchanging this stage significantly impacts the costs of supporting the network after implementation, so it is critical to budget time for staff, and consultants if necessary, to design your Windows 2000 network so that it provides maximum returns. Heavy investing in the first stages of the project will pay large dividends later.

Since Windows 2000 is Plug and Play-enabled, staff time spent installing new hardware and configuring new PCs will be reduced. This may not be a big factor, but you may need to squeeze out all possible savings to come out on top. It is not uncommon for a technician to spend several hours configuring hardware on those troublesome PCs that plague almost every network.

As mentioned earlier in the chapter, many networks will be able to reduce the number of domain controllers on their networks. This means that those systems will never have to upgraded or replaced, and they also might be assigned other roles, such as a dedicated print server, thus increasing the available resources on other servers that may be straining under the current workload. Be sure to think about how you can realize savings that may not be readily apparent at first glance.

Organizations that plan to utilize Active Directory to integrate with other applications will consider cost/benefit analysis from a level that will probably eclipse the scope of most network administrator's responsibilities. In a situation such as this, the network administrators and managers will likely be asked to provide the analysis relevant to their departments, and other departments will contribute to the effort also. However, you will probably need to assist the other team members in finding the information they need since you will be considered the Windows 2000 and Active Directory expert.

There is one important item in particular to which it is really impossible to assign a dollar value—security. With all the security enhancements of Windows 2000, you can protect your network and data to a much greater extent. Many companies derive their income solely on innovative products, and the research and development information is critical to them. They certainly need to keep it from falling into a competitor's hands, but they also need to make it available to their organization. Windows 2000 will enable network administrators to implement security policies and technology to ensure the safety of sensitive data regardless of whether it is on a server's disk or transmitted across the network.

Developing an Upgrade Plan

Now that the right people have been convinced that moving to Windows 2000 is the best thing for your network, the project has been approved, the domain design is complete, and new hardware is arriving daily, it's time to decide exactly how you're going to go about installing Windows 2000 on all those systems.

Goals

Other than primary goal of getting the operating systems upgraded, there are four standard goals for a Windows 2000 upgrade project. Keeping these objectives at the forefront during the planning and execution of the upgrade will help ensure a smooth, successful project.

Goal #1: Minimize Disruption

The users don't exist for the network; the network exists for the users. It is most important to keep user downtime to a minimum. Access to files, printers, and applications should be kept at the top of the priority list. Of course, the user's system will be unavailable while it is being upgraded and that is acceptable due to the fact that it is practically unavoidable. However, some organizations may consider uptime to be so critical that workstations must be upgraded after business hours. Another strategy many upgrade projects employ is to upgrade the system while the user is being trained on its new features.

Resources that exist on servers, however, can be moved to temporary locations while a server is being upgraded. Depending on your environment, this may not be a workable solution. You may have to schedule some downtime or upgrade the server after hours. If users have mapped their own network drives, you may not have an easy way of changing the locations to which their drives are mapped. This is why it is always best to map network drives in logon scripts, or to use Windows NT Distributed File System. Putting these things in place now will enable you to upgrade servers during business hours instead of during weekends and evenings.

Goal #2: Minimize Administration

There can be numerous tasks necessary to upgrade a computer, including inventorying the system, ordering and installing hardware, backing up the system, training the user, upgrading the operating system, creating the user accounts, configuring the user environment, installing applications and printers, and testing. You will want to automate as much of it as possible so that the upgrade team can spend their time completing the tasks that cannot be automated. Once again, well-managed networks will benefit most from the ability to easily develop and rely on an automated upgrade process.

Unless you are completely scrapping your Windows NT domain, you will be able to migrate domain user accounts to Active Directory without changing user passwords or permissions. White papers published by Microsoft will give you more detail on how to do this and issues of which you need to be aware.

One of the best ways to minimize administration is to build a check-list of items that must be completed for each system. When a step is skipped it often requires a trip to the desktop, which slows down the technicians who are upgrading the systems. As the project gets started and you find additional items that may cause problems, add them to the checklist. This is a simple tool that will save you many hours.

Goal #3: Maximize Important Features

There are probably a small number of features really driving the upgrade process, and it is important to keep these in mind when developing your upgrade plan. Organize your plan so that intend-ed beneficiaries can utilize these key elements at the earliest possible time.

Goal #4: Don't Compromise Security

The upgrade process should have as little negative impact on securi-ty as possible. As you move to Windows 2000, you will be able to increase the level of security on workstations and servers. An upgrade project is usually a good time to undertake a thorough security analysis so that you can apply new security policies and procedures with the new operating system.

Exercise 1.2 Upgrading a Server

1. Test all applications running on the server to make sure they function properly under Windows 2000. Secure upgraded versions or replacements if necessary.

2. Check the Windows 2000 Hardware Compatibility List at http://www.microsoft.com/hcl/default.asp to ensure that you don't have an upgrade failure due to hardware issues (see Table 1.1).

3. Make sure that you have the appropriate version, upgrade or full product, for the server you are upgrading.

4. Backup the server for recovery in case the upgrade doesn't work.

5. If the server is a member of a cluster, please check the Windows 2000 Help file for more information about upgrading a cluster.

6. Convert file systems to NTFS if you currently have FAT or FAT32 file systems that you wish to be NTFS in Windows 2000.

7. Disable disk mirroring.

8. Disconnect any UPS devices from serial ports. UPS units may cause problems with the hardware detection process.

9. Start the Windows 2000 upgrade by running Setup.exe and select Install Windows 2000 as shown in Figure 1.12.

Figure 1.12 The Windows 2000 setup.exe welcome screen.

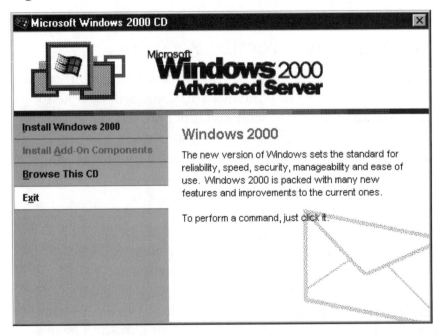

10. The first option is the choice of upgrading or installing a clean operating system. Installing a clean OS will ignore all configurations and installed applications on the current operating system.

11. The end-user license agreement is presented to you next.

12. Setup will warn you of any incompatible items of which it knows in the next prompt (see Figure 1.13).

Figure 1.13 The Windows 2000 Setup incompatible items warning.

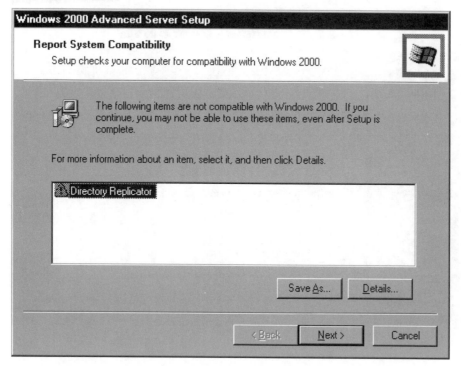

13. Setup will now start copying files, so fill up your coffee cup and come back in a few minutes

14. After file copying, Setup will restart and run the text mode portion of the setup process.

15. Another restart and the GUI mode setup starts, including hardware detection and component setup.

16. If the server you are upgrading is a domain controller, Active Directory setup will start. See Exercise 1-1 for details on Active Directory installation.

17. One final restart and Windows 2000 setup is complete! After you log on, you will see a screen prompting you to configure various Windows 2000 components (see Figure 1.14).

Figure 1.14 After Setup is complete, this dialog appears with selections to configure various components.

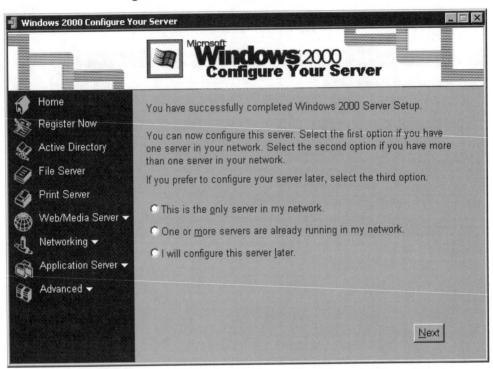

Strategies

There are a few different strategies you can adopt for the actual task of upgrading the systems on your network. Staff levels, user and management requirements, network resources, and other factors will all play a part in determining which approach is best for your network.

Everything at Once

This plan is really only feasible for small networks where everything can be accomplished in a time frame measured by hours or days. Attempting to upgrade both servers and workstations at the same time in a large network could become an unforgettable experience, although you'll want to forget it.

Domain Controllers First

By upgrading domain controllers first, you can get the Windows 2000 domain structure in place and ready to go without other upgrade activities affecting this part of the project. After the domain controllers are upgraded, you can follow with servers and workstations. The workstation upgrade phase is typically the most time-consuming and logistically difficult part of the project. By putting it last, you don't have concerns about overrunning and delaying the server upgrade process.

Please check Exercise 1-3 for more information about upgrading a domain. If you plan to upgrade domain controllers first, there are some important items of which you need to be aware.

Member Servers First

If your Active Directory design team has not completed the domain design but the project time line requires you to get underway immediately, you can upgrade member servers before domain controllers. This will enable you to get some of the grunt work completed without waiting until the design phase is complete. Remember, if the design requires a member server to become a domain controller, you can make the member server a domain controller simply by installing Active Directory. There are really no major disadvantages to this approach except that additional travel is required if the upgrade team must physically visit a remote site to complete the upgrades.

Workstations First

Although we just discussed some reasons opposed to upgrading workstations first, you may find that the priorities of the upgrade project are weighted in favor of the functionality on the desktop. If this is the case, then it may make sense to complete the workstations prior to any server upgrades.

As Required

This approach implies that there really isn't an upgrade project in place, but that Windows 2000 will be installed only when someone can't otherwise fulfill his or her job duties. Despite the undesirability of this method, some networks will be forced to use it due to a lack of resources required to undertake a methodical upgrade project. Nonetheless, planning is still important so that the small steps that are taken can be toward a common goal instead of in different directions. Since Windows 2000 is fully backward-compatible with Windows NT, Windows 2000 servers and workstations can function fully in a mixed environment, so you will basically be operating under the principles of a Windows NT network without the benefits of Active Directory.

Exercise 1.3 Upgrading a Domain

This exercise does not include upgrading member servers, which can be upgraded either before or after the domain controllers.

1. Follow all directions in Exercise 1.2 when upgrading a server.

2. If you have a remote access server, it is advisable to upgrade it sometime before the last domain controller is upgraded. Remote access servers depend on domain controllers for domain user information, and Active Directory security must be weakened in order for a Windows NT 4.0 remote access server to function in a domain where all domain controllers are Windows 2000 computers.

3. Convert any FAT partitions on existing domain controllers to NTFS. According to Microsoft's documentation, you "must use the NTFS file system."

4. See Exercise 1-1 for details on the options that will be presented to you during the installation of Active Directory.

5. Upgrade the primary domain controller first. This is important because your existing Windows NT domain will need a Windows 2000 server to emulate a PDC. Windows 2000 will recognize that you are upgrading a PDC and configure it to emulate a Windows NT PDC.

6. If the Active Directory installation was not able to automatically update the DNS server with SRV records, you will need to append the records saved in %systemroot%\system32\config\netlogon.dns to the appropriate DNS zone file.

7. Upgrade all backup domain controllers. Again, if the DNS entries aren't automatically added you will need to do it manually.

8. When all domain controllers are upgraded, change the domain from mixed mode to native mode. After it is changed to native mode, you cannot install any Windows NT domain controllers.

The Upgrade Team

Upgrading the systems in a network to Windows 2000 will require an organized team effort. A successful project will depend on a group composed of various skills and experience working together to accomplish specific goals. It is extremely important that each member is qualified and willing to do the tasks assigned to him or her. Some members may serve in more than one role, but there are several distinct roles that are necessary for a Windows 2000 upgrade project to be successful.

Project Manager

The role of the project manager is one that requires an individual who has excellent management skills as well as a good understanding of the majority of the technical issues involved in the upgrade process. It is important for the project manager to make good decisions about the technical directions taken in the project, and that cannot be done without a good understanding of networking and Windows. The project manager is responsible for communicating with management regarding the status of the project, assembling and managing the project team, planning the project, assigning roles and responsibilities, and making sure the project is a success. A consultant can fill this role, but it is usually best if it is kept in house. In order to succeed, the project manager often needs to draw on organizational resources that may not be known or available to a consultant.

Domain Designers

Depending on the size of your network and how it is currently managed, you may have one domain designer or a handful. The important thing to consider here is to keep the number of designers as low as possible to eliminate stalemates in the process. It is extremely important that designers thoroughly understand the current domain structure and the Windows 2000 domain model. Any one individual who is not up to speed can cripple a design team by withholding approval due to a lack of understanding. The designers should be considered the "gurus" of Windows NT in your organization.

You also have the option of bringing in consultants to perform this function, but just because they are consultants doesn't guarantee they really know what they're doing! Be sure to adequately research any outside help you get. Writing a performance-based contract is always a good idea. Consultants will need to get a good understanding of your network and its needs, which could take a substantial amount of time.

Software and Hardware Validation

Every piece of software in use on your network must be tested or validated by the publisher to make certain that it will work with Windows 2000. This is a job for someone who has the most knowledge of the software in use on your network. An experienced and reliable desktop support employee is often a good match for testing client software. Network administrators familiar with your server-based software should be assigned the responsibility of testing the backend software.

Use the Hardware Compatibility List to validate hardware. As Windows 2000 matures, newer hardware released by manufacturers may not be included on the list and it will be necessary to test it on your systems. Hopefully you have limited the diversity of systems on your network and eliminated a lot of work already. This role should be staffed by a team member who understands both client and server hardware, and is familiar with the hardware used in your network.

Software Automation

This is a job for someone who loves to make things easy. Almost any software installation can be automated so that no user intervention is required. If you will be doing clean installs on your workstations, you will be installing a lot of applications, and having automated processes will save many man-hours during the upgrade process. Not only does it make each upgrade faster, it makes each upgrade less prone to failure and callbacks due to mistakes made by the installer.

The installation of Windows 2000 can also be automated, which is something you'll definitely want to do if you have a large network. An individual who has experience automating Windows 95 or Windows NT installations will be a shoo-in for this task. An expert in this field will likely be able to automate the entire process so that the operating system and all applications are installed without any user intervention at all. This is a position that can be filled by a consultant with the appropriate skills.

For installation of applications after Windows 2000 is installed, Intellimirror and the Windows Installer can be used for managing application installation. However, depending on the time line, the learning curve for your automation expert may slow the project down; you may not want to use the same person(s) for the upgrade project. Additionally, you may want to make use of Windows 2000's Remote Installation Service if you will be performing clean installs on PCs.

Scheduler

A large upgrade project will need someone to schedule training and upgrades for users. Some of this could be automated with a Web site, but the needs of most organizations usually require a person in this role. An administrative assistant or the systems support organization usually handles this task.

Trainers

If users need training on how to use Windows 2000, you will need to have training available or else beef up your help desk to deal with the aftermath of the upgrade. Many organizations utilize training firms to complete this task, but others choose to keep it internal. The trainer needs to be a pleasant, patient person who knows how users can benefit from the new software and can teach others how to be more productive.

Installers

This is a role that you may not need to fill depending on the amount of software automation you have developed. For instance, if your users are currently using Windows NT 4.0 and you are going to do an upgrade, you can start the upgrade process with a command line delivered via a software distribution system, e-mail, or logon script. If the installation has been automated and you are not installing applications, then there is no need for an installer to visit the client to complete the upgrade. However, if you did not have the time or resources to automate the upgrade, it will probably be necessary to dispatch an installer to the desktop. Some organizations schedule their projects during the summer months so that they can utilize interns for such jobs. Any person who can follow instructions and is comfortable installing software will fill this role well.

Support Services

You will need to staff your support services to handle the post-migration traffic. The amount of additional support you will require depends on the success rate of the upgrade process and the level of training the users received. It will be important to monitor the pilot phase of the project to determine what the impact of the general rollout will be on your support infrastructure.

Summary

Windows 2000 brings a host of new services and capabilities to the Windows computing platform, all of which are designed to make using and managing a Windows network easier, more reliable, more secure, and more scalable. The one new feature that eclipses all others is Active Directory. Active Directory is a database distributed across the forest of Windows 2000 domains that contains information regarding users, computers, and other network devices. Network applications can be interfaced with Active Directory to utilize its directory services, facilitating the ease of application administration.

Despite the great changes that have been introduced in Windows 2000, much will be very familiar to individuals with Windows NT experience. The core of the operating system has not changed significantly, and many services and features of Windows NT are still present, but improved.

Many Windows NT networks will be upgrading to Windows 2000. It is important to understand how Windows NT domains will be included in Windows 2000 forests and trees. Forests and trees are collections of domains that have transitive two-way trusts so that they can either be managed as a whole, or administration can be delegated as needed. Active Directory is the foundation for the domain infrastructure, and all domain configuration and security information is kept in Active Directory.

The other features new in Windows 2000 include enhanced versions of most of the applications that shipped with Windows NT and the Windows NT 4.0 Option Pack. Also, tools for managing and securing data storage, support for network protocols to provide new services and enhance security, system reliability and scalability improvements, desktop management features, and GUI enhancements are new or enhanced. Windows 2000 is a very significant upgrade, and it is important to plan properly for successful deployment so its new features can provide maximum benefits for your network.

FAQs

Q: What are the benefits of upgrading to Windows 2000?

A: Windows 2000 has improved usability, security, scalability, reliability, and manageability over Windows NT 4.0. The specific benefits you will receive will depend on your network and its needs. For instance, a small network will not benefit much from Active Directory, but a large network can experience major improvements because of Active Directory. On the other hand, a small network will be more likely to use network address translation and Internet connection sharing, whereas a large network will probably not use those features of Windows 2000.

Q: Can I still use Windows 95, Windows 98, and Windows NT clients if I upgrade my servers to Windows 2000?

A: Yes! Windows 95, Windows 98, and Windows NT 4 clients can access the Windows 2000 servers without any configuration changes if you allow the domain to run in mixed mode. When you begin upgrading your domain controllers Windows 2000 will operate in mixed mode so that the Windows 2000 and Windows NT domain controllers can interoperate. When all domain controllers have been upgraded, you have the option to change the domain to native mode.

Q: How can I find out if my applications will work with Windows 2000?

A: There are three possible ways of finding out if an application will function properly with Windows 2000. The first way is to check with the software publisher to see if they have any information regarding Windows 2000 compatibility. Secondly, you can use Microsoft's Directory of Windows 2000 Applications at http://www.microsoft.com/windows2000/ready/. The last option is to test it yourself, which can be more time-consuming making it the choice of last resort.

Q: How can I automate the installation of Windows 2000?

A: Microsoft has a white paper entitled "Deployment Guide: Automating the Windows 2000 Upgrade" available at http://www.microsoft.com/windows/professional/deploy/autom ating.asp. The process is very similar to automating Windows 9x and Windows NT installations, so it will be rather easy for someone who is experienced with automating the installation of those operating systems. With a little ingenuity, you can install applications, patches, and other software as part of the same process. If the target computer has no operating system on it, you can use Windows 2000 Remote Installation Services to boot from the server or a floppy disk and start the installation from the network.

Q: Do I really need to learn this Active Directory jargon to work with Windows 2000?

A: As long as you are working with very small networks, you might be able to get by without learning much about Active Directory.

People who intend to implement or manage Windows 2000 in enterprise environments have no choice—they must learn about Active Directory. Understanding Active Directory and how Windows 2000 components utilize it will be the key to successful Windows 2000 implementation.

Q: What is the best way to migrate a network to Windows 2000?

A: The needs of your network, the requirements of management, and the resources you have available to work on the upgrade project will determine which way is best. What is best for a small or medium-sized network may be impossible for a large network, so there is no standard answer to this question. The upgrade project should begin with a thorough analysis of all factors affecting the upgrade process. The planning based on that analysis should make it clear which way will work best for your organization.

Chapter 2

Microsoft TCP/IP 2000

Solutions in this chapter:

- Review of TCP/IP

- Summary of Important New Features of TCP/IP

- QoS

- IPSec

- DDNS

- DHCP

- Performance Enhancements

Introduction

Many of the networking changes in Windows 2000 revolve around TCP/IP and its suite of protocols, including DNS, DHCP, and IPSec. This chapter covers the basics of the new features in Windows 2000 TCP/IP and includes some background on TCP/IP, while later chapters cover DHCP, DNS, WINS, TCP/IP security and routing in detail. Windows 2000 has added and enhanced a number of protocols and services related to TCP/IP; it is important to know about them so that you can get the maximum benefits that Windows 2000 has to offer for your network.

In an ideal world, your network would run only the TCP/IP protocol and Windows 2000 workstations and servers. However, even Microsoft knows that it will be years before even a small percentage of large corporations achieve this goal. Windows 2000 still includes excellent support for Windows 95/98 workstations, Novell 3.x and 4.x servers, and even Macintosh workstations. Gaining a better understanding of the TCP/IP protocol suite is one of the best ways you can sharpen your skills for Windows 2000 and improve your current network.

TCP/IP—A Quick Overview

TCP/IP is a network protocol based on a 32-bit addressing scheme that enables networks to be interconnected with routers. The bits in each address are separated into four sets of eight bits, called octets, which are separated by periods. With the binary number system, 8 bits can be used to signify any number from 0 to 255, so the lowest IP address is 0.0.0.0, while the highest is 255.255.255.255.

Each device, or host, on the network must have a unique IP address to communicate on the network. In order to communicate on the Internet, IP addresses must be registered with the organizations that manage the Internet so that routing can be configured correctly. There are two commonly used network addresses that are reserved for private use and are not routed on the Internet. These two network addresses, 10.0.0.0 and 192.168.0.0, are used on networks that are not connected to the Internet or connected by using network address translation (NAT) or proxy hosts. NAT and proxy hosts have two IP addresses, one on the private network and one registered on the Internet, and handle all communications between the private network and the Internet.

IP Address Classes and Subnets

As you can see in Table 2.1, IP addresses are divided into classes, or blocks of addresses, for administrative purposes, and each class is assigned a default subnet mask. The class structure is simply a way to manage the address space. The United States government, for example, might have one or two Class A address spaces instead of thousands of Class C addresses.

Table 2.1 IP addresses are divided into three usable classes

Class	Range	Default Mask	Addresses per Network
A	0.0.0.0-126.255.255.255	255.0.0.0	16 million +
B	128.0.0.0-191.255.255.255	255.255.0.0	64,000 +
C	192.0.0.0-223.255.255.255	255.255.255.0	254
D	224.0.0.0-239.255.255.255	Reserved for multicast addressing	
E	240.0.0.0-254.255.255.255	Reserved for experimental use	

The subnet mask determines which bits in the IP address are the network address and which bits are the host addresses. If the subnet mask is 255.0.0.0, then the first 8 bits (which equal 255) are the network portion of the address, and the three remaining octets are available for host addresses. As you may know, it is not realistically possible to have 16 million hosts on a single network, or even 64,000, without segmenting the network with routers. Accordingly, networks with Class A and B addresses do not typically use the default mask and their subnet masks usually end up much like those of Class C networks.

When a mask other than the default is used, subnets are created which enable the address space to be split up to create several smaller networks and route traffic between them. A Class B network address could be split into 255 networks by using a 255.255.255.0 subnet mask. The actual number of usable networks, however, is a bit less than 255, due to network and broadcast addresses.

Subnets and Routing

Routers are devices that connect networks together and relay traffic between networks according to routing tables that are configured in their memory. IP networks that are not on the same logical network must have a router to connect them in order for their hosts to communicate. The IP address and the subnet mask determine the logical network, or subnet.

In the example given in Figure 2.1, Network A has a network address of 192.168.10.0 since its subnet mask is 255.255.255.0.

This is a simple case since the first three octets of the subnet mask are 255, meaning that all bits in the first three octets of each IP address are the network address, and the last octet is the host address. The network address of Network B is 192.168.11.0, and since it is on a different subnet (logical network), it must be connected to Network A by a router. In this specific example, the physical networks are parallel with the subnets. However, if both subnets were on the same physical network, either a router would be necessary for hosts on the 192.168.10.0 network to communicate with the hosts on the 192.168.11.0 network, or the routing tables on each computer could be configured

Simple routers may have the capability to only connect two networks, while enterprise-class routers can connect several. Multiple routes can be configured between networks, providing TCP/IP with a measure of fault tolerance. Computers can act as routers if they

Figure 2.1 IP subnets are connected by routers.

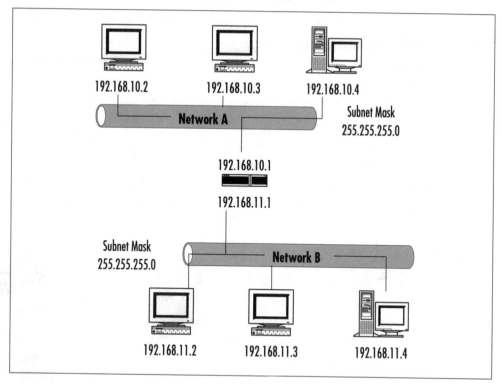

are running software to perform that function. Routers are, in fact, computers designed for the specific purpose of routing network traffic. Windows NT and 2000 computers can also perform the functions of routers with the Routing and Remote Access Service.

Features of TCP/IP

TCP/IP has quickly become the default network transport protocol since the Internet exploded onto the public scene in the mid-1990s. Prior to that time, its use was limited mostly to universities, U.S. government entities, and a few other large organizations. Rather than discuss the entire history of TCP/IP, which you can find in numerous other books, let's look at why TCP/IP has become so popular.

Open Architecture

TCP/IP is not a proprietary protocol, and all information about it is publicly available. Accordingly, there are no business limitations to make it difficult for hardware or software manufacturers to implement TCP/IP on a given computing platform or networking device. Specifications for TCP/IP and related protocols are published in Request for Comments (RFC) papers that are submitted by individuals or groups that wish to implement a change to an existing TCP/IP protocol or introduce a new one. RFCs are approved or rejected by the Internet Engineering Steering Group (IESG), which is influenced by the opinions of the Internet Engineering Task Force (IETF).

Systems Interoperability

Many of the network protocols that have been developed were created by software or hardware companies to enable their systems to talk with systems of the same type. The proprietary nature of these protocols meant that it was often difficult or impossible to get disparate systems to communicate over a network. The short-term solution, when possible, was usually to install multiple protocols on the servers or clients. In fact, Microsoft provided NWLink, an IPX/SPX-compatible protocol, so that Windows NT could more easily be assimilated into a NetWare environment.

Software and hardware manufacturers wanted to sell their wares to the government and universities who were using the Internet, so they began to include TCP/IP interoperability in their products. As this trend continued and as the Internet grew in popularity, network administrators began to remove the old proprietary protocols and use TCP/IP, since it was available on just about every platform and it met the needs of their networks. It is now possible to run just one transport protocol, TCP/IP, and communicate with just about any type of system. Macintosh, NetWare, Windows, UNIX, IBM mainframes, and Hewlett-Packard print servers all have one thing in common—the ability to communicate via TCP/IP (see Figure 2.2).

Figure 2.2 TCP/IP is supported on almost every major business systems computing platform, enabling interoperability between disparate systems.

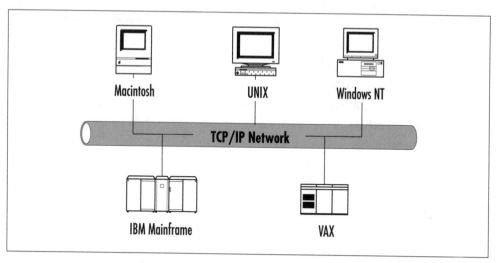

Scalability

So how did TCP/IP become the standard for the Internet? Back in 1983, the authorities of ARPANET, the predecessor of the Internet, began to require the use of the TCP and IP protocols for all ARPANET network traffic. These protocols were selected because they could scale well on the massive network that was destined to span the globe. Only the most visionary individuals of the early 1980s foresaw what we often take for granted today. When you stop to give it some thought, it is amazing that mankind has linked almost every computer on the globe in just a few years. Most of the proprietary network protocols were not designed to be able to connect millions of computers across the most distant places, so TCP/IP was selected because of its ability to do what none of the others could accomplish. Scalability combined with the non-proprietary and high availability features made TCP/IP a wise choice for ARPANET.

High Availability

One of the design goals for TCP/IP was that it be able to continue working even though part of the network might not be functioning. TCP/IP networks can be configured so that there are multiple routes to a given destination, and each route can be given an associated cost.

Accordingly, if the lowest cost route fails, the network will send traffic by a different route. This enables you to have a backup link that will automatically be used if your primary link fails. High availability is a requirement for most networks today, and TCP/IP was designed to meet this need.

The TCP/IP Protocol Suite

As TCP/IP has matured, it has grown to include a number of protocols and applications. Actually, TCP/IP is somewhat of a misnomer because TCP isn't used by every application that communicates on an IP network. As you can see in Figure 2.3, applications use either TCP or UDP to communicate with IP on the Internet layer.

The other Internet layer protocols listed, ARP, ICMP, and IGMP, are used by IP to resolve IP addresses to hardware addresses and route packets. In the transport layer, UDP is a connectionless protocol and does not guarantee delivery of network packets, so most applications do not use it. Therefore, since most applications use TCP, the name TCP/IP has become common usage for referring to IP networks and components. The other common applications and protocols that are usually present in a TCP/IP implementation are included with TCP and IP to comprise what is known as the TCP/IP protocol suite.

The TCP/IP protocol suite grows as new application protocols are introduced to provide functionality for IP networks. Hypertext Transport Protocol (HTTP) was created to transfer Hypertext Markup Language (HTML) documents over TCP/IP, and was introduced in 1991. It quickly became considered part of the TCP/IP protocol suite due to its quick proliferation throughout the Internet community. It is amazing to think that prior to 1991, the World Wide Web did not even

Figure 2.3 The TCP/IP model and protocols compared to the OSI model.

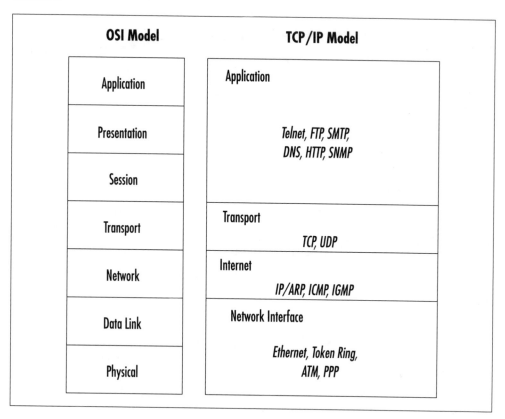

exist, and in less than a decade it has become one of the most popular means of communication. Tim Berners-Lee, the creator of HTTP, can be credited with an invention that has created new jobs and helped many find new jobs, increased competition among businesses, provided entertainment and education for millions, and has even helped some people find their lifetime loves. The impact of this one "very simple" and "restricted," as Tim describes it, protocol has been nothing less than a worldwide revolution, and it is still in its infancy.

Using some of the other TCP/IP applications has been made easier by HTTP technology. Web browser applications have grown to include the ability to use File Transfer Protocol (FTP), which is much simpler than using a command line FTP interface. Web browsers can also be used to access e-mail, which negates the need for users to configure an e-mail client. Although you are probably not intimidated by command line interfaces and SMTP configurations, many users would not even use these applications if it weren't for the World Wide Web.

When viewed from a different perspective, the TCP/IP protocol suite becomes something far greater than just a bunch of protocols. This technology, combined with others, has changed the lives of many people in many different ways. Discussing the details of the technology may be less appealing than considering the way it changes the world. This is a technical book, however, so we must.

TCP/IP Core Protocols

There are a handful of protocols in the TCP/IP suite that are the bread and butter of the system. The protocols handle all of the network connections and routing so that applications are simply concerned with handing data to the protocols at the transport layer.

TCP

Transmission Control Protocol works on the transport layer of the TCP/IP model, providing connection-based communication with other IP hosts. When an application passes data to the transport layer, it is often too much data to transmit in one packet, so TCP segments the data on the sending side and reassembles it at the receiving end according to sequence information that is packaged with the packet. TCP sends acknowledgements to confirm successful delivery, and analyzes each packet according to checksum information to ensure data integrity.

TCP uses a system of ports for applications used to manage communication. Applications bind to a specific TCP port, and any inbound traffic delivered to that port will be picked up by the application. This enables multiple applications on one host to use TCP at the same time, and also standardizes the way a client can connect to a given service on a server. For instance, Telnet's standard TCP port is 23, so Telnet clients try to establish connections on port 23 by default. Port assignments are flexible—that is, you can change the port a client or server uses for a specific application, if needed.

Although Web servers typically use port 80 for HTTP communication, the Web server application can be bound to a different port. Clients will need to know which port to use in order to establish a connection since it differs from the default (see Table 2.2).

Table 2.2 TCP ports used by common applications

TCP Port	Application
20	FTP (data)
21	FTP (control)
23	Telnet
53	DNS zone transfers
80	HTTP
139	NetBIOS session

UDP

UDP also provides transport-layer services, and is a connectionless protocol that does not guarantee delivery or sequencing of data. UDP can be used when data transfer is not critical or when the application is designed to ensure correct delivery of data. Since it does not acknowledge successful transfer, it is faster and uses less network bandwidth than TCP (see Table 2.3).

Table 2.3 UDP ports used by common applications

UDP Port	Application
53	DNS name queries
69	Trivial File Transfer Protocol
137	NetBIOS name service
138	NetBIOS datagram service
161	SNMP
520	Routing Information Protocol

IP

When TCP and UDP are ready to send data, they pass it to IP for delivery to the destination. IP is connectionless and unreliable, which is why TCP is designed to establish connections and guarantee delivery. IP does not try to detect or recover from lost, out-of-sequence, delayed or duplicated packets. IP protocol handles host-to-host communication, but IP addresses for individual hosts are required. IP is the foundation of the TCP/IP protocol suite.

ARP

Address Resolution Protocol is used resolve IP addresses to Media Access Control (MAC) addresses. MAC addresses are unique IDs that are assigned to network interface devices. ARP uses a broadcast to send out a query that contains the IP address of the destination host, which replies with its MAC address. When the request is answered, both the sender and the receiver record the IP and MAC addresses of the other host in their ARP table cache to eliminate the need for an ARP broadcast for every communication.

ICMP

Internet Control Message Protocol is used by network devices to report errors, control, and status information. ICMP messages are delivered by IP, which means that they are not guaranteed to reach their destinations. ICMP is used by routers to indicate that they cannot process datagrams at the current rate of transmission, or to redirect the sending host to use a different route considered better. Most of you are probably familiar with the "ping" utility, which sends ICMP echo requests and displays the replies it receives.

IGMP

Internet Group Management Protocol is used to exchange and update information regarding multicast group membership. Multicasting is a system of sending data to one address that is received and processed by multiple hosts. Multicast addresses are in the Class D IP address range, and addresses are assigned to specific applications. For instance, the 224.0.0.9 address is used by RIP (Routing Information Protocol), version 2 to send routing information to all RIP routers on a network (see Table 2.4).

Table 2.4 TCP/IP core protocols and their related RFCs

Protocol	RFCs
ARP	826
IP	791
ICMP	792
IGMP	1112, 2236
UDP	768
TCP	793

TCP/IP Applications

TCP/IP would be rather useless without applications to run on top of it. In addition to the applications that are considered part of the TCP/IP protocol suite, there are numerous proprietary applications that work on IP networks as well. For instance, NetBIOS over TCP/IP (NBT) is Microsoft's implementation of NetBIOS for IP. Since NBT is typically only found on Windows computers, it is not considered part of the TCP/IP protocol suite. We will discuss the most popular of the TCP/IP applications and protocols, but an entire book could be filled if each application and protocol were covered in great detail.

SMTP

Simple Mail Transport Protocol is a protocol designed for applications to deliver mail messages. SMTP defines the specific commands and language that mail servers use to communicate, and the format of the messages to be delivered. For instance, if an SMTP server receives a mail message that is addressed to a user that is not defined according to SMTP standards, it will reply to the sender and include information regarding the failed delivery.

The SMTP protocol is not used for delivering messages from a server to a user. Once an SMTP server has received the message, a mail application, such as a POP3 server, will provide an interface for user applications to retrieve their mail messages. However, many e-mail clients will typically send mail by using SMTP to communicate with an SMTP server.

Coupled with Multipurpose Internet Multimedia Extensions (MIME), SMTP can be used to deliver file attachments with e-mail messages. This capability greatly increases the functionality of e-mail and has helped make it one of the most popular applications on the Internet.

Most modern server-based messaging software packages include an SMTP server that enables them to send and receive Internet mail. The mail server recognizes SMTP addresses, converts messages destined for other SMTP hosts to comply with SMTP standards, connects to the recipient's mail server or a mail gateway, and sends the mail using SMTP. Messages that are not sent to or received from the Internet are typically kept in the native format and delivered by a proprietary delivery system.

HTTP

The standout of Internet protocols, Hypertext Transport Protocol, is used by Web browsers and Web servers to conduct their business with each other. HTTP defines how browsers request files and how servers respond. HTTP works in conjunction with Hypertext Markup Language (HTML), graphics, audio, video, and other files to deliver the killer application of the 1990s, the World Wide Web.

FTP

File Transfer Protocol is a client/server application designed to enable files to be copied between hosts regardless of the operating systems. FTP can also be used to perform other file operations, such as deletion, and it can be used from a command line interface or a GUI application. The latest versions of popular Web browsers include complete FTP functionality, although many shareware FTP clients offer interfaces that are faster and more powerful.

FTP provides an authentication scheme so that unauthorized users cannot access the FTP server. It supports transferring files in either text of binary mode, and can be used to both upload and download files.

Telnet

Telnet is an application that enables a remote command line session to be run on a server. By using Telnet to log onto a server, you can run programs and perform other operations on the server. It's the next best thing to being there! Telnet is available on most operating systems, and Windows 2000 installs a Telnet server service by default, although it is not started by default. The Windows NT Server 4.0 Resource Kit included a Telnet server service as well, and Telnet clients are installed on Windows computers as part of the TCP/IP protocol.

DNS

DNS is used by most of the other applications in the TCP/IP protocol suite to resolve host names to IP addresses. A Web browser, for example, cannot establish a connection to a Web server unless it knows the IP address of the server. DNS is used to resolve host names, such as www.microsoft.com, to IP addresses.

DNS is a distributed database that is essential for TCP/IP to be used on a massive Internet-size scale. It provides a function that hides the complexity of IP addresses from users, and makes things such as e-mail and the World Wide Web much easier to use.

The best way to describe how DNS actually works is to use an example:

1. An application on a client computer (wks001.windows2000.com) requests a hostname resolution from the local DNS server (ldn001.windows2000.com). DNS servers maintain databases of hostnames and IP addresses for domains over which they are authoritative.

2. If the requested hostname belongs to a domain for which the local DNS server is authoritative (windows2000.com), then it resolves the hostname to an IP address and replies to the client with the results.

3. If the requested hostname belongs to a domain that is not maintained by the local DNS server, it queries a root domain server on the Internet for the IP address of the DNS server that is authoritative for the requested domain.

4. The root domain server replies with the requested information, and the local DNS server then queries the DNS server that is authoritative for the requested host for resolution.

5. The authoritative DNS server replies, and the local DNS server then responds to the client request.

SNMP

Simple Network Management Protocol was designed to provide an open systems management infrastructure for hardware and software vendors to implement on their systems. This enables management software to be developed that can query a host for information defined in its Management Information Base (MIB). Devices running SNMP software can also send *traps*, which are simply messages formatted according to SNMP specifications, to a management server when a certain event occurs. For example, a server may generate a trap when the temperature inside the cabinet exceeds a specified limit. The trap is sent to an SNMP management console that can handle the message according to configured rules, which can send an e-mail, page, or network message to inform administrators of the condition. Since SNMP is an open platform, SNMP management console software can interoperate with systems of various types as long as they comply with SNMP standards.

Windows TCP/IP

Most of you have worked with TCP/IP on Windows NT and other Windows operating systems, so you are familiar with how to use it and TCP/IP-related services such as WINS and DHCP. Microsoft has implemented support for most cross-platform TCP/IP applications such as DNS, SMTP, and FTP, as well as adding one additional service, Windows Internet Naming Service (WINS), which is unique to Windows networks. This section discusses some of the more important Windows TCP/IP services, while the enhancements and new protocols related to TCP/IP are covered in the next.

NBT and WINS

If you have worked with Windows in a network environment, you know that Windows computers have a computer name that is used to identify each system on the network. This computer name is the NetBIOS (Network Basic Input/Output System) name. NetBIOS, which has a history extending back to 1983, is a networking API that was used by Windows computers to register and locate resources. NetBIOS names are 15 characters in length and the namespace is flat, two factors which are severely limiting on a large network.

NBT is simply the application of NetBIOS working on a TCP/IP network, and WINS was introduced to help manage the NetBIOS names on a TCP/IP network. WINS is a service that registers IP addresses with the associated computer names and services in a database, and responds to queries from clients who need to resolve a NetBIOS name to an IP address. Without WINS, Windows clients had to rely on broadcasts or static files located on each PC to resolve names to IP addresses. WINS was introduced to reduce the amount of broadcast traffic on a Windows network and provide the ability to resolve addresses for computers throughout a WAN.

Windows 2000 has taken a big step away from NetBIOS, NBT, and WINS, but they are still there to support existing Windows networks. When your network is completely upgraded to Windows 2000, you will be able remove WINS and disable NBT, since Windows 2000 is designed to use the DNS naming architecture instead of NetBIOS. However, Windows 2000 introduces several new features for WINS that improve its manageability. Chapter 5 discusses WINS and the enhancements you will find in Windows 2000.

DHCP

Windows has long included support for Dynamic Host Configuration Protocol on both the server and client sides, and Windows 2000 is no exception. DHCP enables clients to request the lease of an IP address from a server. The server will also automatically configure other TCP/IP items such as gateways, DNS servers, and WINS servers. Windows 2000 includes several new DHCP features including performance monitor counters, integration with DNS, disabling NBT on clients, and detection and shutdown of unauthorized DHCP servers on Windows 2000 servers by integration with Active Directory. Chapter 3 contains detailed information regarding DHCP, configuring, and managing the DHCP service on Windows 2000 computers.

DNS

Windows NT 4.0 ships with a DNS server service, and organizations that have deployed it will benefit when they upgrade to Windows 2000. As has already been mentioned, Active Directory relies on DNS in order to function and some older versions of DNS servers will not be suitable. In order for Active Directory to work, it must register SRV records with the DNS service, which are not supported on some DNS servers. A detailed discussion of Windows 2000 DNS is presented in Chapter 4.

SNMP

An SNMP service ships with Windows NT and Windows 2000, enabling them to participate as SNMP managed hosts. Third-party software is also available so that a Windows NT or 2000 computer can be an SNMP network management station. DHCP, IIS, and other Windows services install custom MIBs so that they can be managed via SNMP. Microsoft Systems Management Server includes a client service, Event to Trap Translator, which converts Windows NT and 2000 events into SNMP traps. This feature is a very useful tool to integrate Windows NT and 2000 into large organizations that depend on an SNMP management infrastructure.

TCP/IP Printing

TCP/IP printing services enable Windows NT and Windows 2000 computers to act as both client and server in TCP/IP printing environment. TCP/IP printing is commonly used by HP JetDirect print servers and by UNIX and mainframe computers.

Windows 2000 extends TCP/IP printing to the HTTP protocol, enabling users to print documents to print queues on their intranet's servers. It also allows users to print documents to queues on servers across the Internet. This is accomplished through an Internet Information Server ISAPI extension DLL running on the Windows 2000 server that houses the queue.

Exercise 2.1 Configuring TCP/IP on Windows 2000

1. First, you will need to open the Network and Dial-up Connections window. This is accomplished by right-clicking the "My Network Places" icon on the desktop and selecting "Properties."

2. The Network and Dial-up Connections windows displays an icon for each network adapter and dial-up connection you have configured, as well as an icon to create a new connection. Right-click on the adapter you want to configure and select "Properties."

3. The Properties tab for the connection will show the installed network components with a checkbox beside each one (see Figure 2.4). This enables you to unbind a client, service, or protocol from the adapter. Make sure Internet Protocol (TCP/IP) is checked, highlight and click the "Properties" button.

4. The TCP/IP property screen appears with the TCP/IP Properties page that enables you to specify the IP configuration. As you can see in Figure 2.5, the most commonly configured items, IP address, subnet mask, default gateway, and DNS servers, have been consolidated onto one tab.

5. Click on the "Advanced" button to configure additional IP addresses, gateways, DNS servers, WINS servers, IPSec, and filtering.

Figure 2.4 Properties for a Windows 2000 network connection.

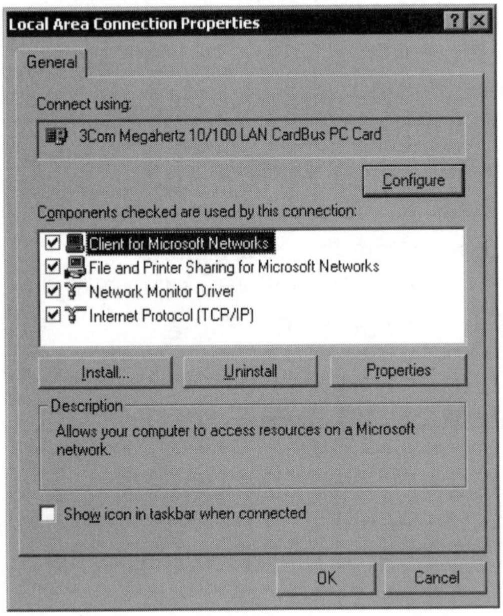

Figure 2.5 The TCP/IP Properties page has changed significantly from Windows NT 4.0.

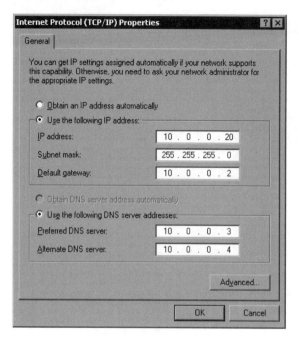

6.   The first tab you see in the Advanced TCP/IP Settings dialog (Figure 2-6) enables you to configure additional IP addresses and gateways for the adapter.

7.   The DNS tab (Figure 2.7) has changed quite a lot from Windows NT 4.0. You can add additional DNS servers and change the order of use, configure how DNS resolves unqualified names, set the DNS suffix for the connection, and specify DNS registration options. To see details regarding an option, click the "?" button in the top right corner and then click on the option.

8.   On the WINS tab (Figure 2.8) you can specify WINS servers, enable LMHOSTS lookup, specify NetBIOS over TCP/IP configuration. Note that you can add more than two WINS servers, which was the limit in Windows NT 4.0.

9.   The Options tab, as shown in Figure 2.9, provides a place for additional TCP/IP items to be configured. To configure an option, select it and click the "Properties" button.

Figure 2.6 Configure additional IP addresses and gateways from the IP Settings tab in the Advanced TCP/IP Settings dialog box.

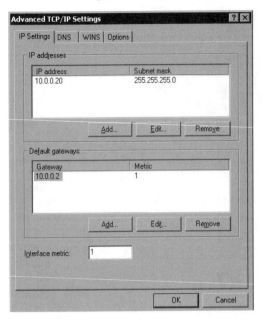

Figure 2.7 The DNS configuration tab has several options new in Windows 2000.

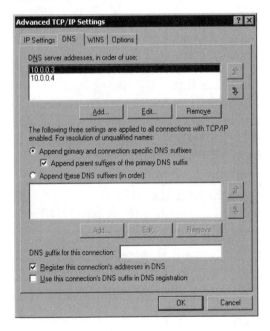

Figure 2.8 WINS, LMHOSTS, and NetBIOS over TCP/IP settings are configured from the WINS tab.

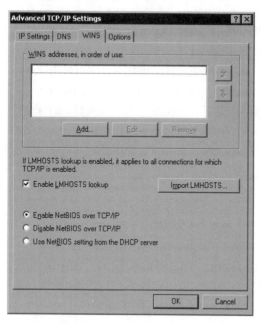

Figure 2.9 IPSec and filtering are configured from the Advanced TCP/IP Setting Options tab.

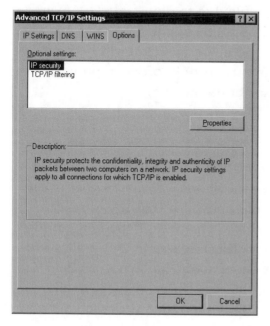

New TCP/IP Features in Windows 2000

Windows 2000 has a number of new features and protocols related to TCP/IP networking. As the uses of TCP/IP have been expanded, it is critical that network operating systems be updated to support the new applications. Additionally, as more and more networks are establishing permanent Internet connections, security is a more urgent concern than ever before and Windows 2000 includes some features that can enhance the security of your network traffic. Some of the new features relate to improved performance and manageability as well.

QoS Admission Control

One important new component in Windows 2000 is Quality of Service (QoS) Admission Control, which is founded on the IETF standard for subnet bandwidth management (SBM). QoS Admission Control enables network administrators to guarantee bandwidth to a client for an application. The primary uses for QoS are currently audio and video applications, which often need to reserve bandwidth to ensure acceptable performance.

Without some control of what network traffic receives priority on the network, a spike in network traffic due to data transfers may interrupt audio or video feeds. As real-time applications become more common on IP networks, services such as QoS will become standard parts of the network infrastructure in order to provide acceptable performance for all uses of the network.

QoS Model

QoS is implemented by clients requesting a bandwidth reservation from an Admission Control Service (ACS) host. The ACS host is configured with a maximum amount of bandwidth that it can reserve for clients, and approves or denies client requests depending on the bandwidth available for reservation. These requests and replies are communicated with the Resource Reservation Protocol (RSVP).

RSVP is also used to distribute the reservation request to all hosts in the path of the traffic flow, and maintains the reservation at each network host. Routers and switches that do not support RSVP simply pass the RSVP traffic along, and if such devices are present in the traffic flow, then there is no guarantee that the QoS reservation will be enforced end to end. Network interface cards must comply with the IEEE 802.1p standard to support QoS; devices not meeting this specification will not be aware of QoS reservations and thus may compromise the integrity of the reservation by using so much bandwidth that there is not enough left to fulfill the reservation.

An RSVP reservation is started by a server, which sends a PATH message to the ACS host. If the request is approved, the ACS host forwards the request to the client, which also establishes the PATH state at each hop, or router, along the path. The client creates a RESV message and sends it to the server along the route as determined by the PATH message it received. Each router receives the RESV message, approves or denies the request, and informs the client that data is to be sent. The client and server send PATH and RESV messages along the route during the session to maintain the reservation (see Figure 2.10).

Figure 2.10 An RSVP reservation requires PATH and RESV messages.

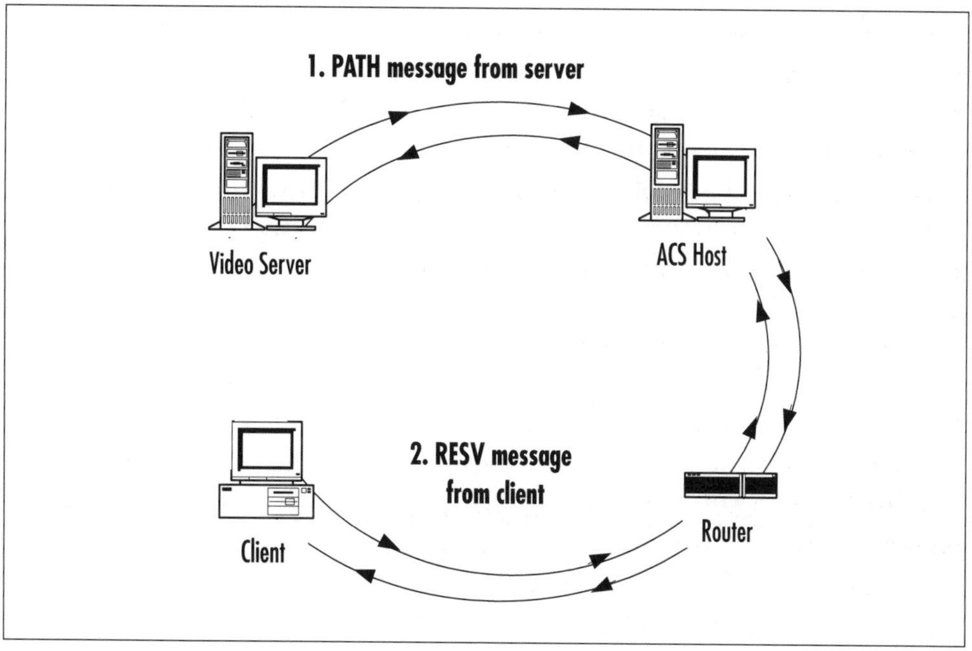

QoS Windows Components

A QoS implementation on a Windows 2000 network is composed of protocols and services working together to request a bandwidth reservation, approve or deny a request for bandwidth, control the traffic, and maintain the reservation until it is no longer needed. The required Windows components are the QoS Admission Control service running on a server, and the Packet Scheduler service on each Windows 2000 and Windows 98 client that will run applications requiring QoS.

The QoS Admission Control service must be installed on a domain controller in each subnet on which you want to provide QoS services. If you have a physical network that includes more than one subnet, you must install QoS Admission Control on a separate domain controller for each subnet. The QoS Admission Control service provides ACS host services, and can service QoS operation from other operating systems that support SBM.

QoS Admission Control Policies

Control policies for QoS are stored in Active Directory, and managed with the QoS Admission Control console. Policies are defined according to both authenticated and unauthenticated users. Unauthenticated users are users who are not logged on to domain accounts. Policies are configured in the enterprise container for these two types of users, and additional exceptions can be made when the enterprise policies are not adequate.

Policies can be defined by the following classes:

- User policy in a subnet
- Group policy in a subnet
- Authenticated user on a subnet
- Unauthenticated user in a subnet
- User in the enterprise container
- Authenticated user in the enterprise container

For IT Professionals

QoS Admission Control

The QoS Admission Control service is a network service in Windows 2000. In Windows NT 4.0, network services were installed on a tab in the Network Properties dialog. In Windows 2000, however, network server services are installed from Control Panel's Add/Remove Programs application by clicking on the Add/Remove Windows Components button. This will invoke the Windows Components Wizard, which will allow you to install or uninstall network services such as QoS Admission Control, IIS, Indexing Service, and Message Queuing. The Packet Scheduler is a network client service, and is installed in the network adapter properties dialog.

The QoS Packet Scheduler is composed of two components. The packet classifier, as its name implies, classifies packets that are then queued to be processed by the packet scheduler. The packet scheduler decides the delivery schedule for each packet queue, creates queues for each particular data flow, and services the queues according to the RSVP reservations in effect (see Figure 2.11).

Figure 2.11 The QoS Packet Scheduler service is installed on client computers.

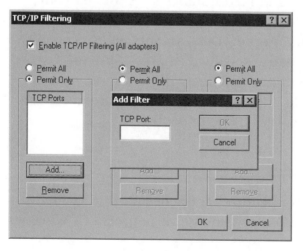

Policies are applied in a specific order, and policy values with a higher priority will always override values with lower priority. If values are not configured at the higher priority, QoS will use the lower priority policy and accumulate values as it continues down the order.

Subnet objects are configured in the QoS Admission Control console, enabling you to define policies that will affect all QoS Admission Control hosts in the subnet. A subnet object also allows you to define user policies on the subnet level.

IPSec

Internet Protocol Security is a set of cryptography-based services and protocols that works at the IP layer. Implementation at this layer provides all TCP/IP applications with secure communication since all network traffic they generate must pass through IP. Implementing security on a lower layer, at the data-link or physical layers, would make it unfeasible to extend the security to remote or mobile users. Cryptography based on a protocol at a higher layer requires applications to be written to interface with it, so it would be realistically impossible to implement complete security at that level as well. Encryption at the IP layer effectively thwarts the use of network sniffers to steal data, since any data they capture must be unencrypted to be useful.

IPSec can be deployed to a limited number of clients on your network or to every computer running Windows 2000, or to mobile or remote clients across the Internet. Departments within your organization that are particularly sensitive, such as Human Resources, R&D, and Accounting, will likely be providing you with the justification necessary to implement IPSec. For more information, see Chapter 6, which covers IPSec in depth.

IP Auto-Configuration

Windows 2000 includes a new feature that is designed to facilitate the use of TCP/IP on small business and home networks. If Windows

2000 is set to use DHCP to obtain IP configuration, it will automatically assign an IP address network if no DHCP server is available. The Windows 2000 DHCP client carries out the IP auto-configuration function.

When the DHCP client fails to contact a DHCP server, it selects an address from the Class B 169.254.0.0 network, which is a reserved network address for such purposes, and uses the default subnet mask of 255.255.0.0. The DHCP client issues a gratuitous ARP request, which is a standard ARP message to determine if an IP address is already in use. If the IP address is already assigned to another computer, the DHCP client will select another IP address and try again.

After an address is selected and bound to the network adapter, the DHCP client continues to attempt to contact the DHCP server. If it is successful, it will replace the auto-configuration assigned address with the DHCP address.

If the client has a valid DHCP lease when it is started, it will try to contact the DHCP server and renew the lease. If it is unsuccessful, it will ping the default gateway that has been configured by the lease. If the gateway ping is successful, the DHCP client will continue to use the leased IP configuration and carry on business as usual. If the gateway ping fails, the DHCP client assumes that the computer has been moved to a different network and uses auto-configuration to select an IP address. The client will continue to attempt to contact a DHCP server in five-minute intervals after auto-configuration.

You must edit the registry in order to disable auto-configuration. Run Registry Editor (regedit.exe) to create the following REG_DWORD value and set the value data to 0 (zero):

```
HKEY_LOCAL_MACHINE\SYSTEM\CurrentControlSet\Services
\Tcpip\Parameters\Interfaces\adapter_name,
IPAutoconfigurationEnabled
```

See Chapter 3 (DHCP) and Chapter 8 (Connecting Small Offices and Home Offices to the Internet) for more information on IP Auto-Configuration.

Large TCP Windows

TCP/IP specifies a window size that indicates the maximum number of packets that can be transmitted without waiting for acknowledgement. Large window support enables the dynamic recalculation and scaling of the window size during long sessions, which increases throughput when the window size is increased. This function is a TCP/IP standard defined in RFC 1323, "TCP Extensions for High Performance."

TCP Selective Acknowledgement

Another TCP improvement in Windows 2000 is the implementation of TCP selective acknowledgements, as defined in RFC 2018. TCP typically acknowledges contiguously received segments, and any missing segment must be retransmitted along with all subsequent segments. Selective acknowledgement allows TCP to deviate from this and only request re-transmission of the specific segments that are missing. The benefits, obviously, are improved performance and less utilization of bandwidth for re-transmitted data.

Improved RTT Estimation

TCP uses Roundtrip Time (RTT) to determine the amount of time needed for round trip communication between two hosts. Windows 2000 uses the Round Trip Time Measurement option, also defined in RFC 1323, to improve RTT calculations. This feature will improve performance over WAN links, where accurate roundtrip estimation is most important.

ICMP Router Discovery

Windows 2000 supports ICMP router discovery, which enables computers to locate the default gateway if none is configured. In order to find the gateway, an ICMP router solicitation message is sent by the client. Routers on the network respond with an ICMP router advertisement, which enables the computer to configure its default gateway. RFC 1256 is the authoritative document on ICMP router discovery.

DNS Caching

The Windows 2000 DNS name resolver caches DNS name queries, and the cache can be viewed with the ipconfig utility. See the next section for specific information on the ipconfig command.

DNS

The Windows 2000 DHCP client includes new functionality for dynamically updating the DNS Service with a host (A) record for the computer. The DHCP Service handles the reverse name lookup (PTR) record update to the DNS server, and can also update DNS for the host records for DHCP clients. The integration between the servers was included in Windows NT 4.0, but now Windows 2000 clients can update the DNS server directly.

On the server side, Windows 2000 DNS, like so many other components of Windows 2000, can integrate with Active Directory, using it to store its zones. See Chapter 3 for more information regarding DHCP and DNS integration in Windows 2000.

WINS

The Windows 2000 WINS Service includes a number of new enhancements that make the service more reliable and manageable. These consist of persistent connections between replication partners, manual tombstoning of records, integration into the Microsoft Management Console (MMC), several management improvements, up to twelve WINS servers configured for clients, and dynamic registration. See Chapter 5 for more information on the WINS Service in Windows 2000.

DHCP

The DHCP service has also been improved with a number of new features. The Windows 2000 DHCP Service is integrated with Active Directory, which is used to authorize DHCP Services for use on the network. If this feature is configured, the DHCP Server will not service DHCP clients if the server is not listed in Active Directory as an authorized server. The DHCP service also includes expanded scope support, option class capabilities, and improved monitoring and reporting.

Windows 2000 DHCP is also integrated with DNS by the implementation of client registration with dynamic DNS servers. The DHCP client now includes IP auto-configuration, about which you just read above. See Chapter 3 for more information on Windows 2000 DHCP features and how to implement them on your network.

TCP/IP Utilities

Windows 2000 comes with a number of command line utilities to assist in troubleshooting TCP/IP network problems. If you have been supporting Windows NT TCP/IP, you are probably familiar with most of these utilities. Some of the utilities have been enhanced, and one new utility, pathping, has been added to the toolset.

Arp

The arp utility is not one that you will use often, but is very useful in certain situations. Arp can be used to display, delete, and add entries in the computer's arp table. The arp table contains IP-address-to-MAC-address assignments, and you shouldn't need to modify it except under extreme circumstances. It can be useful, however, to use arp to view the arp table when an IP address conflict occurs on the network and you don't know what device is using the address. You can use the MAC address it returns to either look up the host with that MAC address (if you have MAC addresses recorded somewhere), or you can determine the manufacturer of the network interface, which may give you an idea of which device is causing the problem. To see information on usage, run the executable without any command line switches.

Hostname

The hostname utility simply returns the hostname of the computer. There are no command line switches except for the /? switch.

Ipconfig

Ipconfig is a utility that can be used to display IP configuration, manage the DHCP client, and manage and display the DNS cache. New switches for the ipconfig command include /flushdns, /registerdns, and /displaydns.

Running ipconfig with no switches displays the IP address, subnet mask, and default gateway for each network adapter. This is especially useful when troubleshooting to see if a client has received a DHCP address or not. Let's discuss some of the command line options since ipconfig is a utility you will probably use more than most of the other TCP/IP utilities.

/?

The /? switch will display command line options, syntax, and examples. This is a very good help screen, so you don't need to worry about memorizing all the switches and how to use them.

/all

Running ipconfig with the /all switch will display the following configuration items for all network adapters:

- Node type
- Primary DNS suffix
- IP routing enabled (Yes/No)

- WINS proxy enabled (Yes/No)
- Host name
- DNS servers
- Adapter description
- MAC address
- DHCP enabled (Yes/No)
- Autoconfiguration enabled (Yes/No)
- IP address
- Subnet mask
- Default gateway
- DHCP server
- Primary and secondary WINS servers
- The time the DHCP lease was obtained
- The time the DHCP lease expires

/renew

You can force the DHCP client to refresh its configuration from the DHCP server by using the /renew switch. All network adapters are refreshed by default, but you can specify an adapter to renew by appending the network adapter name (wildcards can be used) after the switch, e.g. ipconfig /renew Local*. The name of your adapters can be found by running the ipconfig command without any switches. Windows 2000 will report on "Ethernet Adapter Local Area Connection," for example, and the name of the adapter is "Local Area Connection." In order to use a name with spaces, you must use quotes around the name for the utility to work.

/release

The /release switch will remove the IP configuration from all adapters with DHCP configuration. This operation can also be performed on a specific adapter by appending its name after the release switch.

/flushdns

The DNS cache is flushed by using the /flushdns switch with ipconfig. DNS caching is a new feature of Windows 2000, and this switch is available to assist in troubleshooting any cache problems.

/registerdns

The /registerdns switch renews DHCP leases on adapters and performs dynamic registration for DNS names and IP addresses. This will be useful in environments that are utilizing dynamic DNS. The adapter name can also be appended to this command to limit the operation to specific adapters.

/displaydns

The DNS resolver cache can be displayed by using the /displaydns switch. Sample output is included below, but you will find that it will return a large number of records if you have been accessing the Internet even for a short time. To be useful, you may need to pipe this command to a text file so that you can see all of it (ipconfig /displaydns > c:\temp\displaydns.txt).

```
L:\>ipconfig /displaydns

Windows 2000 IP Configuration

    localhost.
    ----------------------------------------------------------
        Record Name . . . . . . : localhost
        Record Type . . . . . . : 1
        Time To Live  . . . . . : 31466765
        Data Length . . . . . . : 4
        Section . . . . . . . . : Answer
        A (Host) Record . . . : 127.0.0.1

    f20.mail.yahoo.com.
    ----------------------------------------------------------
        Record Name . . . . . . : f20.mail.yahoo.com
```

```
Record Type . . . . . : 1
Time To Live  . . . . : 620
Data Length . . . . . : 4
Section . . . . . . . : Answer
A (Host) Record . . . : 128.11.68.226
```

/showclassid

Using /showclassid with the ipconfig command will return information on the DHCP Class ID that is configured on the client. The network adapter name can be appended to this command as well, to
limit output to a specific adapter.

/setclassid

Class IDs on network adapter can be set by using the /setclassid
switch with the network adapter name trailing it. The function of
Class IDs is to control DHCP configuration for specific groups if the
same configuration is not appropriate for all users.

Lpq

The lpq command is used to show the status of a remote lpd queue.
If you are using TCP/IP printing on a server, this command can be
used to view information about a print queue on the server. The
server name and printer name must be specified in the command,
and the –l switch can be used to specify verbose output. The command syntax is:

```
lpq  -Sserver -Pprinter [-L]
```

Nbtstat

Nbtstat is a utility used to view protocol statistics and current
TCP/IP connections using NBT. There are a number of command

line switches available to allow you to view adapter status and name tables of remote computers, local NetBIOS names, the cache of NetBIOS names and IP addresses, names resolved by WINS or broadcast, and session information. Use the /? switch to see syntax information and descriptions of switches.

Netstat

Netstat also displays protocol statistics and current TCP/IP connections, but it is not based on NBT like the nbtstat command. Several command line switches are available to display information such as all connections and listening ports, Ethernet statistics, addresses and port numbers, connections by protocol type, the routing table, and statistics by protocol. Using the /? switch will display information you need to use the utility.

Nslookup

Nslookup is a utility used to troubleshoot DNS issues. This is one command where you cannot use the /? switch to get help on how to use the utility. Nslookup can be used as an interactive utility by running the executable with no command line options. When nslookup is started, you will be greeted with a greater-than (>) prompt. For information on the options available, type "?" or "help" and hit Enter. The Windows 2000 Help file also has information regarding nslookup.

Ping

The ping utility sends an ICMP ECHO request to the specified host and displays statistics on the replies that are received. Ping is one of the first IP troubleshooting tools to use when you are trying to resolve a network problem. See Table 2.5 for command line switch options for this familiar utility.

Table 2.5 Command Line Switches for the Ping Utility

Switch	Description
-?	Displays syntax and command line options
-t	Ping continuously until Ctrl-C
-n count	The number of ICMP ECHO requests to send
-l size	Size of send buffer
-f	Set Don't Fragment flag in packet
-i TTL	Time to Live
-v TOS	Type of Service
-r count	Record route for count hops
-s count	Timestamp for count hops
-j host-list	Loose source route along host-list
-k host-list	Strict source route along host-list
-w timeout	Milliseconds to wait for replies

Route

The route command enables you to view, add, remove, or modify the IP routing table on a computer. The /? switch will display usage options, and the Windows 2000 Help file can be consulted for more information as well.

Tracert

Tracert is a utility that determines the route to a given host by using ICMP ECHO messages. This utility is useful to help determine why two hosts may not be able to communicate. As tracert returns information, you can see any routers that are not responding or any loops caused by misconfigured routers. See Table 2.6 for command line options, or just run the executable without indicating a target system and the command usage will be displayed.

Table 2.6 Tracert Command Line Options

-d	Don't resolve addresses to hostnames
-h max_hops	Maximum number of hops to target
-j host-list	Loose source route along host-list
-w timeout	Milliseconds to wait for replies

Pathping

Pathping, a utility that is new to the Windows operating system, discovers the route to the destination host, pings each hop for a period of time, and then reports the statistics. See the sample output below, and Table 2.7 for command line switch options.

```
L:\>pathping core-snfx1-atm5-0.16.grid.net

Tracing route to core-snfx1-atm5-0.16.grid.net [206.80.187.78]
over a maximum of 30 hops:
  0   THINKLE [209.138.11.38]
  1   usrha-ipls1815.grid.net [207.205.227.135]
  2   core-ipls1-fe0/0/0.grid.net [207.205.227.252]
  3   core-snfx1-atm5-0.16.grid.net [206.80.187.78]

Computing statistics for 75 seconds...
                    Source to Here    This Node/Link
Hop   RTT     Lost/Sent = Pct   Lost/Sent = Pct   Address
  0                                                THINKLE
[209.138.11.38]
                                    0/ 100 =  0%    |
  1   144ms      0/ 100 =  0%     0/ 100 =  0%  usrha-
ipls1815.grid.net [207.205.227.135]
                                    0/ 100 =  0%    |
  2   149ms      0/ 100 =  0%     0/ 100 =  0%  core-ipls1-
fe0/0/0.grid.net [207.205.227.252]
                                    0/ 100 =  0%    |
  3   216ms      0/ 100 =  0%     0/ 100 =  0%  core-snfx1-
atm5-0.16.grid.net [206.80.187.78]

Trace complete.
```

Table 2.7 Pathping Command Line Switches

Switches	Description
/?	Displays pathping options
/n	Do no resolve address to hostnames
/h maximum_hops	Max number of hops to destination
/g host-list	Loose source route along host-list
-p period	Number of milliseconds between pings
-q num_queries	Number of pings per hop
-w timeout	Milliseconds to wait for each reply
-T	Test each hop with Layer-2 priority tags
-R	Test each hop for RSVP awareness

Summary

The proliferation of computers into businesses, governments, academia, and homes that occurred in the 1980s created a great demand to network them together. Government entities and universities were the first organizations to connect their systems into what we now know as the Internet. With the invention of the World Wide Web in the early 1990s, the Internet suddenly became a medium that was attractive to businesses and individuals as well. In less than a decade, the Internet went from a network primarily used by the federal government and universities to a massive, global Web that fueled multi-billion dollar businesses and changed the way many people communicate, research, play, and shop on an everyday basis.

TCP/IP was selected as the protocol suite required for Internet communication in the early 1980s due to its open development and standards, scalability, and reliability. This prompted most systems manufacturers to implement TCP/IP on their platforms, providing a common network protocol for them to communicate with each other. Prior to this time, most networks were closed to a particular vendor's systems and ran on that vendor's proprietary protocols.

Microsoft implemented TCP/IP on the Windows NT platform early in its history, and has improved the IP features and functionality with each new version and service pack of the operating system. Windows NT supports all of the core TCP/IP protocols in addition to services such as TCP/IP printing, SNMP, and DHCP.

Windows 2000 brings a number of new features and enhancements to Windows TCP/IP connectivity. Most important are Quality of Service (QoS), IP Security (IPSec), and IP Auto-configuration. Windows 2000 also provides a handful of TCP/IP standards-based performance enhancements, the pathping utility, DNS caching, and an improved DHCP client that supports dynamic DNS.

FAQs

Q: Are there any new TCP/IP utilities available in Windows 2000?

A: The pathping utility is new in Windows 2000, and is a great way to test the reliability of the route to a host. Pathping discovers the route to a target, tests each hop with a number of pings, and reports the statistics.

Q: What do I need to implement Quality of Service (QoS) on my network?

A: You will need network cards that comply with the IEEE 802.1p standard, routers that support RSVP, QoS Admission Control installed on a domain controller for each subnet, and the QoS Packet Scheduler installed on clients and servers.

Q: DNS caching is new on Windows 2000. How can I see information regarding the DNS cache on a particular PC?

A: Use the ipconfig utility with the /flushdns, /registerdns, and /displaydns switches to view and manage a client's DNS cache.

Q: When can I disable NetBIOS over TCP/IP (NBT)?

A: Microsoft states that you can remove WINS once you have a pure Windows 2000 environment. Since WINS relies on NBT, you cannot disable NBT until you are no longer relying on WINS for name resolution. Additionally, legacy applications and logon scripts often use NetBIOS names, and these must be modified to use DNS name resolution before you can remove NBT. You can disable NBT via DHCP on Windows 2000 clients when you are ready to make the change.

Q: What new TCP/IP features in Windows 2000 improve network performance?

A: Windows 2000 implements three new features that enhance TCP/IP performance: large TCP Windows, improved RTT estimation, and TCP selective acknowledgement. All three of these features are based on TCP/IP RFC standards.

Q: What is an RFC?

A: TCP/IP and Internet standard are established by a Request for Comments process. An individual or group that wishes to have a standard established must submit a document, called an RFC, detailing the proposed standard. The Internet Engineering Steering Group (IESG) approves or rejects the standard. The IESG often asks authors to make revisions after their review before the RFCs are published. RFCs are open to the public and the official publication site is www.rfc-editor.org.

Chapter 3

DHCP Server Management

Solutions in this chapter:

- Overview of DHCP
- DHCP in Detail
- Integration with DNS
- Configuration of DHCP
- Management of DHCP

Introduction

All common network protocols assign each computer a unique identifier. In the case of IPX (Internetwork Package Exchange), this number is assigned automatically by the workstation in a way that is guaranteed to make the number completely unique; NetBEUI uses a 16-character NetBIOS name. The TCP/IP protocol uses an IP address. TCP/IP was designed to connect a relatively small number of servers together. The idea of manually inputting a server address did not seem a problem.

The purpose of Dynamic Host Configuration Protocol (DHCP) is to provide a way to dynamically assign IP Addresses to computers when they connect to the LAN. The availability of a DHCP server on your network makes it easier for users when they move their computer or are visiting another office with their laptops. The DHCP server also gives out other TCP/IP configurations to the client, including the IP address of the gateway, DNS server and the client's DNS Domain Name.

Windows 2000 DHCP is integrated with Microsoft DNS Server. This new feature allows a Windows 2000 DHCP Service to communicate IP addressing and host name information to a Windows 2000 Dynamic DNS (DDNS) Service. This provides dynamic IP addresses to host name registration and resolution. As application standards move toward using the WinSock interface, it is critical in large corporate networks to locate clients by host name and IP address.

DHCP is a mission-critical feature of enterprise networks. Most corporate networks have moved to TCP/IP and rely on DHCP for IP address administration. If DHCP Servers fail, your users may not be able to access their network resources. The successful network administrator must know how to set up and maintain your DHCP servers in optimal configurations.

DHCP Overview

Dynamic Host Configuration Protocol provides IP addressing information for DHCP clients. To obtain IP addressing information, the client must obtain a "lease" from a DHCP server. In this section, we will examine the process of lease assignment and integration of DHCP with DDNS. We will also examine some lease configuration strategies to optimize the allocation of IP addresses.

The Process of Obtaining a Lease

The DHCP client and server participate in a dialog that consists of four primary interchanges:

- DHCPDISCOVER
- DHCPOFFER
- DHCPREQUEST
- DHCPACKNOWLEGEMENT

The result of this dialog is the assignment of an IP address and additional TCP/IP parameters. Let's look at each of these messages in more detail.

DHCPDISCOVER

When the DHCP client initializes, it broadcasts a DHCPDISCOV-ER message to the local segment. The destination address is the limited broadcast address, 255.255.255.255. All DHCP servers on the segment will respond to the DHCPDISCOVER message. The DCHP client does not yet have an IP address, so it includes with the DHCPDISCOVER message its Media Access Control address (identified as the "ciaddr" field in a packet analysis). The following is a list of information included in the DHCPDISCOVER message:

- The client's host name
- A "parameter request list" that includes DHCP option codes the client supports
- The "Hardware type" of the client's Network Interface Card, such as 10MB Ethernet

DHCPOFFER

All DHCP servers on the segment respond to the client's DISCOVER message by offering an IP address from their "pool" of available IP addresses. This offer is made in the form of a DHCPOFFER message. The DHCP client will accept the IP address from the first DHCPOFFER message it receives.

The DHCPOFFER message is a broadcast message. In order for the correct client to receive the information, the destination MAC address is included in the "ciaddr" field. Other information included in the DHCPOFFER message includes:

- DHCP server IP address
- The offered IP address
- The offered subnet mask
- DHCP option information: WINS and DNS servers, Default Gateway
- Lease Interval
- First and second lease renewal intervals (Renewal [T1] and Rebinding [T2] Time Values)

The DHCPOFFER message contains the basic IP addressing information the client computer will use when the TCP/IP stack is initialized.

DHCPREQUEST

The client responds to the offer by issuing a DHCPREQUEST broadcast message. A question might come to mind at this point, "Why use a broadcast message? Doesn't the client now have an IP address?" Recall that all DHCP servers respond to the initial DCHPDISCOVER message. The purpose of the DHCPREQUEST broadcast is to inform other DHCP servers that their offers have been rejected. The rejected DHCP servers then return the IP addresses they offered to their pools of available IP addresses.

The DCHPREQUEST message is a confirmation of the information sent to the client in the DHCPOFFER message. The DHCPREQUEST message includes:

- The client's hardware address
- The DHCP server's IP address
- The client's requested IP address
- The client's host name

DHCPACKNOWLEDGEMENT (DHCPACK)

Finally, the DHCP server responds to the DHCPREQUEST message with a DHCPACK broadcast message. The reason this message is broadcast is because the client doesn't "officially" obtain its IP address until it is acknowledged. Again, the client's MAC address is included in order to identify the proper destination of this message.

The DHCPACK message contains information similar to that included with the DHCPOFFER message, and acts as a confirmation of the DHCPREQUEST message. At this point, the client has leased the IP address and can use it for network communication. The address is marked as "leased" by the DHCP server and will not be leased to any other client during the active lease period.

DHCP Negative Acknowledgement (DHCPNACK)

After a reboot, the client will attempt to renew its lease. The client will broadcast a DHCPREQUEST message in an attempt to retain its current IP address. If the server determines the client can keep this address, it will return to the client a DHCPACK message.

However, if the server decides the client cannot keep its current IP addressing information, (perhaps the address has been given to another computer), then the DHCP server will issue a DHCP Negative Acknowledgement (DHCPNACK). The DHCPNACK message is similar to the DHCPACK message in that it contains the client's MAC address and is a broadcast message. Also included is the IP address of the DHCP server that issued the Negative Acknowledgment.

When the client receives the DHCPNACK, it will broadcast a DHCPDISCOVER message. The message is similar in content and form to the original DHCPDISCOVER message. It is different in that the client will attempt to obtain its previous IP address. This DCHPDISCOVER message contains the field, "DHCP: Requested Address," that was not part of the DHCPDISCOVER message when the client did not yet have an IP address. If the IP address is available again for some reason, the client will receive the same IP address. If the original IP address continues to be unavailable, it will be assigned another IP address from any responding DHCP server's pool of available IP addresses. If the client is unable to obtain a lease from a DHCP server, TCP/IP will be shut down and the computer will no longer be able to participate in network activity.

Integration of DHCP with DNS

The DHCP Service included with Windows 2000 includes enhanced capabilities compared to the Windows NT DHCP server. The most significant is the Windows 2000 DHCP Service's ability to deliver host name and IP addressing information to a Windows 2000 DDNS server.

After assigning a DHCP client an IP address, the Windows 2000 DHCP Server can interact with a Windows 2000 Dynamic DNS Server in one of three ways:

1. It will update the DNS server by providing information to create an "A" address record and PTR (pointer) record on the DNS at the client's request

2. The DHCP server will update both the Address Record and the Pointer Record regardless of client request.

3. The DHCP server will never register information about the DHCP client. However, the client itself may contact the Dynamic DNS server directly with this information.

These configuration options are made at the DHCP server, as pictured in Figure 3.1.

Figure 3.1 Configuring DNS updates from the DHCP Server.

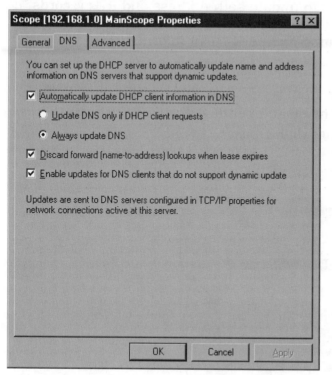

The DCHP/DDNS interaction varies with the type of client receiving the IP addressing information from the DHCP server. The Windows 2000 DHCP Service supports the Client Fully Qualified Domain Name (FQDN) Option (Option Code 81), which allows the DHCP client to communicate its FQDN to the DHCP server. Only Windows 2000 clients support Option Code 81. The interplay between the Windows 2000 client and Windows 2000 DHCP encompasses the following:

1. The Windows 2000 Client broadcasts a DHCPREQUEST message and receives an IP address via a DHCPACK. After officially obtaining a lease, the Windows 2000 client will register its own Address record with the Dynamic DNS Service.

2. The DHCP server will register the client's pointer record (PTR) with the DDNS server. This is the default behavior for a Windows 2000 client and Windows 2000 DHCP Service.

3. Client and Server configuration can be manipulated to allow the DHCP server to update both Address and PTR records. If desired, the DHCP server and DCHP client can be configured so that no dynamic update of client information reaches the DDNS server.

To prevent the client from registering directly with the DDNS server, you must alter the default settings. Figure 3-2 shows the Advanced TCP/IP settings dialog box.

Figure 3.2 Advanced TCP/IP Dialog Box.

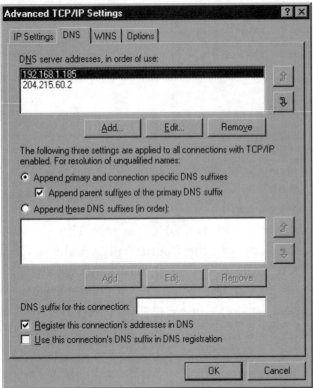

You can remove the checkmark for "Register this connection's addresses in DNS." This will prevent the computer's FQDN as defined in the "Network Identification" tab in the System Properties dialog box from registering directly with DDNS. The second option,

"Use this connection's DNS suffix in DNS registration," refers to entries made in the textbox for the "Append these DNS suffixes (in order)" or those assigned to the specific network connection via DHCP. Each network connection can be customized to provide its own DNS name information. If you remove the checkmark from both of these, it will prevent the client from registering directly with the Dynamic DNS Server.

This is what happens when dealing with pure Windows 2000 clients and servers. However, downlevel clients are not able to communicate "A" Address record information to a DDNS server. In this case, the DHCP server will act as "proxy" and will forward both Address and PTR information to the DDNS Server.

Windows 2000 computers configured with static IP addresses will update their own Address and Pointer records with the DDNS server. If you change the name or IP address of a Windows 2000 client that has a static IP address, you can manually update that client's entry in the DDNS server by issuing the command:

```
ipconfig /registerdns
```

Downlevel clients with static IP addresses are not able to communicate directly with the DDNS server. DDNS entries for these clients must be manually reconfigured at the DDNS server.

What Are Leases?

A lease is an agreement to let someone use something for a specified period. The DHCP client leases IP addressing information from the DHCP server. It does not keep this information forever. This allows the DHCP server to maintain a dynamic pool of IP addresses. The lease process prevents computers no longer on the network from retaining IP addresses that could otherwise be returned to the pool and assigned to other computers.

The length of the lease is defined at the DHCP server. The default lease period on a Windows 2000 DHCP server is eight days. This can be changed depending on the needs of the network administrator.

A DHCP client must renew its lease. The DHCPOFFER and DHCKACK messages include the amount of time a client is allowed to keep its IP address. Also included are times when the client will be required to renew its lease. The DHCPOFFER message included not only the lease period, but also a "Renewal Time Value (T1)" and the "Rebinding Time Value (T2)."

The Renewal Time Value represents 50 percent of the lease period. At this time, the DHCP client will attempt to renew its IP address by broadcasting a DHCPREQUEST message containing its current IP address. If the DHCP server that granted the IP address is available, it will renew the IP address for the period specified in the renewed lease. If the DHCP server is not available, the client will continue to use its lease, since it still has 50 percent of the lease period remaining.

The Rebinding Time Value represents 87.5 percent of the lease period. The client will attempt to renew its IP address at this time only if it was not able to renew its lease at the Renewal Time. The client broadcasts a DHCPREQUEST message. If the server that granted the IP address does not respond, the client will enter the "Rebinding State" and begin the DHCPDISCOVER process, attempting to renew its IP address with any DHCP server. If it cannot renew its IP address, it will try to receive a new one from any responding DHCP server. If unsuccessful, TCP/IP services are shut down on that computer.

The ipconfig Command

The ipconfig command allows you to manually renew and release IP addresses. You might want to release an IP address if you plan to remove a client from the subnet, or if you need available IP addresses. Issue the following command from the command prompt:

```
ipconfig /release
```

This command moves the IP address from the list of leased addresses and makes it available to other machines that may require IP addresses. If a client releases an address, it will not be able to participate on the network. Running IPCONFIG again with no parameters will show that the client has an IP address of 0.0.0.0 (i.e. no address).

The network administrator may at times wish to manually renew an IP address. This is helpful when a change has been made to the DHCP options configured at the DHCP server and you want to immediately deliver them to the clients. Issue the following command:

```
ipconfig /renew
```

This forces a DHCPREQUEST message. The client will gather new DHCP configuration information from the DHCP server.

The Windows 9.x operating systems include a utility with the same functionality as the ipconfig command. The utility is winipcfg. The winipcfg command presents a GUI interface to the renew and release commands. There is no "registerdns" capability since Win 9.x clients cannot directly register their "A" Address records with a Dynamic DNS server.

Leasing Strategy

How you time your leases depends upon the level of dynamism of your network or network segments. The default lease period is eight days for Windows 2000 DHCP Service. This can be reconfigured to meet your needs. Lease periods are configured on a per scope basis. Increase the lease duration for segments that do not add or remove clients frequently. Segments that have a large excess of IP addresses benefit from extended lease periods. You are able to reduce the amount of network traffic due to DCHP broadcasts by lengthening the lease period. Extended lease periods can allow the network administrator more time to fix a "downed" DHCP server before client leases begin to expire.

Shorten the default lease duration if you have segments that see many computers joining and leaving on a frequent basis. The typical example is that of a sales division with many laptop users joining and leaving the network. It would not take much time to exhaust all of the available IP addresses for that scope if their segment had a long lease period. The truncated lease period allows the DHCP server to rapidly reclaim IP addresses from computers that have left the network.Segments that have a narrow required/available IP address ratio benefit from shortened IP lease durations. This maximizes the chance of a computer gaining a lease when the number of available IP addresses is tight.

The definition of "long" and "short" lease periods is debatable. However, consensus dictates that lease periods of 30-60 days are adequate for stable networks, while highly volatile networks might require lease periods of 24 hours or less. Be aware that more broadcast traffic is generated when you shorten the lease interval.

Operating Without a DHCP Server

A TCP/IP network does not require a DHCP server. The DHCP server provides the convenience of IP address allocation and management. In small or very stable networks (such as home or SOHO locations), DHCP server functionality does not enhance ease of use.

Problems commonly associated with decentralized management of IP addressing information include assigning multiple machines the same IP address, or misconfiguring TCP/IP parameters such as WINS, DNS, or Default Gateway.

If you opt against using a DHCP server, Windows 2000 clients can avoid the problem of duplicate IP addressing by using APIPA (Automatic Private IP Addressing).

Automatic Client Configuration

Automatic Client Configuration, or APIPA, allows Windows 2000 computers configured as DHCP clients to assign themselves their own IP addresses. This technology is available on Windows 98SE clients and is now part of Windows 2000. A Windows 2000 DHCP client unable to contact a DHCP server may assign itself an IP address.

There are two scenarios where APIPA finds itself useful. The first scenario occurs when the machine has not previously bound an IP address. In this case:

1. The Windows 2000 computer configured as a DHCP client starts up. A DHCPDISCOVER message is broadcast to the segment. If the machine does not receive a reply, it will attempt to autoconfigure its IP address.

2. The machine will select, at random, an IP address from the Microsoft reserved Class B network ID 169.254.0.0 with the default Class B subnet mask of 255.255.0.0.

3. A "gratuitous ARP" message will be broadcast for this randomly selected IP address. If no machine responds to the ARP request, the machine will bind the new IP address to the network adapter configured as a DHCP client.

4. If a machine responds to the ARP request, the self-configuring computer will choose another IP address and issue another ARP request. It will continue this process for up to 10 addresses. If the machine cannot configure an IP address after 10 attempts, it will stop and disable TCP/IP.

If a DHCP client who has an active lease starts up and cannot contact a DHCP server, the process is a little different:

1. When the DHCP client with a valid lease starts up, it will issue a DHCPREQUEST broadcast to renew the lease.

2. If the client does not receive a DHCPACK from the DHCP server, it will start to PING the IP address of the default gateway configured in its lease.

3. If the default gateway responds, the machine "assumes" there must be a problem with the DHCP server itself. The DHCP client attempts to renew its lease at 50 percent and 87.5 percent of the lease period.

4. If the default gateway fails to respond to the PING, the machine assumes it has been moved. In this case, the machine will abandon its lease and autoconfigure itself as described above.

In both cases, the DHCP client will issue a DHCPDISCOVER message every five minutes attempting to contact a DHCP server. If the client receives a DHCPOFFER message at any time, it will bind a valid IP address from the DHCP server sending the offer.

Windows 2000 DHCP computers communicate with NDIS 5.0 compliant network interface card drivers to obtain information about network connection status. This "media sense" capability allows the operating system to detect whether the computer has been removed from the network. If the operating system senses the computer has been removed from a network and plugged into another, it will begin the lease renewal and autoconfiguration process.

A DHCP client can be configured to not autoconfigure. To suppress autoconfiguration, find the following Registry Key:

```
HKEY_LOCAL_MACHINE\SYSTEM\CurrentControlSet\Services\Tcpip\
Interfaces\adapter_name
```

Once there, add the following value:

```
IPAutoconfigurationEnabled: REG_DWORD
```

```
Set the value to 0
```

Keep in mind that APIPA is only useful on single segment networks where all machines are using APIPA. Otherwise, the self-configuring machines will assign themselves to a different network ID than the other clients on the segment. Please refer to Chapter 8 for more information on how APIPA is used in environments taking advantage of Windows 2000 Internet Connection Sharing (ICS).

Manual IP Addresses

The administrator can completely forgo DHCP and Automatic Client Configuration and manually set IP addressing information on all the computers on the network. Elements which require configuration include: IP address, subnet mask, default gateway, WINS address, DNS address, Alternate DNS address, NetBIOS node type, and many others.

In a large installation with thousands of computers, the manual IP addressing method is a prescription for error. IP addressing information must then be tracked by manual methods. This can be done with the help of tools such as Microsoft Access or Excel. If the network team coordinates their efforts and is assiduous in recording TCP/IP information in a spreadsheet or database, this solution is may be viable.

The vast majority of enterprise networks use DHCP for system-wide IP address assignment and configuration. This avoids the overhead of manual record-keeping and attendant human error.

Design of a DHCP Configuration

Optimal placement of DHCP servers across the organization is pivotal to successful DHCP deployment. When planning the locations for DHCP servers, it is vital to consider the following:

1. DHCP messages are broadcasts.
2. Broadcasts do not traverse routers without special configuration.
3. DHCP servers do not share information with each other, unlike WINS.

DHCP server location must be done with these issues firmly in mind.

Placement of Servers

The simplest setup is the non-routed, single segment network. A single segment will likely represent a single network ID. A single scope on a solitary DHCP server is all that is required. Unless otherwise noted in this text, segment and subnet will be used synonymously.

The complexity of the DHCP server placement problem increases with the number of segments on the network. Allowance must be made for the fact that DHCP messages are broadcast-based. One solution is to put a DHCP server on each segment. This obviates the need for broadcast messages to traverse routers. This solution can be costly and manpower-intensive if there are a large number of subnets to be managed. This distributed approach will complicate issues for the administrator who seeks a more centralized management solution.

However, for a small network consisting of only two or three segments, you might consider placing a server on each segment. In this case, enabling the DHCP service and creating a scope would be a simple task that requires nominal administration.

Another option is to use fewer DHCP servers and place these machines in central locations. To solve the problem of broadcast management, routers can be configured to pass DHCP/BOOTP messages selectively. If one cannot or will not change router configurations, then placing a "DHCP Relay Agent" on each segment allows DHCP clients and server to communicate. The Relay Agent will communicate with a DHCP server and act as a proxy for DHCP messages sent to remote segments.

Link speed is an important issue in DHCP server placement. If you choose to locate the DHCP server remotely from the DHCP clients, you require a fast, reliable path between them. Segments separated by WAN links are typically slower than intranet connections. At least one DHCP server should be placed on each of a WAN link for performance and fault tolerance reasons.

Using DHCP Routers or DHCP Relay Agents

Routers that conform to RFC 2132 (which supercedes 1542) can be configured to pass DHCP/BOOTP broadcast messages. These broadcast packets pass through UDP Port 67. This is known as BOOTP/DHCP relay. Most modern routers support BOOTP/DHCP relay. If your router does not, contact the router manufacturer for a software or firmware upgrade.

If you cannot upgrade routers to support BOOTP/DHCP messages, you can engage a Windows NT or Windows 2000 server to become a DCHP relay agent. The DHCP Relay Agent will listen for DHCP broadcast messages and forward these to a DHCP server on a remote subnet. When the remote DHCP server receives the messages from the DHCP Relay Agent, it forwards replies to the source subnet and requesting client.

The details of this exchange when an RFC-compliant router acts as a Relay Agent:

1. The DHCP client broadcasts a DHCPDISCOVER message.

2. The DHCP Relay Agent intercepts the message. In the message header, there is a field for the gateway IP address. If the field is 0.0.0.0., the Relay Agent will insert its own IP address.

3. The DHCP Relay Agent forwards the DHCPDISCOVER message to the remote DHCP server.

4. When the DHCPDISCOVER message arrives at the DHCP server, the service examines the gateway IP address (giaddr). The server determines whether it has a scope for the network ID specified in the giaddr.

5. The DHCP server prepares a lease for the client, and issues a DHCPOFFER message directly to the address included in the giaddr.

6. Since the client does not yet have an IP address, the local router interface broadcasts the DHCPOFFER to the subnet.

7. The same processes take place for the DHCPREQUEST and DHCPACK messages.

RRAS Integration

The Routing and Remote Access Service (RRAS) is able to call upon a DHCP server to assign IP addresses to RRAS clients. The RRAS server acts as a "proxy" between the RRAS client and the DHCP server. The way the RRAS server uses the DHCP server to distribute IP addresses is different from the way LAN clients receive their IP address information.

If the RRAS server is configured to use DHCP to assign IP addresses, it will obtain a group of IP addresses from the DHCP server as a block. This block of IP addresses is obtained when RRAS services initialize. RRAS clients do not directly receive information from the DHCP server. The number of IP addresses retrieved is equal to the number of RAS ports configured on the RRAS server, plus one. The RRAS server itself uses the additional IP address.

The IP addressing information available to RRAS clients is limited compared to LAN DHCP clients. When the RRAS server obtains its group of IP addresses, any option information sent from the DHCP server to the RRAS server is ignored. Typical DHCP option parameters, such as WINS and DNS server IP addresses, are obtained from the specific RRAS connection itself. Each RRAS connection can be independently configured.

The RRAS client lease is different from the LAN client's lease. There is no effective lease period for the RRAS client. The lease immediately expires after the connection is terminated. You can perform an ipconfig on the client machine to see DHCP configuration parameters the RRAS server has assigned.

Configuring a DHCP Server

A DHCP server becomes functional after a pool of IP addresses is made available to DHCP clients. When so configured, the DHCP server is able to deliver additional information to DHCP clients. DHCP messages are broadcasts, which do not cross routers by default.

We will examine these issues in this section on configuring a DHCP server. We will also examine how a DHCP server provides information to BOOTP clients, the new Vendor and User Class Options, and the special topic of Superscopes.

DHCP Scopes

A scope defines a collection or pool of IP addresses. A single scope includes all the IP addresses that you wish to make available to DHCP clients on a single subnet. Only one scope can be created for each subnet. A single DHCP server can manage several scopes. The server itself does not need to be local to all Scopes it services. Remote hosts can access the DHCP server via RFC-compliant routers or DHCP Relay Agents.

Each scope must consist of at least the following elements:

- Scope Name
- Start and End IP address
- Lease Duration
- Subnet Mask

The scope typically includes all available IP addresses for the network ID or subnetwork ID. An exception to this is when the available addresses are split among DHCP servers to provide fault tolerance for the scope. If you have clients with static IP addresses, such as WINS, DNS, or other DHCP servers, you can configure a range of excluded IP addresses. These excluded IP addresses are removed from the scope and are not available for distribution.

Creating a new scope in Windows 2000 is a much easier task because it is wizard-driven. Most configuration options are included in the wizard, which helps the administrator define and configure the scope.

At the end of this chapter, we will perform a walkthrough on the steps involved in creating a new scope.

Configuring Leases

A lease contains all information provided to the client by the DHCP server. The lease is not permanent, unless you wish to create a permanent lease assignment. The default lease period is eight days for a Windows 2000 DHCP Service. Figure 3.3 shows the lease period configuration panel.

Leases periods should remain short for volatile networks. Longer lease periods are appropriate for stable networks where new clients are not added frequently.

Figure 3.3 Configuring Lease Duration for DHCP clients.

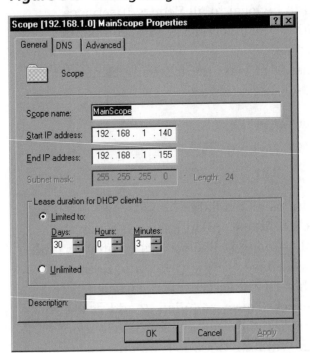

DHCP Options

The DHCP server can deliver to the DHCP client more information than just an IP address. Configuration details such as the IP address of the WINS server, DNS server, and Default Gateway can be included in a client lease. These additional configuration details are referred to as DHCP Options.

There are several levels of DHCP Options. These include:

- Server Options
- Scope Options
- Client Options
- Vendor Class or User Class Options

Each level shares a similar set of DHCP Options. There are a large number of options available in the Windows 2000 DHCP

Service. Microsoft client operating systems support a small number of these options. Of the standard set of DHCP options, Microsoft clients support:

003 Router	The IP address of the Default Gateway
006 DNS	The IP address of the DNS server
015 Domain Name	The DNS Domain Name the client should use
044 WINS/NBNS Servers	The IP address of the WINS server
046 WINS/NBT Node Type	The NetBIOS node type
047 NetBIOS Scope ID	The NetBIOS scope ID

Each of these options is configured at the DHCP server. Let's now look at the different option levels and see how to configure options for each level.

Server Options

Server Options apply to all scopes on a single DHCP server. For example, you have three scopes on your DHCP server for the following network IDs:

192.168.1.0

192.168.2.0

192.168.3.0

You configure the WINS server address to 192.168.1.16. Clients receiving their lease from any of these scopes will be given the same WINS server address.

To configure Server Options:

1. Open the DHCP Management Console.

2. In the left pane, expand the server name, and then click the "Server Options" folder. If there are any existing server options, they will appear in the right pane.

3. Right-click the "Server Options" folder, and select "Configure Options." You should see a dialog box like in Figure 3.4.

Figure 3.4 Setting Server Options.

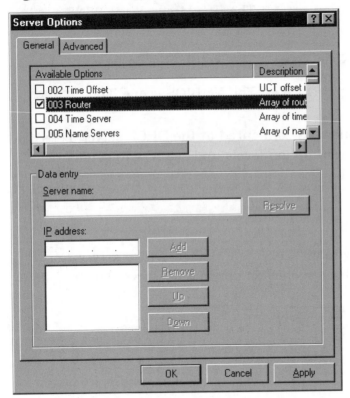

4. Select the desired option and put a checkmark in the box. The "Data entry" pane will change to allow configuration of the option. When completed click "Apply" and then "OK" to close the dialog box.

Scope Options

Scope Options allow you to specify DHCP Options that apply to a single scope. For example, you want the default gateway to be on the same subnet as the clients. Therefore, for each scope you configure a different default gateway. It wouldn't make much sense to assign the same default gateway to all the scopes.

To configure Scope Options:

1. Open the DHCP Management Console.

2. In the left pane, expand the server name, and then expand the Scope folder. You will need to already have a scope in place to do this. Right-click the "Scope Options" folder, and then click "Configure Options."

3. Select and configure options as described above.

Client Options

Client Options are assigned to computers configured to receive the same IP address from the DHCP server each time the client starts. This client is also known as a "reserved client." Creating reserved clients allows you to assign functionally "static" IP address to computers that require these, such as WINS and DNS servers. DHCP servers also require a static IP address. However, the DHCP server itself cannot be a DHCP client. Client reservations allow you to centrally manage IP addressing information on machines that might otherwise require manual configuration.

To create a Client Reservation, perform the following steps:

1. Open the DHCP Management Console.

2. In the left pane, expand the server name, and then expand the Scope folder. You will need to already have a scope in place to do this. Click the "Reservations" folder.

3. Right-click the "Reservations" folder, and select "New Reservation." You should see the New Reservation Dialog box as it appears in Figure 3.5.

Figure 3.5 Creating a reserved client.

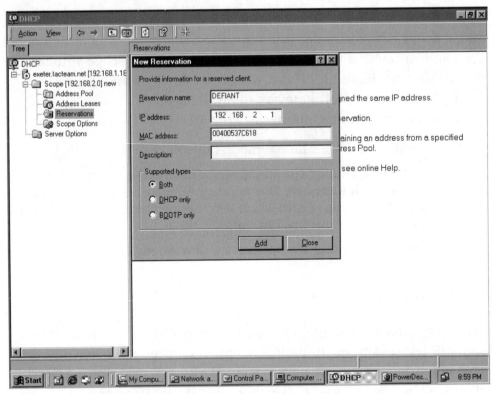

4. In the "New Reservation" dialog box, enter the following information:

    Reservation Name: The host name of the computer

    IP Address: The IP address of the computer

    MAC Address: The Media Access Control address (do not include dashes; MAC addresses might also be written or notated with spaces or colons.)

    Description: An optional field to describe the reserved client

    Support Types: Indicates whether this reservation is for a DHCP client, a BOOTP client, or both.

5. Click "Add" to complete the operation, then click "Close."

A reserved client's IP address must be included in an existing scope. Some administrators conclude that since the reserved client's IP address is not available to any other client, they should exclude its IP address. That is not correct.

Client Options can be now be configured. To create Client Options:

1. Open the DHCP Management Console.

2. In the left pane, expand the server name, expand the "Scope" folder, and then expand the "Reservations" folder. You need to have a scope in place to do this. Right-click the name of the client reservation you want to configure options, and then click "Configure Options."

3. Continue adding options in the same manner as above.

DHCP Options Order of Precedence

There is an order of precedence that applies when conflicts arise among DHCP options. This order is:

1. Client Options
2. Scope Options
3. Server Options

Should a conflict arise among the options delivered to the client, Client Options will override Scope Options, and Scope Options will override Server Options.

BOOTP/DCHP Relay Agent

The Routing and Remote Access Service must be installed prior to configuring the DHCP Relay Agent. After installing RRAS, open the Routing and Remote Access console, expand the server name, expand the IP routing node, then click on the DHCP Relay Agent node. In the right pane, you will see a list of Interfaces listening for DHCP broadcasts. Figure 3.6 demonstrates how the

Figure 3.6 DHCP Relay Agent node in the Routing and Remote Access Console.

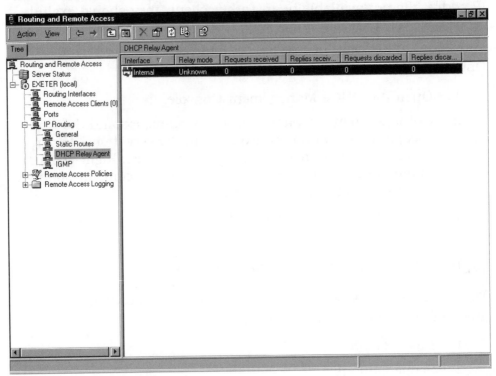

Routing and Remote Access console should appear to you at this point.

Double-click the interface of choice. You see the "Internal Properties" dialog box as seen in Figure 3.7. Put a checkmark in the "Relay DHCP Packets" box to enable DHCP Relay. The "Hop Count Threshold" allows you to configure the number of DHCP relay agents that determines the number of hops a DHCP message can take before being discarded. This prevents DHCP messages from looping endlessly throughout the network. The maximum setting is 16.

The "Boot Threshold" defines the number of seconds the relay agent waits before forwarding DHCP messages. This option is useful if you are using a combination of local and remote DHCP servers, as in the case of fault-tolerant setups. The Relay Agent should forward

Figure 3.7 The DHCP Relay Agent Internal Properties sheet.

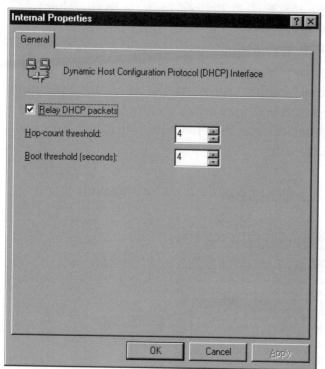

DHCP messages only if the local server becomes unavailable. This setting helps prevent a "flood" of routed DHCP packets. Do not implement both a DHCP relay agent and RFC-compliant router pass-through. If you choose the DHCP relay option, reconnoiter your network and disable BOOTP/DHCP forwarding on your routers to minimize pass-through broadcast traffic.

Vendor-specific Options

RFCs 2131 and 2132 define Vendor Classes, which allow hardware and software vendors to add their own options to the DHCP server. If a manufacturer wants custom DHCP options sent to the DHCP client, this custom option information can be made available when the DHCP client initializes and requests IP a lease from the DHCP server. A DHCP client can be configured to send vendor class identification to the DHCP server. The DHCP server will recognize the vendor's class identifiers and forward the vendor-configured options to the client.

The Vendor Options must be installed and configured on the DHCP server. Microsoft has included Vendor Class Options for Windows 2000 and Windows 98 clients, as well as a generic Microsoft operating system Vendor Class. The latter is used to deliver DHCP options to any Microsoft operating system that includes "MSFT" as a client identifier during the client initialization. You can see these options in Figure 3.8.

Figure 3.8 Server Options dialog box demonstrating built-in Vendor Classes.

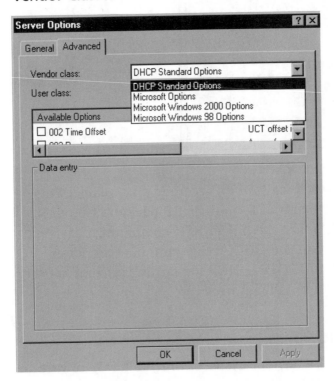

Microsoft vendor-specific options include:

- Disable NetBIOS over TCP/IP (NetBT)
  Allows an option to be sent to the client to disable NetBT.

- Release DHCP lease on shutdown
  Informs the client to release its lease shut down. You might use this with laptop computers that move on and off the network frequently. This will free up IP addresses in the scope.

- Default router metric base
  Sets the default base metric for the DHCP client. This value is used to calculate the fastest and least expensive routes.

- Proxy autodiscovery
  Used only by clients that have Internet Explorer 5.0. This option informs the client of the location of the Internet Explorer 5.0 automatic configuration file.

The administrator cannot create the Vendor Class options provided by the hardware or software vendor. The administrator can implement these options when available.

User Class Options

User Classes are part of a proposed Internet Standard under consideration by the Internet Engineer Task Force (IETF). User Classes allow DHCP clients to identify their "class membership" to a DHCP server. The server can then return to the client a specific set of options relevant to the "class."

Prior to implementing User Classes, you must define the class at the DHCP server. For example, you could classify a group of computers, which should use a specific IP address, subnet mask and default gateway, as "portable" by first creating the "portable" class at the DHCP server. Then define DHCP options at the server, which will be returned to any client that identifies itself as a member of the "portable" class. Next, configure the client to use the class, by issuing the ipconfig /setclassid command at the client.

Microsoft has included some built-in classes that are available "out of the box." These include Users Classes with special options for BOOTP and Remote Access Clients, as depicted in Figure 3.9 below.

Figure 3.9 Server Options Dialog Box demonstrating built-in User Classes.

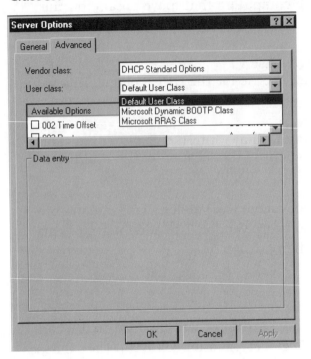

TIP

Scope Options override Server Options, Client Options override Scope Options, and User Class Options override all other options. For example, if we have a machine with a Client Reservation, this machine's reserved client options will override any other options that might be set for the server or for the scope. However, if the reserved client identifies itself as a member of a certain User Class, the User Class Options will override any reserved client options that are in conflict.

To create a new User Class:

1. In the DHCP Management Console, right-click on the server name, and then click "Define User Classes."

Figure 3.10 Creating a New User Class.

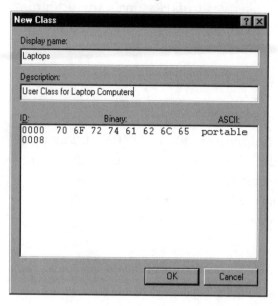

2. The "DHCP User Classes" dialog box appears. Click the "Add" button. You should now see the "New Class" dialog box as seen in Figure 3.10.

3. Enter in the display name of the class, and a description. To enter the User Class ID in ASCII, click on the right side of the lowest text box under "ASCII" and type in the Class ID. This is the Class ID you will use with the ipconfig command on the client to configure them to send their class membership to the DHCP server.

4. Click "OK" and then click Close to close the DHCP User Classes dialog box.

At the client machine, type in the following command to have the client identify itself as a member of the class:

```
ipconfig /setclassid adapter [classidtoset]
```

In the example above, the new class ID was "portable." At the client, we would open a command prompt and type:

```
ipconfig /setclassid DC21X41 portable
```

User Options allow us a greater level of granularity in the assignment of DHCP options. This improved granularity gives the administrator greater control over the TCP/IP parameters configured on the DHCP clients in his network.

BOOTP Tables

BOOTP (Bootstrap Protocol) is the predecessor to DHCP. It was originally designed to provide IP address configuration of diskless workstations, which booted from the server. DHCP was developed to improve on the host configuration services offered by BOOTP, and address some of the problems encountered in using it.

NOTE

BOOTP specifications are defined in RFC 951.

Similarities between DHCP and BOOTP

Because DHCP is based on BOOTP, they are alike in many ways. For instance, the request and reply messages they use are basically the same, using one 576-byte UDP datagram for each message. The headers are almost the same as well, although there is a slight difference in the final message header field that carries optional data: it is called the vendor-specific area in BOOTP, and whereas DHCP calls it the options field. The size of the field differs, too; the vendor-specific area is only 64 octets, while the DHCP options field can hold as much as 312 bytes of information.

Another thing the two protocols have in common is the use of the same UDP ports for communication between server and client. UDP 67 is used for receiving client messages, and UDP 68 is used to accept replies from a server.

Because of these similarities, relay agents generally don't distinguish between BOOTP and DHCP packets, treating them both the same.

Differences between DHCP and BOOTP

Despite the similarities noted above, there are some important differences between the two host configuration protocols. The IP address allocation methods are not alike – BOOTP normally allocates one IP address per client, which it permanently reserves in its database on the BOOTP server. DHCP, as its name implies, leases addresses dynamically, assigning an address to the client from a pool of available addresses and only temporarily reserving it in the server's database.

Many of the differences between BOOTP and DHCP stem from the difference in intended purpose. Unlike BOOTP, DHCP was originally designed to configure addressing information for computers with hard drives from which they could boot, especially laptops and other computers that are moved frequently.

Due to this, BOOTP uses a two-phase configuration process, in which client computers first contact a BOOTP server for address assignment, and then contact a TFTP (Trivial File Transfer Protocol) server to transfer their boot image files to boot the operating system. DHCP clients, which are capable of booting from their own hard drives, use a one-phase configuration process; the client negotiates a leased IP address from the DHCP server, which contains any other needed TCP/IP configuration details (such as subnet mask, default gateway, DNS and WINS server addresses).

Another difference is that BOOTP clients must restart in order to renew the configuration with the server. DHCP clients, however, can automatically renew their leases with the DHCP servers at pre-set intervals. It is valuable for a Windows 2000 administrator to be aware of the characteristics of BOOTP, since it is the foundation upon which automatic host configuration was founded.

Superscopes

Microsoft recommends the use of superscopes when you have more than one DHCP server on a subnet. A superscope is a Windows 2000 DHCP feature that lets you use more than one scope for a subnet. The superscope contains multiple "child" scopes, grouped together under one name and manageable as one entity. The situations in which superscopes should be used include:

- When many DHCP clients are added to a network, so that it has more than were originally planned for
- When the IP addresses on a network must be renumbered
- When two (or more) DHCP servers are on the same subnet for fault tolerance purposes

Using superscopes gives the administrator the flexibility to support DHCP clients in multinet configurations. A multinet is a network configuration in which multiple logical networks reside on the same physical segment. The administrator is able to activate the individual scope ranges of IP addresses used on the network, and provide leases from multiple scopes to the DHCP clients on the same physical network.

Superscopes are valuable in situations where the available DHCP addresses have almost been used up, and there are additional computers that need to join the network. Using a superscope will allow you to extend the address space for the network segment. In this situation, you can create a superscope with two child scopes: the original scope of addresses that is almost depleted, and a new scope for the additional computers that need to join the network.

Windows 2000 includes a "New Superscope Wizard" that guides you through the process. To start the wizard, access the DHCP management console (Start | Programs | Administrative Tools | DHCP), right-click the server name, and select "New superscope..." from the context menu.

Managing DHCP Servers

Managing DHCP servers is easier and more efficient than ever. Windows 2000 DHCP Service include Enhanced Monitoring and Statistical Reporting, as well as Rogue DHCP Server Detection.

Enhanced Monitoring and Statistical Reporting for DHCP Servers

The Windows 2000 DHCP Service supports enhanced ease of use and more statistical counters compared to its NT counterpart. You can view DHCP statistics such as the number of Discovers, Offers, Requests, Acks, and Declines by viewing them through though a window in the DHCP management console. Figure 3.11 shows the DHCP Statistics window.

The Performance Console contains DHCP objects counters including Informs/sec, Nack/sec, Offers/sec, Releases/sec, and Requests/sec as shown in Figure 3.12.

Figure 3.11 The DHCP Statistics Window.

Server 192.168.1.185 Statistics	
Description	Details
Start Time	Thursday, October 21, 1999 6:17:36 PM
Up Time	50 Hours, 28 Minutes, 37 Seconds
Discovers	10
Offers	10
Requests	194
Acks	3707
Nacks	0
Declines	0
Releases	0
Total Scopes	1
Total Addresses	16
In Use	11 (68%)
Available	5 (31%)

Refresh   Close

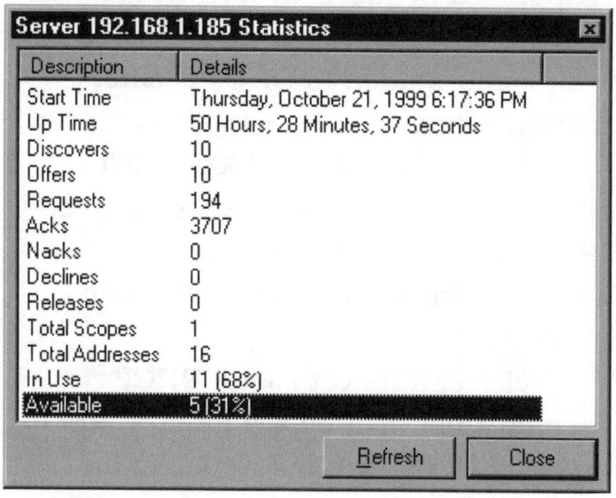

Figure 3.12 The Add Counters Dialog Box.

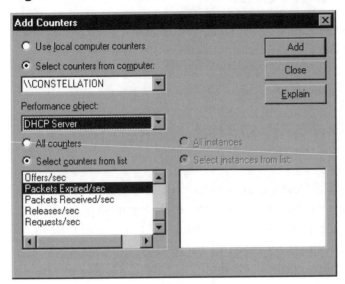

Authorizing DHCP Servers

DHCPDISCOVER is a broadcast message, which means it is indiscriminate. If an "unofficial" DHCP server is introduced to the network, an error in IP address assignment can occur. A "rogue" DHCP server (a DHCP server that has not been approved by the IT department) is likely to contain invalid scopes and DHCP options. Rogue DHCP servers can assign inaccurate IP addressing information to DHCP clients, which may disrupt network communications for these hapless clients.

Windows 2000 networks running only Windows 2000 DHCP Service can recognize and shut down rogue DHCP servers, by keeping a list of "authorized" DHCP servers in the Active Directory. Any DHCP server that starts up and is not included in the authorized list will be shut down automatically.

Only Windows 2000 DHCP Service can detect rogue DHCP servers, and the rogue DHCP server must also be a Windows 2000 computer. Rogue NT DHCP server detection will fail to detect an unauthorized Windows NT DHCP server.

How Rogue DHCP Servers Are Detected

When the Windows 2000 DHCP Service initializes, it broadcasts a DHCPINFORM message to the local segment. The DHCPINFORM message contains vendor-specific option codes that can be interpreted by Microsoft Windows 2000 DHCP servers. These option types allow the Windows 2000 DHCP service to obtain information about the network from other Windows 2000 DHCP servers on the segment.

The DHCPINFORM message submits queries to other Windows 2000 DHCP servers, and when a Windows 2000 DHCP Server on the segment receives this message, it responds to a DHCPINFORM query. This query asks for information about the Enterprise root name and location. The queried Windows 2000 DHCP Server responds by sending back a DHCPACK that includes Directory Services Enterprise Root information.

NOTE

The new DHCP server will receive DHCPACK messages from all the DHCP servers on its segment. This allows the new DHCP Service to collect information domain membership information about all Windows 2000 DHCP servers on its segment.

If the new DHCP server receives information about an existing Directory Services Enterprise Root, it will query the Active Directory, which maintains a list of DHCP servers that are authorized to participate in the domain. If the machine's IP address is on the list, it will successfully initialize DHCP server services. If not, DHCP server services will not initialize.The new DHCP server will start DHCP server services if:

1. There are other DHCP servers on the segment that are authorized DHCP servers and the new DHCP server is listed in the Active Directory's list of authorized DHCP servers, or

2.   The new DHCP server is the only DHCP server on the segment (If the new DHCP does not receive a response to the DHCPINFORM message query, the new DHCP server cannot be made aware of existing Directory Services Enterprise Roots), or

3.   The new DHCP server is on a segment with other Windows 2000 DHCP servers that are workgroup members or all other DHCP servers on the segments are downlevel systems (such as Windows NT DHCP servers).

In the second and third instances, the new DHCP server is unable to contact another DHCP server that has information about a Directory Services Enterprise Root. The "lone" DHCP server will send a DHCPINFORM message every five minutes. If the new DHCP server later receives a DHCPACK from a DHCP server that contains information about the Enterprise Root, the new DHCP server will look to see if it is authorized in the Active Directory and if not, will disable its DHCP server services.

Authorizing A DHCP Server

You must authorize a new DHCP server in the Active Directory. In this exercise, you will authorize your DHCP server.

1.   Open the DHCP Management Console.

2.   Right-click your computer name and click on "Authorize." (see Figure 3.13).

The DHCP server is now authorized. To confirm that the DHCP server was successfully authorized in the Active Directory, perform the following steps:

1.   Log on as Administrator at a Domain Controller in the Domain that the DHCP server was authorized in.

2.   Open the Active Directory Sites and Services Management console. You should see something like Figure 3.14.

3.   Right-click on the top level where it says "Active Directory Sites and Services" and point to the "View" menu. Click on "Show services node." You now see a services node in the left pane.

Figure 3.13 Using the DHCP MMC to authorize your new DHCP server.

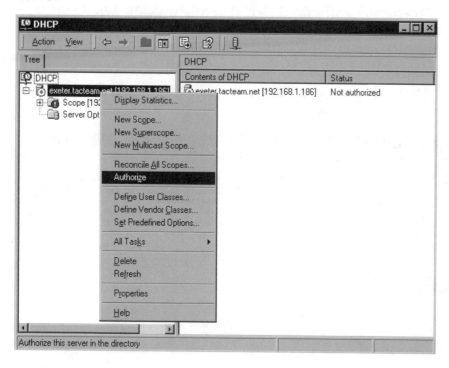

Figure 3.14 Using the Active Directory Sites and Services tool to confirm authorization of the DHCP server.

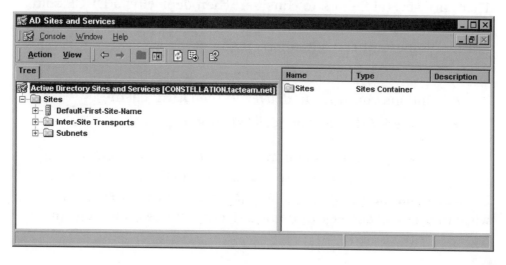

4. Expand the services node and click the folder "NetServices." In the right pane you see the Fully Qualified Domain Name of the newly authorized DHCP server with the type "DHCPClass." In Figure 3-15 you see that exeter.tacteam.net has now been authorized.

Figure 3.15 Finding the FQDN of your newly authorized DHCP Server.

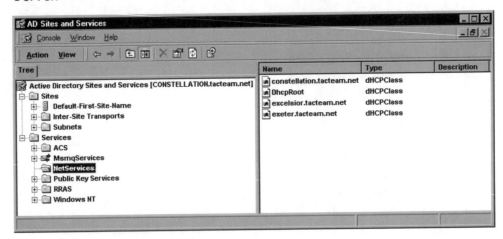

Deploying DHCP

There are several factors to consider when deploying a DHCP solution in an enterprise network that are related to its physical configuration. Important considerations include:

- The number of physical segments on the network
- Options you want to deliver to the DHCP clients
- Where WAN links connect network segments

Within a LAN environment, a single DHCP server can service multiple physical segments. You can place a DHCP Relay Agent on segments that do not house a DHCP server; however, segments without a DHCP server can be negatively impacted if intersegment traffic is interrupted.

If segments are joined by WAN links, it is a good idea to place a DHCP server on each side of the link. WAN links tend to be frail and less reliable than LAN connections. Placing a DHCP server on both sides of the WAN will ensure more reliable lease assignment.

The success of your DHCP deployment depends, to a large degree, on planning. You should determine beforehand what DHCP options you want to assign to each DHCP scope, as well as any global options you that should be assigned. You should also decide in advance what computers will require client reservations and what blocks of IP addresses should be configured from the scope.

DHCP, when properly deployed, can reduce administrative headaches, decrease the time spent on TCP/IP configuration, prevent configuration errors that occur when addresses are entered manually on each client, and help you avoid the problem of IP address conflict. Windows 2000 makes it easier than ever to administer DHCP services with the management console, which integrates the DHCP administration tools into one centralized location. Windows 2000 also includes command line DHCP tools.

Best Practices

The Windows 2000 DHCP Service allows you to customize DHCP in a way that works best for your network. Optimum DHCP lease assignment will depend on the size of the network, its physical characteristics (routed or non-routed), and the nature of its client connections (for example, whether there are remote access clients using DHCP).

Microsoft provides some guidelines and recommendations for the most effective and efficient implementation of DHCP in typical network configurations.

Optimizing Lease Management Practices

The default lease duration of eight days strikes a good medium for most networks. You can customize this value to optimize performance based on the unique characteristics of each network. The administrator can change the lease duration on a per-scope basis. In this section, we will examine when it is advantageous to lengthen or shorten the lease period.

Lengthening Lease Duration

Windows 2000's DHCP Service configuration allows you to change the duration of the leases. If you have a network that is extremely stable, and especially if it consists of multiple physical LANs connected by routers, it may be beneficial to increase the duration of the leases over the default (eight days). You can reduce the overall amount of DHCP-related broadcast traffic on the network by providing for longer lease periods. Extended lease periods can range from 9 to 60 days, depending on the nature of change on your network.

This solution should be used only if there are plenty of extra scope addresses available, to ensure that the longer lease duration doesn't result in a shortage of addresses when the clients "hold onto" their leases for an increased period.

NOTE

It is possible to set the lease duration for an infinite time, but this is not generally recommended.

Shortening Lease Duration

Conversely, when your supply of available IP addresses in the DHCP scope is limited, or if your client configurations are not fixed (such as when computers often change location), it may be best to decrease the lease duration so that addresses are returned to the pool more quickly.

There are also special situations in which you can optimize performance by reducing the duration of the lease for certain clients.

For example, when you have a segment that sees a lot of laptop computers entering and exciting the segment. In this way, their leases will be released more quickly to be available for assignment to other DHCP clients. Another situation in which you would benefit from temporarily shortening the lease period is if you plan on reconfiguring the IP infrastructure of the network (such as changing WINS, DNS, or Domain Controller IP Addresses).

You can create a User Class for laptop computers, as discussed above.

NOTE

Remember that RRAS clients obtain their address lease through the RRAS server, which gets a group of addresses from the DHCP server to distribute to its clients, and the RRAS server can specify options to the clients that use these proxied leases. RRAS Clients do not obtain Option information from a DHCP Server.

Determining the Number of DHCP Servers to Use

The number of clients, segments and WAN links in your organization determines the optimum number of DHCP servers.

There is no hard and fast rule regarding the exact number of servers required, and there is no theoretical limit to the number of clients a single DHCP server can service. However, DHCP is very disk- and CPU-intensive. It is recommended that you use the performance console to assess how your machines are impacted by DHCP services, and add DHCP servers when indicated.

You definitely should place a DHCP server on each side of a WAN or dial-up link, since these links can be slow or unreliable.

If DHCP servers will service remote segments, do not put all of the servers on the same segment. Placing them in different segments will prevent failure of DHCP services if the single segment is isolated from the rest of the network.

Fault-Tolerant Planning

DHCP fault tolerance can be achieved by providing for more than one DHCP server on each subnet. This gives the DHCP clients a "backup," so that if one server becomes unavailable, the other will still be able to grant new leases or renew existing ones.

A good rule of thumb for balancing the load between the servers is the "80/20 Rule." This DHCP design standard recommends that, when spreading a single scope of addresses between two DHCP servers, you should have one server distribute 80 percent of the addresses and have the second server distribute the other 20 percent.

Router Support Required

If you chose to enable pass-through of DHCP messages, you will require a router that is RFC 2132-compliant. Most modern routers support DCHP Relay and can be configured to do so based on the individual router's manufacturer's instructions.

However, older routers may not include software or firmware that supports DHCP Relay. If this is the case, first try contacting the router manufacturer to obtain a software upgrade. You may need to purchase new routers if no upgrade is available. The alternative is to use a Windows NT or Window 2000 computer as a DHCP Relay Agent.

Walkthrough

Installation of a DHCP Server

We will install the DHCP server software in this walkthrough.

NOTE

If you are doing this exercise on a corporate network, you must obtain permission from your network administrator. Installing an unauthorized DHCP server on your network can have severe negative consequences on network function and reliability.

To begin the installation, perform the following steps:

1. Log on as Administrator.

2. Click Start | Settings | Control Panel.

3. Open the "Add/Remove Programs" applet.

4. Click the "Add/Remove Windows Components" icon.

5. This takes you to the "Windows Components Wizard.". Scroll down so that you can see the "Networking Services" option. Highlight it, as shown in Figure 3.16. Do not remove the checkmark from the check box.

Figure 3.16 Add network services in the Windows Components Wizard.

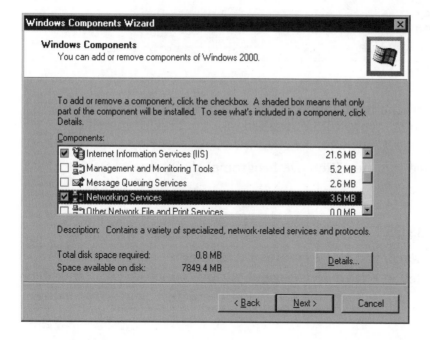

6. Click on the "Details" button in the "Windows Components Wizard" dialog box. Place a check in the box next to "Dynamic Host Configuration Protocol" as shown in Figure 3-17. Then click "OK."

7. After clicking "OK" you are returned to the "Windows Components Wizard" dialog box. Click the "Next" button.

Figure 3.17 Choosing DHCP as the network service to be added.

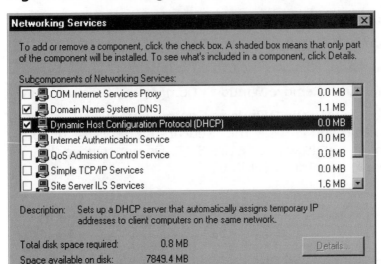

8. When the installation of the DHCP server software is complete, you will be notified of a successful installation. Click "Finish".

9. Close the "Add/Remove Programs" dialog box.

Creating Leases

To create leases, you must create and configure a scope. Windows 2000 includes a "Create New Scope" wizard, which greatly simplifies the process. In this walkthrough, we will create a new scope using the Wizard.

1. Click Start | Programs | Administrative Tools | DHCP.

2. Expand all levels in the left pane. You will see the server name and a folder for "Server Options" as they appear in Figure 3.18.

3. Authorize your server, if you have not already done so.

Figure 3.18 Preparing to configure the DHCP scope on your server.

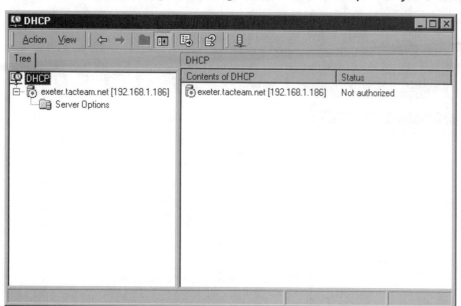

WARNING

If you do not authorize your server, it will be shut down as a rogue DHCP server.

Follow the procedure you read about earlier to authorize your server. After authorization, the server status will be labeled "running."

4. Click on the computer's name. In this example, I clicked on "exeter.tacteam.net." Notice the toolbar changes its appearance. Compare the appearance of the toolbars in Figures 3.18 and 3.19.

5. We will create a new scope, for network ID 192.168.2.0 with a subnet mask of 255.255.255.0 (the default Class C subnet mask, which uses 24 bits). Either right-click on your computer's name and select "New Scope" or click the rightmost icon on the toolbar (it looks like a video screen).

Figure 3.19 Dynamic toolbar changes appearance when different nodes are selected.

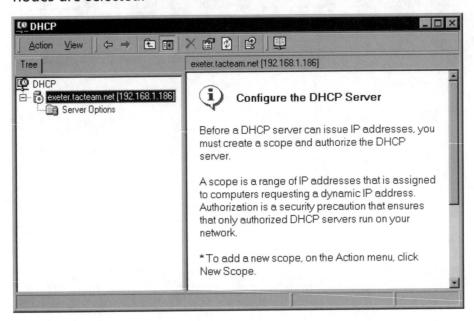

6. This opens the "New Scope Wizard" and you see the Welcome Screen. Click "Next."

7. Enter the name of the scope and a description to help you remember some characteristics of the machines using the scope, as in Figure 3.20. Click "Next."

8. Enter the first and last IP addresses in the range of addresses this scope will "hand out." Include the appropriate subnet mask. Enter 192.168.2.1 as the Start IP address and 192.168.2.254 as the End IP address as seen in Figure 3.21. Click "Next."

9. The Wizard allows us to exclude some IP addresses from the range defined above. Let's exclude the bottom five and top ten IP address. First enter the Start IP address 192.168.2.1 and the End IP address 192.168.2.5 then click "Add." Enter the Start IP address 192.168.2.245 and the End IP address 192.168.2.254 and click "Add." Your screen should look like Figure 3.22. Click "Next."

Figure 3.20 Naming the new scope.

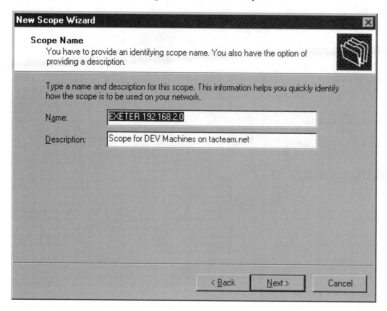

Figure 3.21 Defining the scope address range.

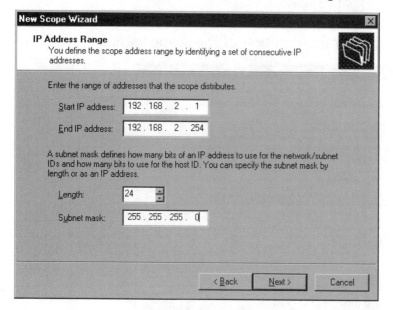

Figure 3.22 Excluding addresses from the scope's range.

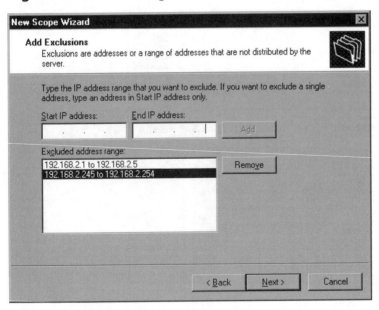

10. Set the lease duration for IP addresses delivered by this scope. Change the lease duration to 14 days, as in Figure 3.23. Then click "Next."

Figure 3-23 Specifying the duration of the scope leases.

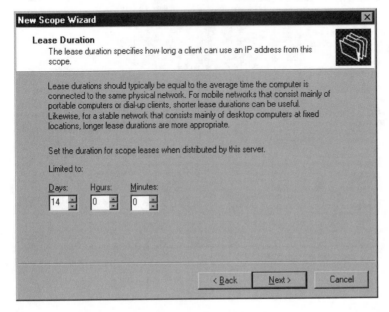

11. This dialog box offers you the opportunity to configure
     DHCP Options. Select the option button for "Yes, I want to
     configure these options now." Then click "Next."

12. The first option is for the Router (Default Gateway). Enter
     192.168.1.16 into the IP address space, and then click the
     "Add" button. You should now see this in the list as shown
     in Figure 3.24. Click "Next."

Figure 3.24 Setting the IP address for the default gateway
(router address).

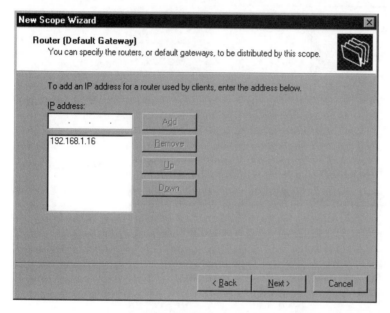

13. Choose the parent domain your DNS clients will use for DNS
     name resolution. You can also configure your DNS server
     name or address. Enter 192.168.1.185 in the IP address box
     as seen in Figure 3.25 below. Then click "Next."

14. Enter the IP addresses or names of your WINS servers. In
     the "IP address" box enter 192.168.1.185 and click "Add."
     Your screen should look like Figure 3-26. Then click "Next."

15. The Wizard asks if you would like to activate the scope.
     Select the option button for "Yes, I want to activate the
     scope now." Click "Next."

16. Click "Finish."

Figure 3-25 Choosing the DNS server.

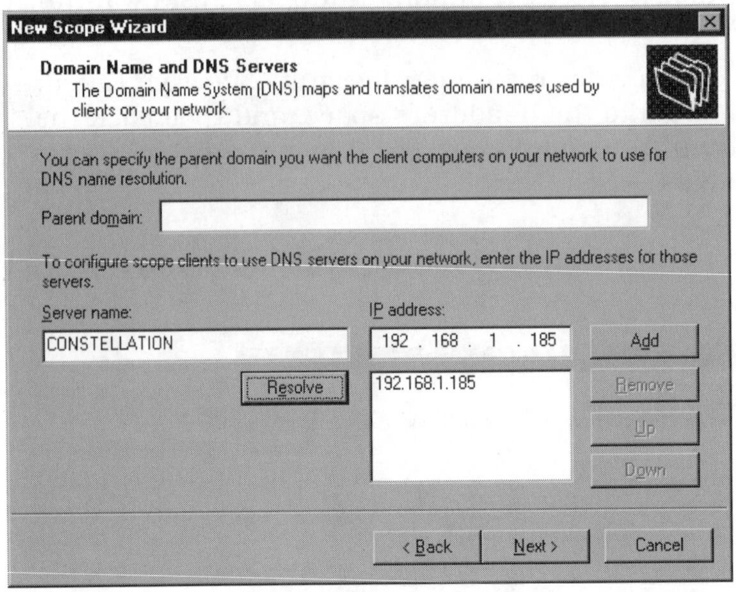

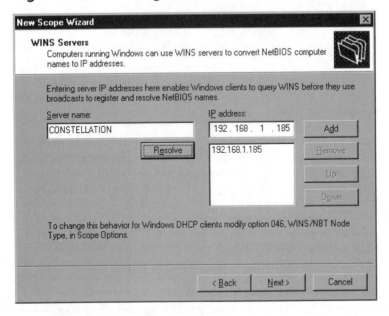

Figure 3.26 Defining the IP addresses or names of the WINS servers.

Return to the DHCP Management Console. Your screen should look similar to Figure 3.27.

Figure 3.27 Viewing the newly created scope in the DHCP MMC.

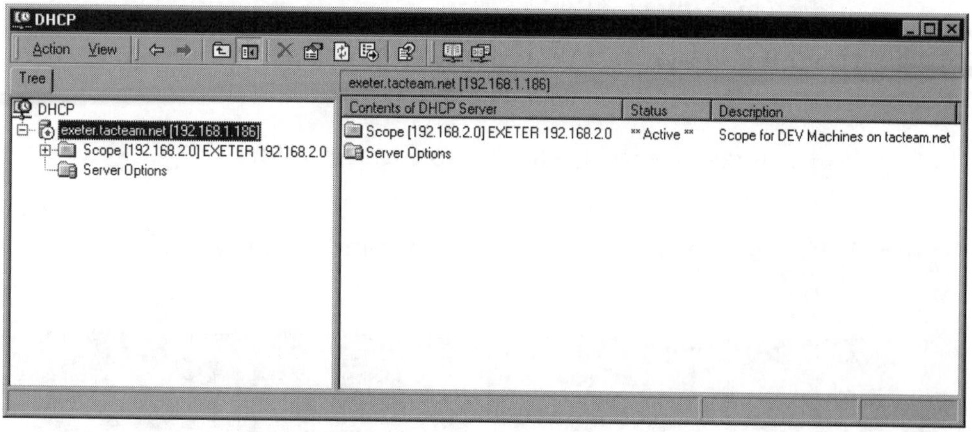

Testing your DHCP Server

In this walkthrough, we will examine what happens when a client moves from manually set static IP addressing information to automatically assigned information via DHCP.

WARNING

Again, do not complete this exercise on a corporate network without the express permission of your network administrator.

You will need two computers for this walkthrough. One will be a DHCP server and the other a DHCP client. The DHCP server must be a member of the Windows 2000 Server family of operating systems. The DHCP client can be either a Windows 2000 Server or Windows 2000 Professional computer.

1. Log on as Administrator at a Windows 2000 computer that is not a Domain Controller. This will be the DHCP client computer.

NOTE

This computer also must not be a DHCP, DNS, or WINS server.

The computer must already have manually configured IP addressing information.

2. Open a command prompt. At the command prompt type:

```
ipconfig /all
```

You will see a screen similar to Figure 3.28.

Figure 3-28 Using the ipconfig /all command to view DHCP information.

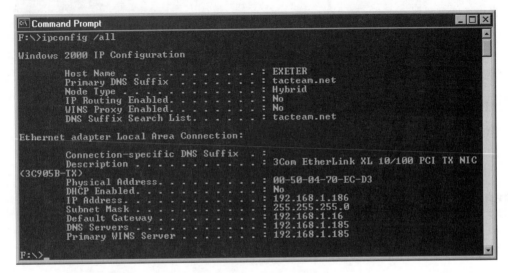

3. Close the command prompt window.

4. Right-click "My Network Places" and click "Properties."

5. You now see the "Network and Dial-up Connections" window. Inside this window is an entry for "Local Area Connection." Right-click the "Local Area Connection" icon and click "Properties."

6. This opens up the "Local Area Connection Properties" dialog box. Click "Internet Protocol (TCP/IP)" and click the "Properties" button.

7. You see the "Internet Protocol TCP/IP Properties" sheet as in Figure 3.29. Write down the IP address, subnet mask, default gateway and the preferred and alternate DNS servers. Click the "Advanced" button.

Figure 3.29 The TCP/IP properties sheet.

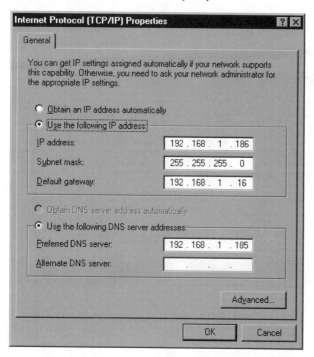

8. You then see the "Advanced TCP/IP Settings" properties sheet. There are four tabs, labeled IP Settings, DNS, WINS and Options. Click each of the tabs and write down the entries for DNS, WINS, and Options.

9. Close the TCP/IP properties sheets.

10. Move to your other computer that is the DHCP server. Log on as Administrator. Then click "Start" | "Programs" | "Administrative Tools" | "DHCP."

11. You see the DHCP administrative console. Expand all nodes in the left pane. Click on the "Scope Options" node and write down settings for each option.

TIP

Make special note of settings that are different from those you saw in the ipconfig /all screen print on the other computer.

The options should look similar to those seen in Figure 3.30.

Figure 3.30 Viewing the settings for the scope options node in the DHCP MMC.

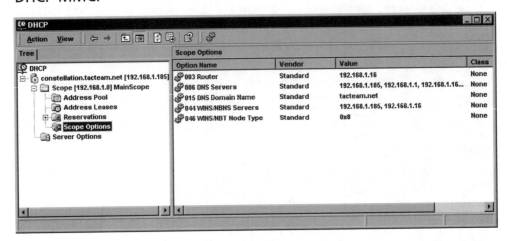

12. Click the "Address Leases" node. Your non-DHCP client is not listed in the right pane.

13. Close the DHCP console.

14. Click "Start" | "Programs" | "Administrative Tools" | "DNS." Expand all nodes in the left pane. Click on your domain name. If your soon-to-be DHCP client computer is listed there, right-click the computer's name and click delete.

WARNING

Do not remove the Domain Controller!

NOTE

After the computer is designated as a DCHP client, it will register itself again automatically in the DNS.

15. Return to the soon-to-be DHCP client computer. Return to the TCP/IP properties sheet. On the "General" tab, select the "Obtain an IP address automatically" option button. Select the "Obtain DNS server address automatically" option button. It should now look like Figure 3-31. Click "OK.". Restart the computer.

NOTE

The machine will immediately obtain its new settings from the DHCP server, but may not reliably register itself in the Active Directory unless you reboot).

Figure 3-31 Configuring TCP/IP properties for the DHCP client.

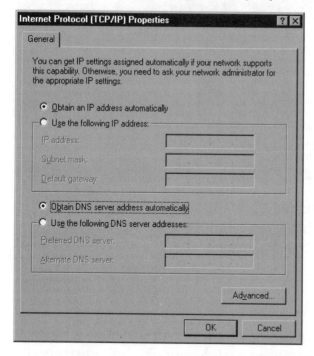

16. Log on again as Administrator.

17. Open a command prompt, and type:

```
ipconfig /all
```

Write down the information on this screen. How does this compare with the information you saw the first time you ran ipconfig? How does this compare with the information you saw when perusing the DHCP options?

18. Return to the DHCP server and log on as Administrator.

19. Open the DHCP console. Click the "Address Leases" node. Note that the other computer is listed in the right pane along with its leased IP address and the date of its lease expiration, as shown in Figure 3-32.

Figure 3.32 Viewing the DHCP lease address information in the DHCP MMC.

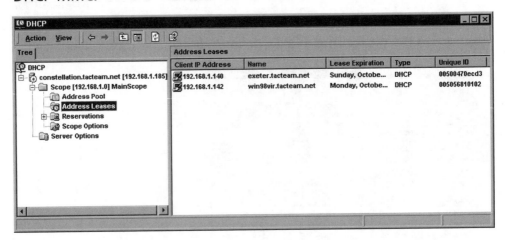

Close the DHCP console and open the DNS console. Click on your domain name. Note that your computer has registered its "A" Address record. Close the DHCP console.

Summary

The Dynamic Host Configuration Protocol was designed to fill the need for automatic and centralized assignment and administration of IP addresses in a large TCP/IP-based network. DHCP is implemented as a client/server protocol. Upon initialization, the DHCP client requests an IP address from a DHCP server, which is configured with a pool of addresses to assign to DHCP clients. The DHCP server can be configured to also send additional information to the DHCP client.

DHCP clients do not usually keep IP addresses indefinitely. Instead, IP addressing information is "leased" to DHCP clients. There are four steps to the lease process: DHCPDISCOVER, DHCPOFFER, DHCPREQUEST and DHCPACK. All DHCP messages are broadcasts.

A client must have a valid lease to retain an IP addresses, and will not be able to continue network activity if is does not retain a valid lease.

A lease will be renewed at 50 percent and 87.5 percent of the Lease period. At 50 percent of the lease period the client will broadcast a DHCPREQUEST message to the DHCP server that issued the lease. If the server is available, the lease is renewed. However, the client will keep its lease even if the server is not available. If the client was not able to renew its lease at the 50 percent mark, it will try again at 87.5 percent of the lease period. If successful, the lease is renewed. If unsuccessful, the client will broadcast a DHCPDIS-COVER message to obtain a new lease from any DHCP server. All TCP/IP Networking services will be shut down if the client is unable to obtain a lease. If the computer is configured to automatically assign itself an IP address, the computer will use the autoconfigured IP address instead of deinitializing TCP/IP.

Remember that broadcast messages do not traverse routers. DHCP messages can be communicated across routers if you configure a router to pass through BOOTP/DHCP messages via Port 67 or if you implement a DHCP Relay Agent. A DHCP Relay Agent intercepts multicast DHCP messages and forwards them as unicast messages to a DHCP server.

The pool of available IP addresses is called a scope. Only one scope is allowed per logical subnet. Scopes typically include all the available IP addresses for a specific network ID. Clients that require static IP addresses can be excluded from the scope. Excluded addresses will not be allocated to DHCP clients.

The DHCP server can deliver additional IP addressing information in the form of DHCP Options. A large number of DHCP Options are available, but Microsoft network clients support only a small number of DHCP Options. An example of DHCP Options information that can be delivered to DHCP clients would be the IP addresses of the WINS server and DNS server.

DHCP options can be configured at several levels. These include Server Options, Scope Options, Client Options, and Vendor Class/User Class Options. Server Options apply to all Scopes configured on a single server. Scope Options apply only to a single scope. Scope Options override Server Options.

A DHCP server can deliver the same IP address to a machine each time it renews a lease, if a client is designated as Reserved. A Reserved Client is a computer whose MAC address and IP address have been configured at the DHCP server. It is useful to create Reserved Client entries for machines that require static IP addresses, such as WINS and DNS servers. A Reserved Client can be configured with its own DHCP Options, and Reserved Client Options override Scope Options.

Vendor Class Options are introduced for the first time in the Windows 2000 DHCP server. They allow for a hardware or software manufacturer to add to the available set of DHCP Options. The DHCP client can identify itself as a member of the Vendor's class, and the DHCP server will send class members a custom set of options.

The DHCP administrator configures User Class Options, which are delivered to machines identifying themselves as a member of a particular User Class. For example, a User Class named "laptops" could be created. All laptops would be configured to send their Class ID to the DHCP server, and DHCP Options configured for the "laptops" User Class are then sent to these machines. Vendor and User Class Options override all other DHCP Options

DHCP clients unable to contact a DHCP server can autoconfigure their IP address. APIPA (Automatic Private IP Addressing) allows DHCP clients to self-assign an IP address from the 169.254.0.0 Class B network ID. When an autoconfiguing DHCP client holding a valid lease is moved to a foreign network, it will PING the address of the default gateway. If successful, it will keep its lease until lease renewal time. An autoconfigured client will broadcast a DHCPDISCOVER message every five minutes in an attempt to obtain a valid IP address. Autoconfiguration prevents TCP/IP from shutting down when a DHCP server cannot be contacted.

Routing and Remote Access Services (RRAS) can use DHCP to assign IP addresses to RRAS clients. The RRAS server obtains a block of IP addresses from a DHCP server during initialization. The RRAS server retains only the IP address itself and all Options information is discarded. Then the RRAS server assigns WINS and DNS settings to the RRAS client based on a connection-specific configuration on the RRAS server. This information does not come from the DHCP server. A RRAS client lease lasts for the duration of the connection.

The Windows 2000 DHCP Service also supports dynamic assignment of IP addresses to BOOTP clients, and Client Reservations can be configured for BOOTP clients, as well. The name of a TFTP server and the location of the Boot Image are configured in the DHCP server Boot Table.

A single physical network containing multiple logical subnetworks is called a multinet. A superscope must be configured to support multinet configurations. To create a superscope, you first create to individual scopes. Then you use the superscope wizard to join the individual scopes into a single administrative unit.

FAQs

Q: Why would I ever not use DHCP?

A: DHCP is the ideal solution for IP address management and allocation for large organizations. Small Offices or home networks that have a small number of clients do not require DHCP services. Automatic Client Configuration is the ideal solution for these environments. Also, if you have computers on the network that need static IP addresses, they should not use DHCP.

Q: What protocol and ports do DHCP use?

A: DHCP uses UDP ports 67 and 68.

Q: How does the DHCP server know what subnet the DHCP request came from?

A: The "giaddr" (Gateway Internet Address) field in the DHCP message includes the source network ID. The DHCP server will use this information to search for a Scope to service the client's request.

Q: Do any Routers have DHCP server functionality?

A: DHCP servers are very disk-intensive. For this reason, it is unlikely that any routers built by the major router manufacturers will include DHCP functionality, either now or in the future.

Q: Can I use DHCP for assigning IP addressing information to my routers?

A: You can do this, but it is not recommended. Gateway IP addresses need to be reliable and accessible to all clients. If the gateway address changes, some clients will not be able to connect to remote subnets.

Chapter 4

Windows 2000 DNS

Solutions in this chapter:

- **Understanding DNS**

- **How Name Resolution Works**

- **DNS and AD Integration**

- **Configuring DNS**

Introduction

The Domain Name System (DNS) is a distributed database that resolves host names to IP addresses. DNS solves a basic problem when connecting to servers on an intranet and on the Internet: names are easier to remember than numbers.

Windows NT 4.0 DNS servers were considered "add-on" products. All previous Microsoft Networks were based on the NetBIOS naming standard. Windows Internet Name Servers (WINS) provided NetBIOS name-to-IP-address resolution. DNS servers were added in the rare event that a WinSock client/server program was implemented. The integration of Active Directory and Dynamic DNS (DDNS) makes DNS services *sine qua non* in the network infrastructure.

Microsoft's stated goal is to eliminate NetBIOS. WINS servers allow NetBIOS clients to dynamically register their NetBIOS names with a WINS server. DDNS allows computers to update their host names dynamically. Dynamic DNS name registration allows administrators to wean their networks from the NetBIOS standard. WINS is included with Windows 2000 to allow downlevel, NetBIOS-based (such as Windows NT 4.0 and Windows 9x) systems to continue working as they did prior to Windows 2000.

If you elect to replace your existing DNS infrastructure with Windows 2000 DNS, you will be responsible for host name resolution, and thus access, not only to your NT Servers but also your Unix servers, mainframe computers, and the Internet.

Understanding DNS

The Domain Name System maps "friendly" names to IP addresses. DNS is like a phonebook. Host names are paired with their IP addresses like people's names are paired with their phone numbers. DNS performs a function similar to the Windows Internet Name Service (WINS). A WINS server matches up or *resolves* NetBIOS names to IP addresses.

During the Internet's early development, *name resolution* (associating a host name with an IP address) was accomplished through a

"HOSTS" file. HOSTS was a flat, text-based database. It contained the names and IP addresses of all the computers on the Advanced Research Projects Agency Network (ARPAnet). The ARPAnet was a forerunner of the Internet.

The HOSTS file faced a major challenge. This static text file had to be updated "by hand." Every computer on the ARPAnet had to download a copy of the HOSTS file after it was updated.

The Stanford Research Institute (SRI) maintained the central copy of the HOSTS file. Traffic to the SRI computer that housed the HOSTS file became problematic. A better approach to host name resolution had to be developed if the Internet was to ever go beyond a few thousand computers.

Clearly, no one person or entity could track the millions of host computers on the Internet. A method had to be developed that would allow distribution of responsibility for tracking and organizing local groups of computers. These groups would have their own database of host names to IP addresses. Others would share in this information. You could join these isolated databases to create a single large "distributed" database.

The distributed database approach would solve another problem. Large flat databases take a very long time to search. Name resolution queries aimed at such a file would take an unreasonable amount of time to complete. Performance would be improved by orders of magnitude by partitioning the database.

Domain Name Space

The Domain Name Space is a hierarchical construct. Examples of familiar hierarchical constructs include the File Name Space you see in the Windows Explorer and the Organizational Name Space in a corporate organizational chart. Comparing the DNS to the File System Namespace, you can consider each domain to be like a folder. Just as a folder can contain files and/or other folders, a domain can contain hosts and/or other domains.

The highest level of the DNS hierarchy is "root." A single period (".") represents the Root domain. Underneath the Root domain are the "Top Level" domains. Frequently encountered Top Level domains include: .com, .net, .org, .edu, .mil and .gov. Other Top Level domain names include a "Country Code" such as .ca or .au, representing Canada and Australia, respectively. Top Level domain names are assigned by the Internet Society (ISOC).

The domain names directly beneath the Top Level domains are the "Second Level" domains. Familiar Second Level domains include microsoft.com, syngress.com, and osborne.com. Assigning second level domain names had been the sole responsibility of Network Solutions, Inc. (NSI, previously known as InterNIC) until 1999. Other organizations can now register Second Level domain names. These are collectively the "Domain Registrars."

The only centralized aspect of the Internet is the management of Top and Second Level domains. Each organization is responsible for managing its portion of the domain name space once it is assigned a Second Level domain name.

Domains under the Second Level domains are called "subdomains." A DNS administrator's primary duty is managing his Second Level domain and the subdomains it contains. You will be responsible for designing, implementing, and maintaining subdomains.

Like any database, the DNS database contains records. Each domain contains "resource records." The resource records contain information about the DNS infrastructure. There are many types of DNS database records. The most common database record is the "A Address" record. The Address record contains a single host name and IP address mapping. Several domains and subdomains can be managed from a single DNS Server. A group of contiguous domains can be managed from a single DNS database file. All domains managed in a single DNS database file are members of the same "zone." We will talk more about zones a little later.

NOTE

A single DNS server can contain information about many domains. A zone may contain multiple contiguous domains. Multiple zone files may be placed on a single DNS server.

Domain Naming Conventions

Each domain name is separated by a "." (referred to as "dot"). Each domain or host name is a *label*. A label cannot be more than 63 octets (or bytes). A single ASCII character consists of 8 bits or 1 byte. Eight bits also defines an "octet." The entire fully qualified domain name cannot exceed 255 octets.

NOTE

A single domain or host label is limited to 63 octets (or bytes). The UTF-8 standard allows a single character to span more than a single octet. This is why it is more accurate to enumerate octets rather than characters.

Windows 2000 DNS Service supports the UTF-8 standard. UTF-8 allows for extended character set entries as DNS labels. Not all DNS servers support the UTF-8 standard. Only use extended characters in DNS labels when your DNS environment contains only Windows 2000 DNS servers. Standard characters for DNS label characters are a-z, A-Z, 0-9, and the hyphen. Note that the underscore is *not* supported. Standard DNS servers are not case-sensitive, www.Blah.com is the same as www.BLAH.com and resolve to the same IP address. File names included in a URL may be case-sensitive depending on the Web server implemented.

WARNING

DNS servers using the standard label character convention do not support the underscore. If your NetBIOS naming scheme includes machines with underscores in their names, now is a good time to rename them. Any new machines introduced into the network should conform to standard naming conventions. This will save you many headaches when you upgrade your domains to Windows 2000.

Host and Domain Names

Microsoft network operating systems are based on the NetBIOS naming standard. Network applications for Microsoft networks were written to the NetBIOS API. These programs accessed networking protocols via the NetBIOS session layer interface. NetBIOS names represent endpoints of communication between two computers using NetBIOS applications.

NetBIOS programs *must* know the NetBIOS name of the target computer to establish a session. Each computer on a NetBIOS network must have a NetBIOS name. The NetBIOS protocols use the NetBIOS name to identify computers on the Network. NetBIOS names represent each computer as a separate and distinct entity. The TCP/IP protocol uses IP addresses and port numbers as endpoints of communication. TCP/IP is oblivious to NetBIOS names.

How do we make TCP/IP "care" about NetBIOS names? This is the function of NetBIOS over TCP/IP or "NetBT." On TCP/IP networks, the NetBIOS name must be resolved to an IP address. Resolution of NetBIOS names to IP addresses can lead to additional broadcast traffic on the network.

Host Names

Applications written specifically for TCP/IP networks use the WinSock session layer interface. WinSock applications do not require the name of the destination computer to establish a session. WinSock applications only require the IP address and port number of the destination computer to establish a session. A WinSock computer name is a *host* name. Host names are *not* required to establish sessions between computers using the WinSock interface. Only the destination IP address and port number are required. A host name is a convenience. Names are easier to remember than numbers. In comparison, NetBIOS names are integral and required in NetBIOS networking. Host names are optional and convenient on IP networks.

You must not duplicate NetBIOS names. Great care had to be taken to ensure that all NetBIOS names were unique. If a second computer tried to join the network with a duplicate NetBIOS name, it would receive a negative name registration response and not initialize its networking subsystems.

The Domain Name System does allow two computers on the same network to share the same host name. This is a function of the hierarchical structure of the Domain Name System. Duplicate host names are not a problem as long as they are not on the same level and branch of the DNS tree. The DNS hierarchical namespace allows us to do this.

Fully Qualified Domain Names

Hosts names are "qualified" by identifying their position in the DNS tree. When a host name is combined with its parent DNS domain name path, it is called a *Fully Qualified Domain Name* (FQDN). In the following example there are two computers with the same host name:

www.tacteam.net

www.microsoft.com

These two computers share the same host name, "www." However, the DNS path to these hosts is different. This is comparable to mailing addresses. Two homes can have the same "house number," such as 123. However, the complete path to the home includes the street and city name. 123 Main St., Dallas and 123 Oak St., Austin are different because the path to 123 is different.

As it is read from left to right, note that the FQDN moves from specific to general. The is the opposite of a File System path that moves from general to specific as it is read from left to right.

Now it is clear why so many Internet servers can share "www" as their host name. This also explains the occasional URL containing an "unusual" host name, such as "www2", which may signify the corporation maintains more than one Web server on the Internet. It should also be evident that the "www" does not represent a protocol or "service." This author has, on more than one occasion, encountered systems engineers who believed the "www" represented a protocol or service. We see here that this is not the case.

WARNING

It is an Internet convention to name hosts by the services they provide. You give a Web server the host name "www." An FTP server is "ftp" and a mail server is "smtp." These host names are not service identifiers. A server named mail.tacteam.net may not have any e-mail function at all. Mail is the host name and nothing more.

Zones

We have now covered host and domain names. Domain names can be Top Level, Second Level, or subdomains. Each domain has its own resources described in resource records. Management of resources within domains is through DNS *zone files.*

A DNS zone file is a database. Each domain or group of domains included in a zone file are members of the same DNS *zone.* There are two standard zone types: forward *lookup* zones and *reverse lookup* zones. A forward lookup zone allows for resource name-to-IP-address resolution. The resource type varies. Examples of resources include Mail Exchangers, Host Addresses, and Aliases. We will discuss the different types of resources later in the chapter. A reverse lookup zone allows for IP-address-to-resource name resolution.

Using Zones

Let's look at an example. The .net domain is the Top Level domain. We have a Second Level domain named tacteam.net. Tacteam has facilities in Dallas, Seattle, and Boston. We want to partition tacteam.net's resources into three domains: tacteam.net, west.tacteam.net, and east.tacteam.net. The west.tacteam.net domain contains resource records for machines in Seattle. The east.tacteam.net domain contains resource records for machines in Boston, and the tacteam.net domain contains resource records for machines at our headquarters in Dallas.

NOTE

Be aware that DNS domain names are not NT 4.0 domains. An NT 4.0 domain represents a security context in which all domain members participate. DNS domains use DNS queries that are used to organize resources so they can be found.

Our main operation is in Dallas. The majority of our employees and computer personnel are located here. The Seattle facility has programmers and a small systems administration division. The consulting division is located there as well. The Boston office has sales and marketing personnel. There are no computer professionals on site in Boston.

We will manage these three domains using two zones to assure accurate and timely management of the DNS database. One zone includes both the tacteam.net and the east.tacteam.net domains. The other zone includes only the west.tacteam.net domain.

The zone containing both the east.tacteam.net and the tacteam.net domains is named the "tacteam.net" zone. Tacteam.net represents the highest-level domain represented in the zone and therefore makes it the "root" domain in the zone. Moreover, the name of the zone is derived from the zone's Root domain. The west.tacteam.net domain is contained in the west.tacteam.net zone. West.tacteam.net is the only domain in the zone and therefore is the root.

Why Partition Three Domains into Two Zones?

This is how we distribute responsibility for maintaining domain resource records to personnel capable of administrating them. Zones and domains are not the same. Domain information is saved in zone files. You can include multiple contiguous domains in a single zone file. A single DNS server can house multiple zone files. Physical disk files contain the zones information. Each domain can be considered as a different table in the zone database.

Reverse Lookup Zones

Reverse lookup zones allow for reverse lookups. Many diagnostic tools such as nslookup and domain security assessment programs make extensive use of reverse lookup queries.

Forward lookup queries resolve an IP address from a host name. A reverse lookup query does the opposite: it resolves a host name from an IP address. Forward lookup zone files are not structured to perform reverse lookups. You need to create a reverse lookup zone to perform reverse lookups.

The reverse lookup zone is contained in a domain known as in-addr.arpa. Subdomains of the in-addr.arpa domain are based on the dotted quad representation of each network ID, but the order of the octets is reversed.

For example: you have a Network ID of 131.107.0.0. The name of the reverse lookup zone would be 107.131.in-addr.arpa. If you had a network ID of 192.168.2, the reverse lookup zone would be 2.168.192.in-addr.arpa. A network ID of 10.1.0.0 would have a reverse lookup zone of 1.10.in-addr.arpa.

Reverse lookup zones are created independently of forward lookup zones. Reverse lookup zones are not mandatory. Reverse lookup zones use Pointer (PTR) records to provide IP address-to-host-name resolution. You can enter pointer records manually, or have a pointer record created automatically each time you enter an "A" Address record to a forward lookup zone.

Zone Transfer

When a zone is created it becomes the master copy of that zone. The DNS server containing this copy is called a *Primary* DNS server. The Primary DNS server has the only read/write copy of the zone database file.

Domain name servers share information via *zone transfer*. The master copy of the zone file can be copied to another DNS server. The DNS server receiving the copy of the zone file from the Primary DNS server is the *Secondary* DNS server.

A *Master* DNS server is one that sends a copy of its zone information to a Secondary DNS server. Note that DNS server can take on multiple roles. A DNS server can be a Primary for one zone, and a Secondary for another zone. A Secondary DNS server can be a Master to another Secondary DNS server when it copies a zone file to another DNS server.

NOTE

A Master DNS server does not need to be a Primary DNS server. Secondary servers can transfer zone files to other Secondary servers. A Secondary Master server copies the zone database to another Secondary.

Primary and Secondary DNS servers allow for fault tolerance. If the Primary DNS server is disabled, DNS clients can access zone information from a Secondary DNS server. Secondary DNS can optimize DNS query performance.

For example, a DNS client is located in a satellite office that is separated from the Primary DNS server via a 56k Frame Relay. The Frame Relay link is often saturated during normal business hours. DNS queries are slow during times of network congestion. A Secondary DNS server can be placed at the satellite location. This avoids reaching across the WAN to query the DNS server. The satellite DNS server receives zone information from the Primary DNS on the other side of the WAN through zone transfer.

Methods of Zone Transfer

Previous versions of Microsoft DNS servers transferred the entire zone database during a zone transfer. The Secondary DNS server initiates zone transfers. The Secondary DNS server sends a "pull" request to the Primary DNS server. The first record the Primary DNS server sends is the *Start of Authority (SOA)* record.

The SOA record contains the "Refresh Interval." The Secondary DNS server waits this time before requesting another update to its zone file. The Refresh Interval determines how often the zone database on the Secondary updates.

When you create a new zone, it has a *serial number* of 1. Each time a change is made to the zone database, the serial number is incremented by 1. Each time the Primary updates the Secondary's zone file, the Secondary's zone serial number updates. The serial number is included in the Start of Authority Record sent by the Primary DNS server. The Secondary examines the serial number in the SOA record and compares it to the serial number of its own zone file. If the SOA number is larger, the Secondary sends an *AXFR* request. An AXFR request instructs the Primary DNS server to send the *entire* zone database.

The Retry Interval

The Primary DNS server may at times be unavailable. The SOA record on the Secondary server includes a *Retry Interval*. The Retry Interval defines the period of time the Secondary should wait until sending another pull request message.

Compatibility of DNS Server Versions

The zone transfer sends a compressed version of the zone database. This speeds file copy over the network. Care must be taken when running a mixed DNS server environment. DNS servers running versions of BIND (Berkeley Internet Name Domain) lower than 4.9.4 do not support this method of transfer.

Incremental Zone Transfers

Windows 2000 DNS Service supports a more efficient mode of zone transfer than AXFR. These zone transfers require the entire zone database to be copied during each update. Zone transfers can con-

sume a significant amount of bandwidth even when the zone database is compressed. This is especially true in large DNS installations and voluminous zone databases.

Windows 2000 DNS Service support *incremental* zone transfers.
An incremental zone transfer sends only new or changed records.
RFC 1995 delineates incremental zone transfer standards.

The Windows 2000 Secondary DNS Service pull request sends an
IXFR query rather than an AXFR query. The Master server responds
to an IXFR query by sending new and changed records.

The Master server keeps a zone database *change history*. Serial
numbers are associated with changes to the zone file. When the
Secondary sends an IXFR query. The Master and Secondary's serial
numbers are compared, and records added or changed since the
Secondary's serial number is transferred. The Secondary updates its
zone database with the new and changed records and the zone serial number updates to reflect that of the Master DNS server's at the
time of zone transfer.

Your existing DNS servers may not support IXFR query requests.
Downlevel DNS servers do not support incremental zone transfer.
They cannot issue an IXFR query to the Master server. Downlevel
DNS servers only issue AXFR query. In this scenario, the Windows
2000 Master DNS Service responds to the AXFR query by sending
the entire zone database.

DDNS Dynamic Updates

You must manually update resource records on downlevel DNS
servers. A DNS administrator enters each record "by hand." There
are significant limitations to manual updates:

1. They can be very time consuming during large-scale DNS
    rollouts or upgrades.

2. It is unrealistic to include DHCP clients in the DNS. DHCP
    clients change IP addresses on a regular basis.

Windows 2000 premieres the first Microsoft Dynamic DNS
Service (DDNS). A DDNS updates resource records dynamically in a
fashion similar to a WINS server. Clients can update their own

Address and PTR record when configured to do so. Dynamic DNS update standards are described in RFC 2136.

A Windows 2000 DHCP Service supports dynamic updates for downlevel clients. When a downlevel Windows 2000 DNS client is also Windows 2000 DHCP Service client, the Windows 2000 DHCP server sends both Address and Pointer record information on the behalf of the downlevel client to the DDNS server.

Only the Primary DNS server can receive dynamic updates in a standard DNS zone. When the DNS zone database is integrated with the Active Directory, any Domain controller in the domain can accept dynamic updates. Windows 2000 DNS client computers send an UPDATE message to the DDNS computer to update their records. Downlevel clients cannot update their own Address records.

Understanding Name Resolution

WinSock applications require the IP address of the destination host to establish a session. Users work with host names rather than IP addresses. The process of finding the IP address for a particular host is *host name resolution*. *Resolver* software formulates and issues query statements sent to the DNS server. Resolver software can be included in the WinSock application, or in the case of Windows 2000, it can be a component of the operating system. Examples of WinSock programs including resolver software are:

- Web browsers (such as Microsoft Internet Explorer)
- FTP clients (such as the command line FTP program found in Windows 2000)
- Telnet clients
- DNS servers themselves.

NOTE

Any program or service that issues DNS queries uses resolver software.

Recursive Queries

When you type a FQDN in the address bar of a Web browser, the resolver sends a query to the client's Preferred DNS server. The DNS server *must* respond to the query either positively or negatively. A positive response returns the IP address. A negative response returns a "host not found" error. A recursive query is one that requires a definitive response, either affirmative or negative. *Referral* is not an option.

Say you were asked, "Who was the 17th president of the United States?" How might you go about answering this question? You could give the correct answer, or admit that you don't know. The former is affirmative and the latter is negative. If you were required to limit yourself to either of those options, you would have been performing *recursion*, and returning a *recursive response*.

Iterative Queries

Is there any other approach you can use to answer the question? You could say, "Hold on, I'm going to find out." Then you would ask other people, who might refer you to other people, who might know the answer. You have this option if I were to issue to you an "iterative" query. Iterative queries allow the DNS server to make a best effort attempt at resolving the DNS query. If the DNS server receiving an iterative query is not authoritative for the domain in the query, it can return a *Referral* response. The Referral contains the IP address of another DNS server that may be able to service the query.

The DNS client sends a recursive query to its Preferred DNS server. If the Preferred DNS server is not authoritative for the host domain in the query, it will issue iterative queries to other DNS servers. Each DNS server can respond with a Referral to another DNS server that brings the query closer to resolution.

Looking up an Address from a Name

The following represents the sequence of events during the host name resolution process using both recursive and iterative queries. In this example, we want to connect to a Web server at tacteam.net:

1. Type exeter.tacteam.net in the address bar of the Web browser, and press "Enter." After pressing "Enter," the resolver formulates a recursive query to send to the Preferred DNS server.

2. The Preferred DNS server will check to see if it is authoritative for the domain in the query. The server will first check its cache to see if it has recently resolved the same host name. If the IP address is not in its cache, and if the DNS server is not "authoritative" (does not contain a zone for the target domain) for the queried domain, it will send an iterative query to an Internet "root" name server. At this point, the Preferred DNS server becomes a DNS client itself. The Preferred DNS server starts the iterative query process in order to complete recursion. Once recursion is complete, a definitive answer can be returned to the client.

3. The root name server is not authoritative for tacteam.net. However, the Internet Root DNS server is authoritative for all Top Level domains. This includes the "net" domain. The Root server sends the IP address of the DNS server authoritative for the domain to the Preferred DNS server.

4. The Preferred DNS server connects to a DNS server authoritative for the net domain. The net domain DNS server is not authoritative for the tacteam.net domain. In a best effort attempt, the net domain DNS server returns to the Preferred DNS server the IP address for the DNS server authoritative for the tacteam.net domain.

5. At this point, the Preferred DNS server queries the DNS server authoritative for the tacteam.net domain. The tacteam.net DNS server checks its zone files for an address record containing exeter.tacteam.net. Exeter is located in the tacteam.net domain, and there is an address record for it in the zone database. The tacteam.net DNS server responds to the Preferred DNS server the with IP address of host computer, Exeter.

6. The preferred DNS server has completed recursion. It responds to the client with a recursive response and sends the IP address of exeter.tacteam.net. You can establish a connection to the destination host because the IP address is known. If the tacteam.net DNS server did not have an address record for Exeter, the Preferred server would have issued a recursive response in the negative.

Note that both the requesting host and the Preferred server acted as resolvers in the above process.

NOTE

The DNS server caches the results of successful queries. This reduces Internet traffic to Internet Root servers. Extended periods of up-time allow the DNS cache to build. DNS requests speed up significantly after the DNS server has built up a large cache of successful queries.

Looking up a Name from an Address

We have examined how we can resolve a host name to an IP address. Occasionally we need to do the opposite, resolve a known IP address to a host name. IP-address-to-host-name resolution can aid in investigating suspicious activity. Many security analysis programs use IP address-to-host-name resolution.

A HOSTS file can be used to map host names to IP addresses. It is simple to search the HOSTS file to find an IP-address-to-host-name mapping. However, this situation becomes much more complex when dealing with a worldwide distributed database.

The primary "index" for the Domain Name System is the domain name. The forward lookup is based on this indexing scheme. Finding a domain name using the IP address as the index value would require an exhaustive search of the entire DNS. Reverse lookups could be accomplished this way, but performance would be so dismal they would be of no use.

The answer lies in creating *another* domain that uses IP address-es as the index value. Then we can search this domain in the same way as we did the forward lookup domain. This is the *in-addr.arpa* domain.

Each node in the in-addr.arpa domain is named after numbers found in the w, x, y, and z octets of the Network ID. Each level in the in-addr.arpa domain can contain 256 domains corresponding to the possible values for each octet. At the bottom are the actual resource records (PTR records) that contain the IP-address-to-host-name mapping.

As we saw above, the in-addr.arpa domain notation is the reverse of the forward lookup domain convention. For example, if tacteam.net has a network ID of 21.18.189.0, the in-addr.arpa sub-domain is 189.18.21.in-addr.arpa. This maps to the domain name tacteam.net.

IP addresses, like domain names, are hierarchical. Network IDs are assigned in a fashion similar to domain names. Like subdo-mains within the Second Level domain, you can subdivide or subnet your Network ID any way you like.

We can delegate authority in the same way as is done for the for-ward lookup domain when we make the leftmost octet the top of the hierarchy. For example, the 126.in-addr.arpa domain contains reverse mappings for all hosts whose IP addresses start with 126. The administrator of network 126 can delegate authority for the 255 subdomains of the 126 domain.

The iterative and recursive query process works the same when performing reverse lookups as it does when performing forward lookups.

WARNING

As the administrator of your own subdomains, you are not required to create or maintain reverse lookup zones. Some network security analysis software will not work correctly if reverse lookup zones are not created.

Active Directory and DNS Integration

To this point, we have focused on traditional DNS zone management. Windows 2000 allows DNS integration with the Active Directory. There are significant advantages to integrating Windows 2000 zones with the Active Directory.

DNS is required for Active Directory-enabled Windows 2000 domains. Windows 2000 Domain Controllers are located via DNS queries. The Netlogon service searches for a log-on server via DNS. Prior to Windows 2000, WINS servers provided this function. However, Windows 2000 is no longer dependent on NetBIOS. Core network functionality is mediated through the WinSock interface.

The more efficient and fault-tolerant Active Directory replication model provides the primary advantage of integrating DNS with the Active Directory. In addition, Dynamic DNS updates can be secured by using Active Directory-integrated zones.

When Active Directory is installed on a Domain Controller, it will seek out a DNS server authoritative for the Domain. If it cannot find an authoritative DNS server, or if the authoritative DNS server does not support Dynamic updates and SRV records, the installer will require you create a DNS server on that machine. Active Directory domain names are DNS domain names.

You are not required to integrate DNS zones with the AD. You have the option of using either standard or AD-integrated zones. As you saw earlier, standard zones are stored in text-based files with the .dns extension.

Zones stored in the Active Directory are located in the Active Directory tree. Each directory-integrated zone is stored in a Microsoft DNS container object, as seen in Figure 4.1.

Microsoft recommends that if Active Directory is implemented on your network, you integrate your DNS zones into the AD to take advantage of multimaster replication and enhanced zone fault tolerance. Also, since workstations are dynamically entered into DDNS via DHCP, there will be many DNS changes (more than when only the servers are entered). Thus, the more efficient

Figure 4.1 An Active Directory integrated zone container object.

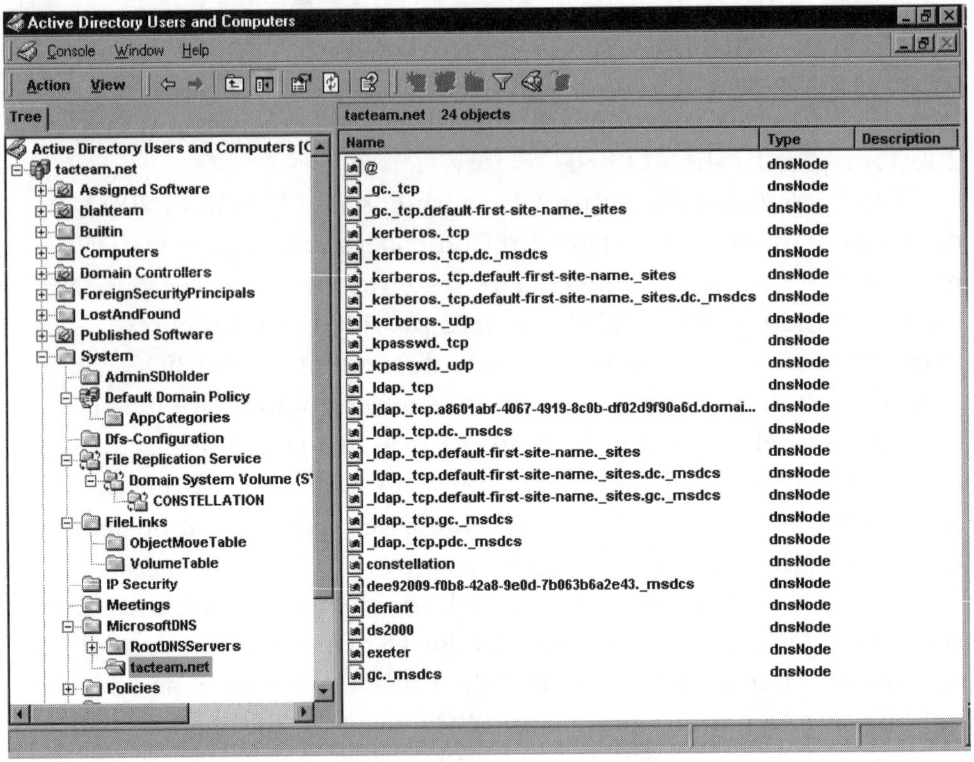

replication scheme finds its best application when DHCP is in widespread use.

Using Active Directory to Replicate and Synchronize DNS

In a standard zone environment, the DNS Primary (Master Zone server) contains the only read/write copy of the zone database. Zone transfer takes place when the Refresh interval has expired. Secondary DNS servers send a pull request to Master DNS servers to receive the zone database. The Secondary DNS server contains a read-only copy of the zone database. This standard zone schema has a single point of failure. If the Primary server for the zone is disabled, accurate zone updates and zone transfers are halted.

The Active Directory integrated zone does not have a single point of failure. DNS zone information is stored in the AD and each authoritative server contains a read/write copy of the zone database. A single "downed" Domain Controller will not prevent zone transfers and zone updates. Updates and transfers continue to take place among all other AD Domain Controllers for the domain.

RFC 2137 Secure DNS Updates

You can implement security measures in AD-integrated zone that are not available in standard zones. RFC 2137 defines the standards for secure updates to an AD-integrated zone. You can control which computers or groups can update resource records by setting access controls in the Active Directory. This prevents unauthorized and potentially malicious attempts to alter information in the zone database. Secure updates are the default for AD-integrated DNS zones.

Zone transfer takes place in a secure fashion immediately upon adding a new AD Domain Controller. You do not need to configure DNS server properties to setup and tune the zone transfer process.

Changing Zone Types

You can easily change the zone type from AD-integrated to standard via the DNS Management Console. You can change a standard zone into an AD-integrated zone, and then change the AD-integrated zone back to a standard zone. The procedure is as easy as making a single click on an option button in the DNS Management Console.

AD-integrated zone management is easier from the planning and design perspective. If you use the Active Directory, and Standard DNS zones, you will need to plan and configure two separate replication strategies: one for AD database replication and the other for

DNS zone database replication. AD-integrated zones provide a unified entity for replication and management of domain and zone information. This also decreases the amount of bandwidth required for zone transfer. AD-integrated zone transfers only replicate property information that has changed. It does not send the entire record.

Integration with DHCP

The Windows 2000 DHCP Service has enhanced capabilities compared to the Windows NT DHCP server. Windows 2000 DHCP server can deliver host name and IP addressing information to a Windows 2000 DDNS server.

The Windows 2000 DHCP Service interacts with a Windows 2000 Dynamic DNS Service in one of three ways after assigning a DHCP client an IP address:

1. It will update the DNS server by providing information to create an "A" address and PTR (pointer) record at the request of the DNS client.

2. The DHCP server will update both the Address and the pointer record regardless of client request.

3. The DHCP server will never register information about the DHCP client. However, the client itself may contact the Dynamic DNS server directly with this information.

The DCHP/DDNS interaction varies with the client receiving the IP addressing information from a DHCP server. The interplay between the Windows 2000 client and Windows 2000 DHCP encompasses the following:

1. The Windows 2000 Client broadcasts a DHCPREQUEST message and receives an IP address. The Windows 2000 client will register its own Address record with the Dynamic DNS server after official obtaining a lease.

2. The DHCP server registers the client's PTR record with the DDNS server. This is the default behavior for a Windows 2000 client and Windows 2000 DHCP Service.

3. Client and server parameters can be manipulated to allow the DHCP server to update both Address and PTR records. If desired, the DHCP server and DCHP client can be configured so that no dynamic updates are made to the DDNS server.

This is what happens when dealing with pure Windows 2000 environment. Downlevel clients are not able to send "A" Address record information to a DDNS server. The DHCP server will act as "proxy" and will forward both Address and PTR information to the DDNS server for downlevel clients.

Windows 2000 computers configured with static IP addresses update their own Address and PTR records with the DDNS server. If you change the name or IP address of a Windows 2000 client with a static IP address, you can manually update the client's entry in the DDNS server by issuing the command:

```
ipconfig /registerdns
```

This command is done from a command prompt window. Downlevel clients with static IP addresses are not able to communicate directly with the DDNS server. You must manually reconfigure DDNS entries for these clients.

WARNING

You must use only Windows 2000 DHCP Service on your network to guarantee that dynamic updates are successful on downlevel clients.

Registration of Server in DNS using the SRV Record

Active Directory Domain Controllers must be registered in the DNS. Domain Controller (DC) entries in the DNS include special SRV records which contain information about their DC status. The

Netlogon service on Domain Controllers automatically registers these SRV resource records via dynamic DDNS update.

These *SRV* (Service Location) records provide a function similar to the service identifier used in the NetBIOS name. For WINS clients, the client could query the WINS database for the service desired by examining the service identifiers recorded in the WINS database. Windows 2000 DCs are able to dynamically update SRV records on a DDNS server and provide information about available services. Examples of such services include LDAP, FTP, and WWW. Domain clients must find a SRV record for a DC in the DNS database in order to find a DC to authenticate logon. There is a SRV record for Kerberos information. This allows Kerberos clients to locate the Key Distribution Service in their domain.

Every Windows 2000–based domain controller dynamically registers a host resource record containing the name of the domain where the domain controller is located. The "A" Address record makes it possible for clients that do not recognize SRV records to locate a domain controller by means of a generic host lookup. Again, the process is similar to the domain name registration done on WINS servers by domain controllers.

There may be times when you will have to manually add SRV records for Domain Controllers. An unfortunate example is the administrator who inadvertently deletes these records. It is important to restore these records on a timely basis, since Domain Clients are dependent on these records for domain activity.

To view the SRV resource records that are created by a domain controller, open and view the *Netlogon.dns* file. The Active Directory Installation wizard created this file during setup. It can be found in:

```
%systemroot%\System32\Config\Netlogon.dns
```

The contents of this file look like those in Table 4.1.

Each record contains the complete AD path. Be sure when creating a new SRV record for a domain controller that the record is placed in the appropriate container object in the AD as indicated by the path defined in the netlogon.dns file.

Table 4.1 Example Contents of netlogon.dns File

```
tacteam.net. 600 IN A 192.168.1.185

_ldap._tcp.tacteam.net. 600 IN SRV 0 100 389 CONSTELLATION.tacteam.net.

_ldap._tcp.pdc._msdcs.tacteam.net. 600 IN SRV 0 100 389
CONSTELLATION.tacteam.net.

_ldap._tcp.a8601abf-4067-4919-8c0b-
df02d9f90a6d.domains._msdcs.tacteam.net. 600 IN SRV 0 100 389
CONSTELLATION.tacteam.net.

dee92009-f0b8-42a8-9e0d-7b063b6a2e43._msdcs.tacteam.net. 600 IN CNAME
CONSTELLATION.tacteam.net.

_kerberos._tcp.dc._msdcs.tacteam.net. 600 IN SRV 0 100 88
CONSTELLATION.tacteam.net.

_ldap._tcp.dc._msdcs.tacteam.net. 600 IN SRV 0 100 389
CONSTELLATION.tacteam.net.

_kerberos._tcp.tacteam.net. 600 IN SRV 0 100 88 CONSTELLATION.tacteam.net.

_kerberos._udp.tacteam.net. 600 IN SRV 0 100 88 CONSTELLATION.tacteam.net.

_kpasswd._tcp.tacteam.net. 600 IN SRV 0 100 464 CONSTELLATION.tacteam.net.

_kpasswd._udp.tacteam.net. 600 IN SRV 0 100 464 CONSTELLATION.tacteam.net.

_ldap._tcp.Default-First-Site-Name._sites.tacteam.net. 600 IN SRV 0 100
389 CONSTELLATION.tacteam.net.

_kerberos._tcp.Default-First-Site-Name._sites.dc._msdcs.tacteam.net. 600
IN SRV 0 100 88 CONSTELLATION.tacteam.net.

_ldap._tcp.Default-First-Site-Name._sites.dc._msdcs.tacteam.net. 600 IN
SRV 0 100 389 CONSTELLATION.tacteam.net.

_kerberos._tcp.Default-First-Site-Name._sites.tacteam.net. 600 IN SRV 0
100 88 CONSTELLATION.tacteam.net.

_ldap._tcp.gc._msdcs.tacteam.net. 600 IN SRV 0 100 3268
CONSTELLATION.tacteam.net.

gc._msdcs.tacteam.net. 600 IN A 192.168.1.185

_gc._tcp.tacteam.net. 600 IN SRV 0 100 3268 CONSTELLATION.tacteam.net.

_ldap._tcp.Default-First-Site-Name._sites.gc._msdcs.tacteam.net. 600 IN
SRV 0 100 3268 CONSTELLATION.tacteam.net.

_gc._tcp.Default-First-Site-Name._sites.tacteam.net. 600 IN SRV 0 100
3268 CONSTELLATION.tacteam.net.
```

Figure 4.2 Adding a new SRV record in the AD-integrated zone.

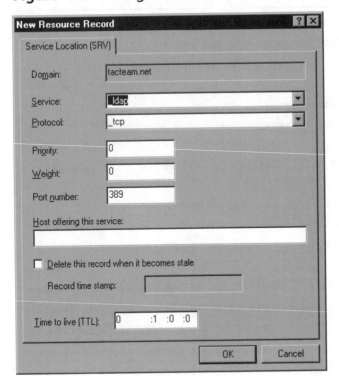

Figure 4.2 shows the "New Resource Record" dialog box used to create SRV entries into the AD-integrated DNS zone database.

Installing DNS Server Service

Installing the DNS server service is a relatively simple affair. The procedure for installing the DNS service on your computer is outlined in a walkthrough at the end of the chapter. Once the DNS server is installed, it will require configuration. Prior to installing the DNS service, you will need to plan the location and roles of the DNS servers on your network. In this section, we'll explore some of the options available for DNS server roles in an enterprise network and configuration options for the DNS service.

DNS Server Roles and Security Topology

You must carefully consider in advance the placement of your DNS servers and what roles these servers will play in the overall DNS infrastructure. We will focus on standard DNS setup in this section. Zone databases can be integrated with the Active Directory. When the zone database is integrated with the Active Directory, many of the concepts discussed in this section will not apply. Further discussion of Active Directory integrated zone databases is included later in this chapter.

A Domain Name Server can take one of several different roles. A single DNS server can assume multiple roles depending on zone topology. A DNS server's principle roles include:

- Primary DNS Server
- Secondary DNS Server
- DNS Forwarder
- Caching Only Server
- DNS Slave Server

Each role determines either how the zone database is maintained on the server and/or how DNS client queries are evaluated.

The IP infrastructure of your internal network is uncovered when an intruder gains access to a DNS zone database. With this information, an intruder can easily compromise internal host systems. It is imperative that your internal DNS servers remain secure. We will discuss different ways to position DNS servers that optimize internal infrastructure security.

Implementation follows the DNS design plan. We will examine DNS configuration options at the end of this section. First, let's examine the different DNS server roles.

Primary DNS Server

A Primary DNS server contains the only write copy of the zone database. A Primary DNS server is *authoritative* for the domain or domains contained in its zone files. Primary DNS servers are authoritative because they can respond directly to client DNS queries. Primary servers do not need to refer DNS queries.

Primary DNS servers share characteristics with all DNS servers, including:

- Zone database information is stored in the <systemroot>\system32\dns directory.
- The ability to boot from either the registry or a boot file
- Caching of resolved queries
- A cache.dns file

All zone files are stored in the %systemroot%\system32\dns directory. Zone file names are based on the name of the zone and are appended with the ".dns" file extension. For example, the tacteam.net zone file is named tacteam.net.dns.

The Windows 2000 DNS Service's configuration information is stored in the Registry. Server configuration is done via the DNS administrative console. This is the default setting.

However, you can administer the DNS server via a file called "BOOT." Unix administrators are accustomed to administrating DNS server by manipulating the BOOT file. You will need to edit the registry if you prefer to administer the DNS server via the BOOT file. The Registry key is:

```
HKEY_Local_machine\System\CurrentControlSet\Services\DNS\
Parameters\BootMethod
```

Set this value to 0 to boot from the BOOT file. Change the registry key back to its original setting if you choose to boot from the registry again.

All DNS servers cache resolved queries. A DNS server can receive and issue query requests. When a DNS server issues an iterative query to another DNS server, the result is placed in the DNS server's cache. Cached information is stored in system memory and is not written to disk. The cached information is lost after a server reboot. DNS servers are most effective when frequent reboots are avoided.

The cache.dns file (also known as the "Root Hints" file) contains host name and IP address mappings for the root Internet DNS servers. If a DNS server receives a recursive query for a domain for which it is not authoritative, it must complete recursion by issuing iterative queries. The iterative query process begins with the root DNS servers. The cache.dns file is located in the same directory as the zone files.

The Internet root server mappings change periodically. You can download the current Internet root server mappings from: ftp://ftp.rs.internic.net/domain/root.zone.gz.

A DNS server can be authoritative for multiple domains. For example, the tacteam.net.dns zone file can contain entries authoritative for tacteam.net and dev.tactem.net. It is authoritative because the server does not need to issue an iterative query in order to resolve recursive queries for tacteam.net and dev.tacteam.net.

A Primary DNS server can act in the role of Secondary DNS server. A Primary DNS server that receives zone transfers from another Primary server acts in the role of Secondary. Any DNS server can contain either or both Primary and Secondary zone files. The only difference between the two is that the Primary zone file is read/write while the Secondary zone file is read-only.

This leads us to the next subject. How do we provide fault tolerance for zone database files? A corporation is highly dependent on reliable host name resolution in order to access both intranet and Internet servers. In order to provide for fault tolerance we configure a Secondary DNS server.

Secondary DNS Server

The Domain Name System should include at least two DNS servers authoritative for each zone. Secondary DNS servers are authoritative for its zones. Secondary DNS servers provide the following functions:

- Fault Tolerance
- Load Balancing
- Bandwidth Conservation

Like Primary servers, Secondary DNS servers contain a zone database file. The copy is received via a "zone transfer." A Primary DNS server for the zone acts as a "master server" and transfers the zone file to the Secondary during a zone transfer. Secondary DNS servers can answer DNS client queries. DNS clients are configured with the IP addresses of both the Primary and Secondary DNS servers for their domain. This provides fault tolerance should the Primary DNS server become disabled. Name resolution services continue without interruption by querying the Secondary server.

Load balancing allows for distributing the DNS query load among multiple DNS servers. A DNS server could be overwhelmed by name query traffic if all client computers were to access a single Primary DNS server simultaneously. Clients on different segments can be configured to query local Secondary DNS servers. This disperses the query load among Primary and Secondary DNS servers for a zone.

Fault tolerance, load balancing, and bandwidth conservation provide cogent reasons to implement Secondary DNS servers. Secondary DNS server placement must be included in every DNS deployment plan you create. If you plan to maintain your own DNS servers on the Internet, the Domain Registrar will require you to have at least one Primary and one Secondary DNS server for your second level domain.

Caching-Only Servers

All DNS servers cache results of queries they have resolved. The caching-only DNS server does not contain zone information or a zone file. The caching-only server builds its database of host names over time from successful DNS queries.

All DNS servers have a cache.dns file containing the IP addresses of all Internet root servers. The Windows 2000 cache.dns file is referred to as the "root hints" file. You can view the contents of the root hints file via the DNS server properties dialog box, as seen in Figure 4.3. The caching-only server uses this list to begin building its cache. It adds to the cache as it issues iterative queries when responding to client requests.

Figure 4.3 The Root Hints tab in the DNS server Properties dialog box.

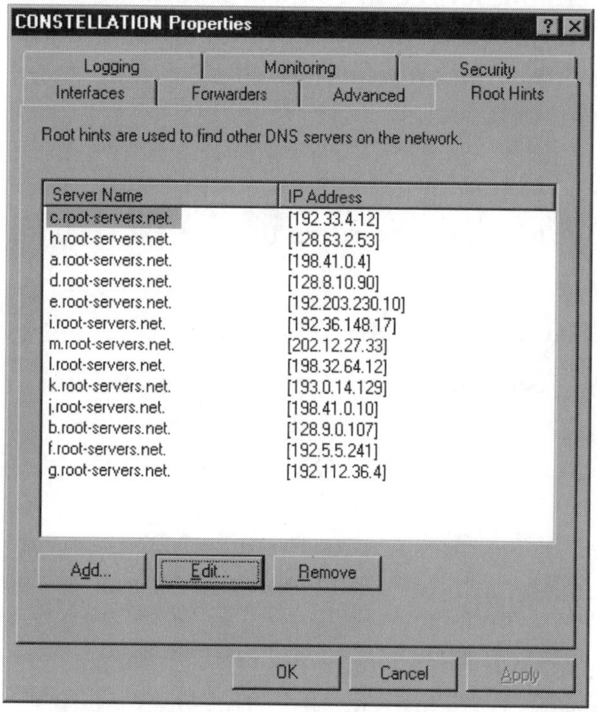

Caching-only servers are valuable because:

- They do not generate zone transfer traffic.
- They are extremely efficient when placed on the far side of a slow WAN link.
- They can be configured as forwarders.

Caching-only servers do not contain zone information, and there-fore are not authoritative for any zone. There is no need for zone transfers to caching-only servers.

Satellite locations are often connected to the main office via slow WAN links. These locations benefit from caching-only servers for a couple of reasons:

1. There is no zone transfer traffic.

2. DNS queries do not have to traverse the WAN after the cache is built from resolved queries.

These caching-only servers do not require expert administration. A satellite office is unlikely to have trained DNS administrative staff on-site. This saves the cost of having an experienced DNS adminis-trator visit the site on a periodic basis.

There is no risk of an intruder obtaining zone information from a caching-only server. Therefore, caching-only servers make excellent candidates for forwarders. We'll cover forwarders in the next section.

DNS Forwarders and Slave Servers

A DNS forwarder is a DNS server that accepts DNS queries from another DNS server. Caching-only servers make good forwarders. A forwarder can be used to protect an internal DNS server from Internet accesses.

A DNS client sends a recursive query to its Preferred DNS server. The request is for a host in a domain for which the DNS is not authoritative.

The DNS server must resolve the host name for the client or return a "host not found" error. You can configure the DNS client's Preferred DNS server to forward all queries for which it is not authoritative. This DNS server issues a recursive query to another DNS server called the forwarder.

Some of the terms used in the forwarding process require clarifi-cation. In our example, the client's Preferred server is "forwarding" the request to the "forwarder." The client's Preferred server is the forwarding DNS server. The DNS server receiving the forwarding server's query is the forwarder. Therefore, the process of forwarding a DNS query involves both a forwarding DNS server and the forwarder DNS server.

The forwarder begins to resolve the host name in the query. It can do this by retrieving the record from its cache, from a zone file, or by issuing a series of iterative queries. If successful, it will answer the recursive query affirmatively and return the IP address to the "forwarding" server. The forwarding server completes its recursion by returning this IP address to the DNS client that initiated the query.

If the forwarder *cannot* resolve the hostname to an IP address, it will return to the forwarding DNS server a "host not found" error. If this happens, the Preferred DNS server (the forwarding server) will attempt to resolve the host name itself. The forwarding server will check its cache, zone files, and perform iterative queries to resolve the host name. If unsuccessful, a "host not found" error is finally returned to the client.

You may not want the forwarding DNS server to issue iterative queries to servers located on the Internet. This may be true when the forwarding server is an internal DNS server. Internal DNS servers that issue iterative queries for Internet host name resolution are easy targets for hackers.

You can configure the forwarding server to not resolve the host names when the forward fails to return a valid IP address. When the forwarding computer is configured in this fashion, it is referred to as a "slave" server. The slave server accepts responses from the forwarder and relays them to the client without attempting host name resolution itself.

Security Considerations and DNS Server Location

You can implement a Slave server/caching-only forwarder combination to protect zone data information on internal DNS servers. A secure intranet is isolated from the Internet by a firewall. The forwarding server is on the intranet side of the firewall. The forwarder is located on the Internet side of the firewall. The forwarder is configured as a caching-only server because of its high Internet visibility.

The firewall must be configured to allow DNS query traffic between the forwarding server and the forwarder. DNS traffic passes through UDP port 53. Therefore, you must configure the firewall to limit pass-through of DNS queries to only the two server's IP addresses. This ensures secure communications.

For example, at tacteam.net we have an internal DNS server we use to resolve internal DNS requests. DNS queries for intranet resources do not represent a security risk. However, what happens when we need to resolve Internet host names?

When the recursive request for Internet host name resolution hits our internal DNS server (which is authoritative for only tacteam.net and dev.tacteam.net) it begins the iterative query process. The Internet DNS servers send their responses to our internal DNS server through the firewall. This exposes our internal DNS server, and its zone data, to the Internet. How can we avoid this potentially disastrous scenario?

We can place a caching-only forwarder on the outside of the firewall and configure the internal DNS server to be a slave server. Now, when a client issues a name resolution request for an Internet host, the internal DNS server will forward the request to the forwarder on the outside of the firewall. The forwarder resolves the fully qualified domain name to an IP address. If successful, the forwarder will return the IP address to the internal DNS server. The internal DNS server will return the IP address to the client. If the forwarder is unsuccessful, it will send a "host not found" error to the internal server, which returns this information to the client. Our internal slave server will *not* issue iterative queries to resolve the host name itself.

At no time does an Internet DNS server send a response to the internal DNS server. In this way, internal zone records are safe.

Configuring DNS Server Options

Installing the DNS server service is a simple procedure that is covered in a walkthrough at the end of the chapter. Configuration parameters are made after installation. Open the DNS Management Console, right-click on the server name, and click on "Properties" to access the DNS server configuration property sheets.

The DNS server Properties dialog box first presents you with the "Interfaces" tab, as seen in Figure 4.4.

Figure 4.4 The Interfaces tab on the DNS server Properties sheet.

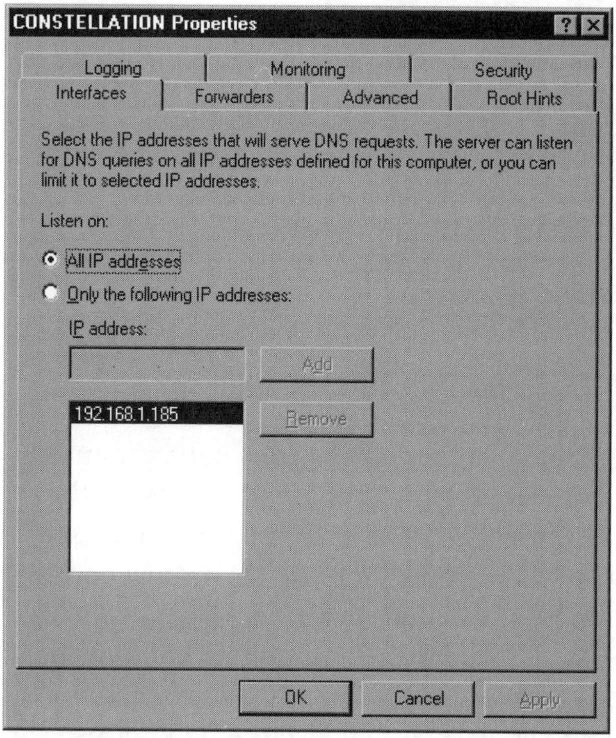

You configure which interfaces the DNS server should listen for queries. This is an issue only for multihomed machines. On multihomed machines you may limit servicing DNS queries to selected adapters by entering the IP addresses of the adapters you wish to accept queries.

Figure 4.5 The Forwarders tab in the DNS server Properties sheet.

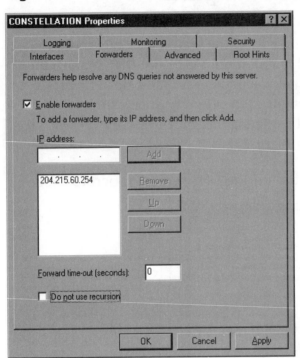

Click on the Forwarders tab and you will see what appears in Figure 4.5.

Put a checkmark in the "Enable forwarders" check box to make the server a forwarding DNS server. Enter the IP address(s) of the forwarder in the "IP address" text box. The "Forward time-out (seconds)" text box allows you to define how long the server will continue attempting to contact and use a listed forwarder. The server will try the next server on the list if the server is unable to contact the forwarder by the end of the time-out period.

This server will be a slave server if you choose the "Do not use recursion" checkbox. Combining slave servers with caching-only servers is an excellent method to ensure DNS zone database security.

The "Advanced" tab includes some extended features of the Windows 2000 DNS service, as seen in Figure 4.6.

Here, you can configure six advanced server options. The details of each of these options are included in Table 4.2.

Figure 4.6 The Advanced tab in the DNS server Properties dialog box.

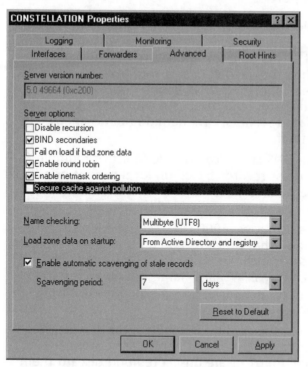

Table 4.2 Advanced DNS Server Options

Option	Properties
Disable recursion	Allows you to disable recursion. Recursion is enabled by default.
BIND secondaries	Allow the Windows 2000 DNS Service to use compression and include multiple records in a single TCP message when transferring zone data to BIND secondary servers. This is the default zone transfer method for the Windows 2000 DNS service.
	BIND-based DNS servers that run versions 4.9.4 and later support this zone transfer method.
Fail on load if bad zone data	Selecting this option will prevent the DNS server from loading zone data if errors are detected in zone records. This is disabled by default.

Option	Properties
Enable round robin	Selecting this option enables DNS Round Robin. DNS Round Robin is used to rotate and reorder a list of multiple "A" Address resource records when the queried host is configured with multiple IP addresses. DNS Round Robin is an ideal vehicle for load balancing all types of WinSock related services. DNS Round Robin is enabled by default.
Enable netmask ordering	The DNS server can reorder a list of multiple A Address records based on local subnet priority if the queried host name is for a multihomed computer. This is enabled by default.
Secure cache response against pollution	The Windows 2000 DNS Service uses a secure option that prevents adding unrelated resource records included in a referral answer to the cache. Typically, any names added in referral answers are cached. This expedites resolving subsequent DNS queries.
	When this feature is enabled, the server will determine if referred names are potentially "polluting" or are unsecured and discard them. The server determines whether to cache the name offered in a referral by determining whether it is part of the DNS domain name tree for which the original queried was made.
	For example, if the original query was for "dev.tacteam.net" and a referral answer provided a record for a name outside of the "tacteam.net" domain name tree, such as syngress.net. The Syngress.net referral would not be included in the cache.

The "Name checking" option allows you to define what are valid DNS name conventions when the DNS server accesses the validity of zone records. Non-RFC (ANSI), UTF-8, and All Names are options for this setting. The "Load zone data on startup" list box configures the boot method the DNS server. Servers running Windows 2000 DNS use registry boot by default. The boot file method is used if you choose to manage the server by manipulating a text-based boot file. The boot file name is Boot.dns and is located in the %SystemRoot%\System32\Dns folder.

A DNS server can retain old or "stale" DDNS registrations over time, in a manner similar to that seen with WINS servers. Put a checkmark in the checkbox for "Enable automatic scavenging of stale records" to allow the DDNS server to clean out these records. When this option is enabled, it sets the default for all zones defined on this server. Each zone can be configured independently of this default setting.

The "Root Hints" property sheet displays the server name and IP addresses for the Internet Root DNS servers. You can add, edit, or remove entries on this list as seen in Figure 4.7.

The "Logging" property sheet allows you to configure advanced debug logging options as seen in Figure 4.8.

Figure 4.7 The Root Hints properties sheet in the DNS server properties dialog box.

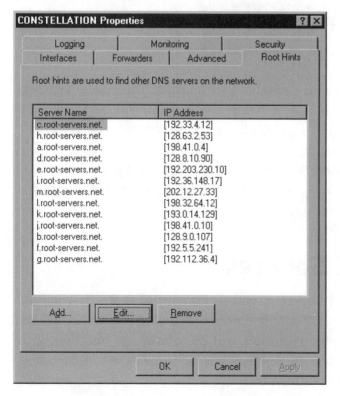

Figure 4.8 The Logging property sheet in the DNS server properties dialog box.

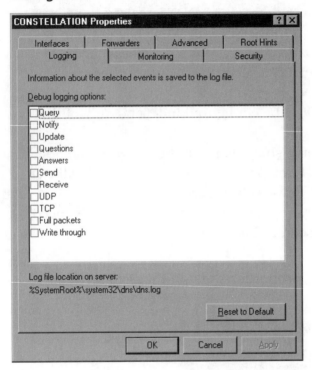

All debugging options are disabled by default. You can selectively enable debugging options. The DNS Server service will perform trace-level logging that aid in debugging the server when error conditions are extant.

These specialized debugging options are disk and processor intensive. Enable them only when you are actively troubleshooting a problem with the DNS server.

Configuring DNS Services

After you install the DNS service, you must configure it. There is a wealth of configuration options available on the Windows 2000 DNS server. Your primary responsibilities will be to manage and configure Forward and Reverse Lookup zones. Let's examine some of the configuration options available for both.

Creating Forward Lookup Zones

A forward lookup zone contains resource records for hosts in domains included in the zone. Each zone can contain one or more domains. The zone database is stored in a file with the zone name and a ".dns" extension at the end of the name.

New zones are easy to configure in Windows 2000. The "New Zone Wizard" walks you through the process of creating a new zone. A walkthrough on how to create a new zone is included at the end of the chapter.

After the new zone is created, you must configure it to meet your specifications. Let's take a look at some of the forward lookup zone configuration options. These options are available after right-clicking on the name of the zone and then selecting properties, as seen in Figure 4.9.

The Zone Properties General Tab reports on the server status. If you need to pause the DNS service without shutting it down you can do it from here.

Figure: 4.9 Zone Properties dialog box, General Tab.

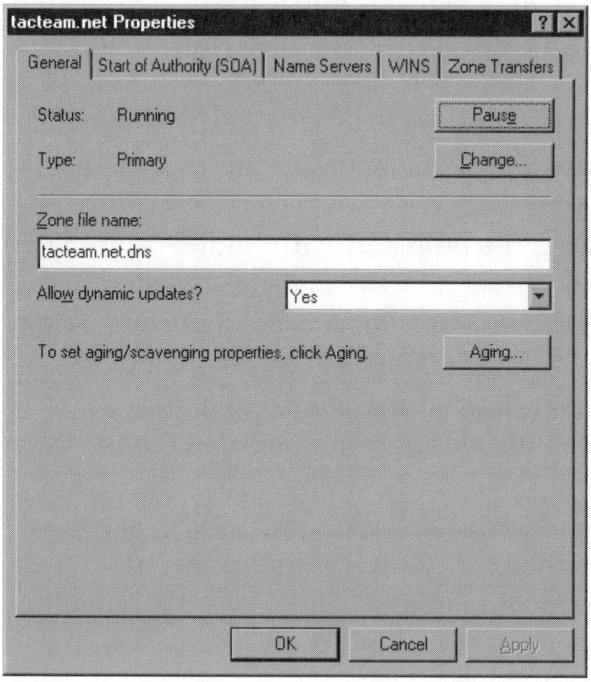

When you create a new zone you are asked if you want that zone to be a Standard primary, Standard secondary, or Directory-integrated zone. If you decide at a later time that you want to change the zone's type, you can do that by clicking the "Change" button. The resulting dialog box allows for the changes seen in Figure 4.10.

Figure 4.10 The Change Zone Type dialog box.

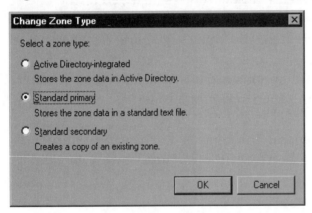

The zone file name can be changed. You might want to do this in order to make a quick backup copy of the zone file. Then change the name back to the original.

Dynamic updates are not enabled by default. To enable dynamic updating of the DNS, click the down arrow in the "Allow dynamic updates?" dropdown box and select "Yes."

Dynamic DNS suffers the same problems with "stale" or outdated records that the WINS server has. If a DDNS client is registers its own Address records and does not shut down properly before being removed from the network, the host's Address record will not be removed from the DDNS server. Laptop users who plug into the network and leave frequently can also leave behind outdated and invalid Address records.

This creates problems similar to those seen with WINS servers. Unlike WINS, there is no method for "tombstoning" a record. Problems arise when too many outdated or "stale" records remain in the database:

- They take up disk space and increase the size of the zone database. This increases the amount of bandwidth required during zone transfer.

- It takes longer to search large zone databases. This impairs the performance of the DDNS server.

- The existence of stale records can lead to incorrect host name resolution.

To solve these problems, you can initiate aging/scavenging of stale resource records. Click the "Aging" button and you see the "Zone Aging/Scavenging Properties" dialog box as seen in Figure 4.11.

Figure 4.11 The ZoneAging/Scavenging Properties dialog box.

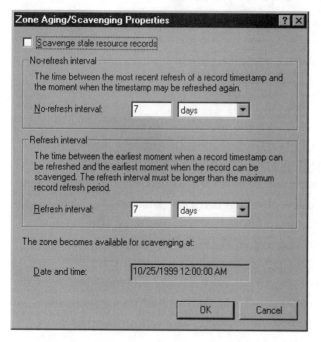

Scavenging is not enabled by default. The administrator should be very careful about enabling scavenging. If the administrator is not fully aware of the implications of scavenging, valid resource records could be removed from the DDNS zone database.

If you click on the "Start of Authority (SOA)" tab, you see what appears in Figure 4-12.

Figure 4.12 The Start of Authority tab in the zone properties dialog box.

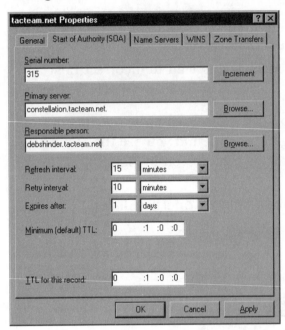

The serial number field is used to track changes to the zone database. Each time there is a change to the zone database, the serial number will be incremented. You can manually increment the serial number by 1 if you click the "Increment" button.

The "Primary server" text box contains the name of the server housing the master copy of the zone. You can change this value by click on the "Browse" button and selecting another server.

The "Responsible person" text box contains the e-mail address of the DDNS server administrator. Include the e-mail address of the DDNS administrator here in FQDN format. For example, if the DDNS administrator's e-mail address were dnsmaster@globalone.net, you would enter dnsmaster.globalone.net.

Secondary DDNS server will check for updates to the zone database on a periodic basis. The amount of time the secondary DDNS will wait between update checks is defined by the "Refresh interval." The default is 15 minutes. You can change this by manipulating the time periods in the appropriate dropdown boxes. If you do not have clients that dynamically update their records, you might want to increase the Refresh interval to a higher number.

If a secondary DDNS server is not able to contact the Master server, it will repeat the zone transfer request. How often this request is repeated is determined by the "Retry interval." The default Retry interval is 10 minutes and should be set to a value smaller than the Refresh interval.

When a DDNS server queries another DNS server, the responding DNS server will send information about how long the record should be considered valid. This is known as the "Time to Live (TTL)." You can set the Time to Live in the "Minimum (default) TTL" text box. This is the default value for records emanating from this server. Individual records can be configured with their own TTL values, which will override the server TTL. The default period is 60 minutes. The SOA record has its own TTL, which you can modify in the "TTL for this record" text box.

Click on the "Name Servers" tab to see a list of name servers that are authoritative for the zone, as seen in Figure 4.13.

Figure 4.13 The Name Server tab in the zone Properties dialog box.

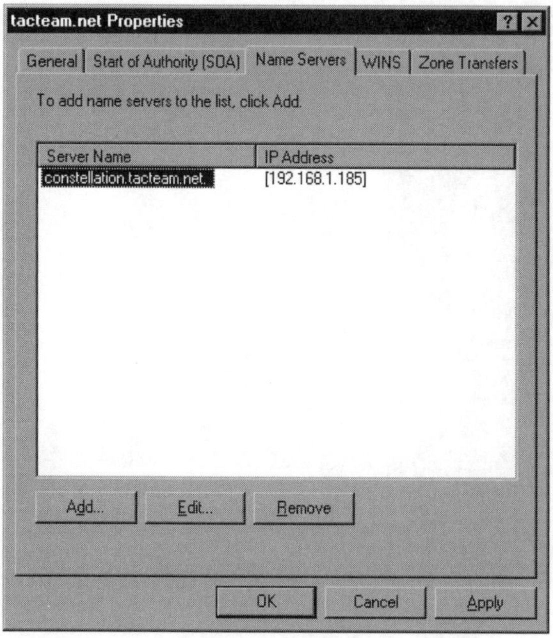

Lists of name servers are configured for either the server or zone. This displays a list of DNS servers configured to be authoritative for the zone. In most cases, this includes all other servers that are configured as zone secondaries. In order to make a server authoritative for a zone, it must have an NS (name server) record configured in the zone.

DDNS servers that cannot locate a resource record for a requested host name can be configured to look up the host name in a WINS database. To configure the DDNS server to use WINS forward lookup (resolving NetBIOS name to IP address) click on the WINS tab, as seen in Figure 4.14.

Place a checkmark in the "Use WINS forward lookup" to enable WINS forwarding. The "Do not replicate this record" checkbox is enabled if you have non-Microsoft DNS servers acting as secondaries. A zone update failure might occur if you include WINS resource

Figure 4.14 The WINS tab in the zone properties dialog box.

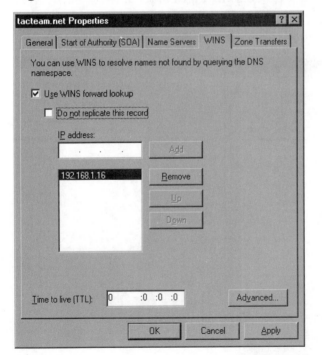

record information in the zone transfer to non-Microsoft DNS servers. If all the secondaries are Microsoft DNS servers, leave the checkbox clear so that WINS resource records are included in the zone transfer.

If you enable WINS forward lookup, enter the IP addresses of the WINS servers to be queried. You can configure an ordered list of WINS servers to be queried. If the first WINS server fails to respond, the next one on the list is tried.

Consider adding a new WINS-enabled DDNS lookup zone dedicated to WINS lookup requests. When naming the zone, use a subdomain added to an existing DNS domain that is used just for WINS-specific referrals added to your DNS domain namespace.

For example, you have a domain named dev.tacteam.net. You will call the new zone wins.dev.tacteam.net. You then use the new WINS referral zone as the root zone for any WINS-aware computers with names not found in other DNS zones.

To make the WINS referral zone work, you need to include its domain name in a DNS suffix search order for your clients. This can be configured manually at the client, or the DNS suffix search order can be configured as an Option delivered by a DHCP server. When the name of the WINS referral zone is included in the DNS suffix search order list, any DNS names not resolved in other zones will be resolved using the WINS referral subdomain.

The Time to Live for a WINS record is configured in the "Time to live (TTL)" text box. The minimum time-out configured on the SOA record is not the time-out for cached WINS records. You can configure cache and lookup time-outs separately by clicking the "Advanced" button.

DDNS servers acting as Master servers are able to transfer their zone databases to configured secondary servers or to other domain controllers. Click on the "Zone Transfers" tab to configure zone transfer options, as seen in Figure 4.15.

To allow zone transfer put a check in the "Allow zone transfers" checkbox. You then decide who is allowed to transfer the zone. The three options are:

Figure 4.15 The Zone Transfer tab in the zone properties dialog box.

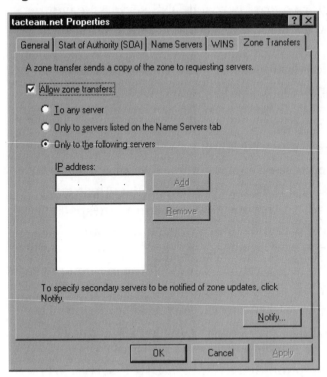

- To any server
- Only to servers listed on the Name Servers tab
- Only to the following servers

If you allow transfer to any server, anyone configuring a DNS server can transfer a zone, whether you desire that transfer or not. The second option allows you to restrict zone transfers to computers that are known authoritative secondaries for the zone. If for some reason you want more granular control of zone transfer, you can enter the IP addresses of selected DNS servers in the "IP address" box under the "Only to the following servers" option.

Without further configuration, DNS servers will only update their zone files according to the amount of time configured in the "Refresh interval." You can configure the Master server to immediately notify secondaries when there is a change to the zone database. Click the

Figure 4.16 The Notify dialog box.

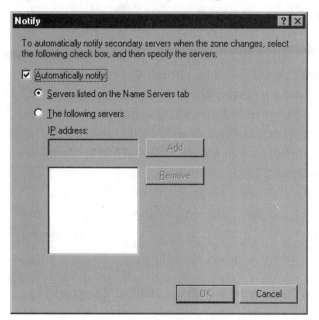

"Notify" button to enable this feature. Figure 4.16 shows the subsequent "Notify" dialog box.

To enable notification, put a checkmark in the "Automatically notify" checkbox. Then select whether you want "Servers listed on the Name Server tab" or a custom set of DNS servers to be notified. If you choose the latter, then enter the IP addresses of those servers.

Creating Reverse Lookup Zones

A reverse lookup zone allows you to find host names via IP addresses. This is the opposite of the forward lookup where you wish to resolve host names to IP addresses. In order to accomplish this, you must configure a reverse lookup zone.

The reverse lookup zone takes on the format of <network_ID_in_reverse>.in-addr.arpa. For example, to create a reverse lookup zone for network ID 192.168.2.0, you would create a reverse lookup zone 2.168.192.in-addr.arpa. Queries directed to hosts located in network ID 192.168.2.0 would be directed to this reverse lookup zone for IP-address-to-host-name resolution. Reverse lookup zones are populated with "Pointer" resource records.

Reverse lookup zones are easy to configure in Windows 2000. There is a "New Zone Wizard" dedicated to creating a new reverse lookup zone. All you need to do is right-click on the "Reverse Lookup Zones" node in the left pane of the DNS administrative console and select "New Zone." The wizard will ask for the network ID, and will automatically create a zone database file with the ".dns" extension based on the reverse lookup zone's name.

Configuration options for the reverse lookup zone are almost exactly the same as those found for forward lookup zones. The only tab that is different in the reverse lookup zone is the WIN-R tab, as seen in Figure 4.17.

Figure 4.17 The WINS-R in the reverse lookup zone properties dialog box.

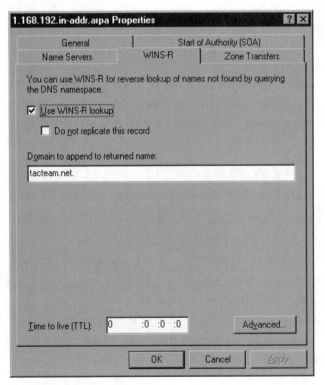

A reverse WINS lookup allows a client to perform IP-address-to-NetBIOS-name resolution. The WINS database is not indexed by IP address. Therefore, the DNS service cannot send a reverse name lookup to a WINS server.

The DNS service solves this problem by sending a "node adapter status request" directly to the IP address implied in the DNS reverse query. A node adapter status request causes the target computer to respond with a list of NetBIOS names registered for the adapter.

The DNS server will append the DNS domain name listed in the "Domain to append to returned name" text box onto the NetBIOS name provided in the node status response. The result is forwarded to the requesting client.

Record Types (i.e. mx, SRV, SOA…)

The DNS forward lookup zones are populated with a variety of resource records. The most common resource records include:

- Host or "A" Address Records
- Pointer (PTR) records
- Service location (SRV) Records
- Mail Exchanger (MX) Records
- Alias or Canonical Name (CNAME) records

Table 4.3 lists the types of records and their functions in the DNS database.

Table 4.3 Resource Record Types

Resource Record Type	Name	Description
SOA	Start of Authority	The SOA identifies the DNS server as authoritative for the data within the domain. The first record in any zone file is the SOA. Several configuration parameters are included in the SOA RR.

Resource Record Type	Name	Description
NS	Name Server	The NS record defines a DNS server that will return an authoritative answer for the domain. This includes the Primary DNS server for the zone, and secondary DNS servers to which you delegate authority for the zone.
A	Address	The Address Record contains the host name to IP address mapping for the particular host. The majority of the records in the zone will be host "A" Address Records
SRV	Service	The SRV denotes a service running on a particular host. This is similar to the "service identifier" in NetBIOS environments. If a host is looking for a Domain Controller for authentication, it will check for a SRV record to find an authenticating server.
CNAME	Canonical Name	This is an alias record. There must be a computer with an existing "A" Address record. For example, you might create an alias for a computer named "bigserver" if that computer is also a Web server. The most common CNAME record for Web servers is "www".
MX	Mail Exchanger	Identifies the domain's preferred mail servers. Several servers in the same domain can have MX records. An order of precedence determines which MX records will be delivered to the client.
HINFO	Host Information	HINFO records provide information about the DNS hardware and software. Entries include: CPU, operating system, interface type, and other server characteristics. This is a primitive resource tracking method.
PTR	Pointer	The Pointer record is created for reverse lookups. Reverse lookups are valuable when doing security analysis and checking authenticity of source domains for e-mail.

The SRV record has been recently introduced to the Microsoft DNS service. The primary purpose at this time is to record the information about Domain Controllers in the DNS. The SRV record is similar in function to the Service Identifier used in the NetBIOS name, which is saved in the WINS database. Examples of such services include LDAP, Telnet, and SMTP. A DNS client can then locate a service with the desired service based on the SRV record entry.

A service record conforms to the following syntax:

```
service.protocol.name   ttl   class   SRV   preference   weight
port   target
```

An example:

```
_ldap._tcp.ms-dcs     SRV  0 0    389 constellaton.tacteam.net
                      SRV 10 0    389 exeter.tacteam.net
```

Two fields of interest are the priority and weight fields. The priority field determines which target hosts are contacted first, in order of priority, for a specific service. The weight field is used to provide for load balancing when multiple servers are listed in the **target** field, and all have the same priority number. When all target servers have the same priority value, this value is used to set an added level of preference that can determine the exact order or balancing of selection for the target hosts used in an answered SRV query. If you use any value but 0, servers of equal priority are tried in proportion to the weight of this value. The range of values is 1 to 65535 for both priority and weight values. Use a value of **0** in the weight field if load balancing is not desired.

Manually Adding Records

At this time, the only resource records that are dynamically updated are the "A" Address, Pointer PTR, and SRV records. The DDNS administrator must manually create all other records.

Adding Resource Records is time consuming but easy to do. To manually add a new RR:

1. Open the DNS Console.

2. Expand all Nodes and right-click on the node you wish to add the new RR. You should see the context menu appear as in Figure 4.18.

Figure 4.18 Context menu for the selected domain.

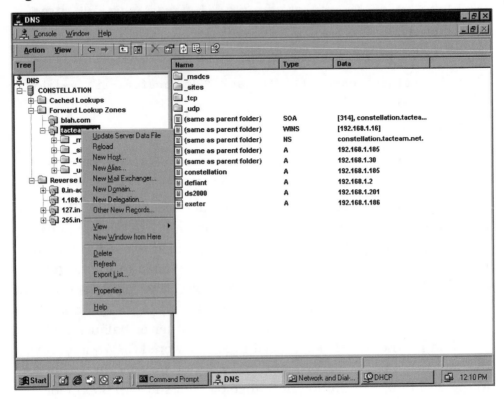

3. Select the type of RR you wish to create. For example, select "New Host." The "New Host" dialog box appears as in Figure 4.19.

4. Enter the host name of the machine in the "Name" text box. Enter the IP address of the host in the "IP address" text box. To have the server automatically enter the Pointer Record for reverse lookups, place a checkmark in the "Create associated pointer (PTR) record" checkbox. You have the option to change the Time to Live for the record here if you wish to change from the default of 60 minutes.

Figure 4.19 Adding a new A Address record to the domain.

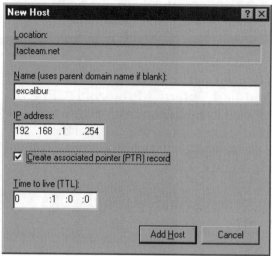

5. Click "Add Host." You will see the new record appear in the DNS Console.

Configuring DNS Client

The DNS client can be configured manually or via a DHCP server. The preferred method is to have the DHCP server automatically configure DNS settings for DHCP clients. This avoids error inherent in going from machine to machine manually configuring DNS settings. We will look at both approaches in this section.

Manually

You must be located at the local machine to perform manual configuration. You can manually configure the client's Preferred DNS by doing the following:

1. Log on with an account that has administrative privileges.
2. Right-click "My Network Places," and then click "Properties."

3. This opens the "Network and Dial-up Connections" window. You should see at least two icons: one for "Make New Connection" and a second for "Local Area Connection." Right-click "Local Area Connection," and then click "Properties."

4. The "Local Area Connection Properties" dialog box appears. Scroll through the list and find "Internet Protocol (TCP/IP)." Click once on the text (not on the checkmark or you may remove it inadvertently), and then click the "Properties" button just underneath it. You will see the "Internet Protocol (TCP/IP) Properties" as in Figure 4.20.

Figure 4.20 Configuring TCP/IP properties and setting the DNS servers.

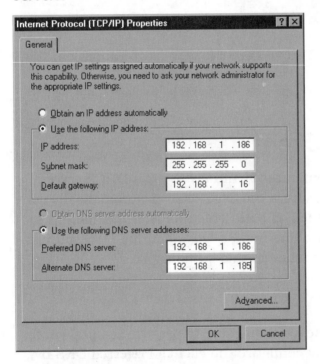

5. Select the "Option" button "Use the following DNS server addresses" and type in the IP for the Preferred DNS server. For fault tolerance, type in the IP address of an Alternate DNS server.

6. Click OK, and then click OK again.

The foregoing procedure allows for basic client configuration. Other client configuration options are available by clicking the "Advanced" button.

After clicking the "Advanced" button, you will see the "Advanced TCP/IP settings" dialog box. The tab we are interested in at this point is the "DNS" tab. After clicking the "DNS" tab you will see what appears in Figure 4.21.

Figure 4.21 The DNS tab in the Advanced TCP/IP Settings dialog box.

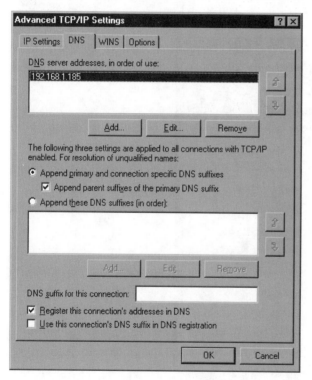

From here you can add additional servers to the DNS servers address list. The search order can be changed by using the up and down arrow buttons on the right side of the DNS servers list.

One area of confusion regarding DNS client setup relates to the three options seen underneath the DNS servers list. The option "Append primary and connection specific DNS suffixes" refers to what DNS "suffixes" should be included in a request to a DNS server if an "unqualified" DNS request is sent to a DNS server.

For example, if you were to type http://constellation in the address bar of your Web browser, that would be considered an unqualified request since there is only a host name, and no domain name included in the request. A DNS server must use a fully qualified domain name in order to process a request. The Primary suffix is the computer's domain membership included in the "Network Identification" tab of the "System Properties" dialog box, as seen in Figure 4.22.

Figure 4.22 The System Properties dialog box.

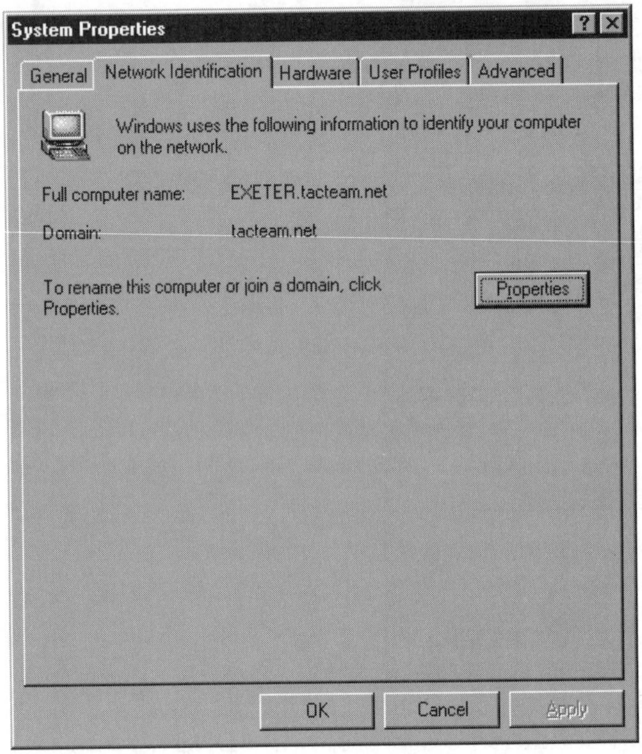

You can change the computer's Primary membership by clicking the "Properties" button. You will then be able to change the machine's domain membership via the "Identification Changes" dialog box, as seen in Figures 4.23 and 4.24. The latter appears after clicking the "More" button.

The connection-specific suffix is one that you enter in the text box to the right of where is says "DNS suffix for this connection."

Figure 4.23 The Identification Changes dialog box.

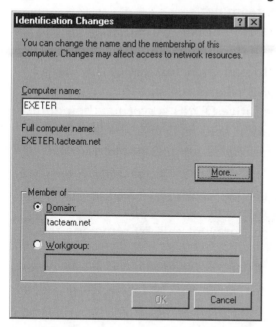

Figure 4-24 The DNS Suffix and NetBIOS Computer Name dialog box.

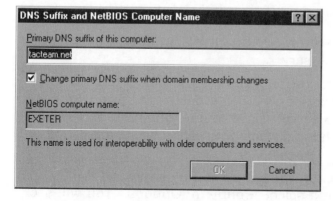

The "Append parent suffixes of the primary DNS suffix" option specifies whether resolution for unqualified names used on this computer includes the parent suffixes of the primary DNS suffix up to the Second Level domain.

For example, your primary DNS suffix is dev.west.tacteam.net. You type ping xyz at a Windows 2000 command prompt. The first fully qualified domain name sent in the DNS query will be xyz.dev.west.tacteam.net. Windows 2000 also queries for xyz.west.tacteam.net and xyz.tacteam.net.

If you choose "Append these DNS suffixes (in order)," you can then configure a customized set of domain names to append to DNS queries. Click the "Add" button to add DNS suffixes to the list.

By default, Windows 2000 DNS clients register their own A Address records with the authoritative DDNS server for their zone. The "Register this connection's addresses in DNS" is selected by default. The domain name for this registration is defined in the "System Properties" dialog box.

Connection-specific domain name registrations can be made as well. By default, each connection-specific DNS suffix is also registered with the DNS server. You can prevent this by removing the checkmark from that option.

Using DHCP

You can avoid a lot of administrative hassle by using DHCP to assign DNS Preferred server addresses. The computers must be configured as DHCP clients. To assign the DNS options at the DNS server:

1. Install a DHCP server. See Chapter 2 on how to install and configure a DHCP server.

2. Create a scope on the DHCP server. It is best to configure DNS server addresses on a per-scope basis. You want clients to use local DNS servers prior to querying remote DNS servers. Instructions on how to create a scope are found in Chapter 2.

3. Expand all nodes in the left pane. Right-click on the "Scope Options" node and select "Configure Options." You will see the "Scope Options" dialog box as it appears in Figure 4.25.

4. Type in the IP address of the DNS servers to be used for the scope. The DNS servers are listed in priority order. Enter the server IP addresses in the "IP address:" text box and then click "Add." Move the Preferred DNS sever to the top by using the "Up" or "Down" buttons.

5. Click "OK." The DHCP console will show the new DNS options in the right pane, as seen in Figure 4.26.

Figure 4.25 Configuring DNS Scope Options.

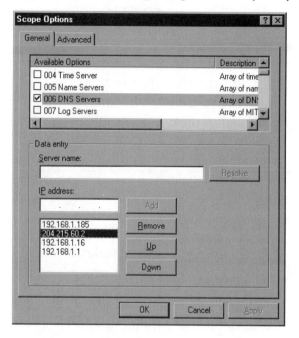

Figure 4.26 The DHCP console showing new DNS server Options.

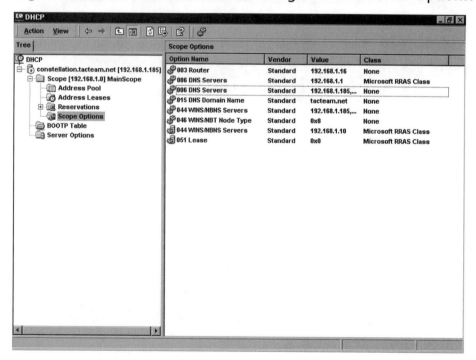

Walkthrough

WARNING

Do not perform any of these Walkthrough Exercises on a production network without the express permission of your network administrator. Some of these exercises have the potential to disrupt or disable network communications or stability.

Installation of a DNS Server

You can install the DNS during the Windows 2000 installation process or can defer installing it until later. This is the procedure for

Figure 4.27 The Add/Remove Programs Dialog Box.

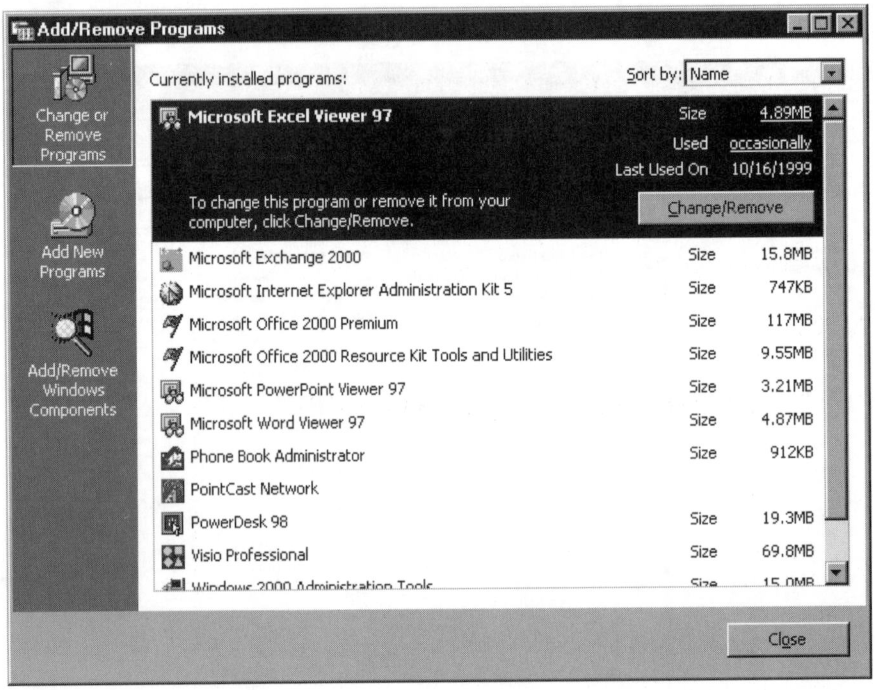

installing the DNS service when it was not included in the Windows 2000 setup.

1. Click Start | Settings | Control Panel | Add/Remove Programs. You will see the "Add/Remove Programs" dialog box, as seen in Figure 4.27.

2. Click the "Add/Remove Windows Components" button. This displays the "Windows Components Wizard." Scroll down until you find "Networking Services" and click it once to select it, as seen in Figure 4-28. Do not to remove the checkmark from the check box.

3. Click the "Details" button. This opens the "Networking Services" dialog box, as seen in Figure 4.29. Click the checkbox to the left of "Domain Name System (DNS)" to place a checkmark there. Click "OK," then click "Next." The service installs now.

4. A dialog box informs that the installation is complete. Click "Finish."

Figure 4.28 Adding Network Services.

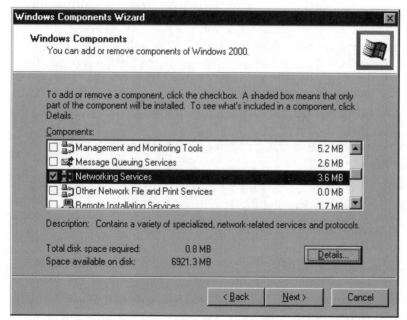

Figure 4.29 Selecting the Domain Name System.

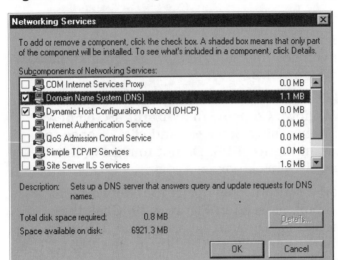

Creating a Forward Lookup Zone

1. Click Start | Programs | Administrative Tools | Computer Management. You should see what appears in Figure 4.30.

2. Expand "Services and Applications." You will see an entry "DNS." Your server name will appear. Expand the computer name. Note if any zones appear in the left pane.

3. Right-click the computer name, and then click "New Zone."

4. The "Welcome to the New Zone Wizard" starts. The Wizard will walk us through the process of creating the new zone. Click "Next."

5. We want to create a Standard Primary Zone, so select this option, as seen in Figure 4.31. Click "Next."

6. The Wizard now asks whether we want to create a Forward lookup zone or a Reverse lookup zone, as seen in Figure 4.32. Always create your forward lookup zone prior to creating the reverse lookup zone. The reverse lookup zone will contain the pointer records for resources in your forward lookup zone. Click "Next."

Figure 4.30 Windows 2000's Computer Management tool.

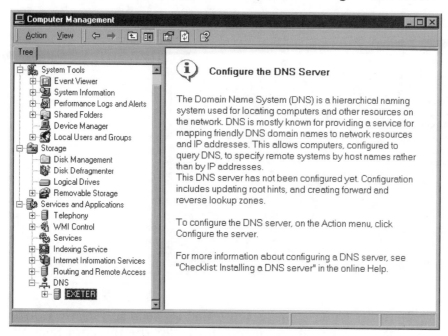

Figure 4.31 Choose the zone type in the New Zone Wizard.

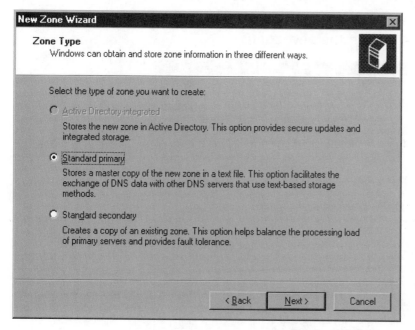

Figure 4.32 Choose Forward or Reverse lookup type.

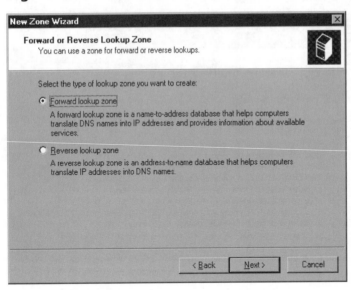

7. Type in the name of your new zone, as seen in Figure 4.33. This DNS server will be authoritative for the tacteam Second Level domain, where the net domain is the Top Level domain. Click "Next."

Figure 4.33 Naming the new zone.

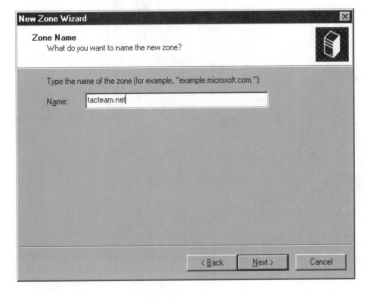

8. By default, the Wizard creates the new zone file based on the domain name, and then appends the ".dns" extension, as seen in Figure 4.34. This file will be stored in the %systemroot%\system32\dns folder. This zone file can easily be transferred to another DNS server if you need to. Click "Next."

Figure 4.34 Creating or selecting a zone file.

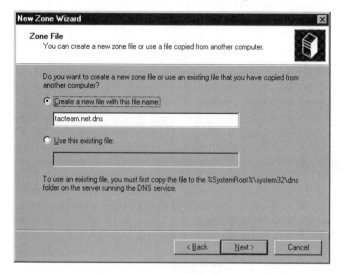

9. The wizard presents a datasheet listing your responses. If everything looks good, click "Finish." If you need to make corrections, click the "Back" button, then click "Finish."

10. Return to the Computer Management Window. Expand all zones to see the new forward lookup zone.

Creating a Reverse Lookup Zone

Now let's configure our reverse lookup zone. Our computers in the tacteam.net domain are located on network ID 192.168.1.0 and use the default Class C subnet mask, 255.255.255.0.

1. Log on with an account that is a member of the local Administrators Group if not already logged on as such.

2. Click Start | Programs | Administrative Tools | Computer Management.

3. Expand all levels in the DNS node.

4. Right-click your computer name and click on "New Zone."

5. The "New Zone Wizard" starts. Click "Next."

6. You are asked whether you want to create a "Standard Primary," "Standard Secondary," or an "Active Directory Integrated" zone. Select "Standard Primary." If you have Active Directory installed, you should select "Active Directory integrated" to take advantage of the benefits of Active Directory. Click "Next."

7. Select "Reverse Lookup Zone." Click "Next."

8. The Wizard requires the Network ID that serviced by this reverse lookup zone, as seen in Figure 4.35.

Figure 4.35 Configuring the Reverse Lookup zone.

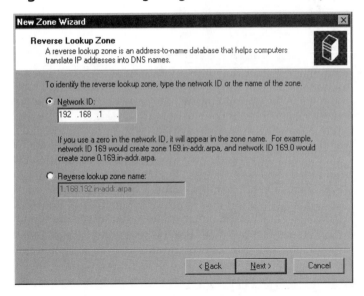

You can type in the Network ID and subnet mask, or directly enter the name of the zone file yourself. If you want to type it in yourself, begin with the network ID in reverse, then a period, then type "in-addr.arpa." For example, if the network ID were 131.107.0.0, the reverse lookup file would be 107.131.in-addr.arpa. Click "Next."

9. The Wizard asks you to confirm the name of the file. Unless you have an old reverse lookup file to import, select the default. Click "Next."

10. The last screen confirms the data entered data. Click "Finish."

Return to the computer management screen to confirm the creation of your new reverse lookup zone.

Testing your DNS Server

Now we need to populate the zone with resource records. A Address records are the most common type of record you will enter. Let's go over the procedure of entering A Address records:

1. Log on with an Administrative account.
2. Click Start | Programs | Administrative Tools | Computer Management.
3. Expand all nodes.
4. Right-click the tacteam.net forward lookup zone. Click "New Host." You should see the "New Host Properties" dialog box as in Figure 4.36.

Figure 4.36 Entering resource records for host computers.

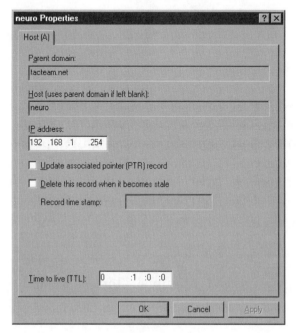

5. Enter the host name "neuro" of the new computer. Enter the IP address of the host. Be sure to put a check mark in the "Create associated pointer (PTR) record" so that DNS will automatically create this record for you and place it in the inverse lookup zone.

6. You have now entered a resource record for host neuro at tacteam.net. Open a command prompt. At the command prompt type:

    ```
    nslookup neuro.tacteam.net
    ```

    You should see the host name successfully resolved as it is in Figure 4.37.

Figure 4.37 Host name successfully resolved with nslookup.

Summary

The Domain Name System is a distributed database that allows for host-name-to-IP-address resolution. Domain names are arranged in a hierarchical structure, with the Root domain occupying the upper-most position in the hierarchy.

Top Level domains lie just beneath Root. Common Top Level domains are .com, .net, and .edu. Second Level domains lie under the Top Level Domains. Second Level domains frequently take on the name of the organization they represent. Microsoft.com is an example of a Second Level domain. Root, Top Level, and Secondary Level namespaces are centrally managed. Administrators of Second

Level domains are responsible for their portion of the DNS database. This distributes the responsibility for managing what would otherwise be an unmanageable database.

Each computer in the DNS namespace has a host name. A fully qualified domain name is the computer host name combined with the full domain path to that computer. Unqualified names do not include a full domain path to the host.

When a DNS client needs to resolve a host name to an IP address, it issues a recursive query to its Preferred DNS server. If the Preferred DNS server is not authoritative for the destination domain, it will issue a series of iterative queries to other DNS servers to find one authoritative for the zone. The response from the authoritative DNS server is sent to the client's preferred DNS server, who forwards the answer to the DNS client.

Each domain's resources are contained in a zone file. Multiple contiguous domains can be included in a single zone. Zone files are stored on DNS servers. DNS clients can query DNS servers containing a zone of interest to look up a resource. A single DNS server can be responsible for multiple zones.

Resource records track domain resources. You use an A address record to add resources to the domain. You use other resource records types to identify zone resources such as mail servers. The NS Resource record defines servers that are authoritative for domains.

The Primary DNS is the one on which the first zone was created. The Primary contains the only read/write copy of the zone database. Read-only copies of the zone database are kept on Secondary DNS servers. Secondary DNS servers allow for fault tolerance in the event the Primary DNS server becomes unavailable. Secondaries are also useful in providing load balancing.

The Primary DNS server copies the zone database to the Secondary. Traditional zone transfer copied the entire zone database file from Primary to Secondary. Windows 2000 DNS Services support incremental zone transfer. Incremental zone transfer copies only new or changed records to the Secondary DNS server.

For IT Managers

Partitioning DNS Namespace

You have some decisions to make about how to partition your DNS namespace if your company maintains an Internet presence. A company can use the same Second Level domain name for both internal and Internet resources. However, this puts your zone information at risk. A DNS server answering Internet DNS queries exposes itself to intruders. These intruders can gain valuable information about your internal DNS structure by accessing information contained in a zone database.

It is better to partition your DNS structure by registering Second Level domain names for Internet *and* intranet resources. For example, your Internet domain can be corp.com and your intranet domain can be corpinc.com. You place all intranet resources in the corpinc.com domain and all Internet resources in the corp.com domain. Position the corp.com DNS servers on Internet side of a firewall, and the corpinc.com DNS servers on the intranet side. This protects the identities of the intranet resources from Internet intruders.

You might wonder why you need to register the internal DNS domain. The internal DNS domain does not require registration with a Domain Registrar. However, you avoid some embarrassing situations by partitioning the corporate resources into two *registered* domains.

Imagine you have a corporation named BigEarth. BigEarth is a big player in the heavy equipment industry. They have a strong Internet presence. You implement DNS for your internal resources using bigearthinc.com and your Internet resources using bigearth.com. You decide to save $35 by not registering bigearthinc.com.

The CEO has a meeting with some outside investors. He wants to show these guests the company's internal Web site, to impress them with BigEarth's technological prowess. However, when the CEO types in www.bigearthinc.com, a

Continued

competitor's Web site displays! That is what can happen when you don't register your intranet domain. If someone else registers the domain, DNS queries will be answered with the IP addresses associated with the registered domain. The only way to avoid this situation is to restrict DNS queries to the intranet. In this case, no one inside the firewall will be able to access Internet resources by host name.

The Windows 2000 DNS Service supports dynamic update of Address records. A Windows 2000 DNS client can update its own Address and Pointer records. Downlevel clients are unable to update their own records in the DNS. Using DHCP as a mediator can provide support for dynamic DNS update for downlevel clients. DHCP will update both Address and Pointer records for downlevel DHCP client.

Zones can be either "Standard" or Active Directory-integrated. Active Directory integrated zones provide for multimaster replication, more efficient zone transfer, and secure updating of the zone database.

AD-integrated DNS servers are all Primary DNS servers. Zone transfer is from AD domain controller to another. The Primary DNS server replicates only change properties, rather than entire records. You provide security on a granular level, and access controls can be placed on objects in the zone database. This prevents updating of resource records without requisite permissions.

FAQs

Q: How do I make DNS rotate through the available addresses for a service, say www.tacteam.net to obtain a load-balancing effect, or similar?

A: Create several A Address records for www.tacteam.net, and give each entry a different IP address. The DNS server will rotate through the entries so that the same server isn't hit twice in a row.

Q: I want to set up DNS on an intranet. Are there any special considerations?

A: You do not need to use the cache hints file included with the Windows 2000 DDNS server. Replace that file with the host names and IP addresses of your internal root servers. This has the advantage of not having to obtain a new cache.dns file on a regular basis.

Q: Where does the caching name server store its cache?

A: The cache is completely stored in memory, it is never written to disk at any time. The cache can become very large in a short period of time in a large organization. DDNS servers dedicated as caching servers must have generous amounts of RAM to respond to DNS client queries on a timely basis.

Q: What happens after I restart my caching DDNS server?

A: The cached entries disappear. It is recommended that a caching DDNS server be very stable and rarely rebooted for this reason.

Q: How many times does a DNS client query a DNS server, and for how long?

A: The DNS client will query each DNS server on the list in order of succession. The client will wait three seconds and then issue another query. Total time spent on each server is 15 seconds or a total of five queries. The client will then move to the next server on the list and repeat the process.

Q: Is DNS necessary in Windows 2000?

A: No. DNS is only required if you implement Active Directory Domain Controllers. Windows 2000 client computers can participate in Windows NT 4.0 domains. Windows NT domains are NetBIOS-based and do not require host name resolution services. DNS is required if you do implement a Windows 2000 domain model.

Q: Can I use "illegal" characters with Windows 2000 DDNS servers?

A: Yes, but they are no longer illegal. New DNS specifications allow for the use of an extended character set for label names. Microsoft Windows 2000 DDNS servers support UTF-8 which is based on the Unicode character set. The Unicode character set allows for characters from virtually all known languages. Great care must be taken if you use non-standard characters because not all DNS servers support the extended character set.

Q: Why should I use Directory Integrated DNS zones?

A: There are many reasons to implement Active Directory-Integrated DNS Zones. The two foremost reasons are secure updates and streamlined directory replication. Non-directory-integrated servers cannot prevent unauthorized dynamic updates. Directory-enabled zones allow the administrator to control access to the zone database on a granular basis. Zone database replication is faster for Directory-enabled zone. Non-Directory-integrated zones can transfers records using either AXFR or IXFR. While IXRF is more efficient than AXFR, the entire record must be sent for those records that have changed. Directory-integrated zones send only changed property information and not the entire record. (see Table 4.4)

Table 4.4 DNS-related RFC Documents

RFC Number	Document Status	RFC Title
1034	Standard	Domain Names - Concepts and Facilities
1035	Standard	Domain Names - Implementation and Specification
1101	Unknown	DNS Encoding of Network Names and Other Types
1536	Informational	Common DNS Implementation Errors and Suggested Fixes
1591	Informational	Domain Name System Structure and Delegation

RFC Number	Document Status	RFC Title
1794	Informational	DNS Support for Load Balancing
1995	Proposed	Incremental Zone Transfer in DNS
1996	Proposed	A Mechanism for Prompt DNS Notification of Zone Changes
2052	Experimental	A DNS RR for Specifying the Location of Services (DNS SRV)
2136	Proposed	Dynamic Updates in the Domain Name System (DNS UPDATE)
2308	Standards Track	Negative Caching of DNS Queries (DNS NCACHE)

Chapter 5

Developing a WINS Strategy

239

Introduction

Windows Internet Name Service (WINS) has been part of each version of Windows NT, up to and including Windows 2000. Its purpose is to provide a method of resolving server names (such as \\LDNNT001) to IP Addresses and to provide the location of Domain Controllers.

Even though Windows NT has supported WINS since the start, many smaller networks did not use it. If your network did not have a router, Windows could use broadcasting and all name resolution would be automatic.

After reading the previous chapter on DNS you may be ready to remove your WINS server from your network and rely exclusively on DNS. Generally, this is not a good idea until you have upgraded all of your workstations to Windows 2000 Professional and your servers to Windows 2000 Server.

Thanks to the improvements in Windows 2000, WINS you will be able to maintain and expand your WINS system with a minimal amount of effort.

WINS Functional Description

The Windows Internet Name Service (WINS) provides NetBIOS name resolution on the network, via a dynamic database that matches "friendly" NetBIOS names to IP addresses. Users prefer names to numbers; it's easier for human beings to think of a particular computer on the network as "MyServer" than as "192.168.0.9." However, computers on a TCP/IP network use IP addresses to communicate with one another. In order for you to be able to type "Connect to another computer" using the "MyServer" name, there must be some way for your computer to discover the IP address of the computer that goes by that name.

TIP

To understand why name resolution is necessary, think of it this way: If you're told you need to deliver a package to someone whose name is "Bertram Cavanaugh," that knowledge alone won't enable you to find his house and give him the package. But you can look up the name in the telephone directory, and find the address where Mr. Cavanaugh lives, and then you can get there and communicate with him. WINS is like the phone book, which matches a name to an address so your messages can get to the proper destination.

IBM introduced the NetBIOS interface in the early 1980's. Microsoft then developed NetBIOS as an Application Programming Interface (API) for MS-DOS programs to use for network communication, and it became a standard for PC Local Area Networks (LANs). NetBIOS uses a flat namespace (in contrast to the hierarchical namespace of DNS) and NetBIOS names are limited to 16 characters in length and used to identify network resources. However, when you create a NetBIOS name (for instance, when you designate a name for your computer during installation of Windows 2000), you can only specify 15 characters. The 16th character is hexadecimal and used to identify the resource type.

NetBIOS names are registered dynamically when the computer starts up on the network or the user logs on. NetBIOS names cannot be duplicated on the network; for instance, if two computers are given the same NetBIOS name, the second one that attempts to log on the network will not be allowed to register its name.

All Windows operating systems prior to Windows 2000 required NetBIOS in order to function in a networked environment. The NetBIOS interface is not a requirement for networking Windows 2000 computers; DDNS can handle all name resolution. However, Windows 2000 supports WINS and includes an improved version of the service, as many Windows 2000 networks will still include "downlevel" computers on the network, which require NetBIOS for network communication.

All Windows operating systems prior to Windows 2000 were dependent on the NetBIOS. This was because all networking components in these "legacy" operating systems were NetBIOS programs. NetBIOS programs required the NetBIOS interface to work with TCP/IP. In contrast, Windows 2000 core networking functions use the WinSock interface, thus disassociating it from the NetBIOS. Computer names are now host names. Host names can be dynamically registered, and queried for, using the new Windows 2000 Dynamic DNS server.

However, NetBIOS is still required for interoperability with legacy or "downlevel" operating systems and applications. To provide support for these clients, Microsoft provides a new and improved implementation of its NetBIOS Name Server (NBNS): The Windows Internet Name Service (WINS).

There are many benefits to using WINS; it provides the administrator with a centralized database of NetBIOS names that is updated dynamically, and WINS reduces broadcast traffic on the network. A Windows 2000 server can be a WINS server, implementing the TCP/IP over NetBIOS (NetBT) standards to register and resolve names for NetBIOS-enabled computers.

NetBIOS Name Resolution

Programs written to the NetBIOS API must know the name of the destination host in order to establish a session. However, the TCP/IP protocol only requires the destination IP address and port number in order to establish a session. The TCP/IP protocol is totally unaware of the presence of NetBIOS names and doesn't care at all about them. NetBIOS programs must communicate via NetBIOS names. The challenge faced by NetBIOS applications on

TCP/IP networks is to match up a NetBIOS name with an IP address. The process of matching up the NetBIOS name with its IP address is called *NetBIOS Name Resolution.*

NetBIOS over TCP/IP, or NetBT, is a component of the NetBIOS interface. When NetBIOS applications sent a request to the network, NetBT intercepts this request and resolves the NetBIOS name to an IP address before the request is sent further down the TCP/IP protocol stack.

Microsoft provides several mechanisms for resolving NetBIOS names. These include:

- NetBIOS Name Cache
- NetBIOS Name Server
- Broadcasts
- LMHosts file
- HOSTS file
- DNS

The order in which these methods are employed depends on the *NetBIOS Node Type* of the host computer. The NetBIOS node types are as follows:

- B-node
- P-node
- M-node
- H-node

Below is a more detailed description of the different node types.

B-Node

B-node clients depend primarily on broadcasts to resolve NetBIOS names. Broadcasts are limited because they do not normally cross router boundaries. They do not use NetBIOS name servers to resolve

NetBIOS names. Microsoft's implementation of B-node is known as "enhanced B-node." The enhanced B-node client preloads entries marked with the #PRE tag in the LMHosts file into the NetBIOS name cache.

The NetBIOS name cache is a reserved area of memory that stores recently resolved NetBIOS names. Entries stay in the NetBIOS name cache for two minutes, unless a destination client is contacted again within that two minutes. Then, the name stays in the NetBIOS name cache for 10 minutes. The maximum time an entry can stay in the NetBIOS name cache is 10 minutes, regardless of how many times the client is contacted.

Microsoft enhanced B-node is the default NetBIOS name resolution method when the client is not configured as a WINS client. The order of resolution for the enhanced B-node client is as follows:

1.   NetBIOS Name Cache

2.   Broadcast

3.   LMHosts file

4.   HOSTS files

5.   DNS

P-Node

A P-node client does not use broadcasts to resolve NetBIOS names. The P-node client depends primarily on a NetBIOS Name Server to resolve NetBIOS name query requests. The following is the order of NetBIOS name resolution methods for P-node clients:

1.   NetBIOS Name Cache

2.   NetBIOS Name Server

3.   LMHosts

4.   HOSTS

5.   DNS

M-Node

The M-node client uses both a NetBIOS name server and Broadcasts in order to resolve a NetBIOS name. The M-node client will broadcast before issuing a NetBIOS name query request to a NetBIOS name server. M-Node implementations might be helpful when there is a small group of computers at a branch office that communicate primarily with each other, and the only NetBIOS name server is on the far side of a slow WAN link. Since the branch office only contains a few computers, broadcast traffic is not significant. In this scenario, broadcasts are faster and more efficient than querying a NetBIOS name server on the far side of a slow WAN link.

The order of NetBIOS name resolution methods for M-node clients is as follows:

1. NetBIOS Name Cache
2. Broadcast
3. NetBIOS Name Server
4. LMHosts
5. HOSTS
6. DNS

H-Node

H-node clients use NetBIOS name servers before they issue a NetBIOS name query request broadcast. When a computer is configured as a NetBIOS name server client, H-node becomes the default NetBIOS node type for Microsoft operating systems. In fact, one might think of H-node as "enhanced H-node." An H-node client parses the LMHosts file at startup and preloads any entries in the LMHosts file that have the #PRE tag into the NetBIOS name cache. The following is the order of NetBIOS name resolution for an H-node client:

1. NetBIOS Name Cache
2. NetBIOS Name Server
3. Broadcast
4. LMHosts
5. HOSTS
6. DNS

Note that all node types will attempt to resolve NetBIOS names using a HOSTS file and a DNS server. HOSTS files contain fully qualified domain name to IP address mappings. DNS servers resolve fully qualified domain names to IP addresses.

When a NetBIOS name is sent to the HOSTS file for resolution, only the host name component of the fully qualified domain name is queried. Similarly, when a NetBIOS name resolution request is sent to a DNS server, only the host name is portion is queried. When a DNS server receives a NetBIOS name to resolve, it only checks its own zone and does not refer the request to other DNS servers for name resolution.

What Does WINS Do?

The Windows Internet Name Service (WINS) is Microsoft's implementation of a NetBIOS name server. WINS provides a centralized mechanism to resolve NetBIOS names to IP addresses. When computers are configured as WINS clients, they automatically register their names and IP addresses with a WINS server. When a NetBIOS client application requires resolution of a NetBIOS name to an IP address, it can query the WINS server to obtain this information.

To configure a computer to be a WINS client, the address(es) of one or more WINS servers can be added in the Advanced TCP/IP properties sheet of the client computer, as shown in Figure 5.1. If the computer is configured to obtain its IP address from a DHCP server, the WINS server address information can be provided by the DHCP server.

Prior to the development of WINS, NetBIOS names could be resolved by broadcast on the local subnet, or by use of an LMHosts file for IP addresses on other subnets.

Figure 5.1 The WINS server address is entered on the WINS tab of the Advanced TCP/IP Settings property sheet.

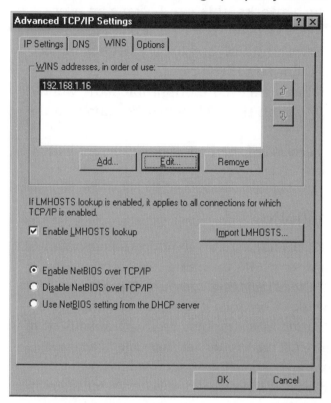

Name resolution using broadcasts is limited because most routers stop NetBIOS broadcast traffic. Broadcast-based name resolution is only useful if the NetBIOS names to be resolved are on the local subnet. If a computer uses only broadcasts for NetBIOS name resolution, it will not be able to resolve NetBIOS names to IP addresses for computers on subnets other than its own.

One solution to the broadcast limitation is the LMHosts files. The LMHosts file contains NetBIOS names and IP address mappings. A computer can examine an LMHosts file for the IP address of remote computers that would otherwise be inaccessible via NetBIOS name query broadcast messages.

LMHosts files are limited by their static nature. In dynamic networks, such as those using DHCP, IP addresses change on a frequent basis for computers throughout the network. Each time a computer changed its IP address, the LMHosts file would need to be updated. On large internetworks, this can become an overwhelming task. In addition, LMHosts files need to be placed on every machine on the network (unless a central LMHosts file is configured). In addition, a flat text file is not the most efficient database structure. This becomes even more problematic when the number of NetBIOS hosts on the internetworks runs into the thousands.

WINS was developed because of the limitations inherent with broadcasts and LMHosts.

Broadcasting versus WINS

One way to resolve a NetBIOS name to an IP address is by using broadcasts. When a computer wants to send a message to a computer named "MyServer," the originating computer sends a broadcast message to the network. A broadcast is a message that does not have a specific destination address; instead it is transmitted to all computers on the subnet. This broadcast message is a name query. It's as if the computer is shouting to a crowd, "Hey, MyServer, are you out there?" If the target computer is on the subnet, it returns a response informing the first computer of its address, and then the message intended for "MyServer" can be sent.

There are two major drawbacks to the broadcast method of name resolution:

- Broadcasts create extra traffic on the networks, since they are sent to all computers on the subnet.

NOTE

In an effort to alleviate some of the traffic congestion caused by broadcasts, a computer in a broadcast-based network (called B-node) will first check its name cache before broadcasting. The cache contains those names which were used recently, or an LMHOSTS file can be configured to preload certain names into the cache by adding the #PRE designation.

- Broadcasts don't normally cross routers, so if the destination computer is on a different subnet on the network, it won't "hear" the broadcast.

This is where the LMHOSTS file, discussed earlier, comes in. LMHosts files can be configured with the names and IP addresses of remote hosts, and therefore circumvents the limitation of local NetBIOS name query requests.

LMHosts versus WINS

The biggest problem with using the LMHosts file for NetBIOS name resolution is the fact that it is a static file. If names and/or IP addresses change, or are added or removed, an administrator must manually edit the file. Manual updating is tedious, time-consuming, and prone to error. Thus LMHosts is a viable method of resolving NetBIOS names only on a small and relatively stable network.

LMHosts is static, but WINS is a dynamic solution to the name resolution dilemma. A WINS server maintains a database with information similar to that in the LMHosts text file, but its name-to-IP mappings are updated automatically. When a WINS-enabled computer comes onto the network, it registers its name and IP address with the WINS server.

The WINS database contains an entry for each name, which is replicated to other WINS servers that are configured to be replication partners.

The following sections explain the interactions a NetBIOS client has with a WINS server.

NetBIOS Name Registration Request

The name registration process is initiated when the WINS client requests to use the name on the network. If the name requested doesn't already exist in the WINS database, the request is accepted and it is entered, time-stamped, given a version ID, and a *Positive Name Registration Response* is sent back to the requesting computer.

If the requested name already exists in the database, one of several things occurs, depending on whether the IP address the name is

registered in the WINS database is the same as that of the requesting computer, and further depending on the state of the entry:

If the IP Address in the Database Is the Same as That of the Requesting Computer

- If the name already exists and the IP address on the entry is
  the same as the one on the request, WINS will check the
  state of the entry to determine whether it is marked active,
  tombstoned, or released. If it is marked active and is owned
  by this WINS server, the time stamp will be updated and the
  requesting computer will get back a positive response, and
  can use the name on the network.

- If it is marked tombstoned (discussed later) or released, or is
  owned by another WINS server, it is treated as a new
  registration. Again, a positive response is returned to the
  requesting client.

If the IP Address in the Database Is Different from That of the Existing Computer

- If the name already exists but the database entry shows a
  different IP address, and the entry is marked tombstoned or
  released, WINS can assign the name to the new IP address.

- If the name already exists with a different IP address and
  the entry is marked active, the WINS server will "challenge"
  the name. First it sends a "Wait for Acknowledge" (WACK)
  message to the requesting computer, specifying an amount
  of time it should wait for an answer to its request. Then the
  server sends a name query to the IP address that is
  registered to the name in the database. If it receives a
  positive response, indicating that computer is still on the
  network and using the name, it will reject the requesting
  computer's request to register the name. If the server does
  not receive a positive response to the name query after three
  tries, it will send the requesting computer a message
  accepting its request and will enter the name and new IP
  address in the database.

Name Renewal

As part of the registration process, the WINS server gives the client computer a Time To Live (TTL), indicating that the registration must be renewed after a certain amount of time or it will expire and eventually be removed from the WINS database.

By default, the TTL is six days. However, WINS clients begin the attempt to renew their registrations when 50 percent of the designated time has elapsed, so renewals will usually be done every three days.

NOTE

Static WINS entries, which were manually entered in the database, do not have to be renewed and do not expire. The renewal process is similar to the initial name registration process. The WINS client sends a refresh request to the WINS server at the 50 percent mark. If there is no response, the client will continue to send requests until it receives a positive response.

The renewal interval is set on the WINS server through the WINS properties sheet. Access the properties sheet as follows:

1. Start | Programs | Administrative Tools | WINS. This will open the WINS console, as shown in Figure 5.2.

Figure 5.2 WINS server settings are made using the WINS console.

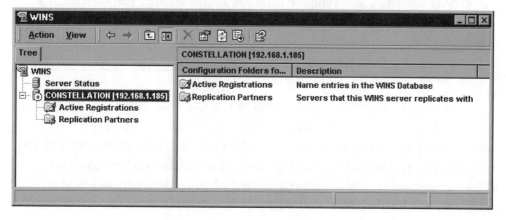

Figure 5.3 The renewal, extinction and verification intervals are set in the WINS properties sheet.

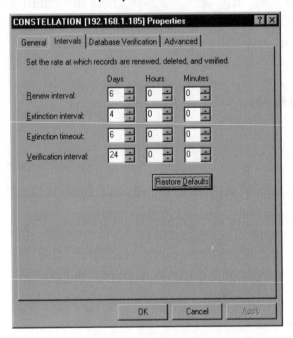

2. To change the interval settings, right-click the WINS server name and select Properties, then select the Intervals tab, as shown in Figure 5.3.

WARNING

If you have multiple WINS servers that are replication partners, they should all use the same renewal interval. If you change the interval from the default, be sure to change it on all partners or network operation may be disrupted.

This property sheet also allows you to set the intervals for extinction and verification, and the extinction timeout. The extinction interval is the amount of time between when an entry is marked as *released* and when it is marked as *extinct* in the WINS database. The extinction timeout is the amount of time between when the entry is marked extinct and when it is scavenged (removed) from the database. The verification interval determines the time after which the WINS server will verify that old names (that are owned by other servers) are still active.

NetBIOS Name Release

When a WINS client shuts down properly, it sends a message to the WINS server releasing its name. The computer user can also cause the name to be released without shutting down the system, by entering "nbtstat -RR" at the command line. When either of these occurs, a message called a *name release request* is sent to the WINS server. The server then marks the registration entry as released and sends a release confirmation message to the client.

If the entry has been marked released, and a computer attempts to register that name with a different IP address, the WINS server will allow the new registration because it knows the name is no longer being used with the former IP address.

If a computer shuts down abnormally, without releasing the name, when it attempts to connect again and register its name, the WINS server will challenge the earlier registration. However, in this case there would be no response to the challenge, so the new registration would be allowed.

The client can also release the name by broadcasting if it sends a release request and does not receive a release confirmation from a WINS server.

NetBIOS Name Query Request

A WINS client will first check its NetBIOS name cache to see if it has recently resolved the NetBIOS name of the computer it is seeking to contact. If the address mapping is not in the NetBIOS name cache, the WINS client will send a NetBIOS name query request to its Primary WINS server. If the Primary WINS server does not respond after three attempts (500ms apart), the Secondary WINS server is tried.

The WINS server searches its records for an IP address mapping for the requested NetBIOS name. If the NetBIOS name-IP Address mapping is contained in the WINS database, a Positive NetBIOS

Name Query Response is sent to the WINS client. If the WINS server does not contain a mapping, a Negative NetBIOS name query response is sent to the WINS client.

If the WINS client receives a Negative NetBIOS Name Query response, it will query a Secondary WINS server. The WINS client continues to query Secondary WINS servers until it receives a Positive NetBIOS Name Query Response.

WINS Configuration

Now that we've touched on what WINS is and what it does, we will discuss WINS configuration in detail.

Configuring Static Entries

A WINS client can lookup up the IP address of another WINS client by querying the WINS database. But what do we do when a WINS client needs to find the IP address of a non-WINS client?

The WINS client will proceed through the NetBIOS name resolution sequence since the non-WINS client's mapping is not in the WINS database. This causes a delay in name resolution. Adding a static mapping for the WINS client into the WINS database solves this problem.

A static mapping is a non-dynamic entry in the WINS database. You must enter the static mapping information manually into the WINS database in the same fashion as entries are made in standard DNS databases. Static mappings are not typically overwritten by dynamic name registrations unless the *migrate on* option is enabled.

The classic scenario involves the Windows-based WINS client that needs to contact a UNIX server running a NetBIOS application. In order for the Windows-based client to establish a session with the UNIX server, its NetBIOS name must be resolved. The Windows client is located on a remote subnet and does not have a mapping for the UNIX host in its LMHosts file. The solution to this problem is to create a static mapping for the UNIX machine in the WINS database. The WINS client is then able to locate a mapping for the UNIX host and resolve its NetBIOS name to an IP address.

The following Microsoft operating systems can be WINS clients:

- Windows 2000
- Windows NT versions 3.5x and 4.0
- Windows 9x
- Windows 3.x with Microsoft TCP/IP-32 add-on
- Microsoft Network client 3.0 for MS-DOS
- LAN Manager 2.2c for MS-DOS

To add a static mapping to the WINS database, right-click the "Active Registrations" node in the left pane of the WINS Management Console and click "New Static Mapping." You are presented with the dialog box that appears in Figure 5.4.

Figure 5.4 Adding a static mapping in the New Static Mapping dialog box.

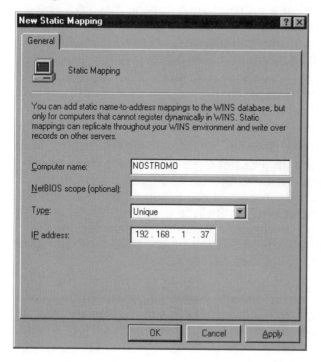

To create a new static mapping, you are required to enter the computer's NetBIOS name, type of mapping, and IP address. Table 5.1 defines the types of static mapping entries you can create. Table 5.2 lists the different NetBIOS names registered in the WINS database.

Table 5.1 Types of WINS Static Mappings

Type	Explanation
Unique	Configure a Unique mapping when a single IP address defines the host computer. Three NetBIOS names arise when you configure a Unique static mapping. A NetBIOS name associating the host name for the workstation service (redirector), messenger service, and server service are created. For example, NOSTROMO will have three entries in the WINS database: NOSTROMO[00h], NOSTROMO[03h] and NOSTROMO [20h].
Group	If the computer is a member of a workgroup, you can configure a Group entry for the machine. The IP address of the host is not included and Group name resolution is performed via local subnet broadcasts only. This known as a "Normal Group."
Domain Name	A Domain Name entry creates a [1Ch] mapping in the WINS database. This mapping points to Domain Controllers in Windows NT environments. A WINS client queries the WINS database for [1Ch] entries for a machine to authenticate a logon.
Internet Group	Configure an Internet Group when you want to create Administrative Groups of shared resources that appear as members of the group when browsing for resources. Examples include grouping file servers and print servers into such Administrative Groups. The Group identifies itself by the shared group name with the [20h] service identifier.
Multihomed	Use the Multihomed mapping to configure multiple IP address for a single NetBIOS host computer. A computer may have multiple adapters or multiple IP addresses bound to a single adapter.

Table 5.2 Some Unique NetBIOS Name Types

NetBIOS Name with Service Identifier	Explanation
computer_name[00h]	NetBIOS clients running the workstation service (redirector) register their NetBIOS name with the [00h] service identifier.
computer_name[03h]	NetBIOS client running the messenger service registers their NetBIOS name with the [03h] service identifier.
computer_name[20h]	NetBIOS clients running the server service register their NetBIOS names with the [20h] service identifier.
computer_name[21h]	NetBIOS clients running the RAS client service register their NetBIOS names with the [21h] service identifier.
domain_name[1Bh]	The Domain Master Browser (typically the Primary Domain Controller) registers its domain name with the [1Bh] service identifier.
username[03h]	Usernames are registered with the WINS server when the user logs on a NetBIOS client. The username is appended with the [03h] service identifier. The messenger service will search for a user when a net send command is issued by searching for the [03h] service identifier attached to the user name.

An "s" attribute denotes a static mapping in the WINS database. When static mappings replicate, replication partners respect their status as static entries and do not overwrite them with dynamic name registrations.

Connecting WINS Servers through Replication

Multiple WINS servers allow for fault tolerance and a more efficient NetBIOS name resolution process. In order to maintain consistency among all WINS servers on a network, there must be a method for sharing information in the WINS databases among the WINS servers. This method of sharing information among WINS servers is known as "WINS replication."

WINS clients typically register their NetBIOS names with their Primary WINS server, and if the Primary WINS server is not reachable, the WINS client registers with one of its Secondary WINS servers. In large networks, multiple WINS servers service the name registration requests of WINS clients near them. Those same WINS servers also answer NetBIOS name queries.

A problem arises when clients register their names with different WINS servers. Imagine that on subnets 192.168.1.0 and 192.168.2.0 all the WINS clients are configured to use a single WINS server at IP address 192.168.1.2. On subnet 192.168.3.0 and subnet 192.168.4.0 all the WINS clients are configured to use a Preferred WINS server at IP address 192.168.3.2.

When clients on the 192.168.1.0 subnet need to resolve a NetBIOS name for a client on subnet 192.168.2.0 they can query the WINS server and a mapping for that client is located in the WINS database. If a client on the 192.168.3.0 subnet needs to resolve a NetBIOS name for a client on the 192.168.4.0 subnet, it can do so successfully because a mapping for clients on both the 192.168.3.0 and 192.168.4.0 subnets are in its WINS database. But what happens when a client on the 192.168.1.0 subnet needs to resolve a NetBIOS name of a client on the 192.168.4.0 subnet?

The client on the 192.168.1.0 subnet issues a NetBIOS name query request to its Preferred WINS server at 192.168.1.2. However, no mappings exist for clients on the 192.168.4.0 subnet exist in its database. To solve this problem, we configure the WINS servers to be replication partners.

Replication partners share their information with each other. In this way, any WINS client will be able to query any WINS server and successfully resolve a NetBIOS name, regardless of what WINS server originally received the NetBIOS name registration.

There are two ways WINS servers are configured as replication partners. These are PULL partners and PUSH partners. The PULL partner receives WINS database information based on a configured replication interval. A PUSH partner sends database information based on how many changes have taken place in the WINS database.

A WINS server is notified by its PULL partner when it's time to request the changes that have taken place in the WINS database since the last time that server received replicated information. This determination is made based on WINS database version IDs. If the PULL partner's WINS database has a version ID higher than the one last PULLed by the WINS server, it will request the changes. If the database version is the same or smaller (an unlikely event, but possible), then records are not replicated from the PULL partner.

PUSH replication causes the PUSH partner to send changes based on how many changes were made in the WINS database. Then, after the minimum number of changes has been made, the PUSH partner sends a message to the WINS server to request the changes. Windows 2000 WINS servers are able to maintain persistent connections, which allow PUSH partners to push changes as soon as they take place.

Microsoft recommends that replication partners be configured as both PUSH and PULL partners. This reduces the chance of inconsistencies occurring in the WINS database. A notable exception to this policy is when WINS servers are separated by slow WAN connections. In this circumstance, it may be more efficient to configure the WINS servers on either side to be PULL partners. These PULL partners can be configured to exchange WINS database information during times of reduced network utilization and therefore not impact normal networking communications to such a large extent.

To configure replication partners, perform the following steps:

1. Open the WINS Management Console and expand all nodes. Right-click the "Replication Partners" node and click "New Replication Partner." You will see the "New Replication Partner" dialog box, as seen in Figure 5.5.

2. Type in the NetBIOS name of the WINS server you want to make a replication partner, or click the "Browse" button and select the WINS server from the Browse list.

Figure 5.5 The New Replication Partner dialog box.

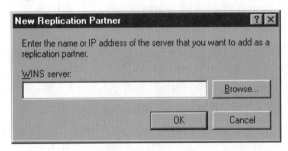

3. You can see the list of replication partners in the right pane of the WINS Management Console in the right pane, as seen in Figure 5.6.

Figure 5.6 The WINS Management Console displaying Replication Partners for Exeter.

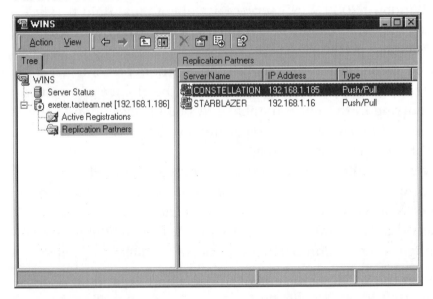

4. Right-click one of the replication partners and click "Properties." On the "Properties" dialog box, click the "Advanced" tab. You should see what appears in Figure 5.7.

5. In the "Replication partner type:" drop-down list box you can select "Push/Pull," "Push," or "Pull." Select the "Push/Pull"

Figure 5.7 Configuring Push and Pull Partner Properties.

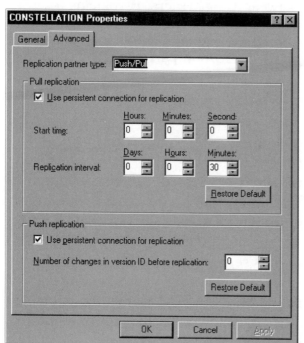

option. This defines CONSTELLATION as the Push and Pull partner of Exeter.

6. After selecting the Push/Pull option, the text boxes for configuring both Push and Pull partnerships are made available. In the "Pull replication" frame, you can configure the "Start time:" and "Replication interval". The "Start time:" represents the time of day on a 24-hour clock. The start time by default is set to midnight, with a replication interval of thirty minutes. So, EXETER will send a Pull notification to CONSTELLATION every thirty minutes to inform it to get any existing WINS database changes.

7. The "Push Replication" frame contains the "Number of changes in version ID before replication" text box. You can configure the number of changes in the WINS database before EXETER sends a Push message to CONSTELLATION so that it will request any existing WINS database changes.

8. For both Push and Pull replication, a persistent connection can be maintained between the partners. By placing a checkmark in the "Use persistent connection for replication" checkbox, you avoid the overhead of opening and closing connections between the replication partners. Replication, therefore, will have less impact on the server as a whole when this option is selected.

Designing a Network of Multiple WINS Servers

Small networks with two or three WINS servers can be configured to have all WINS servers as PUSH and PULL partners. However, larger networks will require configurations that are more sophisticated.

Imagine your organization has 50,000 clients and ten WINS servers. Configuring all ten WINS servers to be PUSH and PULL partners would lead to needless and potentially adverse levels of network traffic during replication. A more efficient method of configuring replication partners in a large network is the "spoke and hub" model of WINS database replication.

The spoke and hub model allows multiple WINS servers to partner with a single "hub" WINS server. The hub collects information from all its partners, and then distributes the information from all the partners back to each one. This is reminiscent of how the Browser services works, with the Domain Master Browser acting as a central point of collection of information from multiple subnets (see Figure 5.8).

In our example, we have three main sites, as pictured in Figure 5.8. Each site has a single "hub" WINS server. Each "hub" WINS server is partnered with three "spoke" WINS servers. Each hub server is configured to be a PUSH and PULL partner to its related spoke servers. Each spoke server is configured to be a PUSH and PULL partners to its related hub server.

The hub servers are also configured to be replication partners. There are several different ways you can configure the hub servers. One approach is to configure one of the hub servers as a "hub" for the hub servers themselves. In Figure 5.8, Dallas could be configured

Figure 5.8 Hub and spoke WINS server deployment.

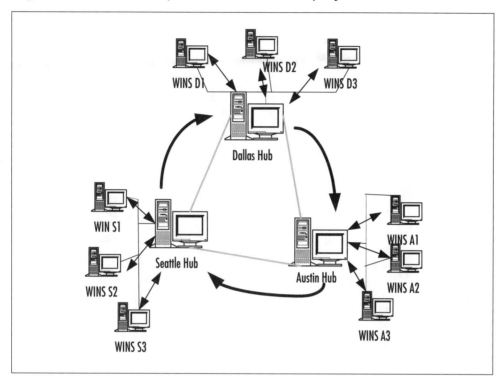

as the hub server with Seattle and Austin as spokes. Each spoke would be a PULL partner of the hub in Dallas, and Dallas would be a PULL partner for the spokes in Austin and Seattle.

Another way to configure the replication relationships among the hub servers is to configure a "chain." The chain arrangement is displayed in Figure 5.9.

In the chain design, the Austin server is configured as a PULL partner of the Dallas server, the Seattle Server is configured as a PULL partner of the Austin server, and the Dallas server is a PULL partner of the Seattle Server. While the chain arrangement consumes less overall bandwidth, convergence time is longer.

When configuring multiple WINS servers in such a distributed fashion, we have to consider the amount of time it takes for database changes to distribute themselves to all WINS servers in our "WINS network." This time period is referred to as "convergence

Figure 5.9 Chain Replication in a WINS Hub Network

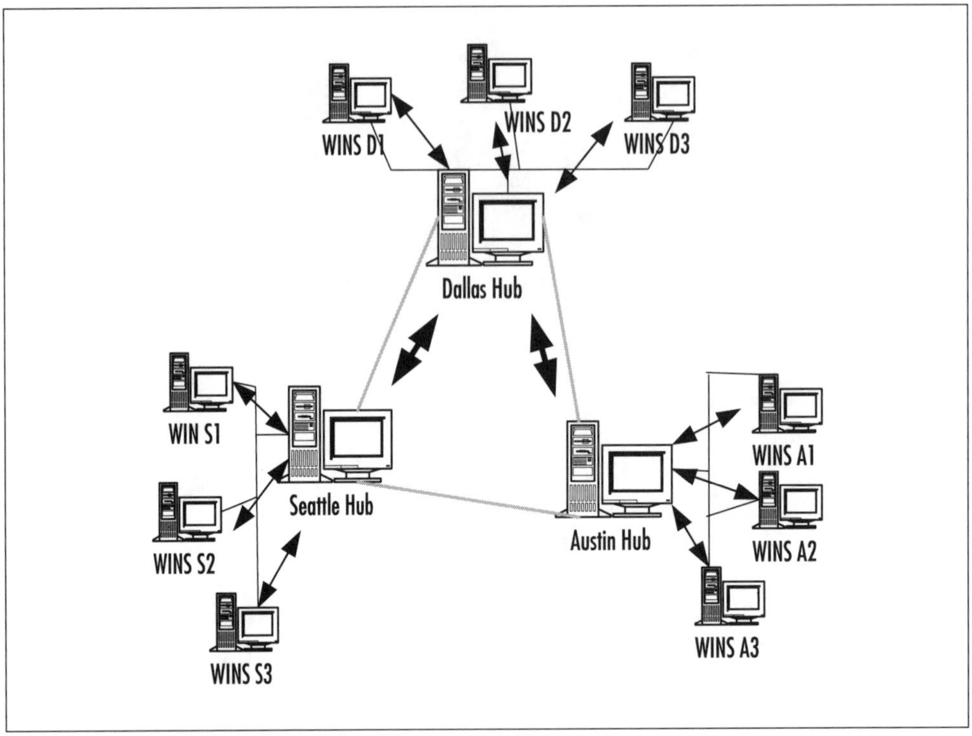

time." This is the amount of time it takes for changes to the WINS database of a single WINS server to converge or be distributed to all other WINS servers in the network.

Let's look at the example in Figure 5.8 again. We will configure the PULL interval between the peripheral spoke servers with their hubs servers to be 15 minutes. Let's configure the Dallas server to be the "hub" of the hub servers, and the PULL interval among the hub servers is 30 minutes. Remember that Dallas is a PULL partner of Seattle and Austin, and Seattle and Austin are PULL partners of Dallas.

How long will it take a change made on one of the spoke WINS servers in Austin to be replicated to one of the spoke WINS servers in Seattle? In a worst-case scenario, the change on the spoke server in Austin will take 15 minutes. That change is replicated from

Austin to Dallas in 30 minutes. The change is then replicated to Seattle from Dallas 30 minutes later, and the Seattle hub sends the change to the Seattle spoke 15 minutes after that. When we add all the intervals together, the worst-case scenario has the convergence time set to 90 minutes.

You need to plan how much time you can allow for full convergence to take place. WINS clients will not be able to resolve NetBIOS names of hosts whose IP address has changed during this interim period. Your decision on how much convergence time is acceptable is dependent upon how dynamic your network infrastructure is. The majority of the problems are related to DHCP. Clients configured with static IP addresses will not send changes to the WINS database, and their records are stable.

Backing Up Your WINS Database

Backing up the WINS database can save you many problems should the database file be corrupted by power fluctuations or disk errors. A large WINS database can take a long time to rebuild. All WINS clients on the network would have to reregister their names with their WINS server. Then all the WINS servers will need to complete the replication process. As you can imagine, this would take a LOT of time to complete.

Make the WINS database folder part of your regular tape backup routine. The WINS database and its supporting files are stored in:

```
%systemroot%\system32\wins
```

You should also keep a local backup copy of the WINS database so that you can rapidly recover in the event the original WINS database file becomes corrupted. Restoring the local copy is faster than searching and restoring a copy from tape.

To backup the WINS database, first create a folder on another physical drive that will contain the WINS database files. Do not use a mapped network drive or the procedure will fail. You can name

Figure 5.10 Selecting the Folder Location to Backup the WINS database files.

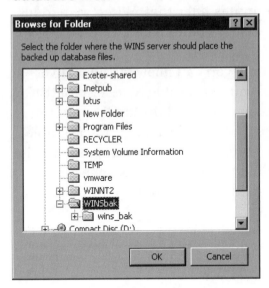

this folder anything you like. Open the WINS Management Console and right-click your WINS server's name in the left pane and click "Backup database." You will see the "Browse for Folder" dialog box, as it appears in Figure 5.10.

Select the folder that you created for the WINS database backup files and click "OK." You will see a dialog box confirming the database backed up successfully.

To restore the WINS database from the local backup, first stop the WINS service. You can stop the WINS server service by going to a command prompt and typing "net stop WINS" or right-click the WINS server name in the left pane of the WINS Management Console and trace to "All Tasks" and then trace over and click "stop."

After stopping the WINS server service, the "Restore Database" command is available. Click "Restore Database." The "Browse for Folder" dialog box appears. Select the directory housing the WINS database backup files, and click "OK." The database is restored and the WINS server service is restarted automatically.

New Features of Windows 2000 WINS

The Windows 2000 WINS server includes all the functionality of previous versions of Microsoft WINS servers and includes additional and enhanced functionality. Windows 2000 WINS servers can maintain persistent connections with replication partners, block replication from selected WINS servers, and have an enhanced user interface. We will look at these features and other new features in the Windows 2000 WINS implementation.

Persistent Connections

Earlier versions of the Microsoft WINS server had to establish a new connection to replication partners each time a replication event took place. The connection closed after completion. This opening and closing of connections between WINS server took processor cycles on both machines. Establishing and breaking down connections on a frequent basis diminished the overall performance of the WINS server.

The Windows 2000 WINS server allows you to configure replication partners to maintain persistent connections. Persistent connections circumvent the need to repeatedly open and close sessions. The server does not need to expend additional processor cycles servicing connection requests. This improves the overall performance of the WINS server.

Another benefit of persistent connections between replication partners is the ability to immediately update partners of WINS database updates. In the past, push updates were configured to a target number known as the "update count" that had to be reached before the push update message was sent to replication partners. This was sometimes set to a high number to avoid frequent opening and closing sessions between partners. An update count of 0 allows persistant connections to obviate this limitation.

A nominal amount of bandwidth is used to maintain a persistent connection because the channel is idle most of the time. When immediate updates are sent, only a small amount of data is sent over the wire, which avoided the negative impact on network communications

There is a walkthrough at the end of chapter where we configure persistent connections for replication partners.

Manual Tombstoning

Tombstoning is the process of marking records in the WINS database as no longer valid. If a WINS client fails to renew its NetBIOS name within the renewal interval, its WINS database record is marked as "released". The record stays in the released state for a duration defined by the extinction interval . After the extinction interval is over the record is marked as "tombstoned." The record remains in the tombstoned state for the entirety of the "extinction timeout" interval. At the end of the extinction timeout interval, the record is removed from the WINS database. Figure 5.11 depicts the lifecycle of a WINS database record.

Figure 5.11 The lifecycle of a WINS database record.

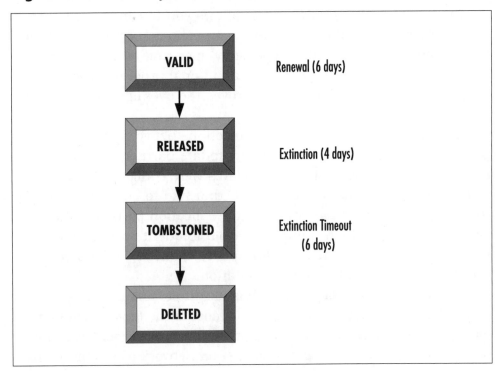

You may wonder "Why tombstone a record? Why doesn't the WINS server just delete the record?" Tombstoning a record prevents that record from being "replicated" back to the WINS server that "owns" it. The owner is the WINS server that received the original NetBIOS name registration from the WINS client.

Imagine you have a computer with the NetBIOS name of W2K1. W2K1 registered with its primary WINS server when it started up. Later, W2K1 is removed from the network. W2K1 releases its NetBIOS name, the WINS server waits the period defined in the extinction interval before marking W2K1's record as tombstoned. When the WINS server that is the owner of W2K1's record replicates, W2K1's tombstoned status replicates as well. After the extinction timeout period has passed, the tombstoned records remove themselves from the owner's WINS database, and from the databases of all its replication partners.

After the extinction timeout, the tombstoned record removes itself from both the server that is the owner of the record and all replication partners receiving the tombstoned record. The record cannot be re-replicated because it removes itself from all WINS databases.

What would happen if we just delete the record, rather than tombstoning it? Let's just delete W2K1's record from the WINS server that owns his record. Consider what has happened before W2K1 went offline. Most likely, W2K1 renewed its NetBIOS name a time or two. In addition, W2K1's Primary WINS server replicated its database during this time. A valid record now exists in the WINS databases of the owner's replication partners.

After deleting W2K1's record from its owners database, the WINS server continues to replicate with its partners. Since W2K1's record is now absent from the database, *no* information regarding W2K1 is included in the replicated records.

However, what happens when W2K1's Primary WINS server receives replication from *its* partners? These WINS servers still have W2K1 in their WINS databases. The record is marked as active in their databases. After replication, W2K1's Primary WINS server receives W2K1's record again. Its status is marked as active! You can see how deleting records, rather than tombstoning

Figure 5.12 The Delete WINS Record dialog box.

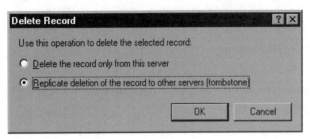

them, can cause them to "loop" back and forth among WINS replication partners.

To manually tombstone a record, open the WINS Management Console. Expand all nodes and click the "Active Registrations node." Right-click one of the records in the right pane of the WINS Management Console and click "Delete." You will see the "Delete Record" dialog box, as it appears in Figure 5.12.

You can manually "tombstone" or mark extinct a record by selecting the option "Replicate deletion of the record to other servers (tombstone)."

It is much better to tombstone records rather than deleting them. Take advantage of this new capability to manually tombstone in the Windows 2000 WINS server.

Improved Management Tools

Window NT 4.0 had the WINS Manager utility for WINS server management. Windows 2000 uses the WINS Management Console. You can access the WINS Management Console features by opening the dedicated WINS Management Console, opening the "Computer Management" Console, or creating a new console and adding the WINS plug-in.

Several new features have been added to the WINS Management Console that allow you to control how WINS records are replicated in your WINS network. These include the ability to overwrite or update static WINS entries and the ability to prevent records from specific WINS servers from replicating.

Static mappings allow you to add WINS records for machines that are not WINS clients or for those machines that have client reservations on a DHCP server. When a machine has a static mapping, it does not dynamically update its WINS records and is not required to renew its name. By default, if a machine tries to overwrite a static mapping, it will fail.

When a WINS server receives a Name Registration Request, it searches its database for another computer claiming the same NetBIOS name. If another record is found with the same name, the WINS server will send a challenge message to the IP address of the owner. If the owner of the NetBIOS name doesn't respond, the Name Registration Request is honored, and the new computer is allowed to register its NetBIOS name and IP address. When the entry in the WINS database is a static mapping, the results of the challenge have no bearing on the result; the new computer will not be allowed to register its name.

When static mappings replicate, they are marked as static mappings. All WINS servers that receive the static record honor the "no overwrite" status of a static mapping. No WINS server tombstones the static mapping. Therefore, static mappings replicate indefinitely unless manually tombstoned. You must tombstone the record because static mappings are not subject to extinction or extinction timeouts. Normally this is not a problem. When you want to remove a static mapping, you just right-click its entry in the WINS database and select the tombstoning options.

But, what if the WINS server went offline and you do not plan to bring that machine back on line? All the static mappings on that machine have replicated to its WINS replication partners. Those partners will continue to copy the static mappings indefinitely until you manually delete all of them. Also, any machine that needs to claim the NetBIOS name will be denied registration because of the statically-mapped computer's entry in the WINS database.

To solve this problem you could go to every WINS machine in your WINS infrastructure and delete the record manually, or you could tombstone the record and wait for the convergence interval to complete. However, there is a less labor-intensive way to accomplish your goal of removing these static entries and allowing dynamic updates of the NetBIOS names to which they lay claim.

You could choose to make the records owned by the absent WINS server "Persona Non Grata." This blocks the replication of records owned by WINS server marked as such. In Windows NT 4.0, the Persona Non Grata value had to be entered manually into the Registry. In Windows 2000 you can enter the IP address of the removed WINS server to block replication of the records it owns. Figure 5.13 shows where to configure Persona Non Grata servers, and Figure 5.14 shows a WINS record and owner information. After adding IP addresses of the computers for which you want to block entries, restart the WINS service to ensure the settings take effect.

While this solves the problem involving replication of static mappings own by absent or disabled WINS servers, it does not allow computers to update or overwrite the information contained in the static mappings. In order to accomplish this goal, you must enable what was known as *Migrate On* in Windows NT 4.0.

Figure 5.13 Configuring the Persona Non Grata server.

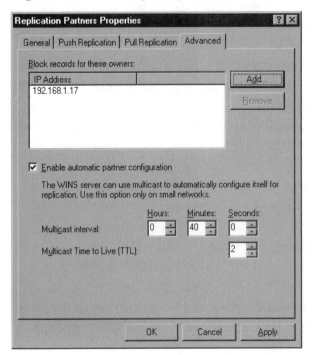

Figure 5.14 WINS record with IP address of owner.

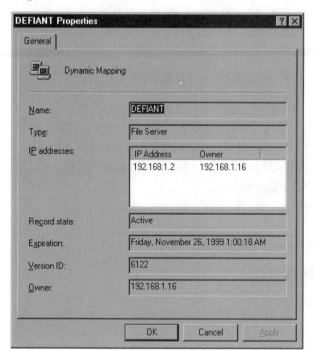

The Migrate On feature is called the "Overwrite unique static mappings at this server (migrate on)" option in Windows 2000. When enabled, WINS clients can register the NetBIOS name and IP address when a client with a static mapping fails to respond to the WINS server challenge. Some types of static mappings will not be overwritten, such as those WINS entries designating a computer as a Domain Controller [1Ch].

Higher Performance

The WINS service now uses the "jet blue" database engine. This is the same database technology used by the Active Directory and Exchange server. The more efficient database design improves the speed and efficiency of the Windows 2000 WINS server compared to its predecessors.

The WINS Management console itself is more flexible than its ancestors. The WINS console is a multithreaded application that allows multiple tasks to engage simultaneously. While you are waiting for a task on one WINS database to complete, you can start work on another WINS server listed in the WINS management console.

Enhanced Filtering and Record Searching

Large WINS installations can gather tens of thousands of WINS records in the WINS database. In the past, if you wanted to find a record or a group of records in the WINS databases, you had to sift through the list manually. Windows 2000 WINS servers have enhanced record finding and filtering.

Figure 5.15 shows the "Find by Name" dialog box.

Figure 5.15 The Find by Name dialog box.

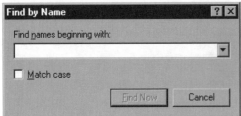

If you want to find all servers that begin with LAX, all you need to do is type LAX in the "Find names beginning with" text box and click "Find Now." The right pane in the WINS manager will display the results of the query. If you want to see all the records in the database, you can type an asterisk (*) in the text box instead of a computer name string. Note that this is the only "wildcard" type of search you can do. The only searches done by the "Find by Name" dialog box are for the entries beginning with the letters typed in the text box.

Figure 5.16 shows the "Find by Owner" dialog box.

Using this search tool, you can find all records owned by selected servers, or view records owned by all servers. The IP address of the server and the highest version ID number is also included on this list.

Figure 5.17 shows the contents of the "Record Types" tab in the "Find by Owner" dialog box. You can filter and view records that

Figure 5.16 The Find by Owner dialog box.

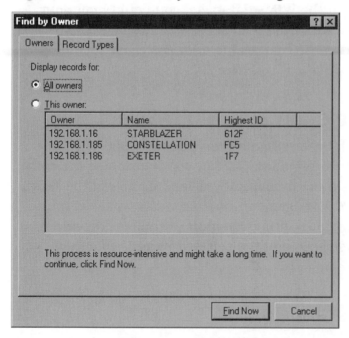

Figure 5.17 Selecting records by service identifier.

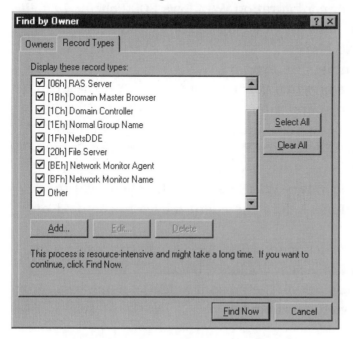

have specific service identifiers. So, if you wanted to find all domain controllers registered in the WINS database, you could limit your search for only entries with the [1Ch] service identifier.

The find and filter feature makes life a lot easier for the administrator in a large enterprise environment.

Dynamic Record Deletion and Multi-Select

Deleting records is a lot easier using the Windows 2000 WINS Management Console. In Windows NT 4.0, you had to use the command line utility winscl.exe to manually delete records in the WINS database. In the WINS Management Console, you can select multiple records by holding down either the shift or the ctrl key on the keyboard and then right-clicking the selected records to either delete or tombstone them.

Increased Fault Tolerance

You can configure Windows 2000 WINS clients with up to 12 "secondary" WINS servers. Downlevel clients support only Primary and Secondary WINS server configuration. Windows 2000 clients benefit from a higher level of fault tolerance for NetBIOS name resolution by supporting more WINS servers.

A WINS client contacts its Primary WINS server when registering its NetBIOS name or when resolving a NetBIOS. If the primary WINS server fails to respond after three attempts to contact it, the client will contact the Secondary WINS server. In addition, the client will contact Secondary WINS server when the Primary WINS server returns a negative NetBIOS name query response. If there are multiple Secondary WINS servers, the client will try each of these three times before the client moves to the next one on the list.

Assigning multiple Secondary WINS servers appears to be a no-lose situation. You must strike a balance between fault tolerance and speed of name resolution. The normal NetBIOS name resolution process for H-node machines includes:

1. Checking its own NetBIOS name
2. Searching the NetBIOS name cache
3. Querying configured WINS server(s)
4. Issuing a Broadcast
5. Searching the LMHosts file
6. Searching the HOSTS file
7. Querying the Preferred DNS server

The efficiency of name resolution depends on services available on your network. It may be more efficient for a WINS client to move through the entire NetBIOS name resolution algorithm than to query up to 12 WINS servers. Consider this when configuring clients with multiple Secondary WINS server addresses.

Burst Handling

WINS servers can be overwhelmed with NetBIOS name registration requests. The typical example is after a system-wide power outage takes place and all machines come online simultaneously and attempt to register their NetBIOS names with their WINS server. The WINS server can cache a certain number of requests, after which it will begin to drop subsequent requests.

Windows NT 4.0 WINS servers with Service Pack 3 and above support high volume WINS registration requests via a process called "Burst Handling." Windows 2000 WINS servers also support WINS server Burst Mode responses.

When a large number of NetBIOS name registration requests arrive at a WINS server in rapid succession, the WINS server will not be able to complete processing of each request in a timely fashion. The WINS server holds these requests in a "queue" for processing until the requisite resources on the server become available. Then the requests are fully processed and written to disk in the WINS database.

The number of virtually simultaneous requests may be so great that the efficiency and accuracy of name registration may suffer.

In this scenario, the WINS server will switch into Burst Mode. When the WINS server is in burst mode, any name registration requests received over a predefined number receive immediate acknowledgement. However, the WINS server does not check the NetBIOS against the WINS database; it does not issue a challenge against duplicate names and it does not write an entry to the WINS database.

The default queue size is 500. When the number of pending registration requests exceeds 500, the WINS server switches into Burst Mode and immediately acknowledges the WINS client's request for NetBIOS name registration. For the first 100 registrations over 500, the clients are given a name renewal period of five minutes. For the next 100 pending name registrations, the WINS clients receive a name renewal interval of 10 minutes. This pattern of incrementing the name renewal period by five minutes per 100 pending requests continues until the TTL reaches 50 minutes (1000 pending registrations). Then the process starts all over with the WINS server sending the next 100 pending registration requests a TTL of five minutes.

The maximum number of queued responses is 25,000. After that point, the WINS server starts dropping the requests.

Note that when the WINS clients receive an immediate acknowledgement, there is a risk of registering duplicate NetBIOS names on the network. This is because the WINS server does not challenge duplicate names in the WINS database prior to acknowledging the client while in burst mode. The assumption is that the WINS server will be less impacted when the client attempts to renew its name, and then the WINS server will be able to complete the normal process of the NetBIOS name registration request.

Figure 5.18 shows the configuration options for WINS server burst handling.

The configuration options are: Low, Medium, High, and Custom. Each configuration option determines how many name registration requests can be in the queue before burst mode is enabled. Low allows 300, Medium 500, and High 1000. You may also select a custom value by entering it into the textbox next to the Custom option.

Figure 5.18 Configuration options for WINS server burst handling.

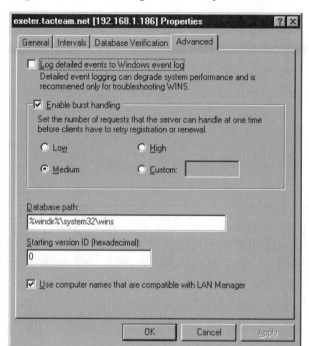

Dynamic Re-registration

You have to restart Windows NT 4.0 clients in order to reregister or update their WINS records after NetBIOS names or IP addresses change. Windows NT clients with Service Pack 4 and above, as well as Windows 2000 WINS clients, support reregistration without restarting the client machines.

To reregister a WINS client's entry in the WINS database, open a command prompt and type:

```
Nbtstat   RR
```

If the name conflicts with another active registration in the WINS database, TCP/IP is disabled on that adapter. In this case, selectively disconnect that adapter from the network and change the NetBIOS name of the computers. Reconnect to the network and reregister the client again.

Walkthrough

Install and Configure a WINS Server

WARNING

Do not perform any of these Walkthrough Exercises on a production network without the express permission of your network administrator. Some of these exercises have the potential to disrupt or disable network communications or stability.

In this walkthrough, we'll install and configure a WINS server, and then configure a Windows 2000 client to use the new WINS server.

In order to complete these exercises you'll need two computers: one Windows 2000 server family computer to install the WINS server, and a second computer to use as a WINS client. The WINS server computer should have a static IP address. If you don't have a second computer, you can configure the WINS server machine as a WINS client pointing to itself.

1. Log on as Administrator at the computer that will be the WINS server.

2. Click Start | Settings | Control Panel.

3. In the Control Panel, open the "Add/Remove Programs" applet. You should see something similar to Figure 5.19.

4. Click on the "Add/Remove Windows Components" button on the left side of the "Add/Remove Programs" applet. You will see for a moment a "please wait" info box.

5. After the "please wait" info box clears, you will see the "Add Components Wizard" window, as seen in Figure 5.20. Scroll down the list of components and find the "Networking Services" entry.

6. Click once on "Networking Services" to select it. Do not click on the checkbox or you may inadvertently remove some networking components. Click on the "Details" button. You

Figure 5.19 The Add/Remove Programs Applet.

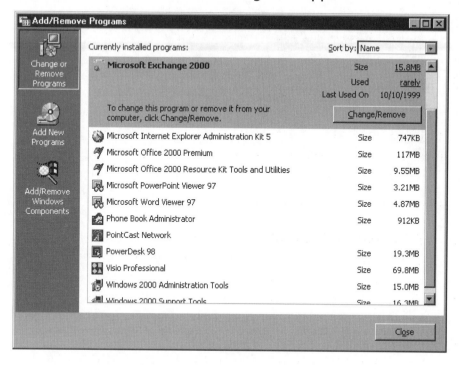

Figure 5.20 The Windows components Wizard dialog box.

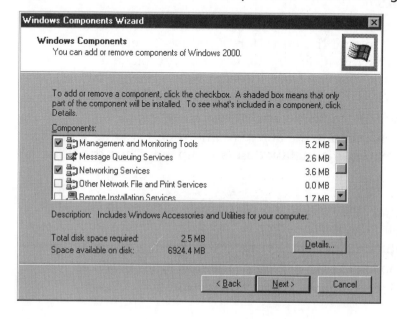

Figure 5.21 The Networking Service dialog box.

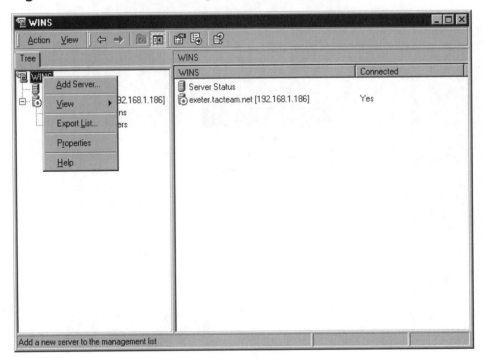

will see the "Networking Services" dialog box, as seen in Figure 5.21.

7. Scroll down the list of "Subcomponents of Networking Services" to find the entry for "Windows Internet Name Service (WINS)." Click in the checkbox to place a checkmark for "Windows Internet Name Service (WINS)." Then click "OK." Then click "Next" in the "Windows Components Wizard."

8. The wizard installs the software and then presents a dialog box indicating the installation is complete. Click the "Finish" button.

This completes the installation of the WINS server. In this section, we configure the WINS server to meet the specifications of our network environment. We focus primarily on configuration settings for the WINS console, WINS server status checking, WINS server properties, and replication partner properties.

1. Click Start | Programs | Administrative Tools | WINS.

2. The WINS administrative console is now open. First, add a server to the WINS console. You can manage all WINS servers from a single location. Right-click the WINS node at the top of the left pane, and click "Add Server," as seen in Figure 5.22.

Figure 5.22 Adding a WINS sever to the WINS Management Console.

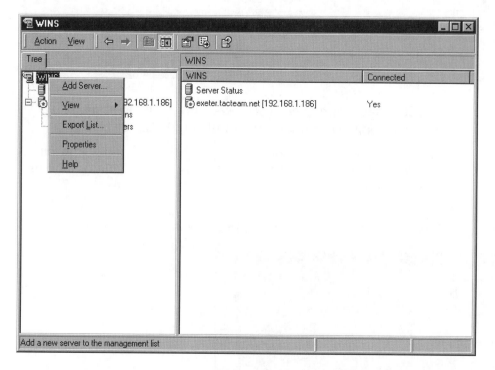

3. You see the "Add Server" dialog box. Click the "Browse" button. You see the "Select Computer" dialog box, as seen in Figure 5.23. In the "Look in:" list box, be sure to select your domain. Scroll through the list of computers and select your WINS server computer. Click "OK," and then click "OK" again to close the "Add Server" dialog box.

4. Expand all nodes. If you see an error message saying that you cannot connect to the server, click on the "Action" menu and click "Refresh." If that does not correct the problem, then right-click your computer name in the left pane, trace down

Figure 5.23 The Select Computer dialog box.

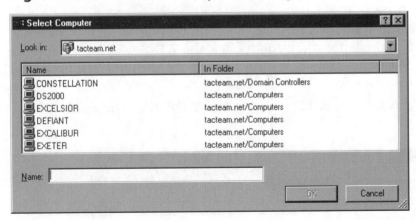

to "All Tasks," and then trace over and click "Restart." Click "Refresh" one more time if you still see the error.

5. Right-click the "WINS" node on top of the left pane and click on "Properties." You see the "WINS Properties" dialog box as seen in Figure 5.24.

Figure 5.24 The WINS Properties dialog box.

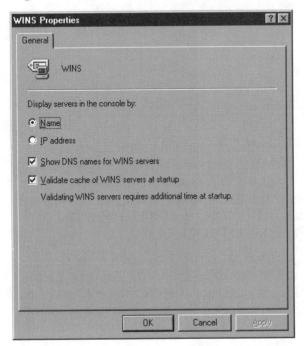

6. Choose to display servers by name and put a check in the "Show DNS names of WINS servers." Put a checkmark in the "Validate cache of WINS servers at startup" to have the system check for the status of WINS servers added to the console at system startup. Click "Apply" and then "OK."

7. Right-click your WINS server name and then click on "Properties." You will see the Properties sheet of your WINS server, as seen in Figure 5.25.

Figure 5.25 The WINS Server properties sheet.

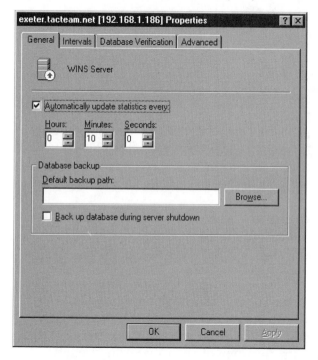

8. Ensure there is a checkmark in the "Automatically update statistics every:" check box and change the update interval to 15 minutes. In the "Default backup path:" text box, type "c:\WINSbak" and place a checkmark in the "Back up database during server shutdown" box. You must create the WINSbak directory manually before the WINS database will back up to that location.

9. Click on the Intervals tab and examine the Renew, Extinction, Extinction timeout, and Verification intervals, as seen in

Figure 5.26 The Intervals tab of the WINS server Properties dialog box.

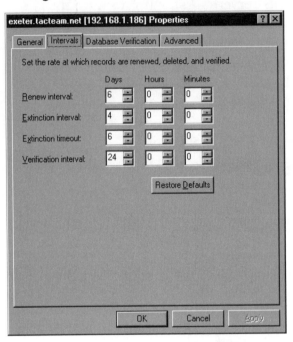

Figure 5.26. The defaults are adequate for most situations and do not need to be reconfigured

10. Click on the "Database Verification" tab. You will see what appears in Figure 5.27.

11. Put a checkmark in the "Verify database consistency every:" check box and set the number of hours to 24. Start verifying at 2 A.M. by changing the value in the "Hours" text box to 2. Change the "Maximum number of records verified each period:" value to 30,000. Select "Owner servers" to whom you will "Verify against."

12. Click the "Advanced" tab to see what appears in Figure 5.28. Put a check in the "Log detailed events to Windows event log." This takes extra disk and processor time; so do not leave this setting on for an extended period. Set burst handling to "Medium." This will allow up to 500 name registration requests to stay in the queue before activating burst mode handling. Leave the checkmark in the "Use computer names that are compatible with LAN Manager."

Figure 5.27 The Database Verification tab.

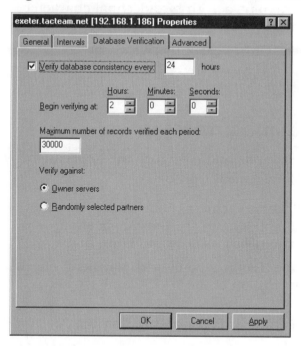

Figure 5.28 The Advanced tab.

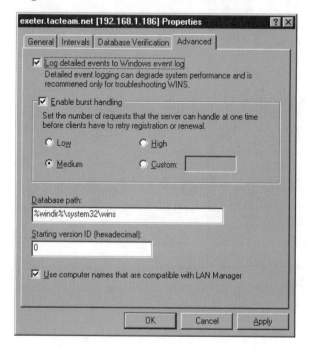

LAN Manager compatible computer names include 15 user configurable characters, plus a 16th hexadecimal character use as a service identifier.

13.   Click "Apply" and then "OK" to clock the WINS server properties dialog box.

Configuring Replication Partners

In the next exercise, we will examine and configure the Replication Partners node in the WINS Management Console.

1.   Right-click the "Replication Partners" node in the left pane and click "Properties." You should see the "Replication Partners Properties" dialog box as seen in Figure 5.29.

2.   Put a checkmark in the "Replicate only with partners" check box to ensure that replication of the WINS database takes

Figure 5.29 The Replication Partners Properties dialog box, General tab.

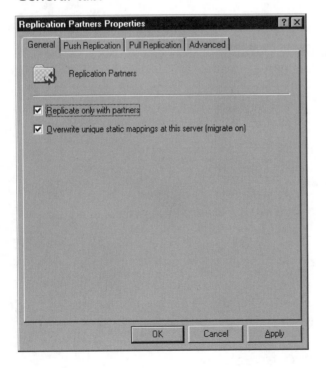

place only among configured WINS replication partners. Put a checkmark in the check box for "Overwrite unique static mapping at this server (migrate on)." The migrate on configuration allows dynamic mappings to overwrite static mappings. This is useful for a network transitioning from an LMHosts name resolution configuration to a dynamic WINS name resolution scheme.

3. Click on the "Push Replication" tab to see what appears in Figure 5.30.

Figure 5.30 The Push Replication tab.

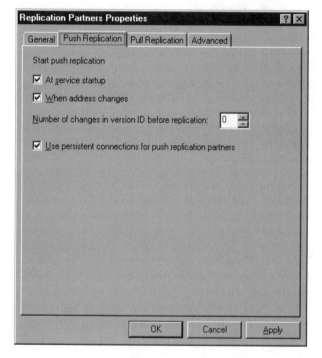

4. Put a checkmark in the check box for "At service startup" to start push replication with replication partners at startup. To immediately update replication partners every time a record is updated, put a checkmark in the check box for "When address changes." If you choose not to update immediately, put a number in the "Number of changes in version ID before replication" text box. Put a checkmark in "Use Persistent connections to push replication partners."

Figure 5.31 The Pull Replication tab.

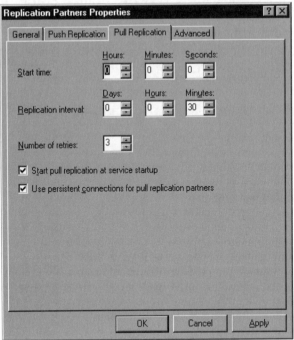

5. Click the "Pull Replication" tab to see the dialog box pictured in Figure 5.31.

6. Enter the time of day when you want a Pull Replication to take place in the "Start time:" text boxes. Enter the amount of time you want to pass between pull requests to replication partners in the "Replication interval:" text boxes. The "Number of retries:" text box determines how many times the WINS server will try to establish failed connections. Put a checkmark in the "Use persistent connections for pull replication partners" check box to enable persistent connections between configured replication partners.

7. Click the "Advanced" tab and you will see what appears in Figure 5.32.

8. If there are WINS servers that you want to "block" or prevent replication from, click the "Add" button to add their IP addresses. (This was known as "persona non grata" in Windows NT 4.0, and had to be set in the registry.)

Figure 5.32 The Advanced tab.

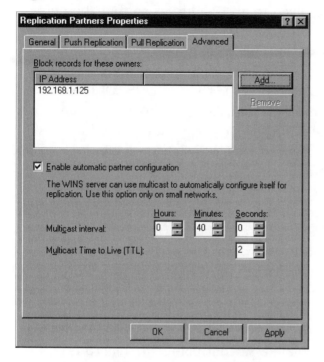

Automatic Partner configuration uses multicast addresses to allow WINS servers to automatically use themselves as replication partners. All WINS servers will identify themselves as part of the same multicast group. Configure how often you want WINS servers to announce themselves as members of the multicast group in the "Multicast interval:" text boxes. Autoconfigured partners will pull records from each other every two hours.

9. Click "OK" to close the Advanced tab.

Summary

NetBIOS programs must know the name of the destination host before a session can be established. In order to establish a session between two TCP/IP hosts, the TCP/IP host must know the destination IP computer's IP address. In order for NetBIOS programs to function on TCP/IP-based networks, the destination computer's NetBIOS name must be resolved to an IP address so that the network request passes down the stack successfully.

Windows 2000 provides a number of methods to resolve NetBIOS names to IP addresses. Those methods include: the NetBIOS Name Cache, WINS, Broadcast, LMHosts, HOSTS, and DNS. Of these choices, WINS is the superior solution. A WINS server maintains a database of NetBIOS names and their corresponding IP addresses.

When a computer is configured as a WINS client, it can register its name and IP address automatically on startup with a WINS server. The host accomplishes this via a NetBIOS Name Registration Request. A NetBIOS name registration refreshes in order for its record to remain valid in the WINS database. If the NetBIOS host computer does not refresh its NetBIOS name within the period known as the "Refresh Interval," its name is marked as "Released" in the WINS database. A released name then becomes available to any other computer that wishes to register the same name in the WINS database.

The NetBIOS name continues to be marked as released until the "Extinction Interval" is completed. At that point, the record is marked as "tombstoned." The tombstoned record remains in the WINS database for the period defined in the "Extinction timeout" interval. When the Extinction timeout interval passes, the record is removed from the WINS database.

WINS clients issue a name query request to resolve a target computer's NetBIOS name to an IP address. The first WINS server the client contacts is the Primary WINS server. If the Primary WINS server fails to respond after three tries, the client contacts a Secondary WINS server. Windows 2000 WINS clients support up to 12 Secondary WINS servers. Use caution when configuring multiple Secondary WINS servers. Too liberal assignments of Secondary WINS servers can extended the time required to resolve a NetBIOS name to an IP address.

A WINS client will send a NetBIOS name release message to its WINS server. This marks the NetBIOS name release and makes it available to other WINS clients for registration.

Networks large enough to require multiple WINS servers require a method to ensure all WINS servers maintain the same entries in their databases. WINS servers are able to share information by replicating database records to configured replication partners. WINS replication takes on two forms: Push replication and Pull replication. You configure WINS servers as Push partners, Pull partners, or both.

A Push partner sends a trigger to its replication partner to pull records from its WINS database after certain numbers of changes have taken place in the WINS database. The WINS administrator configures this number. Windows 2000 WINS servers allow for "persistent connections." You can take advantage of persistent connections between Push partners and send immediate updates of each change. Persistent connections avoid the overhead inherent in establishing and breaking down connections among replication partners.

A Pull partner is configured to send a trigger to its partner at a certain times, and then at regular intervals after the start time. In general, it is wise to configure replication partners as both Push and Pull partners. However, a Pull partner relationship only may be advantageous when defining replication parameters for WINS servers separated by a slow WAN connection.

Enterprise environments may require more than two or three WINS servers. These environments are likely geographically distributed and connected by a variety of slow- and high-speed links. To optimize WINS replication in such a distributed environment, a WINS network based on the "hub and spoke" model works best. You configure Spoke WINS servers as Push/Pull partners of their respective hubs; hub servers are configured in a chain, ring, or star arrangement of Pull partners.

The amount of time required to synchronize all WINS servers in a WINS network is the "convergence time." NetBIOS name query requests can be in error for some WINS clients until the convergence time is over. Configuring the Push and Pull parameters for the participants in the WINS network alters convergence time. Stable networks do not demand quick convergence, while highly dynamic networks that make widespread use of DHCP may require quicker convergence.

The Windows 2000 WINS server includes several new features unavailable or improved upon from the Windows NT 4.0 version of the WINS server: persistent connections, manual tombstoning of records, easier-to-configure burst handling, and an improved interface in the form of the WINS Management Console. Many of the functions that required registry edits (such as persona non grata records and burst handling) can now be configured via the WINS Management Console's GUI interface.

FAQs

Q: I thought Dynamic DNS replaced WINS in Windows 2000. Why is it still included?

A: While Microsoft's stated goal is to eliminate NetBIOS from Windows-based networks, it is not realistic to do so at the present time. The majority of network-enabled applications created for Microsoft networks are NetBIOS-based. To run a mixed network environment that includes Windows 2000 and downlevel network clients, you must enable NetBIOS support on your Windows 2000 network. DNS only resolves host names, not NetBIOS names. To allow optimal NetBIOS name resolution on your Windows 2000 network, you should run WINS.

It will be several years before NetBIOS is completely eliminated from Microsoft Networks.

Q: I have a number of multihomed servers on my network. Is there any way to have my clients rotate through the adapters they connect to on each multihomed server?

A: Yes. The Windows 2000 WINS server supports rotation through IP addresses assigned to a single multihomed server in a manner similar to that seen with DNS Round Robin. When WINS client query a WINS server for multihomed clients, they will receive the list of IP addresses in a different order each time, and try to connect to the first IP in the list. This balances the load on each network adapter connected to the multihomed server.

Q: What is a WINS Proxy Agent?

A: A WINS Proxy Agent intercepts NetBIOS name query requests. This is of particular help when you have non-WINS-enabled client that needs to resolve NetBIOS names. The WINS Proxy Agent will intercept the name query request and forward it to a WINS server. The WINS server will respond to the WINS Proxy Agent, which in turn will return the answer to the client issuing the original request.

The WINS Proxy Agent caches the results of WINS queries. This reduces the amount of query-related traffic. The WINS Proxy Agent also checks the name of the requesting non-WINS client for duplication in the WINS database; it does not register the name in the WINS database.

To make your machine a WINS Proxy Agent, use a Registry Editor (e.g. regedt32.exe) to open HKEY_LOCAL_MACHINE\ SYSTEM\CurrentControlSet\Services\NetBT\Parameters and set the EnableProxy parameter to 1.

Q: Can I put multiple adapters in a WINS server?

A: Yes, but you may have problems with a multihomed WINS server. Specifically, there are problems with WINS replication and name conflicts on a multihomed WINS server. For more information on issues related to multihomed WINS servers, check Microsoft TechNet online at:

http://www.microsoft.com/technet, or
http://technet.microsoft.com

Search for article IDs: Q185786, Q184832, and Q150737.

Q: Am I required to have a WINS server on my network?

A: No. A WINS server is not required. If you must enable NetBIOS name resolution on your network, you can open up UDP Ports 137 and 138 and TCP Port 139 on your routers, or you can implement LMHosts files. A WINS server is a superior solution to LMHosts and NetBIOS broadcast passthrough.

If your network does not require NetBIOS name resolution, you can completely disable NetBT by making a configuration change in the TCP/IP properties on all computers on the network. If you use DHCP for IP addressing, Microsoft provides vendor-specific options that allow you to disable NetBT on DHCP clients.

Keep in mind that although the Windows 2000 core networking components do not require the NetBIOS interface to be enabled, all non-WinSock applications require NetBIOS name resolution. Therefore, NetBT must be enabled to support these applications.

Q: How do my dial-in clients know which WINS server to use?

A: RRAS clients can be configured with a static entry for their WINS server or receive their WINS server settings from the RRAS server's connection-specific settings. RRAS servers can use DHCP to option IP addresses for RRAS clients. The RRAS server ignores DHCP option information sent by the DHCP server. You configure DHCP options such as WINS and DNS servers for the RRAS specific connection.

Now, the RRAS server ignores the RRAS user class options. This situation may be ameliorated in future releases of the product.

Q: Can I use a WINS server to resolve Internet names?

A: Yes and No. WINS cannot resolve fully qualified domains names used on the Internet. However, WINS is useful on an intranet when integrated with a DNS server. You can configure a DNS server to refer to a WINS server to resolve the host name portion of a FQDN. In this way, the WINS server resolves part of a computer's "Internet Name" (FQDN).

Chapter 6

Secure TCP/IP Connections

Solutions in this chapter:

- VPNs
- PPTP
- SSL

Introduction

Security requirements and implementation have changed significantly in the past 10 years as LANs expanded into WANs and WANs joined the Internet. Within the last five years, most corporations and small businesses have connected their networks to the Internet to access services ranging from e-mail to electronic commerce, or e-commerce.

Businesses now share data with partners, allow customers to access account information, and provide dial-up access to the corporate network for employees. ISDN, ADSL, and cable technologies have replaced modems. TCP/IP security standards evolve at a rapid pace. Windows 2000 incorporates many of the new TCP/IP security mechanisms developed in the last five years.

Virtual Private Networks have revolutionized business communications. These *"VPNs"* allow companies to communicate securely over a public network infrastructure (the Internet). By taking advantage of the Internet as their transit network, companies save large sums of money compared to the amount they had to spend to implement private links to branch offices and partners.

In this chapter, we examine several technologies that make communication secure on an intranet and on the Internet. These include Secure Sockets Layer (SSL), Point-to-Point Tunneling Protocol (PPTP), and Layer 2 Tunneling Protocol/Internet Protocol Security (L2TP/IPSec). Each of these provides secure data communication between computers on either a public or a private network. We cover both the theory of each technology and its implementation in Windows 2000.

Security is a rapidly changing field. You can think of security technologies as "antibiotics" for your network. The problem with antibiotics is that the germs develop a resistance to them, and new antibiotics are required to treat the same bacteria. Intruders are the "disease" of your network. Present technologies demand frequent upgrades, and new technologies need implementation as they are developed. In this vein, you should be sure to check the Microsoft

Security Web site on a regular basis for warnings and patches to the security components of the operating system.

SSL

The Secure Sockets Layer (SSL) describes an encryption technology widely used on the Internet to secure Web pages and Web sites. In this section, we will take a high-level look at SSL and discuss methods used by SSL to encrypt information to keep it secure.

Overview of SSL

The Secure Sockets Layer is classified as a Transport Layer security protocol. SSL is a Transport Layer protocol because it results in securing the Transport Layer as well as information generated at the Application Layer. SSL provides secure communications for applications supporting its use. It provides mechanisms supporting the basic elements of secure communications. These are:

- Authentication
- Integrity
- Confidentiality

Authentication ensures that the information you receive is indeed from the individual you think you are receiving it from. *Integrity* guarantees the message you receive is the same message that was sent. *Confidentiality* protects data from inspection by unintended recipients.

SSL lies between the Application and the Transport Layer. It protects information passed by Application protocols such as FTP, HTTP, and NNTP. An application must be explicitly designed to support SSL's security features. Unlike Layer 3 protocols (such as IPSec), it is not *transparent* to Application Layer processes.

The Secure Sockets Layer uses several protocols to provide security and reliable communications between client and server SSL-enabled applications. The *handshake* protocol negotiates levels and types of encryption, and sets up the secure session. These protocols include SSL protocol version (2.0 or 3.0), authentication algorithms, encryption algorithms, and the method used to generate a shared secret or *session* key.

SSL uses a *record* protocol to exchange the actual data. A shared session key encrypts data passing between SSL applications. The data is decrypted on the receiving end by the same shared session key. Data integrity and authentication mechanisms are employed to insure accurate data is sent to, and received by, legitimate parties to the conversation.

SSL uses an *alert* protocol to convey information about error conditions during the conversation. It is also used by SSL hosts to terminate a session.

How a Secure SSL Channel Is Established

To understand how a secure channel is formed, let's examine how an SSL client establishes a session with an SSL Web server:

1. You enter a URL into the Web browser using *https* rather than http as the protocol. SSL uses TCP port 443 rather than port 80. The https entry informs the client to access the correct port on the target SSL Web server.

2. The SSL client sends a client *Hello* message. This message contains information about the encryption protocols it supports, what version of SSL it is using, what key lengths it supports, what hashing algorithms to use, and what key exchange mechanisms it supports. The SSL client also sends to the SSL server a *Challenge* message. The challenge message will later confirm the identity of the SSL-enabled server.

3. The server sends the client a *Hello* message. After examining methods supported by the client, the server returns to the client a list of mutually supported encryption methods, hash algorithms, key lengths, and key exchange mechanisms. The client will use the values returned by the server. The server also sends its *Public Key*. Its public key been signed by a

mutually trusted authority (a digital *certificate* of authenticity).

4.   The client verifies the certificate sent by the server. After verifying the server certificate, the client sends a *Master Key Message*. The message includes a list of security methodologies employed by the client and the session key. The session key is encrypted with the server's public key (which the server sent earlier in the server *Hello* message).

5.   The client sends a *Client Finished* message indicating that all communications from this point forward are secure.

Almost all messages to this point have been sent in "clear text." Anybody listening in on the conversation would be able to read all parts of the exchange. This is not a problem, because no information other than the session key is secret. Moreover, the session key is safe because it is encrypted with the server's public key. Only the server is able to decrypt the session key by using its *Private Key*. The next series of events takes place in a secure context.

1.   The server sends a *Server Verify* message to the SSL client. This message verifies that the server is indeed the server with which the client wishes to communicate. The server verify message contains the challenge message the client sent earlier in the conversation. The server encrypts the challenge message with the session key. Only the legitimate server has access to the session key. When the client decrypts the challenge message encrypted with the session key, and it matches that sent in the challenge, then the server has verified itself as the legitimate partner in the communication.

2.   The last message used to set up the secure SSL channel is the *Server Finish* message. The SSL server sends this message to the SSL client informing its readiness to participate in data transmission using the shared session key. The SSL session setup is complete, and data passes through a secure SSL channel.

The setup procedure is dependent on several security technologies including Public Key encryption, symmetric encryption, asymmetric encryption, message "hashing," and certificates. In the following sections, we'll define these terms and see how SSL uses them to create a secure channel.

Symmetric and Asymmetric Encryption

The two major types of encryption algorithms in use today use either symmetric or asymmetric encryption keys. Symmetric techniques use the same key to encrypt and decrypt information, and asymmetric methods use different keys to encrypt and decrypt data. We will examine both types of encryption methodologies in this section.

Symmetric Encryption

Symmetric encryption uses the same "key" to lock and unlock data. In order to encrypt data, you need two things: an encryption algorithm and a key. Let's look at a very simplistic encryption scheme. I want to send you a secret message. I will encrypt the message using an algorithm that "adds" letters to the original letter. The encryption key is the number of letters added.

For example, the secret message is "red," and the encryption key is 1. To encrypt this message with our encryption algorithm, I must add one letter to each of the letters in "red." The result is "sfe." When you receive the message, you decrypt it by performing a reverse operation, by adding —1 letters to the secret message. After decrypting it, your message reads "red."

The most commonly used symmetric encryption algorithm is the Data Encryption Standard (DES). There are actually several "flavors" of DES. Each uses different encryption key lengths and methodologies. "Plain" DES uses a 56-bit encryption key. A stronger form of DES, known as "Triple DES" or "3DES" uses a 168-bit encryption key. Triple DES provides a higher degree of security at the expense of being slower. In general, symmetric encryption algorithms are faster than asymmetric ones.

How do you know the value of the encryption key? I could send it to you with the message. Then if someone intercepted the message he would have access to the key. That would not be good. This is like writing your PIN on the back of your automated teller machine card. I could send you the key via Federal Express. However, that would take a while, and is expensive. It also would make it difficult to change keys frequently. We need to be able to change keys frequently in case an intruder discovers the identity of our key.

Asymmetric Encryption

We need a secure mechanism to exchange the shared session key that is fast and inexpensive. The session key is used to encrypt data passing between secure partners. To provide secure passage for shared session key exchange, we use "asymmetric" or "Public Key" encryption.

A *Public Key Infrastructure* uses key pairs: a *Public Key* and a *Private Key*. The public key is available to anyone and everyone; it is not secret. The private key is secret. It is available only to the rightful owner of the private key. If the private key is stolen, it is no longer valid and any messages from the owner of that private key are suspect.

Messages can be encrypted using either the public key or the private key. When you encrypt a message using a public key, you are sending a secret message that cannot be read by anyone other than the holder of the corresponding private key. By encrypting a message with someone's public key, you are assured that no one else but the owner of the corresponding private key can read it. Encrypting a message using the recipient's public key provides a *digital envelope* for the message.

If you want others to be sure you are the one sending a message, you encrypt it with your private key. Anyone with your public key can open the message. When you encrypt a message with your private key, you *sign* that message. No one else can sign a message with your private key since you are the only one that has access to it. Encrypting a message with a private key provides a type of *digital signature*.

NOTE

Messages encrypted with a user's public key are secret, and can only be read by the holder of the corresponding private key. Messages encrypted with a Private Key can be read by anybody. The private key encryption provides a way of signing a message.

I want to send you a message. The message is "Hello World!" I want this to be a secret message. To make this a secret message, one that only you can read, I will encrypt it with your public key. I send you the message encrypted with your public key. When you receive it, you decrypt it with your private key. No one else has access to your private key. Therefore, the message remains private between you and me. Encrypting a message with a public key provides *confidentiality*.

How do you know it was I who sent you the message? Maybe it was someone pretending to be me. To assure you that the message was from me, I will encrypt the message with my private key. The only way you can read the message is by decrypting it with my public key. Only messages encrypted with my private key can be decrypted with my public key. If you cannot open the message with my public key, then you know it is not from me. When a message is encrypted using a private key, you can *authenticate* the source of the message.

Hash Algorithms

How do you know that the message I sent to you was "Hello World!"? What if someone intercepted the message and changed the contents to read "Hello Smurf!"? We need a mechanism to confirm the "integrity" of communication. A communication loses its integrity if it is changed during transit. We need to know that the message we receive is indeed the same as the message sent.

We use "hash" algorithms to accomplish this task. The two most commonly used hash algorithms are Message Digest 5 (MD5) and Secure Hash Algorithm 1 (SHA-1). These hash algorithms take the content of a message and convert it to a constant-length string.

These hashes are safe to transmit because the hashed output cannot be reversed-engineered to reproduce the original message. We can use the hashed output to create a digital signature for the document. To create a digital signature, we take the hashed output (also known as the *message digest*) and encrypt it with our private key. I then send you the digitally-signed document.

When you receive the document, you run the message through the same hash algorithm. After running the hash algorithm on the message, a message digest based on the document you received is created. Then you decrypt the digital signature with my public key. Finally, compare the digest I sent you with the one you created. If they are the same, the document you received is the one I sent. If the digests differ, then the message has been altered in transit. The content of the document is not valid.

As you can see in this example, the digital signature provides two functions: authentication and message integrity. I am authenticated because you were able to decrypt the message digest using my public key, and the message integrity was ensured because the digest you calculated was the same as the one I sent to you.

We must solve one more problem. Recall how you received my public key. I sent it to you. How do you know it was really I who sent you the public key? Maybe it was some mad scientist pretending to be me. He would send you messages encrypted with his private key, and you would decrypt them with his public key, thinking all the while that you were decrypting them with *my* public key.

We solve this problem by using *digital certificates* of authority.

Digital Certificates

A digital certificate is a public key signed by a *mutually trusted third party*. The trusted third party signs your public key by first hashing your public key, and then encrypting the message digest with its private key. If I can open the message digest using the mutually trusted third party's public key, and successfully encrypt messages with your public key, then I know for sure that you are the one that sent the message. I am able to authenticate you by virtue of your digital certificate.

Suppose you want to verify my identity. You ask me for my public key. I respond by providing you my public key that has been signed by a party we both trust. This trusted third party has confirmed my identity. You already have the public key of the trusted third party. You use that public key to decrypt the message digest of my public key. If they match, you have confirmed my identity. You have "authenticated" me.

A certificate contains more information than just the public key with an encrypted message digest. It includes several "fields" of information. Table 6.1 shows some of the included fields in a digital certificate.

Table 6.1 Selected Fields Included in a Digital Certificate

Field Name	Explanation
Certificate Version	There are several versions of the certificate standard. This field contains information about the version of the certificate
Serial Number	The serial number is a unique identifier assigned to each certificate assigned by the certificate authority. No two certificates can have the same serial number.
Signature	This is the digital signature of the trusted third party that validates the certificate. It specifies the hash and public key encryption algorithms used to sign the document. This signature is placed on the end of the document (digital certificate).
Issuer Name	This is the X.500 "Distinguished Name" of the issuer of the certificate (the certificate authority).
Validity Period	This field contains the beginning and end dates of the certificate. The certificate is valid at the beginning date, and expires after the end date. Certificates are not forever, and need to be renewed.
Subject Name	The name of the owner of the certificate. This is the owner's X.500 "Distinguished Name."
Subject Public Key	This is the public key itself. The document actually includes two public keys: one to use for digital signatures and the other for use in exchanging shared session keys.

Certificate Authorities

A certificate authority (CA) is responsible for verifying the identities of those that hold certificates signed by them. A certificate authority is a trusted third party. You can create your own key pair, and submit it to them for signing, or you can request the certificate authority to create a signed key pair for you. The certificate authority will verify your identity via phone, personal interview, e-mail, or a combination of the above.

The public key of the CA must be signed too. How do you know the public key from the certificate authority is valid? Because its certificate is signed too! Certificate authorities can consist of a chain of certificate authorities. On top of this chain or hierarchy is the *root* certificate authority. "Sub-authorities" are *child* authorities. Each child authority has its digital certificate signed by a certificate authority above it in the hierarchy. These higher-level certificate authorities are *parent* authorities.

The single point of failure for security in this scheme is the certificate root authority. If the private key of the root authority is compromised, all signed certificates from the root, and all its child authorities, are suspect and should be considered invalid. Similarly, whenever a private key from any child authority is breached, all signed certificates from that child authority, and all of "its" children are also compromised, and must be considered invalid.

One method to protect against fraud when private keys of certificate authorities are compromised is to publish a Certificate Revocation List (CRL). The certificate authority makes public the serial numbers of invalid certificates. The CRL contains a list of serial numbers from certificates that are no longer valid for reasons other than that they have expired.

SSL Implementation

Windows 2000 Server family includes a Certificate Server that can be used to grant certificates to Web site operators. After the Web site operator has a digital certificate, he can implement SSL and protect the contents of communications between the Web server and Web client.

The Windows 2000 root certificate authority must be installed on a Domain Controller running active directory. Child certificate authorities can be created on member servers. In this exercise, we will install the certificate server on a member server.

1. Log on as administrator at a member server in your domain.

2. Open the "Control Panel," and then open the "Add/Remove" programs applet.

3. In the "Add/Remove Programs" applet, click the "Add/Remove Windows Components" button on the left side of the window.

4. You now see the "Windows Components Wizard" window. Put a checkmark in the "Certificate Services" check box. After you do this, you will see the warning message seen in Figure 6.1. This warning informs you that you cannot change your domain membership after installing certificate server. Click "Next."

Figure 6.1 A warning dialog box when certificate server is installed on a member server.

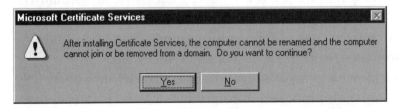

5. You now choose what Certificate Authority type you wish to be. Since we are installing certificate server on a member server, we cannot be the Enterprise Root CA. Select "Enterprise subordinate CA," as seen in Figure 6.2. Click "Next."

6. Enter your identifying information in all the fields, as seen in Figure 6.3. Click "Next."

7. Specify the local paths for the certificate database and the certificate database log. Then click "Next." Here you decide how you want your certificate request processed. You can sent the request directly to a parent certificate authority, or you can save the request to a file that can be sent later to a

Figure 6.2 Selecting the Certificate Authority type.

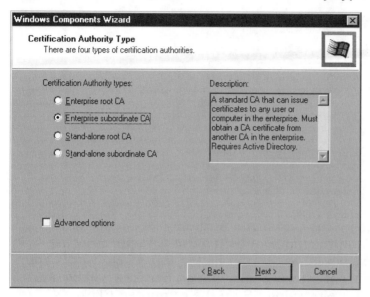

Figure 6.3 Entering identifying information.

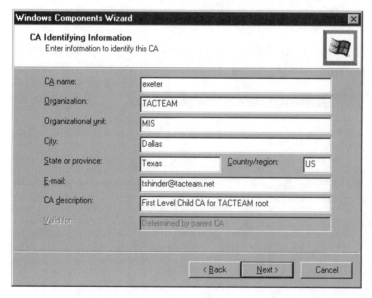

parent certificate authority. In this example, select the "Send
the request directly to a CA already on the network" option
button. Click the "Browse" button to select a Certificate
Authority to send the request to, as seen in Figure 6.4.

Figure 6.4 Selecting a Certificate Authority to sent the request to.

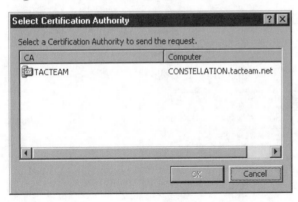

8. After choosing the Certificate Authority, the name of the computer and the name of the parent CA appear in the request text boxes, as seen in Figure 6.5. Click "Next." You are warned that Internet Information Services will be shut down if you are running IIS on the computer. Click "OK." Insert the Windows 2000 CD-ROM or point to the location of the Windows 2000 installation files and following the on-screen instructions.

Figure 6.5 Computer name and Parent CA are automatically filled in after selecting the parent CA.

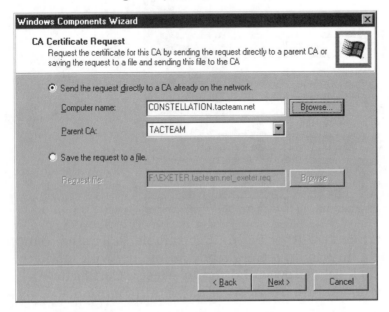

9. The wizard completes the installation of the Certificate Server and presents a dialog box informing you of this. Click "Finish" to complete the installation.

10. To confirm successful installation of the certificate server, open the Certificate Server Management Console, which is located in Administrative tools. You should see what appears in Figure 6.6, and there should be a green checkmark on the certificate server's name indicating that it is functioning correctly.

Figure 6.6 The Certificate Server Management Console.

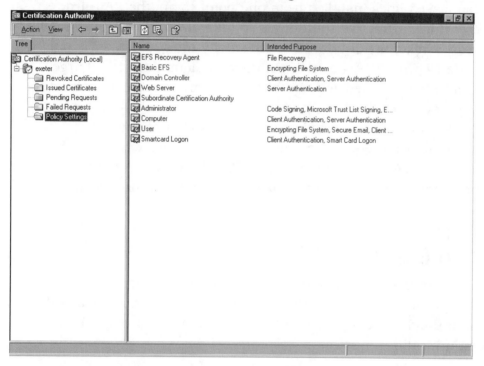

The installed certificate server can now issue certificates that will enable Web sites to use SSL for secure communications.

Secure Communications over Virtual Private Networks

Remote connectivity is becoming a popular solution to a variety of problems: the need for sales personnel to access company databases while on the road, the need for traveling executives to stay in touch with the office, the need for telecommuting employees to view and manipulate files on the corporate servers. The ability to connect to a local area network from offsite locations is becoming not just a luxury, but a necessity in today's business world.

There are several ways to establish a remote connection to a private network. One option is to dial in directly over the public telephone lines, using a modem on the remote computer to connect to a modem on the company server. Another possibility is to have dedicated leased lines installed from one point to another. A third, increasingly attractive solution, is to take advantage of the widespread availability of Internet connectivity to establish a Virtual Private Network (VPN), which circumvents long distance charges, doesn't require expensive capital outlays, and can be done from virtually anywhere.

In the past, a VPN was looked upon as a somewhat exotic, high-tech option that required a great deal of technical expertise. With Windows 2000, setting up a Virtual Private Network connection is much easier—there is even a wizard to guide you through the process.

Tunneling Basics

A VPN can use the public network (Internet) infrastructure, yet maintain privacy and security through encryption and encapsulation of the data being transmitted, or "tunneled" through the public communications system.

VPN Definitions and Terminology

To understand how a VPN works, it's important to first define the terms used in conjunction with this technology.

Tunneling Protocol

A *tunneling protocol* is used to create a private pathway or "tunnel" through an internetwork (typically the Internet) in which data packets are encapsulated and encrypted prior to transmission to ensure privacy of the communication. Windows 2000 supports two tunneling protocols: PPTP and L2TP.

NOTE

These are the tunneling protocols supported by and included with Windows 2000. However, other technologies exist for establishing tunnels, as well as non-Microsoft implementations of PPTP and L2TP. In fact, IPSec can perform Layer 3 tunneling for cases in which L2TP cannot be used.

For more information on PPTP and L2TP, and the differences between the two, see the section "Windows 2000 Tunneling Protocols" later in this chapter.

Data Encryption

Encryption is just a fancy word for the conversion of data into a form that cannot be easily recognized or understood except by persons authorized to receive it. Encryption involves using a cipher, sometimes referred to as a code, to scramble or rearrange the data in such a way that it can be decrypted by someone who has the correct *key*, the algorithm that reverses the encryption process and restores the data to its original form.

The earliest Virtual Private Networking technologies attempted to provide security through encrypting every packet, using encryption hardware that sat between the LAN and the WAN router. There were many drawbacks to this solution, including the fact that private (unregistered) IP addresses on the LAN were generally not supported.

Modern VPN technologies use both encryption and encapsulation to provide an easier-to-implement and more flexible way to transmit private data over the public network.

In a Windows 2000 VPN using the Point-to-Point Tunneling Protocol (PPTP), encryption keys are generated by the MS-CHAP or EAP-TLS authentication process, and Microsoft Point-to-Point Encryption (MPPE) is used to encrypt a PPP frame.

Data Encapsulation

Encapsulation means putting one data structure inside another. VPN technology encapsulates private data with a header that provides routing information that allows the data to travel over the Internet to the private network.

In a VPN, the data packets (IP, IPX or NetBEUI, depending on the LAN protocol used by the private network to which you are connecting) are encapsulated in a tunneling protocol such as PPTP or L2TP; these packets are then packaged by an IP packet which contains the address of the destination private network. The local ISP or other access provider will assign the user an IP address, so the user can keep the unregistered internal address for communications on the LAN. The encapsulated packets can be encrypted using IPSec or another security protocol.

The encapsulation process conceals the original packet inside a new packet. Then the new packet provides the routing information to allow it to go through the Internet or another internetwork without regard to the final destination address that is contained in the original packet header. When the encapsulated packet arrives at its destination, the encapsulation header will be removed and the original packet header will be used to route the packet to its final destination. Tunneling protocols are sometimes referred to as encapsulation protocols.

NOTE

See RFC 1483 for more detailed information on protocol encapsulation.

How Tunneling Works

Tunneling emulates a point-to-point connection by wrapping the datagram with a header that contains addressing information to get it across the public network to the destination private network. The data is also encrypted to further protect the privacy of the communication. The "tunnel" is the part of the connection in which the data is encapsulated and encrypted; this becomes the "virtual private network."

NOTE

It is possible to send a PPP frame through a tunnel in plain text, with no encryption, but this is not recommended for VPN connections over the public Internet, as the confidentiality of the communication would be compromised. This would actually be considered a "virtual" network, but technically is not a VPN, because the element of privacy is missing.

Data encryption is performed between the VPN client and the VPN server; thus the connection from the client to the Internet Service Provider does not need to be encrypted.

IP Addressing

The VPN connection will use a valid public IP address, usually supplied by the ISP's DHCP server, to route the data. This data packet, containing internal IP addresses of the sending and destination computers, is inside the "envelope" of the VPN, so even if you are using private (non-registered) IP addresses on the private network, they will never be "seen" on the Internet. Encryption and encapsulation protect the addresses of the computers on the private network.

Security Issues Pertaining to VPNs

The concept of using an open, public network like the vast global Internet to transfer sensitive data presents obvious security concerns. For virtual networking to be feasible for security-conscious organizations, the privacy component must be ensured. Security over a VPN connection involves encapsulation, authentication of the user, and security of the data.

Encapsulation

The encapsulation of the original data packet inside a tunneling protocol hides its headers as it travels over the internetwork, and is the first line of defense in securing the communication.

User Authentication

Windows 2000 VPN solutions use the same authentication protocols used when connecting to the network locally; authentication is performed at the destination, so the security accounts database information is not transmitted onto the public network.

Windows 2000 can use the following authentication methods for VPN connections:

- CHAP: Challenge Handshake Authentication Protocol, which uses challenge-response with one-way hashing on the response, allows the user to prove to the server that he or she knows the password without actually sending the password itself over the network

- MS-CHAP: Microsoft CHAP, which also uses a challenge-response authentication method with one-way encryption on the response.

- MS-CHAP v2: An enhanced version of Microsoft-CHAP, which is a mutual authentication protocol requiring both the client and the server to prove their identities.

- EAP/TLS: Extensible Authentication Protocol/Transport Level Security, which provides support for adding authentication schemes such as token cards, one-time passwords, the Kerberos V5 protocol, public key authentication using smart cards, certificates, and others.

NOTE

Data will be encrypted by MPPE in a PPTP connection only if MS-CHAP, MS-CHAP v2, or EAP/TLS authentication is used, as these are the only authentication protocols that generate their own initial encryption keys.

Data Security

Data security is provided through encapsulation and encryption, but the higher the security, the more overhead and the lower the performance. IPSec was designed to work with different encryption levels and provide different levels of data security based on the organization's needs.

NOTE

PPTP uses Microsoft Point-to-Point Encryption (MPPE) to encrypt data. When using L2TP for VPN connections, data is encrypted by using IPSec.

L2TP over IPSec uses certificate-based authentication, which is the strongest authentication type used in Windows 2000. A machine-level certificate is issued by a Certificate Authority, and installed on the VPN client and the VPN server. This can be done through the Windows 2000 Certificate Manager or by configuring the CA to automatically issue certificates to the computers in the Windows 2000 domain.

Windows 2000 Security Options

Windows 2000 provides the network administrator with a great deal of flexibility in setting authentication and data encryption requirements for VPN communications. Table 6-1 shows possible security settings combinations for both PPTP and L2TP.

Table 6.1 Authentication and Encryption Requirement Settings

Validate My Identity Using	Require Data Encryption	Authentication Methods Negotiated	Encryption Enforcement
		PPTP	
Require secured password	No	CHAP, MS-CHAP, MS-CHAP v2	Optional encryption (connect even if no encryption)
Require secured password	Yes	MS-CHAP, MS-CHAP v2	Require encryption (disconnect if server declines)
Smart card	No	EAP/TLS	Optional encryption (connect even if no encryption)
Smart card	Yes	EAP/TLS	Require encryption (disconnect if server declines)
		L2TP	
Require secured password	No	CHAP, MS-CHAP, MS-CHAP v2	Optional encryption (connect even if no encryption)
Require secured password	Yes	CHAP, MS-CHAP, MS-CHAP v2	Require encryption (disconnect if server declines)
Smart card	No	EAP/TLS	Optional encryption (connect even if no encryption)
Smart card	Yes	EAP/TLS	Require encryption (disconnect if server declines)

These settings are configured by using the Security tab of the Properties sheet for the VPN connection, as shown in Figure 6.7. To access this dialog box, from the Start menu select:

```
Settings | Network and Dialup Connections | [name of your
VPN connection].
```

Then click the "Properties" button and select the "Security" tab.

Figure 6.7 To customize security settings for a VPN connection, select "Advanced" and click the "Settings" button.

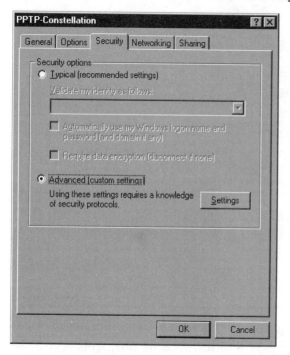

Selecting the "Advanced" radio button and clicking the "Settings" button will display the Advanced Security Settings dialog box shown in Figure 6.8, where the authentication and encryption setting combinations can be adjusted.

This dialog box allows you to select whether encryption is optional, required or not allowed, whether to use EAP or allow

Figure 6.8 Selecting the desired custom security settings in the Advanced Security Settings dialog box.

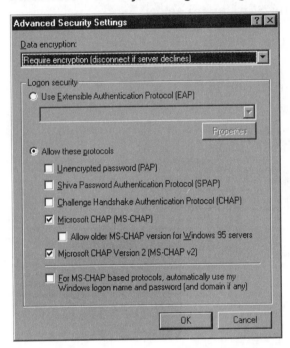

other designated protocols, and whether to automatically enter the logged-on account's Windows user name and password for MS-CHAP authentication.

WARNING

The settings should not be changed from the Typical (recommended) settings unless you thoroughly understand the security protocols and what effects your changes may have.

If you choose to use EAP (for instance, to enable authentication via smart card), you will need to configure the properties for the smart card or other certificate authentication, as shown in Figure 6.9.

You can choose from a list of recognized root certificate authorities (CAs).

Figure 6.9 Setting Smart Card or Certificate properties when using EAP.

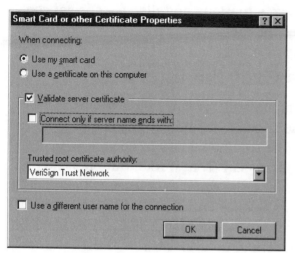

A CA is an entity entrusted to issue certificates to individuals, computers, or organizations that affirm the identity and other attributes of the certificate. VeriSign is an example of a remote third party CA recognized as trustworthy throughout the industry.

Common Uses of VPNs

Virtual Private Networks are commonly used by companies to provide a more cost-effective way for employees, customers, and other authorized users to connect to their private networks. The VPN is a viable alternative to direct dial-in, which incurs long-distance charges, or the hefty initial and monthly expense of a dedicated leased line.

VPNs are typically used to allow a standalone remote user to connect a computer, such as a home desktop system or a laptop/notebook computer when on the road, to the corporate network. However, VPNs can also be used to connect two distant LANs to one another using their local Internet connections, or to connect two computers over an intranet within the company.

We will look at each of these situations and discuss special considerations and best practices for each.

Remote User Access Over the Internet

A typical scenario is the telecommuter, traveling employee, or executive who takes work home and needs to connect to the company's network from a remote location. The traditional way to do so was to dial in to the company RAS server's modem. That works, but often was costly if the remote user was not in the company's local calling area. If the remote user has an Internet Service Provider local to his location, however, he can avoid long distance charges by dialing the ISP instead of the company's modem, and setting up a VPN through the Internet.

See Figure 6.10 for an illustration of this common situation.

Figure 6.10 A user can access the company network from home through a VPN.

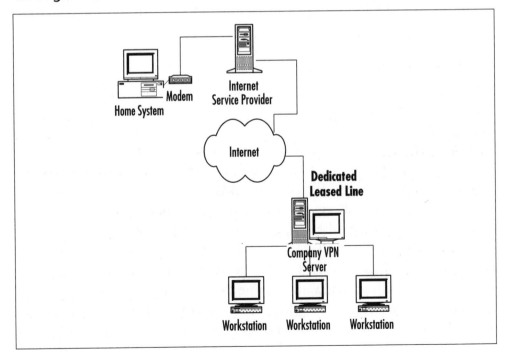

See Chapter 8 for instructions on setting up a client computer to use a Virtual Private Networking connection.

NOTE

An active Winsock Proxy client will interfere with the creation of a VPN by redirecting data to the proxy server before the data can be processed by the VPN. You must first disable the Winsock Proxy client before attempting to create a VPN connection.

Connecting Networks Over the Internet

Another use of the VPN is to connect two networks through the Internet. If you have offices in two cities with a Local Area Network at each office location, you may find it advantageous to connect the two LANs so users at both locations can share one another's resources. One way to do that would be to purchase a leased line such as a T1 line to connect the two networks, but this would be expensive.

Sharing a Remote Access VPN Connection

If both offices already have Internet connections, perhaps through dedicated ISDN lines or DSL service, you can use the existing connection to the Internet to set up a VPN between the two offices and transfer data securely.

Figure 6.11 illustrates a situation where the VPN would be used to connect two distant networks.

In this case, setup will be slightly more complicated than connecting a single remote computer to a company network.

In order to give all the computers on both LANs access to the resources they need, you can set up a VPN server on each side of the connection, then configure a VPN client connection on each side as well. The VPN client connection can then be shared with the rest of the LAN via Internet Connection Sharing.

Figure 6.11 A VPN connection can be used to connect two LANs in distant locations.

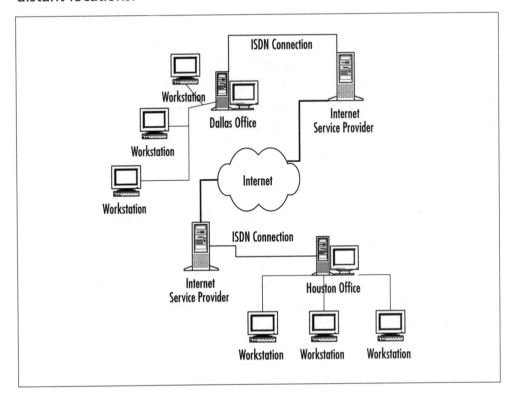

You can also, if you wish, restrict access by remote access VPN clients to only the shared resources on the VPN server and not allow access to the network to which the VPN server is attached.

Using a Router-to-Router Connection

Another way to connect two networks via a VPN is to use a router-to-router VPN connection with a demand-dial interface. The VPN server then provides a routed connection to the network of which it is a part. RRAS is used to create a router-to-router VPN connection, so the VPN servers acting as routers must be Windows 2000 servers or NT 4.0 servers with RRAS.

Mutual authentication is supported, so that the calling router (VPN client) and answering router (VPN server) authenticate them-

Figure 6.12 The VPN server can provide a routed connection to the network to which it belongs.

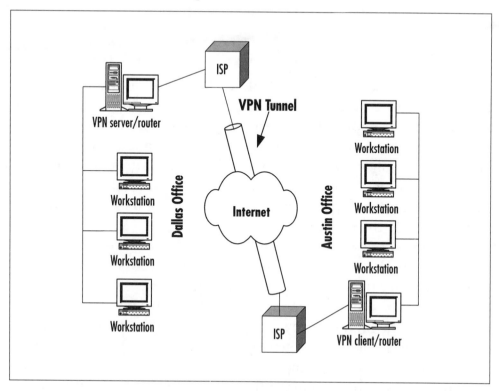

selves to one another. Figure 6.12 illustrates how a router-to-router connection can be used to connect two networks.

In a router-to-router connection, the VPN works as a data link layer link between the two networks. In the illustration, the Windows 2000 computer, acting as a router to the Austin office, is the VPN client that initiates the connection to the VPN server, which is the computer acting as a router to the Dallas office.

NOTE

The VPN server will need to have a dedicated connection to the Internet, unless the ISP supports demand-dial routing to customers, which is not common.

The endpoints of a router-to-router connection are the routers, and the tunnel extends from one router to the other. This is the part of the connection in which the data is encapsulated.

Connecting Computers over an Intranet

A less common scenario, but one that will be useful in some instances, is to provide for a virtual private network over an internal intranet. This is appropriate when you have certain departments or divisions that deal with particularly sensitive data and as a result are not physically connected to the company's intranet. This provides the necessary security but also prevents authorized users from accessing the department's data from computers physically located outside the department.

One way to solve this problem is to physically connect the department to the intranet but set up a VPN server between the department and the rest of the network. In this way, users who have permissions to do so can use the VPN connection to access resources in the high-security department and the encapsulation and encryption will protect their communications used by the tunneling protocol. The department's resources will not show up as network resources to users outside the department who do not have permissions to access them.

Figure 6.13 illustrates this use of VPN connectivity. The VPN connection in this example uses the network's IP connectivity, so you don't have to establish the connection over phone lines or a public network.

TIP

You can restrict access to intranet resources for IP traffic by using packet filters based on a remote access policy profile. For more information about using remote access policies, see Chapter 8.

Figure 6.13 Using a VPN connection to hide a high-sensitivity department from the intranet.

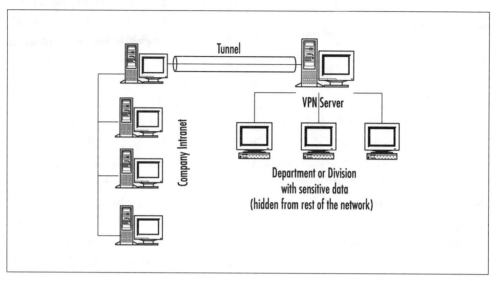

Tunneling Protocols and the Basic Tunneling Requirements

Establishing a secure tunnel through a public or other internetwork requires that computers on both ends of the connection be configured to use Virtual Private Networking, and they must both be running a common tunneling protocol. Windows 2000 Server can be a VPN client, or it can be a VPN server accepting PPTP connections from both Microsoft and non-Microsoft PPTP clients.

Windows 2000 Tunneling Protocols

As mentioned earlier, Windows 2000 supports two tunneling protocols for establishment of VPNs: PPTP and L2TP. A primary difference between the two is the encryption method: PPTP uses MPPE to encrypt data, while L2TP uses certificates with IPSec.

Point-to-Point Tunneling Protocol (PPTP)

The Point-to-Point Tunneling Protocol (PPTP) was developed as an extension to the popular Point-to-Point Protocol (PPP) used by most ISPs to establish a remote access connection to the Internet through the provider's network. PPTP allows IP, IPX, and NetBIOS/NetBEUI datagrams or frames to be transferred through the tunnel. From the user's perspective, the tunneling is transparent.

PPTP allows for NT 4.0 secure authentication, using Password Authentication Protocol (PAP), Challenge Handshake Authentication Protocol (CHAP), and Microsoft's version of CHAP, MS-CHAP.

PPTP support became available in NT Server in 1996, and client software is available for DOS, Windows, and most PPP clients. The PPTP specifications were developed by the PPTP Forum, made up of Microsoft and networking equipment vendors such as Ascend, 3Com/Primary Access, ECI-Telematics, and US Robotics. PPTP is an open standard

Layer 2 Tunneling Protocol (L2TP)

The Layer 2 Tunneling Protocol (L2TP) provides the same functionality as PPTP, but overcomes some of the limitations of the Point-to-Point Tunneling Protocol. It does not require IP connectivity between the client workstation and the server, as PPTP does. L2TP can be used as long as the tunnel medium provides packet-oriented point-to-point connectivity, which means it works with such media as ATM, Frame Relay, and X.25. L2TP can authenticate the tunnel end points, and can be used in conjunction with secure ID cards on the client side and with firewalls on the server side.

L2TP is an Internet Engineering Task Force (IETF) standard, which was developed in a cooperative effort by Microsoft, Cisco Systems, Ascend, 3Com, and other networking industry leaders. It combines features of Cisco's Layer 2 Forwarding (L2F) protocol with Microsoft's PPTP implementation.

L2TP can utilize IPSec to provide end-to-end security (see the section on IPSec for more information).

Using PPTP with Windows 2000

PPTP is installed with the Routing and Remote Access Service (RRAS). It is configured by default for five PPTP ports. You can enable PPTP ports with the Routing and Remote Access wizard. The PPTP ports will be displayed as WAN miniports in the RRAS console, as shown in Figure 6.14.

Figure 6.14 PPTP ports in the Routing and Remote Access (RRAS) console.

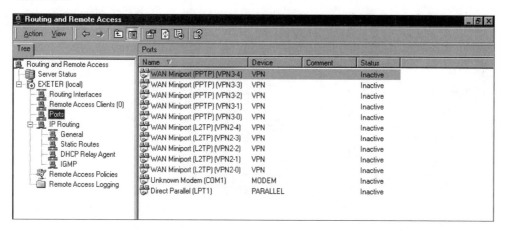

You can view the status of each VPN port, and refresh or reset it by double-clicking on the port name to display the status sheet and clicking on the appropriate button.

How to Configure a PPTP Device

To configure a port device, right-click "Ports" in the left panel of the console and select "Properties." A dialog box similar to Figure 6.15 will be displayed.

Highlight the RRAS device you wish to configure and then click the "Configure" button. You will see a dialog box like the one in Figure 6.16.

In the device configuration dialog box, you can set up the port to be used for inbound RAS connections and/or inbound and outbound demand-dial routing connections.

Figure 6.15 Configuring the properties of a PPTP port device.

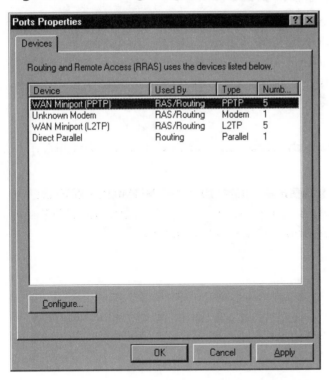

Figure 6.16 Using the WAN miniport (PPTP) configuration dialog box.

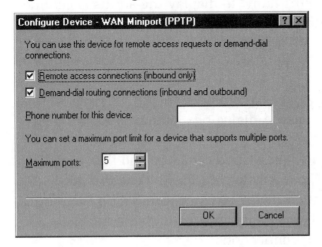

NOTE

A device can be physical, representing hardware (such as a modem), or virtual, representing software (such as the PPTP protocol). A device can create physical or logical point-to-point connections, and the device provides a port, or communication channel, which supports a point-to-point connection.

A standard modem is a single port device. PPTP and L2TP are virtual multiport devices. You can set up to 1000 ports for PPTP and L2TP devices. Five is the default number of ports.

TIP

When you change the number of ports on the PPTP or L2TP WAN miniport device, the computer must be rebooted before the change will be effective.

Using L2TP with Windows 2000

Layer 2 Tunneling Protocol (L2TP) over IPSec gives administrators a way to provide end-to-end security for a VPN connection. L2TP doesn't rely on vendor-specific encryption methods to create a completely secured virtual networking connection.

How to Configure L2TP

To enable the server to be a VPN server for L2TP clients, you must first install Routing and Remote Access (RRAS), if you haven't already.

Open the RRAS console: Start | Programs | Administrative Tools | Routing and Remote Access.

In the left pane of the console tree, right-click the server you want to enable, and click "Configure and Enable Routing and Remote Access." This will start the wizard, which will guide you through the process. After the service is installed and started, configure the properties of the server by right-clicking the server name and selecting "Properties." You will see a properties sheet similar to the one in Figure 6.17.

Figure 6.17 The RRAS properties sheet for the selected remote access server.

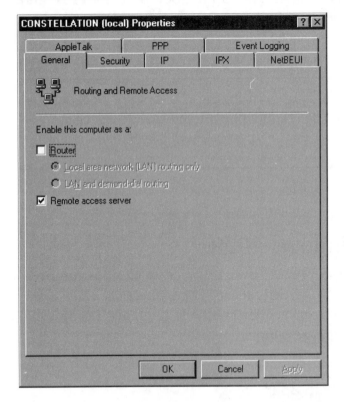

On the "General" tab, be sure that the "Remote access server" check box is selected.

Figure 6.18 Choose either Windows Authentication or RADIUS as your authentication provider.

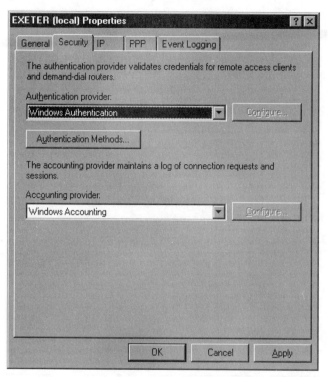

On the "Security" tab, under "Authentication Provider," you can confirm the credentials of RRAS clients by using either Windows 2000 security (Windows Authentication) or a RADIUS server. If RADIUS is selected, you need to configure RADIUS server settings for your RADIUS server or RADIUS proxy.

In the "Accounting Provider" drop-down box, choose "Windows" or "RADIUS" accounting. You can then record remote access client activity for analysis or accounting purposes.

Next click the "Authentication Methods" button, and choose the authentication methods that are supported by the RRAS server to authenticate the credentials of remote access clients, as shown in Figure 6.19.

Figure 6.19 Select the authentication method that will be used by the RRAS clients.

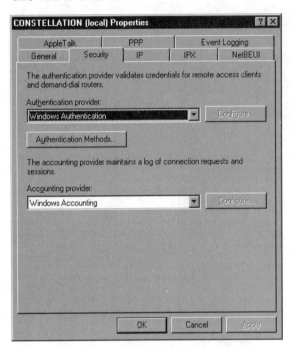

TIP

Microsoft remote access clients generally will use MS-CHAP authentication. If you want to enable smart card support, you need to use EAP authentication.

On the "IP" tab, verify that the "Enable IP routing" and "Allow IP-based remote access and demand-dial connections" check boxes are both checked, as shown in Figure 6.20.

Next you should configure the L2TP ports for remote access. In the RRAS console, right-click "Ports" and select "Properties." Select the L2TP ports, as shown in Figure 6.21.

Click the "Configure" button and you will see the dialog box displayed in Figure 6.22.

You can also configure remote access policies to control access to the VPN server. See Chapter 8 for more information about using remote access policies.

Figure 6.20 You should enable IP routing and allow IP-based remote access and demand-dial connections.

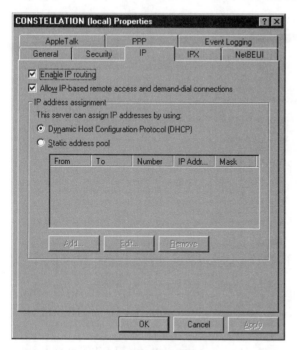

Figure 6.21 Select the WAN Miniport (L2TP) for configuration.

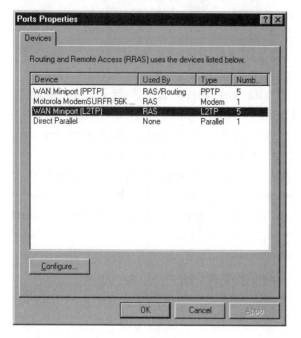

Figure 6.22 Configuring the L2TP ports to allow remote access and/or demand-dial connections.

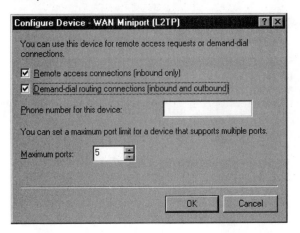

How L2TP Security Differs from that of PPTP

L2TP is similar to PPTP in many ways. They both support multi-protocol VPN links and can be used to create secure tunnels through the Internet or another public network to connect to a private network that also has a connection to the internetwork. L2TP can be used over IPSec to provide for greater security, including end-to-end encryption, whereas Microsoft's PPTP connections are dependent upon MPPE for encryption. L2TP is derived from L2F, a Cisco Systems tunneling protocol.

With L2TP over IPSec, encapsulation involves two layers: L2TP encapsulation and IPSec encapsulation. First, L2TP wraps its header and a UDP header around a PPP frame. Then IPSec wraps an ESP (Encapsulating Security Payload) header and trailer around the package, and adds an IPSec authentication trailer. Finally an IP header is added, which contains the addresses of the source (VPN client) and destination (VPN server) computers. The data inside the IPSec ESP header and authentication trailer, including the PPP, UDP and L2TP headers, is all encrypted by IPSec.

Data authentication is available for L2TP over IPSec connections, unlike for PPTP connections. This is accomplished by the use of a cryptographic checksum based on an encryption key known only to the sender and the receiver.

Interoperability with Non-Microsoft VPN Clients

A Windows 2000 VPN server can accept client connections from non-Microsoft clients, if the clients meet the following requirements:

- The clients must use PPTP or L2TP tunneling protocol.
- For PPTP connections, the client must support MPPE.
- For L2TP connections, the client must support IPSec.

If these requirements are met, the non-Microsoft clients will be able to make a secure VPN connection. You do not have to make any special configuration changes on the VPN server to allow non-Microsoft clients to connect.

IPSec

IPSec allows for secure networking for the enterprise with a minimum of overhead. IPSec secures packets at the network layer of the OSI model. Because security is applied at the network layer, the entire process is transparent to applications and users do not need to be aware of IPSec. IPSec is often said to provide "Layer 3" protection (corresponding to the third layer the OSI model).

IPSec provides "end-to-end" security for communicating hosts. Intermediary hosts do not need to be aware of IPSec because security applies only to the source and destination hosts. This allows you to implement IPSec in a large variety of environments, from corporate intranets to host to host secure communications over the Internet. Devices on the transit internetwork do not need reconfiguration for IPSec to function properly.

NOTE

IPSec provides protection of the data transmission from end-to-end. This is different than the PPTP model that only protects the link.

This end-to-end protection can be applied to different communication scenarios. These include:

- Client-to-Client
- Client-to-Gateway
- Gateway-to-Gateway

IPSec can be configured to operating in either of two modes: *transport mode* or *tunnel mode*. In transport mode, the source and destination machines represent the endpoints of secure communications. Each host must use TCP/IP as its transport protocol for this to work.

IPSec works in *tunnel mode* when gateways represent the endpoints of secure communication. A secure tunnel is created between the gateways, and host-to-host communications are encapsulated in IPSec tunnel protocol headers. Tunnels can be created using IPSec as the tunneling protocol, or you can combine IPSec with the Layer Two Tunneling Protocol (L2TP). In this case, L2TP rather than IPSec creates the tunnel.

IPSec protects the information traversing a transit network (such as the Internet). Packets are protected as they leave the proximal gateway, and then decrypted or authenticated or both at the destination network gateway. In this scenario, the host and destination computers to not employ IPSec, and can use any LAN protocol supported by IPSec (IPX/SPX, AppleTalk, NetBEUI, TCP/IP). The tunnel will encapsulate the LAN protocols during the intergateway transit.

Data Encryption Options

IPSec ensures secures communications by using a variety of cryptographic methods. Kryptos is Greek for "hidden." Cryptology is the study of the "hidden." Cryptography is the practice of hiding or "scrambling" messages so that they cannot be read on casual inspection.

There are several component features of a good security system. The IPSec security architecture is designed to provide support for three cardinal features of secure communications:

- Integrity
- Confidentiality
- Authentication

Message Integrity

Message integrity implies that the contents of a message have not changed during transit. If a message changes contents between the source host and the destination host, it has lost its integrity.

Creating a digital signature can protect message integrity. This digital signature is like a fingerprint. This fingerprint represents the contents of the message. If someone were to capture and change the contents of the message, the fingerprint would change. The destination host could detect the fraudulent fingerprint and would be aware that "other hands" had touched the document. The assumption is that if other hands have touched the document then the message is invalid. It has lost its integrity.

Hash algorithms create these fingerprints.

Hashing Messages

Messages are "hashed" by running them through a hashing algorithm. When the contents of a message are combined with a keyed hashed algorithm, you can create a digital signature of the document. When the exact same message is run through the same keyed algorithm on another machine, the result will always be the same.

The result of a hash is a fixed-length string known as a "message digest." The message digest represents the hashed output of a message. You cannot "reverse engineer" the hashed output of a message. This means that you cannot ascertain the contents of a message by analyzing the message digest. Even if some third party were to gain access to the message digest, they would not be able to access the contents of the message.

Message digests are also known as "Hash Message Authentication Codes" (HMAC). To derive an HMAC, Microsoft's implementation of IPSec uses one of two algorithms:

- Message Digest 5 (MD5)
  Message Digest 5 was developed by Ron Rivest of MIT and is defined in RFC 1321. MD5 processes each message in blocks of 512 bits. The message digest ends up being 128 bits.

- Secure Hash Algorithm (SHA-1)
  Secure Hash Algorithm processes messages in blocks of 512 bits. However, the resulting message digest is 160 bits long. This makes the message more secure. It is more processor-intensive, and therefore slower than MD5.

Each partner in the communication must use the same "key" in order to come up with the same hashed result. We will see later how the use of a "public key" infrastructure allows the exchange of secret keys.

Message Authentication

When a host is authenticated, its identity is confirmed. While integrity is concerned with the validity of the contents of a message, authentication is aimed at confirming the validity of the sender. It would be of little value to receive a message of uncompromised integrity from an imposter.

IPSec can use any of the following methods to authenticate the sender:

- Pre-shared Key Authentication
- Kerberos Authentication
- Public Key Certificate-Based Digital Signatures

Pre-shared Key Authentication

Pre-shared Key Authentication schemes depend on both members of the communication having pre-selected a secret "key" that will be used to identify them to each other. Data leaving the sending computer is encrypted with this agreed-to key, and is decrypted on the other end with the same key.

You can use the preshared key to authenticate a computer using the following procedure:

1. The sending computer hashes of a piece of data (a challenge) using the shared key and forwards this to the destination computer.

2. The destination computer receives the challenge, performs a hash using the same secret key, and sends this back.

3. If the hashed results are identical, both computers share the same secret and are thus authenticated.

Preshared keys are effective and simple to implement. They circumvent potential complications introduced when other authentication schemes are used. However, the shared-key approach isn't very scaleable or mutable. The shared-key must be manually entered into every extant IPSec policy. If you had a large number of organizational units, all using different IPSec policies, it would be hard to keep track of all the keys. In addition, you must change these keys frequently in order to protect your data from crackers. Manually changing the keys can be an arduous process in a large organization.

Kerberos Authentication

The Kerberos authentication method is also based on the "shared secret" principle. In this case, the shared secret is a hash of the user's password.

Public Key Certificate-Based Digital Signatures

Earlier, we saw that running the contents of a message through a keyed algorithm creates a message hash. When a private key encrypts that hash, the message digest becomes a digital signature. You authenticate a message after it is decrypted with the source's public key and then run it through the hash algorithm.

In a public key infrastructure, each computer has a public and a private key. The public key is open and available to the public at large; it is not secret. The private key is a secret key that is only available to the owner of the private key. The private key must remain private. If the private key is ever compromised, all messages from the owner of that private key should be considered suspect.

A viable public key infrastructure includes elements:

1. Secret Private Keys

2. Freely available Public Keys

3. A trusted third party to confirm the authenticity of the public key

The trusted third party digitally signs each party's public key. This prevents people from providing a public key that they "claim" is theirs, but is in fact not the public key of the person they are impersonating.

The mutually trusted third party digitally signs each user's public key. In this way, if I send to you my public key, you can be sure that it is truly mine. A trusted third party has already confirmed my identity and signed my public key. This third party is a Certificate Authority (CA).

Public key authentication is used when non-Kerberos-enabled clients need to be authenticated and no preshared key has been established. You must also use public key authentication when using L2TP tunneling and IPSec.

Confidentiality

Neither integrity nor authentication is concerned with protecting the privacy of our information. Confidentiality is about keeping your private information private. In order to ensure confidentiality, you must encrypt your information using an encryption algorithm.

Data Encryption Standard (DES)

The DES algorithm is an example of a symmetric encryption algorithm. A symmetric encryption algorithm has each side use the same key for encryption and decryption. Contrast this to a public key infrastructure, where the two different keys are used. The public key approach is an "asymmetric" encryption scheme.

DES works on 64 bits "blocks" of data. The DES algorithm converts 64 input bits from the original data into 64 encrypted output bits. While DES starts with 64 bit keys, only 56 bits are used in the encryption process. The remaining 8 bits are for parity.

You can have a higher level of encryption using another form of DES. This is 3DES or "triple" DES. Triple DES processes each block three times, which increases the degree of complexity over that found in DES.

Cipher Block Chaining (CBC)

DES encrypts blocks of data in chunks of 64 bits each. These chunks must be joined or chained before transmission. The chaining algorithm combines the unencrypted text, the secret key, and the "ciphertext" (the encrypted text).

A chaining algorithm solves an important problem. Imagine someone is sniffing electronic transactions. The individual being "sniffed" is transferring a personal paycheck into their online account. This transaction is performed at the same time each week. The transactions are always encrypted with DES. The sniffer would see the same ciphertext each week. However, what if the person got a raise or changed the amount of money transferred for some reason? The sniffer could assume that the person's financial situation has changed. This information can be integrated with other "facts" obtained during an "investigation."

In order to prevent each block from being identical, DES is combined with the Cipher Block Chaining (CBC) algorithm. This DES-CBC algorithm makes each ciphertext message appear different by using a different "initialization vector" (IV). The IV is a random block of encrypted data placed at the start of each chain. This makes each message's ciphertext appear different, even if we send the exact same message a hundred times.

IPSec Security Services

IPSec uses two protocols to implement security on an IP network:

- Authentication Header (AH)
- Encapsulating Security Payload (ESP)

Authentication header only authenticates messages. The Encapsulating Security Payload can authenticate and encrypt messages.

Authentication Header (AH)

The Authentication Header insures data integrity and authentication. The AH does not encrypt data and provides no confidentiality. When the AH protocol is applied in transport mode, the Authentication Header is inserted between the original IP header and the TCP header, as depicted in Figure 6.23. The entire datagram is authenticated using AH.

Figure 6.23 Datagram after applying the Authentication Header in Transport Mode.

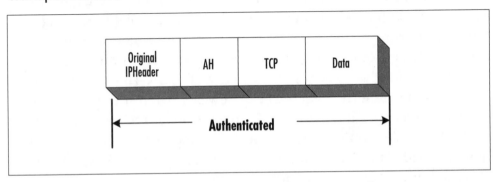

Encapsulating Security Payload (ESP)

The Encapsulating Security Payload protocol provides authentication, integrity, and confidentiality to an IP datagram. Note that the original IP header is not authenticated when using ESP. In transport mode, the ESP header is placed between the original header and the TCP header, as seen in Figure 6.24. Only the TCP Header, Data, and ESP trailer are encrypted. If authentication of the original IP header is required, you can combine AH and ESP.

Figures 6.23 and 6.24 show AH and ESP packet structures in transport mode. Transport mode is used when end-to-end security is required. Tunnel mode is used when the encryption and authentication take place at gateway machines.

In tunnel mode, an additional IP header is added which denotes the destination tunnel endpoint. This tunnel header encapsulates

Figure 6.24 Datagram after applying the Encapsulating Security Payload Header in Transport Mode.

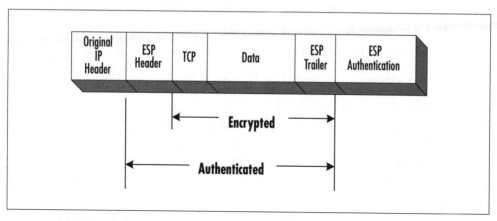

the original IP header, which contains the IP address of the destination computer. A packet constructed for tunnel mode appears in Figure 6.25.

Figure 6.25 Datagram with ESP header in tunnel mode.

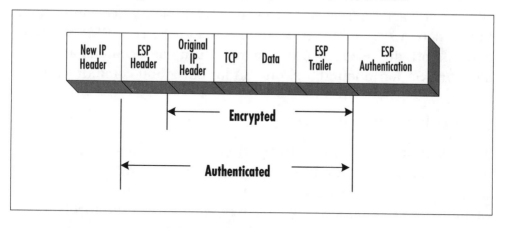

Security Associations and IPSec Key Management Procedures

Computers must come to an understanding regarding what algorithms and protocols will be used when IPSec is employed. The terms of this agreement are contained within a Security Association (SA). One SA is established for each connection made to an IPSec-enabled machine. If a file server has multiple IPSec connections, SAs will be created for each active connection.

Each Security Association contains the following parameters:

- An Encryption Algorithm (DES or 3DES)
- A Session Key (via IKE)
- An Authentication Algorithm (SHA1 or MD5)

A Security Parameters Index (SPI) tracks each SA. The SPI uniquely identifies each SA as separate and distinct from any other IPSec connections current on a particular machine. The index itself is derived from the destination host's IP address and a randomly assigned number. When a computer communicates with another computer via IPSec, it checks its database for an applicable SA. It then applies the appropriate algorithms, protocols, and keys and inserts the SPI into the IPSec header.

An SA is established for outgoing and incoming messages, necessitating at least two security associations for each IPSec connection. In addition, a single SA can be applied to either AH or ESP, but not both. If both are used, then two more security associations are created, one SA for inbound and one SA for outbound communications.

IPSec Key Management

Encryption keys are central in the development of a secure channel. In order for data to move between computers in a secure context, the computers participating in the conversation must exchange encryption keys. We use Key Management protocols to define how keys are formed, key strengths, key mutability, and key expiration. The Key Management protocol provides us with a shared secret key that is used to pass encrypted data. These Key Management techniques allow us to automatic the process of key assignment and creation. In this way, we overcome the limitations of the preshared key model.

Automated Key Management uses a combination of the Internet Security Association Key Management Protocol (ISAKMP) and the Oakley Protocol (Oakley). This combination of protocols is called the Internet Key Exchange (IKE). The IKE is responsible for several things:

1. Exchange of "keying material" (number on which keys will be based)

2. Management and creation of session keys

3. Negotiation of Security Associations

4. Authentication of IPSec peers

The Internet Key Exchange has two phases: Phase 1; the two computers agree upon mechanisms to establish a secure, authenticated channel, and Phase 2; Security Associations are negotiated for security protocols, either AH, ESP, or both.

The first phase establishes what is called the ISAKMP Security Association (ISAKMP SA), and the second phase establishes the IPSec Security Association (IPSec SA).

Phase 1—The ISAKMP SA

The following takes place during the ISAKMP SA:

1. The computers establish a common encryption algorithm, either DES or 3DES.

2. A common hash algorithm is agreed upon, either MD5 or SHA1.

3. An authentication method is established. This can be Kerberos, public key encryption, or prearranged shared secret.

4. A Diffie-Hellman group is agreed upon in order to allow the Oakley protocol to manage the key exchange process. Diffie-Hellman provides a mechanism for two parties to agree on a shared "master" key, which is used immediately or can provide keying material for new master keys. Oakley determines key refresh and regeneration parameters.

Phase 2—The IPSec SA

The ISAKMP SA creates a secure channel. After the secure channel is established, the IPSec SAs are established. The procedure is similar to that in Phase 1, except that a separate IPSec SA is created for each security protocol (AH or ESP) in each direction (inbound and outbound). Each IPSec SA establishes the "rules" of secure communication for each connection. These rules contain the encryption algorithm, hash algorithm, and authentication method.

One important difference is that each IPSec SA uses a different shared secret key from the one negotiated during the ISAKMP SA. The IPSec SA uses mutable or changing secrets. It is important that the secret keys change on a regular basis so that if the key is "cracked," the intruder only has access to a small part of the communication. There are two ways to generate mutable keys:

1. Repeat the Diffie-Hellman exchange.
2. Reuse the keying material obtained during the ISAKMP SA.

All data transferred between the two computers will take place in the context of the IPSec SA.

IPSec and Active Directory

IPSec configuration and deployment is intimately intertwined with the Active Directory and Group Policy. You must create a policy in order to deploy IPSec in your organization. A policy can be applied to a forest, a tree, a domain, an organizational unit, or to a single computer.

It is within the group policy that we can choose from built-in policies or create custom policies to meet our specialized needs. We configure these policies by creating an MMC console and then using the appropriate MMC plug-in.

Example of Where You Would Use IPSec

As mentioned earlier, there are two primary scenarios where we employ IPSec security:

- Host-to-Host
- Gateway-to-Gateway

The Host-to-Host allows for secure end-to-end communications between two computers. An example of this type of interaction is a pair of computers participating in a client-server computing interaction. Both computers are IPSec-enabled. The typical configuration would be to have the Server using the Server or Secure Server IPSec policy, and the client machine using the Client (Respond Only) IPSec policy.

In a small office environment that does not use a domain model for security, they could use a pre-shared key. Larger environments that enable the Active Directory can use Kerberos Public Key infrastructure for authentication.

Gateway-to-Gateway solutions provide for a secure channel as data moves between intranet gateways. The most useful application of Gateway-to-Gateway security is when the gateway edge servers connect a VPN over the Internet. The source and destination computers do not employ IPSec in this scenario, because it is assumed that the intranet is secure. However, the Internet is not secure, so the gateways must establish a secure channel between themselves.

When the non-IPSec-enabled source machine sends a message to the Internet gateway, that message is encapsulated with a secure tunnel protocol header. The tunnel header provides either authentication or confidentiality or both to the information inside the tunnel header. The tunnel header contains the IP address of the destination gateway. When the message arrives at the destination gateway, the tunnel header is removed, and the destination host's IP address is exposed. The message is sent to the destination host from the destination gateway.

There are times when a corporation must physically separate networks in order to secure information on one of the networks. An example might be that of securing the legal department's network from the rest of the organization in order to obtain the highest level of security. While this method is effective for protecting the information on the legal departments segment, it does make it difficult for the legal department employees to access information in other areas of the corporation, since they are physically disconnected.

IPSec policy can be set so that all information entering and exiting the legal departments segment is encrypted. In this way, individuals with network sniffers will not be able to plug into any available Ethernet port and listen in on the data flow between the legal department and other departments. This also prevents unauthorized access to any resource located on any of the segments identified as those belonging to the legal department.

Interoperability with Non-Microsoft Version of IPSec

The IETF RFC IPSec tunnel protocol specifications did not include mechanisms suitable for remote access VPN clients. Omitted features include user authentication options or client IP address configuration. To use IPSec tunnel mode for remote access, some vendors chose to extend the protocol in proprietary ways to solve these issues. While a few of these extensions are documented as Internet drafts, they lack standards status and are not generally interoperable. As a result, customers must seriously consider whether such implementations offer suitable multi-vendor interoperability.

Building an IPSec Policy

IPSec uses policy to determine how and when secure communications are employed. IPSec policy is built either at the local machine, or in the Active directory. IPSec policies created in the Active Directory take precedence over local IPSec policies. The IPSec policies themselves are driven by Filter Lists, Filter Rules, and Filter Actions.

Each IPSec policy can contain multiple rules that determine the security settings of a secure connection when the link matches parameters set in the rule. For example, we can create a policy called "Secure from Legal to Accounting." In this policy we can create a list of rules to apply. Each rule contains its own "filter list." The filter list determines when the rule is applied. Rules can be set up for IP Address, Network ID, or DNS name. You could set up a filter list that includes the Network IDs of the legal and accounting departments. Whenever the source and destination IP address of a communication matches this filter, the authentication methods, filter actions and tunnel settings for that rule go into effect.

Let's take a look at how we can configure a custom IPSec console that we can use to configure IPSec policy and monitor significant IPSec-related events.

Building an IPSec MMC Console

1. Click the "run" command and type "mmc." Click OK.

2. Click the console menu, then click "Add/Remove Snap in." Click the "Add" button, select "Computer Management" and click "Add." A dialog box will appear that will want to know what computer the snap-in will manage. Select "Local computer" (the computer this console is running on). Click "Finish."

3. Scroll through the list of available snap-ins and select "Group Policy" and click "Add." At this point the wizard will query you on what group policy object you want to manage. Confirm that it says "Local Computer" in the text box and click "Finish."

4. Scroll through the list of group policy objects again, and select "Certificates." Click "Add." The Certificate Snap-in dialog box asks for the kind of certificate you want to manage (Figure 6.26). Select "Computer Account," click "Next," and then select "Local Computer" for the computer you want the Snap-in to manage. Click "Finish."

5. Click "close" on the "Add Standalone Snap-in" dialog box and then click "OK" in the "Add/Remove Snap-in" dialog box. Expand the first level of each of the snap-ins. You should see something similar to Figure 6.27.

We can configure and manage IPSec policy from the custom console. Note that in this example, we've chosen to manage IPSec policy for this single machine. This might be appropriate if you were configuring IPSec policy for a file or application server. If you wanted to manage policy for an entire domain or organizational unit, you would make the appropriate selection in the "Group Policy" snap-in configuration.

Figure 6.26 Confirming Certificate Management Plug-in for local computer.

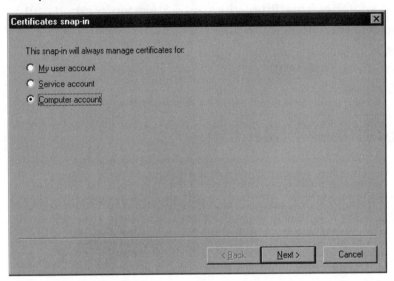

Figure 6.27 Custom IPSec Security Management Console.

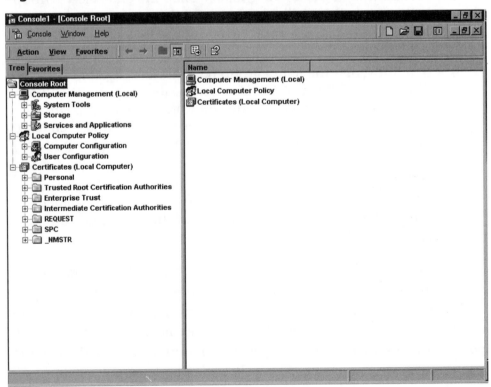

Security Policies

We can build our own IPSec policy or choose from one of the three built-in policies. Let's take a moment to understand the built-in policies.

To find where IPSec policies are defined, expand the "Local Computer Policy," expand the "Computer Configuration" object, expand the "Windows Settings" object, and then click on "IP Security Policies on Local Machine." In the right pane, you will see listed the three built-in IPSec Policies: Client (Respond Only), Secure Server (Require Security), and Server (Request Security). Your screen should look like that seen in Figure 6.28.

The Client (Respond Only) policy allows you to have a computer use IPSec when another computer requests it to use IPSec. For example, you want to connect to a file server that requires IPSec connections.

Figure 6.28 The IPSec Security Console demonstrating the three built-in IPSec Policies.

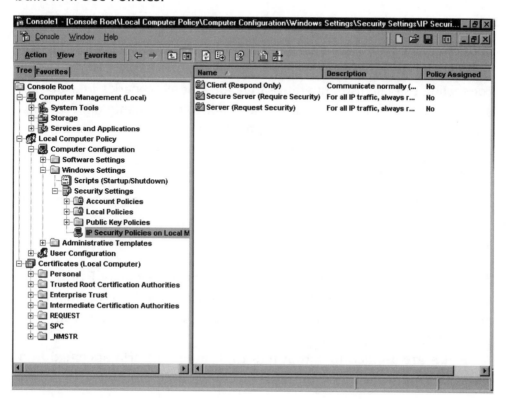

The workstation that has the built-in client policy enabled will negotiate an IPSec security association. However, the workstation never demands IPSec itself; it will only use IPSec to secure communications when another computer asks it to use IPSec.

The Server (Request Security) policy is used to request IPSec security for all connections. The Server policy would be used when you need to enable IPSec-aware and -unaware clients access to the server. If an IPSec-aware client establishes a connection, the session is secured. Unsecured sessions will be established with non-IPSec-aware computers. This policy can be used for networks transitioning from NT to Windows 2000 and finds its best use in a mixed environment.

Use the Secure Server (Require Security) policy to demand that all connections to the machine use IPSec. Examples include file servers with highly sensitive information, and security gateways at each end of an L2TP/IPSec tunnel. Secure Server policy will always request a secure channel. Connections are denied to computers unable to respond to the request.

NOTE

Security policies are bi-directional. If a Secure Server attempts to connect to non-IPSec-aware network servers such as DNS, WINS, or DHCP, the connection will fail. It is imperative that you test all scenarios in a lab that simulates your production environment prior to implementing IPSec policies on your life network. During the testing phase, you must be assiduous in checking the event logs to ascertain what services fail because of IPSec policies.

Rules

An IPSec policy has three main components: IP Security Rules, IP Filter Lists, and IP Filter Actions. Double click the "Server Policy" to see the "Server (Request Security) Properties" sheet, as seen in Figure 6.29

Rules are applied to computers that match criteria specified in a filter list. An IP filter list contains source and destination IP

Figure 6.29 The Server (Request Security) Properties Sheet.

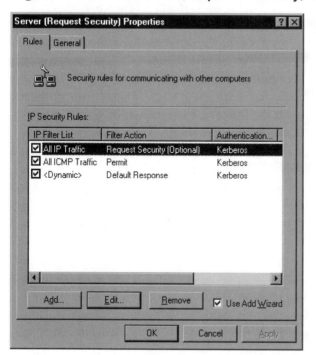

Addresses. These can be individual host IP addresses or network IDs. When a communication is identified as a participant included in an IP filter list, a particular filter action will be applied which is specific for that connection.

The "All IP Traffic" filter list includes all computers that communicate with the server via TCP/IP. Any instructions in the "Filter Action" associated with "All IP Traffic" will be applied. Let's look at some of these actions.

First, double click the "All IP Traffic" filter list. This opens up the "Edit Rule Properties" dialog box for the "All IP Traffic" filter. You should see a tabbed dialog box consisting of five tabs, as seen in Figure 6.30.

The option button for the IP filter list is selected and a description is included which explains the purpose of the list. Double-click on the "All IP Traffic" filter list to see the details of the "All IP Traffic Filter." The name, description, and the details of the filter are displayed here, as depicted in Figure 6.31.

Figure 6.30 The "All IP Traffic" Edit Rule Properties dialog box.

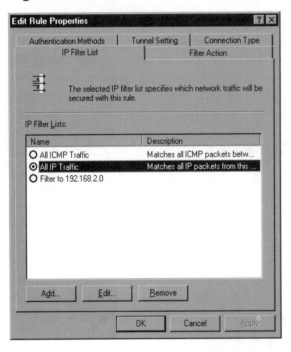

Figure 6.31 The IP Filter List Details dialog box.

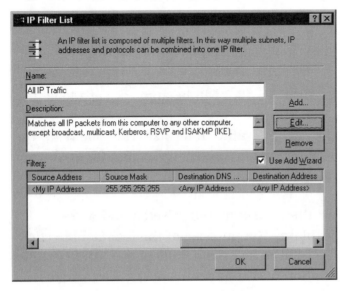

If you want to see more details regarding the addressing, protocol, and description of the filter, you can click the "Edit" button. Click "Cancel" twice to return to the Edit Rules Properties dialog box.

Walkthrough

WARNING

Warning: If you are doing this exercise on a corporate network, you must obtain permission from your network administrator. Installing an unauthorized server on your network can have severe negative consequences on network function and reliability.

Set up IPSec Conversation Between Two Computers

In these practice exercises, we will perform a packet analysis of IPSec-secured communications. To complete these exercises, you will need two Windows 2000 computers. Be sure that neither of these computers needs to be accessed by others on your network while completing these exercises. Downlevel operating systems do not support IPSec; therefore, you must use Windows 2000 machines.

Before we start analyzing IPSec communications in the Network Monitor, let's set up a custom console to use for the exercises.

1. Click Start | Run. Type "mmc" in the run command text box.

2. Click the "Console" menu, then click "Add/Remove Snap-in."

3. In the "Add/Remove Snap-in" dialog box, click the "Add" button. In the "Add Standalone Snap-in" dialog box, select "Computer Management" and click the "Add" button.

4. You are asked whether the snap-in will manage a local or remote computer. Select "Local computer: (the computer this console is running on)" option button, and click "Finish."

5. You are returned to the "Add Standalone Snap-in" dialog box. Scroll through the list and select "Group Policy," then click "Add." You are presented with the "Select Group Policy Object" dialog box. Make sure that "Local Computer" is listed in the "Group Policy Object" text box. Click "Finish."

6. You are back at the "Add Standalone Snap-in" dialog box again. Scroll through the list and select "Certificates" and click "Add." The snap-in will manage certificates for the local computer, so select the "Computer account" option button and click "Finish."

7. Click "Close" to close the "Add Standalone Snap-in" dialog box.

8. Click "OK" to close the "Add/Remove Snap-in" dialog box.

9. Click the "Console" menu and click "Save." In the "Save As" dialog box, name the file *IPSecPractice* and save it to your desktop to make it easy to find.

Enabling Auditing of Logons

When IPSec communications take place, an event will be written to the event log. We can use the event log to see if IPSec is working properly and to troubleshoot IPSec-related events. Perform the following steps so that logons are recorded to the event log. If both computers are part of the same domain, be aware that domain policies override local policies. In this example, both computers will be handled as if they are stand-alone servers. Perform the following steps on both computers:

1. In the IPSecPractice Console expand the "Local Computer Policy" node, expand the "Computer Configuration" node, expand the "Windows Settings" node, and expand the "Security Settings" node. Click on the "Audit Policy" node.

2. Double-click the "Audit log-on events" policy in the right pane. In the "Local Security Policy Setting" dialog box, put a checkmark in both the "Success" and "Failure" checkboxes.

3. Double-click the "Audit object access" policy in the right pane. In the "Local Security Policy Setting" dialog box, put a checkmark in both the "Success" and "Failure" check boxes.

Create a Custom IPSec Policy

In this exercise, we will create a custom IPSec policy. This policy will ensure secure communications between the two computers. The computer that we will run network monitor on will be referred to as NETMON. The other computer we will call NETCLIENT. You do not need to change the names of your computers. The names are used to distinguish the two computers for monitoring purposes.

Perform the following steps on the NETMON machine:

1. In the IPSecPractice Console, expand "Local Computer Policy," expand "Computer Configuration," expand "Windows Settings," and expand "Security Settings," and click "IP Security Policies." In the right pane, you will see the built-in Security Policies.

2. Right-click "IP Security Policies" and click "Create IP Security Policy."

3. The "IP Security Policy Wizard" welcome screen appears. Click "Next."

4. Enter the name and a description of the Security Policy, as seen in Figure 6.32. Click "Next."

Figure 6.32 Naming the IP Security Policy.

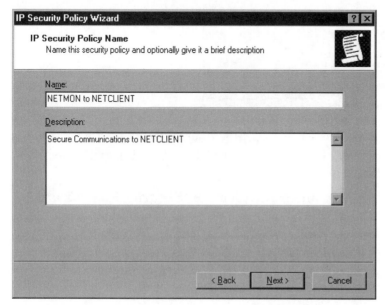

5. You are asked if you want to "Activate the default response rule." Remove the checkmark from the check box for this option. We will create our own rule that will secure communications with NETCLIENT. Click "Next."

6. The wizard is done. Be sure there is a checkmark in the "Edit properties" check box. Click "Finish."

7. You now see the "NETMON to NETCLIENT Properties" dialog box, as see in Figure 6.33.

Figure 6.33 The NETMON to NETCLIENT Properties dialog box.

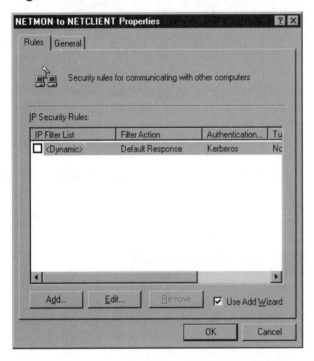

8. Click the "Add" button to add a new IP Security Rule. Be sure there is a checkmark in the "Use Add Wizard" check box.

9. You see the Welcome screen for the "Security Rule Wizard." Click "Next."

10. The wizard asks if you want to specify a tunnel endpoint. We will not be using IPSec tunneling in the exercise. Select "This rule does not specify a tunnel." Click "Next."

11. The wizard now asks for what type of network connections should use this IP Security Rule. Select the "All network connections" option button. Click "Next."

12. Now we need to decide the initial authentication method. The default is Kerberos V5. Select the "Use this string to protect the key exchange (preshared key)" option button. In the text box below, type in "12345" as seen in Figure 6.34. Click "Next."

Figure 6.34 Defining a preshared Master Key.

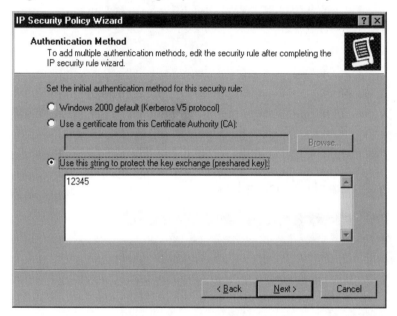

13. You now must define when the Security Policy will be applied. The decision to apply an IP Security Policy is determined by a filter list. If the communicating computer meets the criteria on the filter list, the IP Security is applied. Click the "Add" button as seen in Figure 6.35.

14. This opens the "IP Filter List" dialog box depicted in Figure 6.36. Here you can create multiple filters that can be combined into a single "applied" filter. We want to create a new filter so that our IP Security Policy is applied when communicating with NETCLIENT. In the "Name" text box type "NETCLIENT." Type a description in the "Description"

Figure 6.35 The IP Filter List selection box.

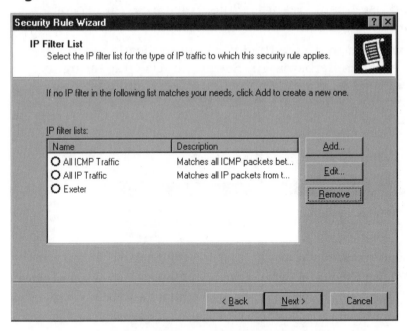

Figure 6.36 The IP Filter List dialog box.

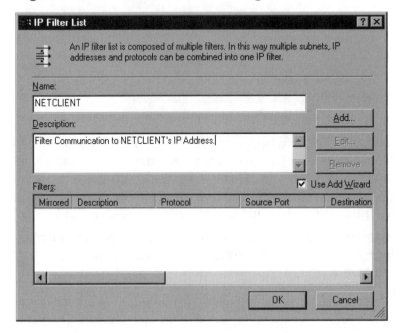

text box. Ensure that the checkmark is in the "Use Add Wizard" and click the "Add" button.

15. The starts the "IP Filter Wizard" and you are presented with a welcome screen. Click "Next."

16. The wizard asks what the source address of IP traffic should be. In the "Source Address" drop down list box, click the down arrow and select "My IP Address." Click "Next."

17. Now enter the destination IP address of NETCLIENT. In the "Destination address" drop down list box, click the down arrow and select "A specific IP Address." Enter the IP Address of the NETCLIENT computer, as seen in Figure 6.37.

Figure 6.37 Entering the IP address of IP traffic.

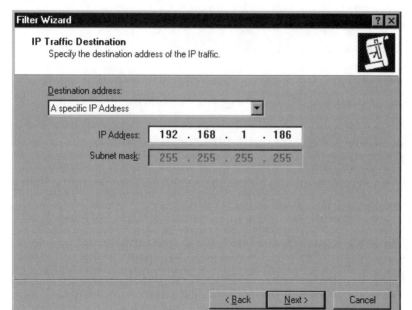

18. The wizard now needs to know what protocols should trigger the IP Security Policy. In the "Select a protocol type" drop down list box select "Any." Click "Next."

19. The wizard has finished collecting information. Click "Finish." Your "IP Filter List" dialog box should appear, as in

Figure 6.38 The completed IP Filter List dialog box.

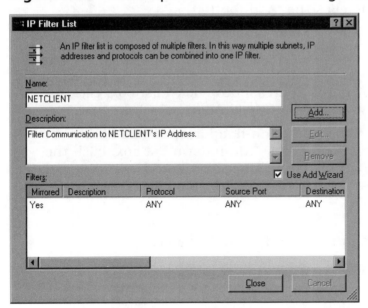

Figure 6.38. Click "Close" to close the "IP Filter List" dialog box and return to the "Security Rule Wizard."

20. The "Security Rule Wizard" dialog box now has an entry for "NETCLIENT." Click the option button next to the NETCLIENT entry and click "Next."

21. Decide on what action is to be taken when the Security Rule is activated. Select the option button next to "Request Security (Optional)" as seen in Figure 6.39. Click "Next."

22. The "Security Rule Wizard" has completed gathering information. Click "Finish." You are returned to the "NETMON to NETCLIENT Properties" dialog box, as seen in Figure 6.40. If there is a checkmark in the "<Dynamic>" IP Filter List, remove it now. Click "Close."

Now that you are back at the IPSecPractice Console, you should see an entry for your new IPSec Security Policy. In order for that policy to take effect, you have to "assign" it. To assign the policy, do the following:

1. Right-click the NETMON to NETCLIENT Policy.

2. Click "Assign."

Figure 6.39 Defining the Filter Action.

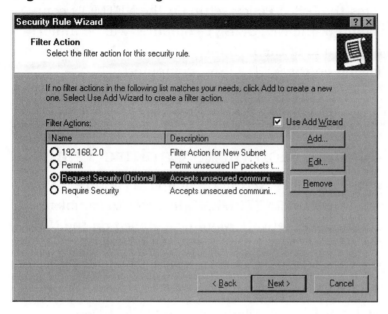

Figure 6.40 The completed NETMON to NETCLIENT Properties box.

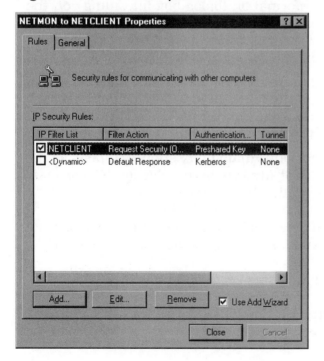

In the right pane, you will see "Yes" in the "Policy Assigned" column. This completes the IPSec Policy setup on the NETMON computer. The preparation of the NETCLIENT computer will be much simpler. We will assign one of the Build-in Policies to the other computer. Do the following on the NETCLIENT computer:

Examine Packets to Ensure Encryption

Configure Network Monitor to Capture Traffic

In this section we will configure Network Monitor to capture traffic passing between NETMON and NETCLIENT. In order to complete this exercise you must have Network Monitor installed on the NET-MON machine. This can be done through the "Add/Remove" programs applet in the Control Panel. Perform the following procedures to configure Network Monitor:

1. Click Start | Programs | Administrative Tools | Network Monitor.

2. Click the "Capture" menu, then click "filter." You are presented with an information dialog box informing you that you can only capture information moving out of, and coming in to, the computer you are working on. Click "OK" to move past this dialog box.

3. You now see the "Capture Filter" dialog box, as seen in Figure 6.41. Click on the line that says "[AND] (Address Pairs)" to select it. Now click on the "Address" button that sits inside the "Add" frame on the right side of the dialog box.

4. The "Address Expression" dialog box should appear as it does in Figure 6.42. Study this figure closely. Notice that near the top of the dialog box, there are two option buttons: "Include" and "Exclude." Make sure that the "Include" option is selected because we want to *include* in our capture any packets moving between NETMON and NETCLIENT.

    Note that there are three sections under the "Include" and "Exclude" options. These are the "Station 1," the "Direction," and the "Station 2" sections. Station 1 is the

Figure 6.41 The Capture Filter dialog box.

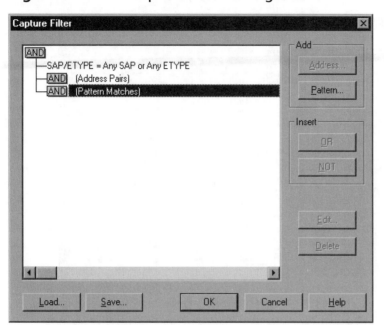

computer you are using now; you cannot make any changes to the entries in that section. Notice that the NetBIOS name of the computer is entered with its corresponding IP, IPX, and MAC addresses. The "Direction" section allows you to indicate what packets you want to capture based on their direction in or out of the computer. The → captures packets leaving the computer, the ← captures packets arriving to the computer, and the ← — → captures packets leaving and arriving to the computer.

Click the entry in the Station 1 section corresponding to your computer's NetBIOS name and IP address. Then click the ← — → symbol in the "Direction" section.

The third section contains addresses for the "other" computer. We need to add an entry for our NETCLIENT computer.

5. Click the "Edit Addresses" button. You will see the "Address Database" dialog box, as pictured in Figure 6.43. We need to add an entry for the NETCLIENT computer. Click the "Add" button in the "Address Database" dialog box.

Figure 6.42 The Address Expression dialog box.

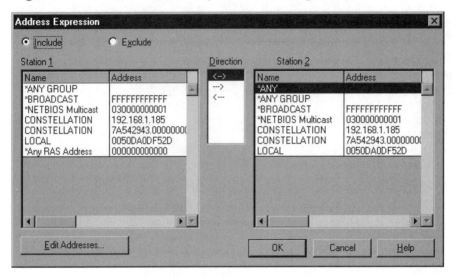

Figure 6.43 The Address Database dialog box.

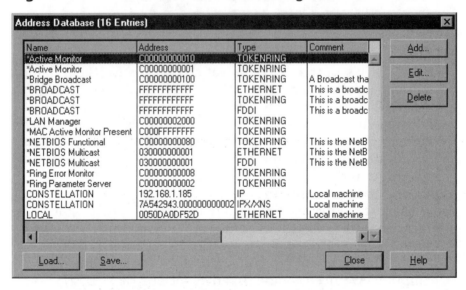

6. The "Address Information" dialog box appears, as seen in
    Figure 6.44. In the "Name" text box, enter "NETCLIENT" as
    seen in the figure. Click the down arrow in the "Type" drop
    down list box, and select "IP." Type the IP address your
    NETCLIENT computer. You can also type in a comment

about this entry in the "Comment" text box. Click "OK" to close the "Address Information" dialog box and return to the "Address Database" dialog box. Click "OK" to close the "Address Database" dialog box and return to the "Address Expression" dialog box.

Figure 6.44 The Address Information dialog box.

7. In the Station 2 section, select "NETCLIENT." Your "Address Expression" dialog box should look like that seen in Figure 6.45. Click "OK" to return to the "Capture Filter" dialog box, which should now look like that in Figure 6.46.

Figure 6.45 The completed Address Expression dialog box.

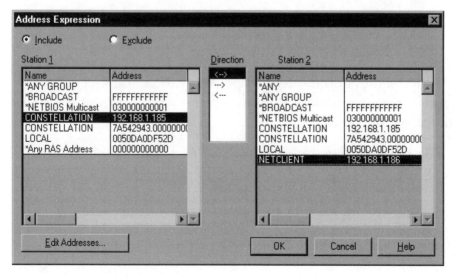

Figure 6.46 The completed Capture Filter dialog box.

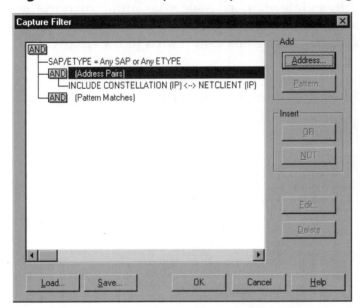

8. Click the "Save" button in the "Capture Filter" dialog box. This will save the filter so that we can use it later. In the "Save Capture Filter" dialog box, type in "*IPSecCaptureFilter*" in the "File name" text box, and save it to the Desktop so you can find it easily. Click "OK" to close the "Capture Filter" dialog box.

Capturing Secured Traffic

Let's generate some traffic between NETMON and NETCLIENT and examine the results of the interchange. We will use the net send command at the command prompt to send some data from the NETMON to the NETCLIENT computer.

1. Click Start | Programs | Accessories | Command Prompt. You should see both the "Command Prompt" and the "Network Monitor" icons on your taskbar.

2. Make Network Monitor the active window by clicking the "Microsoft Network Monitor" taskbar icon. Click the "Capture" menu and then click "Start."

3. Click the "Command Prompt" taskbar icon. In the "Command Prompt" window, type:

```
net send <destination_NetBIOS_name> Hello World!
```

and press "Enter." Your Command Prompt windows should look like that seen in Figure 6.47.

Figure 6.47 The Command Prompt window after issuing the net send command.

4. Switch back to the "Network Monitor" window. Click the "Capture" menu, and then click the "Stop and View" command. You should see what appears in Figure 6.48. Notice the Protocols in the "Protocol" column. The ESP protocol exchanges data between the machines, and the ISAKMP protocol is involved with Key Exchange. Double-click one of the ESP frames (such as Frame 4 in this example).

5. After clicking one of the frames, you should see a "tri-paned" window like that in Figure 6.49. The top window shows the Frame Capture Summary; the middle windows shows the Capture Detail; and the bottom window, known as the "Hex" window shows the contents of the frame in both Hex and ASCII formats.

6. Expand all of the lines that have the plus (+) sign and study the contents of the middle pane. Notice information about the Security Parameters index, the protocol type, and the source and destination address. In the bottom window, notice that you cannot read the contents of the net send message that you sent.

Figure 6.48 The Frame Capture Summary Window.

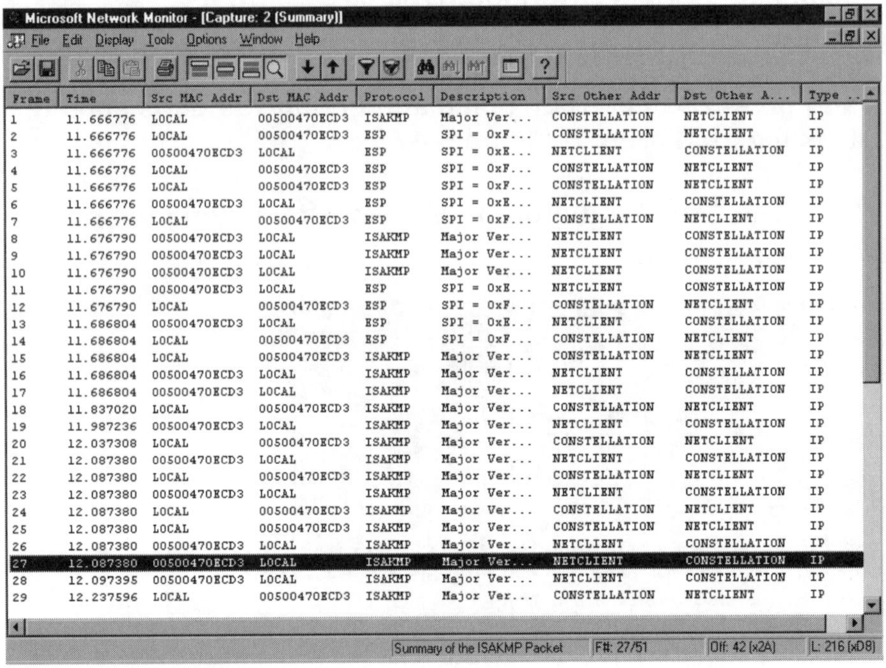

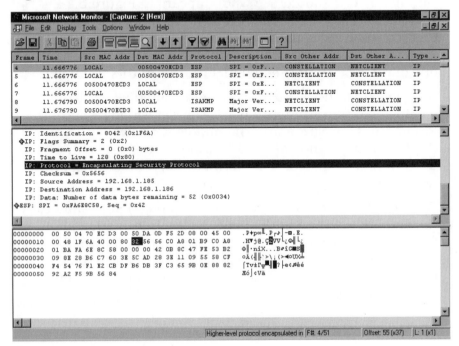

Figure 6.49 Frame Capture in tri-pane view.

7. If you would like to save the frame and all its contents for
    later analysis, you can click on the frame of interest in the
    top window, click the "Edit" menu, and then click "Copy."
    Open up Notepad, or any other text editor, and paste the
    contents of the frame there, as shown in Figure 6.50. This
    makes searching and analyzing packets a lot easier.

Figure 6.50 Captured frame contents pasted into Notepad.

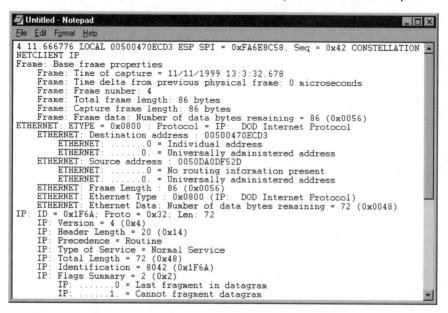

As you can see, if you want to sniff out the contents of a secured
message, you're going to be disappointed. IPSec has encrypted the
contents of the message so routine packet analysis cannot display
the contents of a message. Next, let's examine what we can see
when the packets cross the wire with the aid of IPSec.

Capturing Unsecured Traffic

In this exercise, we'll capture traffic over an unsecured link and see
what we can find in the captured packets. In order to do this, we
need to change the IPSec policy on both computers.

1. From the NETMON computer, open your IPSecPractice
    console and click on the "IP Security Policies" node in the
    left pane.

2. Right-click the "NETMON to NETCLIENT" policy in the right pane and click "unassign."

3. Move to the NETCLIENT computer. Open the IPSecPractice Console you created there and click on the "IP Security Policies" in the left pane. Right-click the "Client (Respond Only)" policy and click "unassign."

No IPSec policies are in effect. The changes should take place immediately.

Move back to the NETMON computer and perform the following steps:

1. In the "Network Monitor" windows, click the "Capture" menu, then click "OK."

2. Return to the command prompt and type:

    ```
    net send <netbios_name_of_NETCLIENT> Hello World!
    ```

3. Switch back to Network Monitor, click the "Capture" menu and click "Stop and View." Your screen should look something like that seen in Figure 6.51.

4. You'll notice packets from different protocols. The net send command transfers information via SMB so double-click on one of the SMB packets similar to Frame 6 in the example above.

5. Look at the contents of the frame in the "Hex" window. You should see something similar to Figure 6.52.

6. See something familiar? To the right of the "Hex" code, you see the ASCII translation. At the end of the ASCII translation is our message, complete with the source and destination NetBIOS names.

This provides a simple but effective demonstration of the ease with which unsecured communications can be captured and read. When capturing packets from all machines on a segment, you would want to limit the received packets, because the frame buffer is limited to the amount of RAM on the machine running Network Monitor. You can limit the number of captured packets when observing all machines on the segment by setting up a "pattern" filter. In that

Figure 6.51 Captured packets from unsecured session.

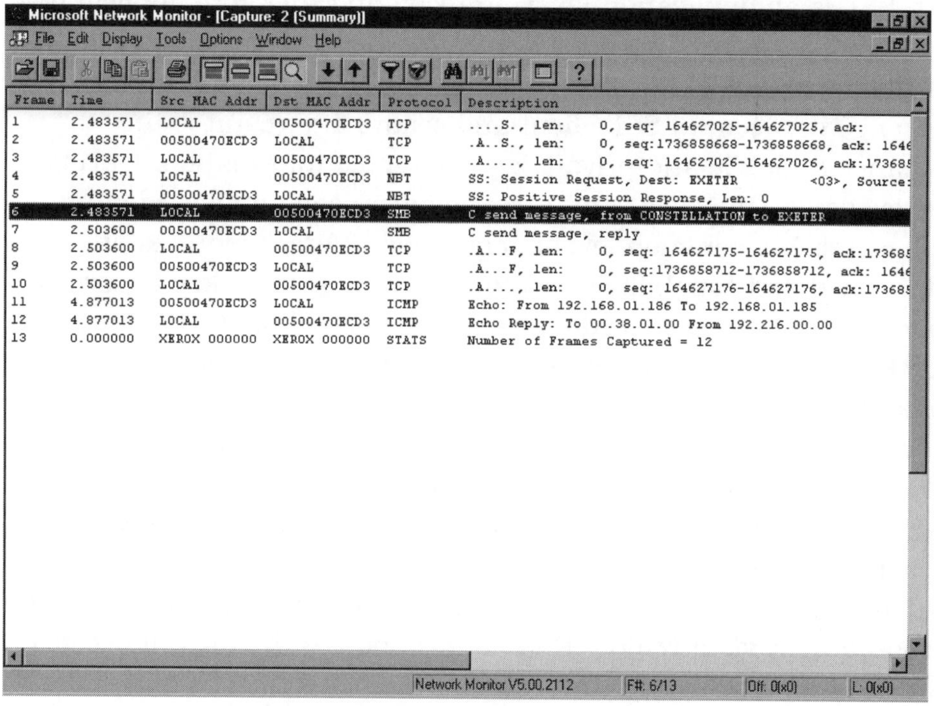

Figure 6.52 Contents of the Hex Pane.

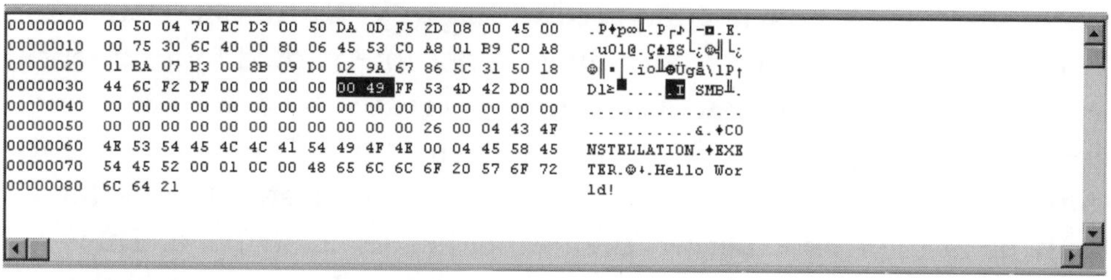

way you only capture packets that contain information of interest, regardless of what computer on the segment they came from.

Summary

The Secure Sockets Layer provides for public key-based security for Web sites. SSL allows users to interact with SSL-enabled Web page to send information such as credit cards numbers, in a secure context. SSL is an application layer protocol, and therefore applications must be "SSL-aware" in order to use the mode of data encryption.

Like other public key-based encryption methods, the initial exchange between an SSL client and secure site requires the exchange of public and private key-encrypted information. During this exchange, the client and server confirm each other's identity and establish a common level of encryption. After identities are established and capabilities are confirmed, a session key is agreed upon, and all subsequent data exchange is encrypted with the session key. The session key was established during the initial development of a secure session.

Virtual Private Networks (VPNs) allow protected communications to take place over a private intranet, or across the public Internet. The networks are "virtual" because a user connects to a network over media other than direct connection to the local network infrastructure. A common example is that of a user who connects to the corporate VPN via a remote RAS connection. To the user, its seems that he or she is directly connected to the network. The only difference is that the network seems a bit slower than usual.

A VPN is private because all data transferred between the VPN client and VPN server is encrypted within a "VPN" tunnel. Data encryption ensures that information is not intercepted by unintended parties while in transit. The tunnel is created by adding a tunnel header to each packet leaving the client machine. The tunnel header contains the IP address of the VPN server as its destination. After arriving at the tunnel server, the tunnel header is stripped. This exposes the original IP header, which contains the address of the destination computer.

Windows 2000 allows you to create a VPN using different technologies. One of these is the Point-to-Point Tunneling Protocol (PPTP). You can create a secure tunnel with PPTP, which uses Microsoft Point-to-Point Encryption (MPPE) algorithm for encryption. Almost any supported protocol can be tunneled within the PPTP channel, including NetBEUI, NWLink, and TCP/IP. These other pro-

tocols are encapsulated within the IP tunnel. The practical signifi-
cance is that a client can be using NetBEUI to dial into a NetBEUI
network via the PPTP tunnel. The original LAN protocol headers are
encapsulated within the PPTP tunnel.

You can use PPTP to protect data that is moving out of, or into,
networks that employ Network Address Table translation (NAT). This
is an important consideration when planning to employ VPN technology, because the other tunneling protocol available in Windows
2000, L2TP/IPSec cannot function when data is moved in or out of
a NAT network.

Another VPN technology available with Windows 2000 is
L2TP/IPSec. IPSec has some advantages and some disadvantages in
comparison to PPTP. IPSec provides for stronger encryption. This
encryption is also "end-to-end." This end-to-end encryption allows for
a secure data channel between the client and destination computer,
rather than just between the client and destination server. One disadvantage of using IPSec-secured tunnels is that they cannot be used
on NAT-translated networks, because the translation process cannot
access secured headers and will invalidate packets when applied.
IPSec is a Layer 3 encryption methodology, which allows it to be
completely transparent to applications. Contrast this with the SSL
encryption model, where applications (such as Microsoft Internet
Explorer) must be explicitly designed to work with SSL.

FAQs

Q: Does SSL have any drawbacks?

A: Yes. The Secure Sockets Layer provides strong security for Web
pages and Web sites. However, SSL is enabled on a per-page
basis, which can be time consuming to configure, and difficult to
audit for large and comprehensive Web installations. Another
limitation of SSL is that it is processor-intensive. You might have
noticed reduced responsiveness when connecting to SSL-enabled
Web pages. Processor cycles used by a single SSL process affect

all services running on the machine. If you are planning to use SSL, be sure to benchmark all processes on that machine while SSL is active. This will provide you with an accurate assessment of how your server's overall performance will play out in a production environment.

Q: In what environment would I use the Microsoft Certificate Server?

A: You can use Microsoft Certificate server to create your own digital certificates of authenticity. However, these certificates are of limited use when running an Internet Web site. The Microsoft certificate server finds its best use in a corporate intranet. You can create certificates for both servers and users. A server certificate authenticates a server for the users connecting to it. A client certificate authenticates the users connecting to an SSL-enabled server. You can "map" user certificates to Windows 2000 user accounts. This provides granular control over intranet server resources. Another scenario where certificate server is helpful is the corporate "extranet." You can create a user certificate to a corporate partner, and then require that certificate when the partner accesses an "order entry" system on your SSL-enabled IIS server. If that partner were to fall in arrears in payments, you could revoke that partner's certificate.

Q: Why can't I use L2TP/IPSec when running NAT?

A: You cannot use IPSec on the inside of a NAT network. NAT (Network Address Translation) allows an intranet to use IP addresses assigned to Private Networks to work on the Internet. A Private IP Address is not recognized as valid by Internet routers, and therefore cannot be used for direct Internet communications. A server running a Network Address Translator will map intranet client's IP addresses to a request, and then forward the request to the destination using its valid Internet address. The destination Internet host responds to the

NAT server by sending the requested information to its IP address. The NAT server then inserts the intranet client's IP address into the destination header, and forwards this response to the client.

Incoming packets are sent to a single IP address, which NAT maps to a private IP address. When using ESP or AH or both, IPSec must be able to access the Security Parameters Index associated with each internal connection. The problem is, when NAT changes the destination IP address of the packet, this changes the SPI, which invalidates the information in the Auth trailer. IPSec interprets this as a breach, and the packet is dropped.

Q: Can I use IPSec to secure communications with my Win 9x machines?

A: No. At this time, only Windows 2000 clients and servers can participate in IPSec-secured communications. Microsoft source material suggests that Windows CE may support IPSec in the future, but there are no plans to support downlevel clients.

Q: Does my VPN server require a dedicated connection to the Internet?

A: Your VPN server requires a dedicated IP address. In most instances, this means your VPN server needs to be connected to the Internet at all times. A small number of ISPs support "on demand" routing, which will cause the ISP to dial up your VPN server when incoming requests are received for its IP address. However, to ensure highest availability, it is best to have a dedicated connection. Remember that the VPN clients will "dial-in" to your server using its IP address, and therefore that IP address must be constant.

Q: Is there a way to force the use of strong authentication and encryption for VPN users and a different set of authentication and encryption constraints for dial-up users?

A: Yes — you can do this by setting remote access policies. With remote access policies, you can grant or deny authorization based on the type of connection being requested (dial-up networking or virtual private network connection).

Q: Is there a way for me to monitor the IPSec connections to my server?

A: Yes. Microsoft provides a tool called ipsecmon.exe. You can start this tool from the "run" command. Figure 6.53 shows the ipsecmon window.

Figure 6.53

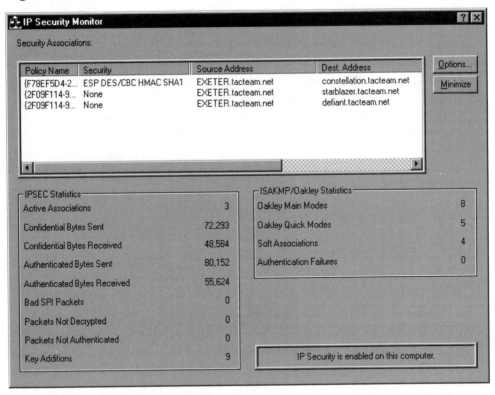

The IP Security Monitor allows you to assess when failures take place in negotiating security associations, when bad Security Parameters Index packets are passed, and many other statistics. The Oakley Main Mode indicates the number of Master Keys exchanged, and the Quick Mode number indicates the number of session keys. The "Options" button allows you to configure the update interval of the displayed statistics.

Q: My VPN clients cannot access network resources beyond my VPN server. What might be causing this?

A: There are several reasons why this might happen. One possibility is that the clients are not running the same LAN protocols used by the internal network. For example, the VPN client is running only the TCP/IP protocol. The internal network runs only NWLink. The VPN client is able to connect to the VPN server because they both run TCP/IP. However, when the VPN client tries to access a server on the internal network, the connection fails because the internal server runs only NWLink.

Another circumstance that can lead to VPN client access failures is when VPN clients are assigned IP addresses via DHCP, and the DHCP server becomes unavailable. If the VPN server has Automatic Private IP Addressing enabled, VPN clients will be assigned IP addresses in the Class B address class 169.254.0.0. Unless there is a route for this network ID in the VPN servers routing table, communication with the internal network will fail.

Also, make sure that your RRAS policies do not filter TCP/IP incoming and outgoing packets to and from the VPN clients. Be careful to open the ports for the control channels used for your VPN connections as well.

Chapter 7

External Network Connections

Solutions in this chapter:

- Connecting to the Internet
- PPTP Over the Internet
- RAS
- Securing NT Servers

383

Introduction

When Windows 95 and Windows NT 4.0 were introduced, software was included to connect to the Internet either directly or via dial-up connection. These connection tools have slowly been improved through various service packs and releases of Microsoft's Dial-up Networking (DUN) software.

In 1995, the typical Internet user connected using a 14.4 kilobits per second modem and impressed friends by sending e-mail and "surfing" Web sites. The content and connection options today are amazingly different. Today, high-speed connections are available for reasonable prices in many major metropolitan areas of North America, Asia, and Europe. Windows 2000 has been updated with excellent support for these new connection methods, making them easier, more functional, and more secure.

Organizations supporting work-at-home employees are finding VPN connections to be a great solution for functional, secure remote access. This is very practical in areas where cable and ADSL (Asynchronous Digital Subscriber Line) modems let home-based users connect to the Internet for approximately the cost of a second phone line.

Remote Connection Options

A number of options exist for establishing a connection to the Internet, and the method that is best for your network will depend on the amount of bandwidth you need, availability in your area, and the amount of money you can justify spending to establish and maintain your connection. Cable modems and ADSL are the new-comers to the field and they are not available in many areas. However, cable and phone companies are pushing the deployment of these media as they try to gain the early advantage over one another. Accordingly, it would be a smart move to do some research regarding available and upcoming options in your neck of the woods.

There are several ways to establish a connection to the Internet that are either not widely available or not commonly used and will not be covered in this book. These include wireless connection options that are currently being deployed in a few cities around the world, and satellite connectivity, which is an option that is typically only used in remote areas or for other special circumstances.

Modems

Of all the different ways available to connect to the Internet, you are probably most familiar with standard modems that work over POTS (plain old telephone system). The word "modem" is derived from the functions it performs, *modulation/demodulation*. Modems were one of the first methods used to connect computers together, and 300 bps (bits per second) modems were the first commonly used units. Over the years, modem speeds increased to 1200 bps, 2400 bps, 4800 bps, 9600 bps, 14.4 Kbs (KiloBits per second), 19.6 Kbs, 28.8 Kbs, 33.6 Kbs, and finally 56 Kbs. Although 56k modems are in wide use, connection speeds often do not reach the full potential of the modems due to line quality issues and FCC regulations.

Modems are connected to computers in one of a number of different ways. Internal modems connect into one of a computer's ISA or PCI bus slots, while external modems connect via a serial port or, the newest way, a USB port. Laptop computers typically use PC Card modems or have a proprietary modem connection built on the system board. Modems haven't commonly been integrated onto system boards due to the upgrade cycle, and such integration isn't likely to occur, as the next generation of connectivity options makes standard modems obsolete.

ISDN

Integrated Services Digital Network (ISDN) connections are capable of doubling the speed achieved by the best modems. An ISDN connection can bond the two 64 Kbs B channels of an ISDN link to establish a 128 Kbs connection to another ISDN device, or it can be configured to use one B channel for voice traffic and one for data. This makes ISDN more flexible and enables you to have a permanent Internet connection without needing an additional line. ISDN devices will not operate on POTS lines, so in order to use it you must first have an ISDN line installed. Monthly charges for ISDN lines are higher than for regular telephone lines. The installation fees and monthly costs vary from region to region, but they are costly enough so that ISDN hasn't gained wide acceptance for home use.

ISDN can be configured to establish a permanent connection or to connect on demand. Some ISDN plans have a flat fee structure, while others charge by the minute. Obviously, it could get rather costly to maintain a permanent connection if by-the-minute fees are accruing, so dialing on demand is necessary in some cases. ISDN connections are established much faster than modem connections, only two or three seconds, so dial-on-demand does not cause much delay when the link is first established. Dial-on-demand configurations are typically set to drop the connection after five or ten minutes of inactivity.

ISDN network connections are commonly used for the following purposes:

- Small businesses to connect to the Internet
- Businesses to connect small offices
- Home-based workers
- Internet "power users"

ISDN interfaces can be installed in computers and routers, enabling them to establish connections by dialing the number of an ISDN line that is connected to another ISDN device. Once the devices are connected and working properly, any problems that occur are most likely due to line problems that require the intervention of the telco providing the ISDN service. ISDN has a number of configuration options that are set by the telco that will be provided to you so that you can configure your ISDN adapters to meet the specifications of their network. ISDN is not an extremely reliable service, a fact that you will want to keep in mind as you consider your connection requirements. (see Table 7.1)

Table 7.1 ISDN is Composed of Three Channels, Two of Which Carry Data

ISDN Channel	Bandwidth	Use
D	16 Kbs	Signaling
B-1	64 Kbs	Bearer
B-2	64 Kbs	Bearer

Leased Lines

Leased lines are full-time, dedicated connections provided by bundles of telephone lines that provide reliable network links from 56 Kbs on up. Actually, leased lines with speeds lower than 56 Kbs have been available, but as modem speeds have increased over the years, 56 Kbs has become the functional entry-level speed for leased lines. Telephone companies provide leased lines, and the deregulation of the phone industry in some countries has enabled competitive providers to offer leased lines to customers, although they typically contract with a traditional phone company to install and maintain the lines.

From a physical network perspective, the point at which you need to consider about leased lines is the *demarcation point*. This is a device installed at your site, beyond which the phone company is not responsible. It is typically smaller than a shoe box and has various LED status lights to assist the phone company technicians with troubleshooting. An RJ-48 cable will connect it with the CSU/DSU (Channel Service Unit/Data Service Unit).

The CSU/DSU is simply a device that converts the telco's network signal into a signal that the router can use. The CSU/DSU is connected to the router via a serial link, and the router, of course, is connected to your network via a network adapter. As you have guessed, the

Figure 7.1 Leased lines utilize a CSU/DSU to connect network routers to the telco network.

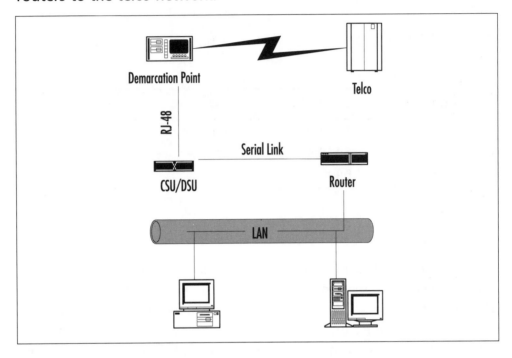

ISP or remote office to which you are connecting will look the same, although they may be using different brands or models of equipment.

As the Internet has become more important to many companies and organizations, dedicated connections have become more commonplace. Leased lines that provide 1.54 Mbs (MegaBits per second) connectivity are called T1 lines. A T1 is composed of 24 copper wires, each of which is capable of 64 Kbs, for a total of 1.536 Mbs. A T1 can be partitioned for voice and data, so if you only need 768 Kbs for data, you can use the other 12 lines for telephones. You may hear someone referring to a fractional T1, which is simply the use of anything less than all 24 lines. Accordingly, you can get any amount of bandwidth between 64 Kbs and 1.54 Mbs in 64 Kbs increments. Although 1.54 Mbs doesn't seem like much compared to 10 Mbs and 100 Mbs LAN speeds, it is usually plenty for most small- and medium-sized companies since most Internet applications are designed to conserve bandwidth.

Some parts of the world have an E1 leased line standard, which contains 32 channels, for a total of 2.048 Mbs. E1 links are found in Europe, Africa, and other areas.

A T3 connection is composed of 28 T1s, for a total of 44.736 Mbs. Internet and WAN connections of this type are typically only feasible for very large entities, such as a large university or a large company that uses the Internet as its primary means of business. As you might assume, it does not always make sense for the phone company to use copper phone wire end-to-end to provide the T3 connection, which would be 670 pairs. Fiber optic cable, microwave transmission, and coaxial cable are used in many cases. The T3 connection is not the highest point of available bandwidth. Speeds in the gigabits per second range are available if you have the need and the money.

Cable Modems

Cable modems have been around since the mid-nineties, although they did not become commonplace until the very late nineties, with only a couple million modems in homes by the turn of this century. Cable modems are used on cable TV systems that provide an Internet connection and cable TV over the existing coaxial cable. Although they are being called "modems," cable modems are not modulation/demodulation devices, so they aren't really modems. The term is being used so that consumers will readily understand the general purpose of the device, which is to connect to the Internet. Cable companies had to upgrade much of their equipment and wiring to deliver this service, but the resulting high-speed Internet connection that will be provided to many homes will eventually replace most modem usage, except in rural areas where cable networks don't exist.

Cable modem connections will not only be available in homes, but will be offered to businesses as well. Bandwidth varies depending on the particular cable network, but speeds are typically around 3 Mbs. Most cable modems are designed to interface with the coaxial cable and provide an Ethernet port for connectivity to a network adapter on your computer. In addition to the bandwidth, the permanent connection status will change the way many people use the Internet.

Entities will be able to utilize cable modems to connect remote offices by establishing VPNs across the Internet. This capability will bring WAN networking to many organizations that could not justify the expense of a high-speed leased line. (see Table 7.2)

Table 7.2 Approximate Speeds of Various Types of Connections

Type of Connection	Speed (Kbs)
Standard modem	56
ISDN	128
ADSL modem	1,500
Cable modem	3,000
T1 leased line	1,500
E1 leased line	2,000
T3 leased line	45,000

ADSL

Asynchronous Digital Subscriber Line services were introduced in the late nineties, and this high-speed access option is considered to be the main competitor of cable modem access. ADSL uses existing telephone wires in your house or business, although phone companies must upgrade some of their equipment in order to support this technology. ADSL, like the cable modem, can provide an "always on" network connection, and although it utilizes your phone lines, you can still use the telephone as you would normally while your ADSL connection is active. This will enable you to eliminate that extra phone line you may now have dedicated for Internet dial-up. Another similarity to the cable modem is the network interface that is used to connect to a computer or router. ADSL modems are commonly an external device with a port for the phone line and an Ethernet port for the RJ-45 cable that connects to your network.

ADSL speeds are generally advertised in the 1 to 1.5 Mbs range, and bandwidth is split between upstream and downstream traffic. ADSL's greatest handicap is that it is limited by distance to the phone companies switch. ADSL will not operate at full capacity beyond approximately three miles from the phone switch, so most rural and some suburban areas will not be able to use ADSL.

ADSL will enable businesses to replace short-distance leased lines with a less expensive ADSL connection. In fact, other DSL technologies have been in use since the mid-nineties to provide connectivity between networks that are not too distant from each other, but they haven't gained widespread acceptance in home and small business use yet.

Other DSL technologies may become market players in the future, although ADSL currently has the spotlight. HDSL (High bit-rate Digital Subscriber Line) modems have been available for short WAN links for quite some time, and you may find it an attractive alternative for your network.

Connecting to the Internet

The specific procedures for configuring a workstation to access the Internet depend on the whether you are using a dial-up, ISDN, cable, ADSL, or leased line connection. All of the methods except for dial-up utilize a network adapter, so configuration will be exactly like setting up a system for a LAN. The ISP providing your cable or ADSL connection will provide you with all of the information regarding the TCP/IP settings you will need to communicate on their network.

If your network is connected to the Internet via a router, the IP configuration of the workstation is not dependent on the type of connection that is used. Since the workstation only needs to know the gateway address, it is unaware of whether the connection is ISDN, dial-up, leased line, etc. However, IP configuration will vary depending on whether NAT (Network Address Translation), proxy, or registered IP addresses are used to access the Internet.

Connecting via a standard modem is a special case since there is no real network adapter involved. A dial-up network connection is configured, and IP configuration relevant to that connection is entered. Whenever a particular dial-up connection is initiated, the computer creates a virtual network adapter that is bound to the modem and uses the IP configuration assigned to that dial-up connection. Many ISPs utilize DHCP, so there is very little to configure. In some cases it is only necessary to specify a phone number to dial, and then provide a username and password. Some ISPs require a script to run to authenticate to their network (see Figure 7.2), and they will provide you with the necessary information, if that is the case.

Figure 7.2 Scripting support is configured from the Security tab of a dial-up connection's properties dialog box.

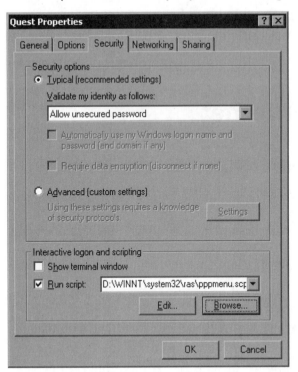

Security Concerns

Once you are connected to the Internet, your computer can be accessed by almost anyone on the Internet, just as if your computer and theirs were on the same LAN. With Windows 2000, you can disable the Client for Microsoft Networks on dial-up connections, which will provide you with a minimum level of security. With this option disabled, other users cannot browse your computer to see shares, printers, or user accounts. This is the only universal setting specific to dial-up networking that you can use to secure your dial-up Internet connection.

If you are running applications such as a WWW or FTP server, you will need to consider the security implications of offering these services to Internet users. See the section later in this chapter regarding this particular security concern for more information.

Windows 2000, like other Windows operating systems, allows you to configure the dial-up connection to use specific authentication protocols, but this setting will depend on what protocols are supported by your ISP. Contact your ISP for information regarding the protocols they support if you are interested in securing your connection. Authentication protocols are configured by clicking on the Advanced button on the Security tab of the dial-up connection's properties dialog.

Exercise 7.1 Creating a dial-up Internet connection

This exercise will walk you through the steps to create a dial-up connection to the Internet and assumes a modem is already installed. Please make sure you understand security implications for your computer and your network before establishing a connection to the Internet.

1. Click on the "Start" menu, select Settings, Network and Dial-up Connections, Make a New Connection.

2. Click "Next" when you are greeted by the Network Connection Wizard with a welcome dialog box.

Figure 7.3 Disabling the Client for Microsoft Networks from the dial-up network connection provides entry-level security.

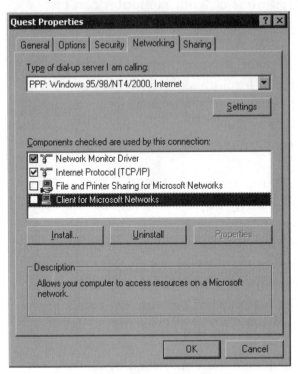

3. You are now presented with five choices, as shown in Figure 7.4. Select "Dial-up to the Internet" for this exercise, and click "Next."

4. The Internet Connection Wizard starts, which is included with Internet Explorer 5.0, so you may be familiar with it already. Select the third option to set up a connection manually and click "Next."

5. Despite the fact that you already specified this information in Step 3, you are now asked if you will connect to the Internet through a modem and phone line or through a LAN. Select the phone line and modem option and click "Next."

6. You are now presented with the opportunity to enter the phone number to which you wish to connect. Enter the phone number and click the "Advanced" button.

7. The Advanced Properties Connection tab allows you to specify the type of connection (PPP, SLIP, or C-SLIP) and the log-on

Figure 7.4 The Network Connection Wizard walks through configurations for various network connections.

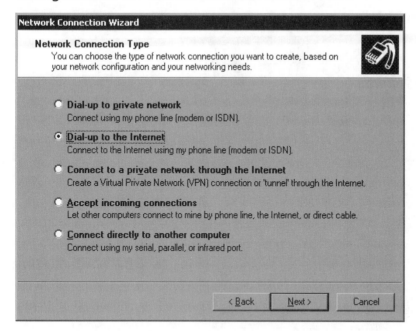

script, if necessary. Most ISP's use PPP without log-on scripts, so you will not likely need to change these options.

8. The "Addresses" tab (Figure 7.5) enables you to specify the IP address and DNS server addresses for the connection. Almost all ISPs use DHCP to supply the IP address, although many still require the DNS servers to be configured manually. Complete the configuration as necessary and click "OK."

9. Now you are back to the phone number dialog box. Click "Next" to move on.

10. You are now prompted for a user name and password. Your ISP will supply these items. If you specified a script to run and the username and password are included in the script, you will not need to enter the username and password here. Click Next when you are done entering the username and password.

11. You are now asked to supply a name for the connection. This will be the name displayed in the Network and Dial-up Connections folder for this connection. Enter a name and click "Next."

Figure 7.5 Specifying IP address and DNS server configuration on a dial-up connection.

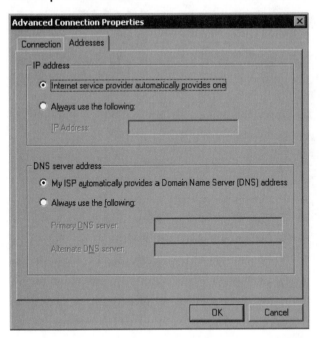

12. The Wizard continues and asks if you wish to set up an Internet mail account. Since we are just concerned with creating the Internet connection, select "No" and click "Next."

13. The next dialog box is the last, which gives you the opportunity to initialize the connection when you click "Finish." Deselect the check box and click "Finish."

14. To configure the connection to disable the Client for Microsoft Networks, click Start, Settings, Network and Dial-up Connections, and select the dial-up connection you just created.

15. The properties for the connection appear (Figure 7.6), allowing you to change the phone number, configure the modem, etc.

16. Click the "Networking" tab and clear the Client for Microsoft Networks check box (see Figure 7.6).

17. You should now be back at the dial prompt. Click "Dial" to test the connection.

Figure 7.6 Configuring general dial-up network connection items.

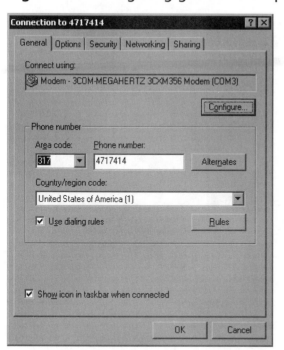

Sharing Internet Connections

Windows 2000 has the ability to share an Internet connection on a workstation with other computers on the network. This feature will be useful for homes and small offices that need an inexpensive method to connect a few PCs to Internet.

Internet Connection Sharing is enabled from the Sharing tab of the Connections Properties dialog box. Simply check the "Enable Internet Connection Sharing for this connection" option, and you can be off and running. The "Enable on-demand dialing" option will invoke the connection whenever another user on the network attempts to access the Internet when the connection is not active.

The Settings button brings up a dialog box in which you can specify additional applications that can be used through the shared connection. These are configured by defining the TCP ports used for the application. Services can also be added, and there are a few pre-defined, but not enabled by default, such as FTP, mail, and Telnet (see Figure 7.7).

Figure 7.7 Sharing an Internet connection with Windows 2000.

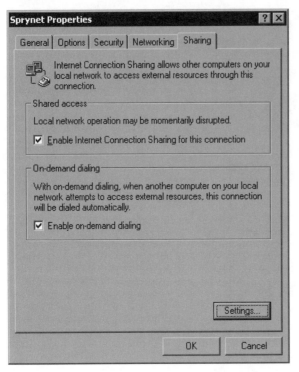

Enabling Internet Connection Sharing will change the IP address of your network adapter to 192.168.0.1 with a subnet mask of 255.255.255.0, a feature designed to discourage its use in all but the smallest networks. Additionally, the share connection service provides DHCP addressing services on the network, so you don't want to enable this feature in an environment that is currently using DHCP. Computers that will access this shared connection can also be configured manually with IP addresses in the same network, and the gateway and DNS server addresses set to 192.168.0.1.

Currently, many small offices have modems in each computer that needs Internet access because it is usually less expensive than purchasing third-party proxy or NAT software and paying a network technician to install and configure it. Windows 2000 will tip the scales in favor of connection sharing and may actually save money for small offices by eliminating some phone lines. See Chapter 8 for more information on connection sharing.

Establishing VPNs Over the Internet

As you learned in Chapter 6, virtual private networks provide the capability to securely join separate physical LANs into one logical network across the Internet. In this chapter, we will take a look at exactly how this can be accomplished, and we will also look at the simpler task of connecting one client to a LAN via a VPN over the Internet.

PPTP and L2TP

Before you begin implementing a VPN solution, you must first gather requirements and decide what type of VPN you are going to deploy. Windows 2000 supports VPNs based on PPTP and L2TP, and while one is easier to implement for most Windows platforms, the other is less proprietary.

PPTP VPNs are supported in Windows 2000, Windows NT 4.0, Windows 95, and Windows 98. However, Windows 2000 is the only Microsoft operating system that is capable of establishing an L2TP VPN. Consequently, you will need to provide PPTP services for legacy Windows systems in your organization.

PPTP relies on proprietary encryption, and Windows systems that support PPTP use Microsoft Point-to-Point Encryption (MPPE). Since MPPE is built in to the networking components of the operating system, it requires fewer steps to implement. A VPN that uses L2TP relies on IPSec for encryption, and accordingly must have security certificates installed on VPN servers and clients.

A Windows 2000 server providing VPN connections can support both PPTP and L2TP connections at the same time, so it won't be difficult to provide for both. You may want to plan on installing certificates on all computers that get upgraded to or delivered with

Windows 2000. This will enable you to use L2TP for these machines, and when your network no longer has any legacy Windows systems, you can remove the PPTP ports on the VPN server, effectively forcing all VPN connections to be L2TP-based.

An L2TP VPN is established as described in the following steps:

1. An IPSec security association is generated.

2. An L2TP tunnel is created between the client and server.

3. A challenge is sent by the server.

4. An encrypted response is sent by the client.

5. The response is compared to the user accounts database.

6. The server accepts the connection if the remote access policies and user account properties are appropriate.

PPTP connection attempts are processed in the following order:

1. A PPTP tunnel is created by the client with the VPN server.

2. A challenge is sent to the client from the server.

3. An encrypted response is sent to the server from the client.

4. The response is compared to the user accounts database.

The server accepts the connection if the remote access policies and user account properties are appropriate.

As you can see, the only major procedural difference between PPTP and L2TP is that L2TP establishes an IPSec association before creating the tunnel. This is not to say that the two protocols are identical otherwise—they certainly aren't. This extra step provides another layer of authentication since IPSec is based on computer certificates.

VPN Solutions

Windows 2000 VPNs can be implemented in two different ways: client-to-server, and server-to-server. The type that you select will depend on the needs of your network and the hardware available for use.

Client/Server VPN

To provide remote clients with access to your LAN, you can implement a client-to-server VPN, which enables a client PC to access all
resources on the VPN server's LAN. This connection can be made
through the Internet, so any client connected to the Internet via any
method can establish a VPN connection. This type of VPN is used
primarily to provide mobile users, or a single computer on a separate LAN, access to your LAN resources. Windows 2000 components
for a client-to-server VPN include RRAS (Routing and Remote Access
Service) on the server with VPN ports configured, and a VPN network connection configured on the client. If a VPN utilizing L2TP
and IPSec is used, each computer must also have a security certificate installed (see Figure 7.8).

Figure 7.8 A client-to-server VPN logically makes a remote
computer a host on a LAN.

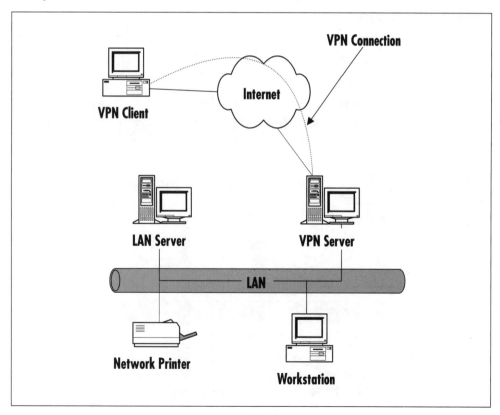

Server/Server VPN

A server-to-server (or router-to-router) VPN is used to create one logical network out of two or more physical networks across the Internet, an intranet, or another public network. With this method, you can create a WAN without buying expensive dedicated connections between physical locations. Each office participating in the VPN simply needs to have an Internet connection and a Windows 2000 Server computer running RRAS with the VPN connections and appropriate routes configured.

As illustrated in Figure 7.9, creating a VPN connection between servers requires that you configure a demand-dial interface to establish the VPN connection when the server starts. Demand-dial interfaces can be configured to dial when network traffic needs to be routed to the other network, or to remain connected continuous-

Figure 7.9 A server-to-server VPN fuses two physical networks into one logical network.

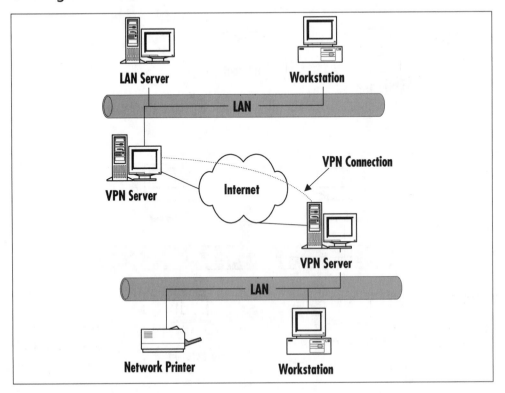

ly. The demand-dial interface configuration includes the IP address or host name of the remote VPN server, the dial-up connection association if it is a dial-up link, a username and password to authenticate, and protocol information. The terminology may be a bit misleading here, since a demand-dial interface may not actually be dialing anything if it doesn't require a modem-based connection. A demand-dial interface for a VPN may use either a permanent network connection or a dial-up connection.

It is important to remember that the appropriate routes must be configured in RRAS for the VPN servers to properly forward traffic to other networks. This requires a fundamental understanding of IP routing concepts and a familiarity with RRAS configuration (see Figure 7.10).

Figure 7.10 Demand-dial interfaces that establish server-to-server VPN connections are created in the RRAS management console.

Creating a VPN Router

In order to create a VPN, you must first have a VPN router. Creating a VPN router with Windows 2000 is a rather simple task, detailed in Exercise 7.2. VPN connections are available through configuring

Routing and Remote Access Service and will allow clients and other routers to establish VPNs across the Internet, an intranet, or by dial-up. Most VPN implementations will be over the Internet, so that will be our focus in this chapter.

Exercise 7.2 Creating a Windows 2000 VPN Router

1. Run the Routing and Remote Access Management Console by clicking Start, Programs, Administrative Tools, Routing and Remote Access.

2. Expand the tree below your server. If it does not expand and shows a red dot on the server, then you must enable RRAS. Do this by right-clicking on the server and selecting "Configure and Enable Routing and Remote Access."

3. Click "Next," select "Virtual private network (VPN)" server, and then click "Next."

4. The available protocols to be tunneled are displayed, and you are given the opportunity to add more protocols. Click Next when all of the protocols are displayed.

5. The next dialog box contains a list of available network connections (Figure 7.11). Select the interface that is connected to the Internet. If you do not have a specific interface that is connected to the Internet, then select "<no internet connection>." Click "Next" after you have made your selection.

6. If you selected "<no internet connection>" or if you have more than two network adapters, you will now be asked to select the network to which clients must be assigned for addressing purposes. This is the network with which the VPN will be established. Select the appropriate network connection and click "Next" to continue.

7. Now you need to select the method for assigning IP addresses to VPN clients. You can choose either automatic assignment or specify a range of addresses. Select the method you want and click "Next."

8. If you selected DHCP and the network connection you selected earlier has a static IP address, you will see a warning urging you to make sure the DHCP addresses will

Figure 7.11 Selecting the Internet connection during RRAS VPN configuration.

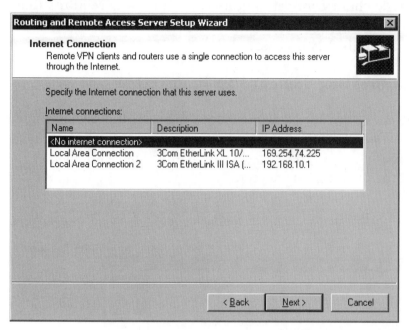

be compatible with the static address of the network connection.

9. If you selected a specified range of addresses, you will now need to create the address ranges to assign to clients.

10. Click "Next" to proceed, and you will see a dialog asking if you want the server to use an existing RADIUS server. For this exercise, we will select No, and click Next to move ahead.

11. Click "Finish," and click "OK" at the message notifying you of the need to configure the DHCP Relay Agent to support relaying DHCP messages from remote access clients.

12. The RRAS service starts, and you now have a VPN server! Expand the tree under your server in the Management Console and you will see the various RRAS components. Click on "Ports" to see the VPN devices. When a VPN connection is active, the status column for that port will change to Active, and you will be able to see details by double-clicking the port.

Connecting a VPN Client

Creating a single client connect is quite easy, and only requires that you know the name or IP address of the VPN router. Exercise 7.3 will take you through this process.

Exercise 7.3 Creating a client VPN connection

1. Right-click the "My Network Places" icon on the desktop and select "Properties."

2. Double-click the "Make New Connection" icon and click "Next" at the welcome screen.

Figure 7.12 Specifying VPN as the type of network connection to create.

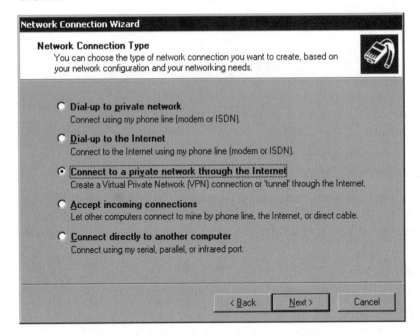

3. Select "Connect to a virtual private network through the Internet" (Figure 7.12).

4. You will now be prompted to select a dial-up connection to use for the VPN connection, or to not dial any connection. Select the appropriate method and click "Next."

5. Enter the IP address or host name of the VPN server or router to which you are connecting and click "Next."

6. Select whether you want the VPN connection to be available for all users or only to the currently logged-on user and click "Next."

7. Give the connection a descriptive name, and uncheck the box at the bottom if you don't want a shortcut to the connection created on the desktop. Click "Next" to continue.

8. A "Connect" dialog box will now appear. Enter a username and password for an account on the remote server that has dial-in permission enabled. Click "Connect" to establish the VPN connection.

9. An icon in the "Network and Dial-up Connections" window is now available for the VPN connection (Figure 7.13). Right-click the new icon and select "Properties."

Figure 7.13 VPN connections are signified by the cloud in the connection icon.

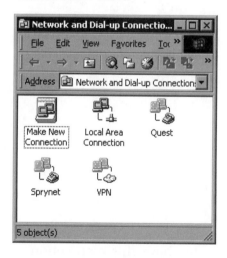

10. The "General" tab can be used to change the IP address of the VPN server, or to configure the connection to connect using another network connection (dial-up to the Internet, for example).

11. Click the "Options" tab to configure whether the connection displays connection progress, prompts for

username and password before connecting, and redial options.

12. Select the Security tab if you need to set specific encryption and authentication protocol settings. To see the advanced settings, select "Advanced" and click the "Settings" button.

13. Click the Networking tab to select the type of VPN and to see the transport protocols, network clients, and services enabled for the connection (Figure 7.14).

Figure 7.14 The Networking tab of a VPN connection Properties enables you to select the type of VPN to which you are connecting.

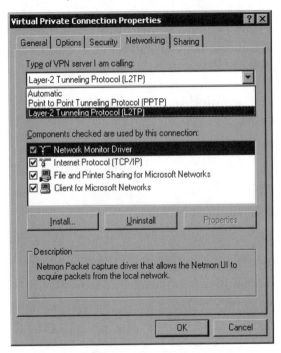

14. Select the Sharing tab if you wish to share this connection with other clients. This may be used in very small branch offices to enable other clients to use the VPN connection. For everything other than very small offices, a server running RRAS would be the appropriate solution.

15. Click "OK" when you are finished configuring the VPN connection.

Tunneling Non-TCP/IP Protocols

Despite the popularity of TCP/IP, some networks still use IPX and NetBEUI on some workstations and servers. These computers can still be accessed via a VPN since these protocols can be tunneled across the Internet. A computer can transmit an IPX or NetBEUI datagram, which will be encapsulated in an IP datagram, transmitted to the remote network, unencapsulated, and delivered to the destination. As you saw in Figure 7.14, you can enable or disable each protocol for use over the VPN connection.

Dial-Up Access

The Windows Remote Access Service (RAS) enables computers to establish modem connections with servers or workstations on a LAN, and makes all network resources on the LAN available to the dial-up client. RAS became very popular with Windows NT 4.0, and those of you who have experience with Windows NT 4.0 RAS will find the Windows 2000 implementation of dial-up network services a bit different. However, you are still dealing with essentially the same devices and services, so it won't take you long to learn how to configure and manage RAS services in Windows 2000.

RRAS first became available as a downloadable add-on for Windows NT 4.0, and enabled Windows NT 4.0 Server to become a full-fledged router and provide VPN services. If you have used RRAS in Windows NT 4.0, then you'll find the transition to Windows 2000 RAS a bit easier, since RAS is integrated into Routing and Remote Access Service (RRAS).

The simplest RAS implementations of RAS will have only one or two modems, and the only hardware configuration required is for the system to recognize and install the modems. An enterprise RAS server, however, may have dozens of modems connected to interface cards that provide a COM port for each modem. In this case, the COM port adapter must be correctly installed before the modems will be recognized by the system. The hardware manufacturer will provide you with drivers and information regarding the configuration of the COM port adapter.

Configuring RAS

When RRAS is enabled on the server (see Exercise 7.2 for information on enabling RRAS), it creates an icon in the Network and Dial-up Connections window (see Figure 7.15), which enables you to select modems and ports for inbound access, to change users' connection permissions, and to configure network protocols, clients, and services.

Figure 7.15 An Incoming Connections icon is created when RRAS is enabled.

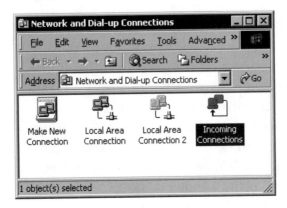

To change the ports available for incoming connections, right-click the "Incoming Connections" icon and select "Properties." The "Properties" dialog box will list all of the available modems and ports, and the check box beside each item will indicate whether it is enabled for incoming connections (see Figure 7.16). The layouts of the Users and Networking tabs are similar, with check boxes designating which users have dial-in permissions and which network protocols, clients, and services are bound to incoming connections.

Within the RRAS Management Console you can view the status of RAS modems in the list of ports (see Figure 7.17) and see the details of a port by double-clicking it. The detailed status provides

Figure 7.16 Configuring ports for inbound access.

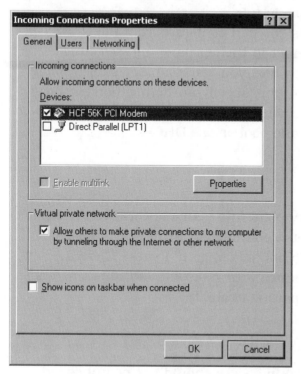

Figure 7.17 RAS port status is viewed in the RRAS Management Console.

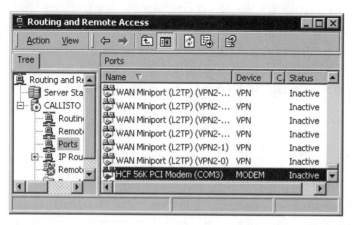

information on the connection speed, bytes in and out statistics, error statistics, and protocols in use.

There are several options you can configure from the RRAS console by right-clicking the server in the left pane and selecting "Properties." From this dialog box, you can enable/disable remote access, enable/disable IP routing, specify authentication methods, authentication providers, accounting providers, and whether to assign IP address from a static pool or use DHCP.

Security Concerns

Since RAS provides an entry point into your network, you need to make certain that an acceptable level of security is established so that unauthorized users are not able to gain access. There are several things you can do to reduce your risks without imposing additional administration or impairing usability.

Secure the Phone Number

Phone numbers used for dial-in access should not be published. Since this is the first thing an intruder needs in order to attempt a RAS break-in, the number should not be readily available to anyone who searches for it. This is one example of why it is advantageous to have Windows NT or Windows 2000 on the laptop computers that have dial-up connections configured. In order to see the dial-up configuration to get the number, an intruder must first be able to log on to the system. A stolen laptop running Windows 95/98 will not provide much of a challenge for a savvy user to get the dial-up information.

User Accounts

Users must be given dial-in permission, which is not granted by default when a user account is created. It is beneficial to grant dial-in permission only to those who actually need it, instead of giving it to everyone, since intruders need to compromise a username and password to gain access. The risk of having an account compromised is greater if a hacker can select any user account for RAS access. If only one of every ten users has dial-in permission, any attempts at brute force will be less likely to succeed, since there is only a one-in-ten chance the account they are trying to compromise can even use RAS.

Password security is also very important. Please see the section in this chapter on Internet security for more information regarding passwords.

Account lockout is another feature that you will want to have enabled to secure a VPN server. This is not related to the account lockout feature that is associated with the user account on the Windows domain. With account lockout enabled, attempts by unauthorized users to establish a VPN connection will be thwarted after a specified number of bad password attempts. Unfortunately, this feature can only be configured by editing the registry on the RAS server. Set the MaxDenials entry to the number of failed attempts to allow before account lockout in the following registry key:

```
HKEY_LOCAL_MACHINE\SYSTEM\CurrentControlSet\Services\RemoteAccess
\Parameters\AccountLockout
```

The ResetTime (mins.) value is set to 48 hours by default, and specifies the length of time before the failed attempts counter is reset. To reset a user account that has been locked out, delete the following registry key:

```
HKEY_LOCAL_MACHINE\SYSTEM\CurrentControlSet\Services\RemoteAccess
\Parameters\AccountLockout\domain name:user name
```

A malicious individual can use the account lockout feature to deny VPN services to authentic users. If someone obtains valid usernames, they can simply make multiple bad log-on attempts and cause the account to be locked out. Although they have not gained access to your network, they have denied service to an authorized user and have created some work for you. If this becomes a problem, you would have to pursue a time-consuming investigation to determine who is causing the problem.

Authentication and Encryption

There are a number of encryption and authentication methods that can be configured on a Windows 2000 server providing RAS services. Windows 2000 includes some new protocols, such as MS-CHAP version 2 (Microsoft Challenge Handshake Authentication Protocol), and EAP (Extensible Authentication Protocol) that are not compatible with legacy Windows systems, so you will have to enable other protocols to support them.

Caller ID and Callback

If you have a known set of numbers from which users will be calling, you can enable caller ID security in Windows 2000. Caller ID security is dependent upon the proper hardware and drivers to support it, so you will need to do a little homework before enabling it. If caller ID security is enabled, the user must be calling from a specified phone number for the connection to be accepted. For VPN access, caller ID can be enabled to accept connections only from specific IP addresses. Caller ID security will be applicable for home users who dial in to the corporate network, but will not be a good option for mobile users since the phone numbers from which they dial are always changing.

Outsourcing Dial-up Access

Since using VPN connections provides secure access to your network over the Internet, you have the option of using an ISP to provide mobile users access to your LAN. Many organizations maintain their own remote access servers, which requires a significant hardware investment and ongoing maintenance. Additionally, remote users out of the local calling area must connect using long distance or a toll-free number. The cost of these items, in addition to the monthly cost of the phone lines, floor space for equipment, etc. can easily be greater than a flat monthly fee per user charged by a national ISP.

Outsourcing dial-up services can provide you with some significant savings, but there are a few issues that can create more support work if outsourcing is not carefully planned and deployed. First of all, the provider you select must have an easy method for users to select the phone number that is local. When a user travels from one city to another, it is not reasonable to expect him or her to look up the dial-up number for that city and manually change the configuration. Several of the national ISPs provide software that keeps a database of dial-up numbers so users can easily find and dial a local number. This is definitely an option you want to look for when selecting a dial-up provider.

You will also need to create VPN connections on every client that will be using this method to access your network. This will require either the time of support personnel, detailed instructions for users to follow, or development of an automated process. It is important to know how this will be accomplished before you plan a timeline for the project to outsource dial-up access. Additionally, support personnel must be trained in order to assist users with problems they may experience. The ISP will handle any issues regarding dial-up access to their network, but any problems with establishing a VPN connection must be resolved internally.

RADIUS

RADIUS (Remote Authentication Dial-in User Service) is a standards-based protocol defined in RFCs 2138 and 2139 that provides accounting, authentication, and authorization services in a distributed dial-up networking environment. RADIUS is most commonly used by Internet service providers, and enables a dial-up server acting as a RADIUS client to receive user authentication and authorization from a RADIUS server.

Windows 2000 RAS includes RADIUS client capabilities, enabling deployment in RADIUS environments. RADIUS authentication and accounting can be configured separately, so you can utilize either component or both depending on your needs. These items are configured on the Security tab of the server Properties dialog box in the RRAS Management Console.

Windows 2000 Internet Authentication Service (IAS) provides the RADIUS server component. IAS will enable you to contract with an ISP that will provide Network Access Servers (NAS) to which your users can connect when they are mobile. Using RADIUS, the NAS will contact your Windows 2000 server to authenticate your users and report accounting information. The advantages are: you are able to control which users are authorized to use the ISP's network, and data regarding usage of the service is up-to-date on your system.

Security for Internet-Connected Networks

Connectivity to the Internet presents several challenging security issues to networks of all sizes. Security must be addressed from several different layers; it is important to review current information about the systems you maintain on a regular basis. Good security is not a project that lasts for a definite period of time, but an ongoing concern that will require periodic research and scheduled reviews.

Types of Attacks

There are several different methods that can be used to compromise your network security, so let's take a quick look at each. It is important that you are aware of and address each kind of potential threat to your network, because disregarding just one can make you vulnerable.

Social Engineering

This is a popular method used to get an authorized user to divulge his or her password. Many hacker stories are colored with incidents of how easy it was to simply call a user and obtain his or her password by pretending to be from the IT department and asking for their current password. With the popularity of e-mail, it is now easier than ever to engage in social engineering, since it takes less time to send an e-mail to numerous users than to call them.

The only way to guard against this type of attack is to periodically remind users that they should never give their password to anyone, and that IT will never ask for it. Additionally, users should be instructed to notify the IT or security department if they encounter password solicitation.

Once hackers have a valid username and password, they may be able to exploit system bugs to gain access to an account with administrative privileges. Accordingly, it is important to keep your systems current with the latest hotfixes and service packs to prevent a user from doing this.

Social engineering can also be used to obtain dial-up numbers for remote access. If procedures are not in place to control the distribution of dial-up information, support personnel will usually give the information to anyone who asks, including unauthorized users. As mentioned earlier in this chapter, dial-up numbers should not be published for perusal to everyone in the company, but should be given only to those individuals who are authorized to use dial-up services.

Account Thievery

A username and password can easily be stolen if the information is sent over the network in clear text. A government system break-in was recently publicized, and this method was used to steal the administrator's username and password when he logged in via FTP from a remote location to move some files. Telnet and FTP are perhaps the two most common applications that present a security risk for account thievery.

There are a few ways to guard against account thievery, the most important of which is education. All users, especially administrators, should understand which applications are safe to use from remote locations. Although you can take steps to disable the use of insecure applications from remote locations, an individual with admin privileges may be able enable them without the knowledge of others.

Although remote use of insecure applications is particularly vulnerable to account thievery, it can also occur within the confines of your own network. An individual with access to a wiring closet or an unused jack could place a device on the network that records traffic, which could be analyzed later to find usernames and passwords. Authorized users can even run software on their PCs to gather network traffic in an effort to steal an administrator's password. As you can see, use of applications that send unencrypted passwords can be dangerous even within the bounds of your network, so good physical security is important to thwart account thievery.

Some of the best ways to protect against account thievery are to use switches, VPNs, and IPSec. This will effectively eliminate the possibility of account thievery by network sniffers, since all data transmitted across the network, including clear-text passwords, is encrypted.

There are some security technologies that require the user to provide a number from a small device that periodically (every 30 seconds or so) generates a new number based on a secret algorithm. This number is checked against a server that also knows the algorithm, and authentication is granted accordingly. While these devices control access through authorized methods of access, they do not control access through unauthorized methods of access and they may not encrypt traffic. Accordingly, a network sniffer on a network could steal a clear-test username and password after the authentication is established, which could be used to log on by dialing an unauthorized remote access number or connecting directly to an unused network jack.

Brute Force

This method is also sometimes referred to as a *dictionary attack,* and utilizes a program to repeatedly attempt system logons using every password specified in the dictionary. Theoretically, a program could generate and attempt logons with every possible combination of characters, but it would take so long that, currently, it isn't very feasible. Lengthy, complex passwords and account lockouts are the two primary methods of securing against brute force attacks. Other, more extreme measures, such as limiting user logons to certain workstations, can be implemented if necessary.

Denial of Service

Denial of service attacks take various forms, and are designed to render a system unusable to authorized users by overloading it or causing it to fail. There are two types of denial of service attacks: exploiting the intended functionality of a system, and exploiting system defects.

For instance, a malicious user could run an application that continuously sends e-mail messages with large file attachments to a specific e-mail address. This abuses the intended functionality of an e-mail server, and at the least will cause the e-mail server to respond more slowly to users. If the attachments contained one or more viruses, virus-scanning software on the attacked e-mail server would also add to system utilization and further erode system performance. Additionally, the targeted mailbox will quickly exceed any size limitations imposed by the administrator and deny additional use to the mailbox owner. If the attack continues long enough, it can also cause the e-mail server to fail due to running out of free disk space or exceeding a maximum database size.

There are too many possible abuses of system functionality to list all of them. Almost every system device and application is vulnerable to this type of attack. The important things are to know that they can occur, to understand the applications and devices on your network so that you can recognize when it is happening, and to have a plan for blocking attacks when they are identified.

Many client/server applications have flaws that cause them to crash when they receive certain data, and hackers will use these bugs to perpetrate a denial of service attack. Good software companies will provide patches, service packs, or hotfixes to eliminate defects as they are discovered, so it is important to periodically review the available updates for applications you have in service on your network. This is perhaps one of the easiest things that can be done to enhance network security.

Application Exploit

An application exploit is an attack that utilizes vulnerable system or application architecture to do something it was not intended to do. In the early days of the Internet, this type of attack was very commonly used against poorly written UNIX-based e-mail server software to cause it to run commands with system privileges. The most common exploits currently take advantage of Web browsers, application macros, and e-mail applications. Malicious macros are typically classified as viruses, and most virus protection software is designed to recognize and repair infected files. Again, the importance of updating the applications in use on your network cannot be emphasized enough. As applications add new features, they become vulnerable in new ways, so it is important to apply the latest fixes from vendors, as well as maintain current virus definitions.

Automated

Users can be tricked into running an application on their computer that will damage files or compromise security. This is commonly called a Trojan horse method since it encourages the user to run a program that has a motive other than the obvious one. An executable that displays an amusing animation or game could also install service on a computer that makes its files available to a remote user, and could send an e-mail message to the perpetrator to report the IP address of the computer on which it has been installed. These attacks can be delivered via e-mail or Internet download, so it is important to educate users about the security risks of running unknown software. Again, these are commonly classified as viruses, and up-to-date virus protection software will help protect your systems from this type of attack.

Physical Access

Although it is not obvious that physical security is important when discussing Internet security issues, physical points can be used to provide entry to unauthorized users on the Internet. For instance, a user with access to a server room may be able to install an application or disable security features if a server console is logged-on with administrative privileges. And as mentioned earlier, a network sniffer could be placed in an insecure wiring closet to capture data for analysis at a later time, which may yield information enabling an unauthorized log-on over the Internet. So while physical access is by definition not an Internet security risk, it can be used as a beginning step in the process to compromise your systems over the Internet.

Unknown

Undoubtedly, the future will bring new ways for hackers to infiltrate networks. Being aware of potential threats is the first and most important step in implementing good security. It is extremely important that you stay informed of the risks associated with the infrastructure, applications, and users on your network so that you can address new types of attacks in a timely manner.

Table 7.3 Network Attacks and Methods to Defend Against Them

To Protect Against	Use This Defense
Physical	Building access policies, locked doors, disabled ports
Denial of Service	Update software, firewall, NAT, plan for contingencies
Social Engineering	User and support personnel education
Account Thievery	IPSec, VPN, education, physical security
Brute Force	Account lockout policies, disable unused accounts
Application Exploit	Update software, application security, firewall, NAT
Automated	Education, virus protection software, application security

Types of Defenses

So now that you understand how your systems can be attacked, it's time to discuss how they can be protected. Each layer of your network—physical, network, and applications—must be addressed to ensure security. You will need to employ several different technologies and implement policies and procedures to make certain that security is enforced properly.

Education

Perhaps the most important thing that can be done to enhance network security is to promote education of network security issues by training or self-study. Network administrators are not the only ones who should be concerned about education, but users, IT managers, and executives should also have an appropriate understanding.

Users need to be adequately trained about procedures they will need to follow because they will attempt to do it "the old way" if they have problems. They also need to understand the risks that are associated with recording passwords on paper, giving passwords to social engineers, etc. Since users are in control of the majority of systems on your network, it would be a big mistake to ignore the need to educate those users.

Network administrators obviously need to understand the technical details of network security and how to make the network as secure as is reasonable. Managers and executives, on the other hand, need to be generally aware of security issues so that security-related projects can get the proper priority for allocation of resources. Security projects are usually an easy sell to corporate executives who generally have a good understanding of the value of the organization's data. They often don't realize how vulnerable it is, though, and will go to great lengths to secure that valuable data when adequately informed.

Application Security

Various client and server applications have security settings that will help prevent unauthorized access and violation of system integrity. Web browsers, for instance, can be configured to implement certain restrictions depending on the Web site being viewed. Database servers often have user accounts separate from LAN access, and a hacker may simply try to break into a database without bothering to steal a LAN user account. Understanding the vulnerabilities and capabilities of your client and server applications is crucial to providing a secure network environment.

Physical Security

Access to wiring closets, server rooms, and even offices by unauthorized users presents a tremendous security risk. Keeping doors locked and unused network ports disabled are starting points. Many corporate buildings have security personnel and require badges for access. If the enforcement of building access is lax, intruders won't need to attack via the Internet; they will just walk in and attach a laptop computer at a vacant desk.

Firewalls, Proxy Servers, and NAT

Many organizations implement firewall software on a server or router that is configured with rules that determine what type of traffic is allowed to pass between their network and the Internet. Firewalls enable administrators to completely block traffic on specific ports, or to filter certain types of traffic on specific ports. Typically, firewalls are configured to deny all traffic except for the ports specified by the administrator, and separate rules can be defined for both inbound and outbound network traffic. Figure 7.18 shows very generally how a firewall works, with traffic being filtered by the rules configured on the firewall device.

Proxy servers are used to process all Internet traffic, and can log information about the Internet sites your users are accessing. Proxy servers can also fill the role of a firewall by limiting the types of traffic that are allowed to pass between networks. Proxy servers can also be used to reverse host or reverse proxy WWW and FTP sites from internal servers to the Internet. Reverse hosting and reverse

Figure 7.18 Firewalls filter both inbound and outbound Internet traffic.

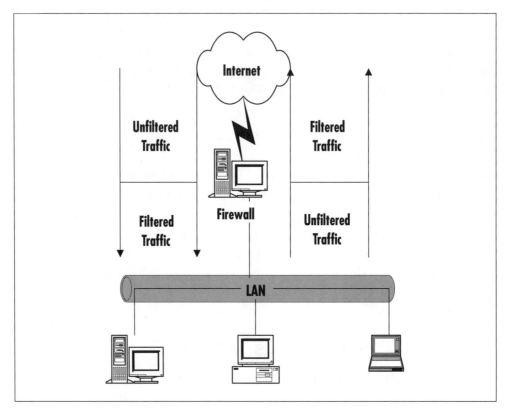

proxying provide a limited measure of security since users can never access your internal servers directly.

Network address translation (NAT) is a service provided by a server or router that enables networks utilizing private IP address ranges to communicate on the Internet. The NAT host has two network interfaces, one connected to the Internet with a registered IP address and one on the local network. Systems on your network are configured to use the NAT device as the gateway, and it handles the traffic by translating the source network address to that of its Internet-connected interface. When the remote host replies, the NAT

For Managers

TCP/IP and Ports

TCP/IP uses software ports to direct network traffic received by a computer to the appropriate application. Applications that use TCP/IP to communicate are assigned default ports so that other computers can easily access services by establishing a session on the default port. For instance, Web servers use port 80 by default, so Web browsers try to establish sessions using port 80 unless otherwise specified. Applications can be configured to use ports other than the default, however, which can be either a security strength or weakness depending on the circumstances. Firewalls and proxy servers can specify exactly which ports are allowed to exchange traffic between your network and the Internet. By keeping the number of allowed ports to a minimum, you can secure many of your applications from external attacks.

A firewall will not protect your network from every type of attack since it does not block all traffic, but it will limit your risk significantly. For example, if your organization utilizes VPNs for mobile users to access the network, the firewall must be configured to allow VPN connections. If an unauthorized user obtains a valid username and password and establishes a VPN connection, the firewall then does nothing to inhibit the intruder, since the intruder is a virtual node on the network.

device forwards the traffic to the computer on your network that established the session. Since computers on the Internet cannot directly access your computers, they cannot initiate a session with them, and thus cannot easily attack them. Windows 2000 RRAS can perform NAT, and Microsoft Proxy Server is a BackOffice product that can be purchased separately.

Updating Software

As has been mentioned numerous times thus far in this chapter, updating operating systems and applications with the latest service packs and hotfixes is very critical. As vendors become aware of security vulnerabilities within their software, they often provide appropriate updates to address the security concerns of their customers. Once an application flaw is discovered, it quickly becomes widely publicized and is available to anyone who wishes to find a back door into your systems. Keeping software up-to-date is perhaps the easiest thing you can do to improve system security.

Most software publishers maintain updated security-related information on their Web sites. The latest information regarding Microsoft products can be found at http://www.microsoft.com/technet/security/default.htm.

Access Permissions

Applying access permissions to resources is important so that a successful intruder will not have access to everything. If the perpetrator is not able to compromise an administrative account, access permissions will protect files that are not available to the account that has been stolen. You should limit the use of the Everyone and Domain Users groups, as well as the Guest account. Refer to Figure 7.19 to see the user account Properties Dial-in tab, where dial-in permission is denied or granted.

The most secure way to implement access permissions is to deny access unless it is explicitly needed. This is especially true for dial-in privileges. By limiting remote access permissions, you will limit the number of accounts available to steal by a hacker who wants to compromise your network by creating a VPN.

Figure 7.19 Specifying remote access permissions for dial-in and VPN connections.

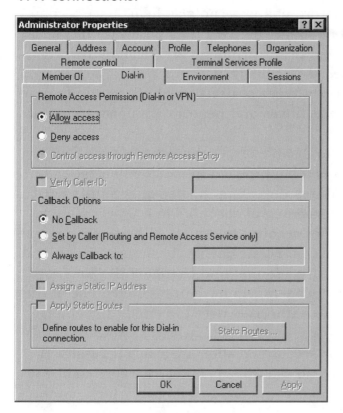

User Account Security

Users should have a fundamental understanding of the types of passwords that provide good security, as well as the discipline to not write their passwords where an intruder could find it. Additionally, administrators can implement minimum password lengths, periodic password changes, and custom password filters. However, forcing difficult, lengthy, and oft-changed passwords can tempt users to write them down since they are more difficult to remember. Be cautious about making password requirements that, although they may seem to be tightening security, will effectively loosen it.

Additionally, administrators can help secure user accounts from brute force attacks by imposing account lockout policies. Requiring periodic password changes can also help, since a compromised account can no longer be used if its password has been changed. Using Group Policies in Windows 2000 configures account lockout policies. Accordingly, account lockout settings can be different for various types of users, enabling you to impose tighter restrictions on executives and network administrators, for example.

It is also important to disable or delete user accounts that are no longer needed. This is a big problem in many organizations, and policies and procedures regarding the use of accounts need to address the decommissioning of accounts in a timely manner. If a perpetrator can gather account information, he or she may be able to identify a user account that has not been used for several months and trick support personnel into changing the password for them. At this point, invaders will have unrestricted use of the account since there is no authorized user to periodically change the password.

Strong procedures for account creation are also a necessity. A hacker should not be able to call up support services pretending to be a manager and have an account created. Proper written or otherwise secure authorization should be necessary for the creation of new accounts.

Encryption

With the arrival of IPSec in Windows 2000, hackers will have a tremendous challenge ahead of them to break into networks that utilize the encryption it provides. Using VPNs for remote access and IPSec for all LAN traffic will effectively secure your network from any intrusion by individuals who try to gather information with network sniffers. See Chapter 6 for additional information on implementing IPSec on Windows 2000 computers.

Summary

There are many choices to be made when considering Internet access for your network. You must determine which type of access will best suit your needs and budget, whether it is dial-up, ISDN, leased line, or one of the newer technologies such as cable and ADSL modems. Each method has advantages and disadvantages, which can vary depending on your needs and your location. Some of the access methods, such as cable and ADSL modems, are not currently available in all areas, but will be available in most metropolitan areas soon.

Windows 2000 has several Internet connection technology improvements, including NAT functionality in RRAS, a new VPN based on RFC-standard technologies, IPSec, Internet Connection Sharing, and more. Establishing a secure and functional connection to the Internet is easier than ever, and many organizations will be using Windows 2000 to provide secure services to remote users.

A permanent Internet connection brings with it the potential for hackers to access your network from their own homes. It is extremely important that network administrators understand the various types of attacks that can occur to disrupt services or gain unauthorized entry, and further, to understand the defenses to implement to protect against each type of attack. While some defenses are implementations of applications such as proxy servers and network encryption, other defenses include policies, procedures, education, and simply locking doors.

FAQs

Q: What are the primary uses of VPNs?

A: VPNs are used to create secure connections between computers across the Internet or another untrusted network. VPN connections can be initiated by mobile users who have established dial-up connections to the Internet via an ISP, or by another server or router that is connected to the Internet. If a server-to-server VPN is established with Windows 2000, the LANs to which it is connected will become a virtual LAN if the routing is configured properly.

Q: Cable, ADSL, leased line, ISDN...There are so many ways to connect to the Internet. Which type should I use?

A: You will need to learn about the advantages, disadvantages, availability, and costs of each in order to select the connection that best suits your needs. Don't rely solely on the information provided to you by the companies who are selling the services. Even leased lines, which are traditionally the most reliable, still occasionally experience downtime. The newest types of connections (ADSL and cable modems) may suffer from inexperienced service technicians as well as immature policies and procedures regarding system administration and maintenance, which could result in unwanted downtime.

Q: How can I secure my systems against malicious attacks if my network is connected the Internet?

A: There are a number of technologies, policies, and procedures that need to be in place to provide adequate security in an Internet-connected environment. At the very minimum, you will need a firewall, which is software that allows or denies IP traffic between networks based on rules configured for various ports. It is also important to keep operating system and application software updated so that you have the latest security-related fixes available. This applies to both server and desktop applications.

Q: What is the best way for a few computers in a small office to access the Internet via dial-up?

A: A Windows 2000 computer can share an Internet connection with other computers, providing DHCP, DNS, and NAT services. This is not intended for use on networks with more than just a few computers, so be sure to understand its capabilities and limitations before proposing it as a solution. Chapter 8 covers Internet Connection Sharing in detail.

Q: How can I use Windows 2000 to connect a larger network to the Internet?

A: By using Routing and Remote Access Service, a component of Windows 2000, you can configure a computer to establish a connection to the Internet and perform routing for your network. RRAS can also perform NAT services if your network uses private IP addresses.

Q: What is RADIUS, and why would I need it?

A: RADIUS is a protocol used by dial-in servers to authenticate and collect accounting data about usage. If you have a large number of dial-in users, you can contract with an ISP who uses RADIUS to provide dial-in servers, which will utilize RADIUS to contact your Windows 2000 computer for user authentication. Accounting information is also sent to your server, providing you with detailed, updated information about dial-up sessions established by your users. Of course, ISPs may also use Windows 2000 RADIUS, since the RAS component includes a RADIUS client.

Chapter 8

Connecting Small Offices and Home Offices to the Internet

Introduction

Using Windows 2000 to connect your small network to the Internet is remarkably easy. Connecting your network to the Internet was more complicated with Windows 95 and Windows NT. You had to purchase additional software (or use freeware), download Routing and RAS Server, or use a Proxy Server such as Microsoft's Proxy Server.

Windows 2000 and Windows 98 (Second Edition) make it much simpler by providing "Connection Sharing," which allows you to quickly connect several computers to each other, and to the Internet. The cost savings for a small company connecting to the Internet with this technology can be significant. Using one phone line and one Internet account, a small group of users can access the Internet for research, faxing and e-mail — without added expense or a high level of technical expertise. There are two basic ways to connect a small office or home office to the Internet: either through a routed connection or through a translated connection (often referred to as NAT). This chapter will focus on the latter — but even then, you have choices. Windows 2000 provides two ways to configure a translated connection. For a simple workgroup situation where there are no domain controllers, DNS servers, or DHCP servers on the network, the Internet Connection Sharing feature of Network and Dial-up Connections can be enabled. If a more sophisticated configuration is needed, Routing and Remote Access Service (RRAS) can be configured to use NAT (Network Address Translation). We will take a look at each of these, and compare the two, so that you can make the best choice for your own situation.

The cost of providing Internet connectivity to a small network should be minimal, as most offices already have at least one computer with a modem connected to the Internet. At the end of this chapter, we will walk you through the steps involved in getting your networked computers connected to the world "outside."

Connecting a Workgroup to the Internet

Providing your employees with access to the Internet has many advantages. They will be able to communicate with clients, suppliers and others outside the business via e-mail. The Web contains a wealth of research resources that will save trips to the library or phone calls to ferret out needed information. They can engage in live conversations using Web phone technology, without the company incurring high long distance charges. Sophisticated software programs even make it possible to use video-conferencing or project collaboration with team members who are miles — or continents — away.

In the past, if you had a small office with only a few computers operating as stand-alone systems or connected in a peer-to-peer network, there was no easy and inexpensive way to provide Internet access to all of them. Many businesses resorted to the installation of a modem and phone line for each computer, and to paying for multiple accounts with an Internet Service Provider (ISP), as well as extra phone company charges. Others bought expensive routers or struggled with difficult-to-configure proxy software. And others, unable to justify the cost, designated one computer as the shared Internet machine, and employees had to wait in line in order to use it.

Now, if you use Windows 2000 (or Windows 98SE) as your operating system, setting up a workgroup and then connecting all the computers to the Internet through one computer's modem or ISDN/DSL adapter is simple and requires no extra hardware or software. In fact, access sharing is a new, compelling reason to network a small company's computers that were previously operating in a stand-alone capacity.

WARNING

When you connect your small network to the Internet, you are providing more than just a way for your users to get to the outside world. You also provide a way for "outsiders" to get to you! Refer to Chapter 6, "Secure TCP/IP Connections," for information on how to protect your newly connected LAN from hackers and snoopers.

Internet Connection Sharing (ICS)

With ICS, all the computers in your workgroup will be able to access the Internet simultaneously. ICS works with e-mail clients, Web browsers, and most other Internet client software. Different users can access different Web sites (or FTP sites, mail servers, etc.) at the same time, without interfering with one another's activities.

What Do You Need to Use ICS?

In order to use ICS to connect your small network to the Internet, you must have one computer with an Internet connection. This can be either a dial-up or dedicated connection. Only this Internet-capable computer must be running Windows 2000 (or Windows 98SE); the other computers on the network can be running Windows 95 or 98 (although using Windows 95 will require some extra work since it doesn't support automatic IP addressing). Many small businesses and home networks will use ICS with regular analog phone lines and a standard modem, but it will also work with an ISDN terminal adapter or other high-speed access methods.

The Internet-capable computer must also have a connection through a Network Interface Card (NIC) to the Local Area Network (your workgroup). Internet sharing must be enabled on this NIC. Later in this chapter, we will walk through the steps necessary to enable ICS and configure the other computers to go through the ICS gateway from your LAN to the Wide Area Network (the Internet). First, though, we will discuss some of the concepts involved in sharing an Internet connection. We will look at characteristics of ICS as it applies to Windows 2000 and Windows 98SE, and then we will examine NAT (Network Address Translation), which is available as part of the Windows 2000 Server operating systems. You will then be able to determine which option will work best for you.

NOTE

If you have a one-way Internet connection device, such as certain types of cable modems that download data via the cable connection and use a separate dial-up modem for uploading, you may not be able to use ICS. However, you can use ICS with external one-way cable modems that incorporate the dial-up modem and then connect to a NIC installed in the computer.

Internet Connection Sharing uses the TCP/IP protocol and utilizes IP autoconfiguration, in conjunction with private network addressing, to make it possible for your workgroup computers to simultaneously use the same dial-up or always-on connection. Let's take a look at each of those components, and how they are used in Windows ICS.

TIP

Before attempting to set up connection sharing, you should ensure that you can access the Internet from the ICS host computer. Much time and effort can be wasted troubleshooting the ICS connection when the problem is actually that the primary computer has lost its connection to the Internet.

TCP/IP Protocol

For computers to communicate with each other on a network, they must all be running a common *protocol*. A protocol is just a set of rules governing the communication process. Most large networks, and an increasing number of smaller ones, use the Transmission Control Protocol/Internet Protocol (TCP/IP) as their common "language." This is due in large part to the fact that TCP/IP is the protocol of the Internet, and must be used if you want to connect a computer to that global network of networks.

In order to use ICS, you will need TCP/IP installed on the computer that connects to the Internet, and bound to both the Internet connection device (modem or ISDN/DSL adapter) and to the NIC that connects the computer to the LAN. You will also have to install TCP/IP on the other computers on your local network, even if they have previously been communicating with one another using a different protocol, such as NetBEUI (NetBIOS Extended User Interface).

Checking Protocol Settings

To ensure that TCP/IP is on your computers, double-click the "My Network Places" icon on the desktop, and click "Network and Dialup Connections." You can also access the same screen from the Start menu: Start | Settings | Network and Dial-up Connections | Local Area Connection.

Right-click your local area connection and select "Properties." You will see a dialog box, like the one shown in Figure 8.1 below.

Figure 8.1 TCP/IP must be installed on the NIC used for your LAN connection.

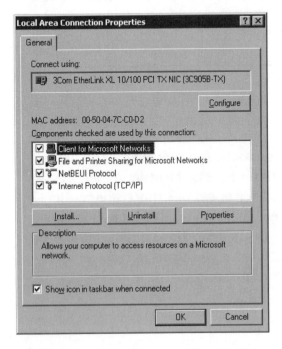

Be sure the TCP/IP protocol is installed for your Local Area connection. If it is not, you can install it by clicking the "Install" button, selecting "Protocol" as the Network Component Type to be installed, and then selecting "Internet Protocol" (TCP/IP). You may be prompted to insert your Windows 2000 CD-ROM, some files will then be copied to your computer, and the new protocol will appear in the Properties box as shown above in Figure 8.1. For more information about TCP/IP, see Chapter 2.

Autoconfiguration IP Addresses versus DHCP

TCP/IP uses a standardized, complex addressing scheme to identify computers and the subnets they belong to on the network. This logical address, called the IP address, is a 32-bit binary number, usually expressed in dotted decimal. Each computer on a network must have a unique IP address, or it will be unable to communicate via the TCP/IP protocol.

What DHCP Does

IP addresses can be manually configured on each computer (called static IPs) or they can be automatically assigned. Administrators who have worked with Windows NT and other major networking operating systems will be familiar with DHCP, or Dynamic Host Configuration Protocol. This is the service which, running on a server, automatically assigns IP addresses to computers that are set up to use the TCP/IP protocol and get their IP addresses from a DHCP server. See Figure 8.2, which shows the TCP/IP properties sheet of a Windows 2000 Professional computer that is configured as a DHCP client.

NT Administrators may be less familiar with a new feature called Automatic Private IP Addressing (APIPA), first available in Windows 98 and now a part of Windows 2000's networking services. It is important to understand what automatic addressing is and how it differs from the address autoconfiguration used by ICS.

Figure 8.2 TCP/IP is set to obtain an IP address automatically using DHCP.

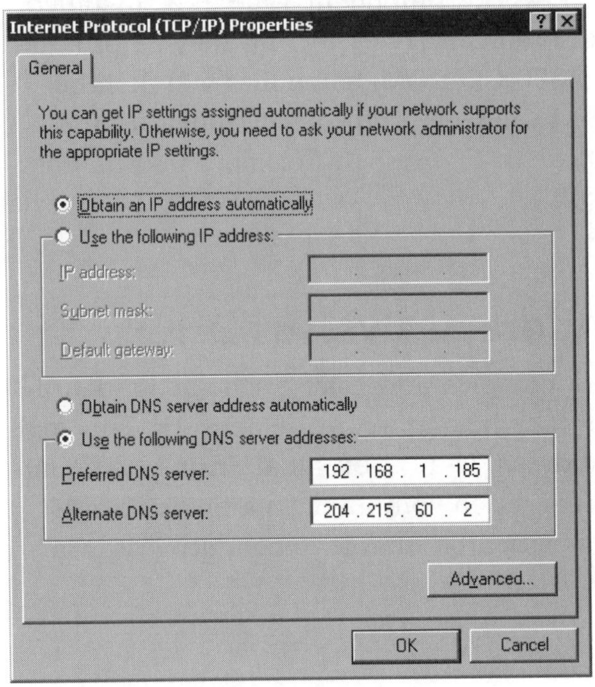

How APIPA Works

APIPA is used in conjunction with DHCP to automate the IP configuration of computers on a TCP/IP network. If a computer's TCP/IP properties are set up to obtain an IP address automatically, when that computer is booted up and comes online it will first attempt to contact a DHCP server. If a DHCP server is found on the network, the computer will go through the process of negotiating to lease an IP address from the range of addresses that has been specified by the administrator on the DHCP server. See Chapter 3 for more information about DHCP and the lease process.

With Windows 95 and NT Server and Workstation clients, if no DHCP server was located, the TCP/IP connection failed. The computer was not able to participate in the network using the TCP/IP protocol, because it had no way of obtaining an IP address. That's where APIPA comes in — with a Windows 2000 (or 98) client, the inability to reach a DHCP server is not fatal. The computer goes to Plan B, assigning itself an address in the range 169.254.0.1 — 169.254.255.254 and the subnet mask of 255.255.0.0 after checking to determine that the address is not being used by another APIPA computer on the network.

NOTE

This range of IP addresses is reserved for use with APIPA, and addresses within this range are not used on the Internet.

This self-assigned address can be used until a DHCP server is located, allowing the computer to communicate on the network, although with some limitations. The computer will only be able to communicate with other computers that are also using APIPA, or that are manually configured with IP addresses on the 169.254.0.0 subnet.

Together, DHCP and APIPA make the configuration and maintenance of a small TCP/IP LAN easier, and provide for more reliable connectivity.

ICS Address Autoconfiguration and the DHCP Allocator

When Internet Connection Sharing is enabled on a computer so that it can connect to the Internet and other computers on its local network can share its connection, that computer becomes a DHCP allocator. It has a pre-set range of IP addresses that it can "hand out" to the other computers as they come online.

A DHCP allocator differs from a DHCP server because its IP address range is predefined, and a Windows 2000 Professional computer or a Windows 98SE computer with ICS enabled can be a DHCP allocator, even though not running a server operating system.

The use of the DHCP allocator for ICS connections also differs from APIPA, where the DHCP-enabled computer assigns itself an address after failing to find a DHCP server. These three concepts all relate to automatically assigning IP addresses, but it is important that you understand the differences between them, and when and where each is used.

Private Network Addresses versus Public Addresses

One of the advantages of using Internet Connection Sharing instead of a routed connection (aside from the cost of the router itself) is the ability to use private IP addresses on your internal network. Instead of having to purchase a block of addresses from your ISP, you only need one valid public address, which will be used by the computer that acts as the gateway from your LAN to the Internet (the Windows 2000 or 98SE computer on which ICS is installed). This can result in substantial savings in time as well as cost, considering the administrative effort involved in changing the internal IP addresses in order to access the Internet.

For more information about how a private or public address is defined, see the section entitled "What is a Private Network Address?" below.

Using Internet Connection Sharing

ICS was designed to be easy to set up and use. On a Windows 2000 Professional or Server computer, you just select a dial-up connection or Virtual Private Network (VPN) connection that you've already configured (for example, your modem connection to your ISP). Then, you enable ICS on the "Internet Connection Sharing" tab (in Windows 2000 Professional) or "Sharing" tab (in Windows 2000 Server). We will walk through these steps one by one as part of the exercise at the end of this chapter.

Using ICS with a VPN Connection

Typically, ICS is used to share a dial-up connection to the Internet. However, you can also share a Virtual Private Network connection using ICS, if you want the ICS client computers to be able to connect to a private network, such as your company network, through a secure "tunnel" over the Internet.

You can set up the VPN connection on the Windows 2000 ICS gateway, using either Point-to-Point Tunneling Protocol (PPTP) or L2TP (Layer 2 Tunneling Protocol), both of which are supported by Windows 2000. The tunneling protocol encapsulates the packets, which can then be using any protocol used on the private LAN (TCP/IP, IPX/SPX or even NetBEUI).

For detailed information on setting up a Virtual Private Network, see Chapter 6.

WARNING

If your connection to the Internet is through a second NIC instead of a modem (for instance, with some types of cable Internet connections), it is very important that you make sure ICS is enabled on the correct network adapter. That is the one adapter that participates on your internal network. If ICS is enabled on the wrong NIC, your computer's DHCP allocator may attempt to assign IP addresses to external computers, which will cause problems for those systems on their own networks.

On-demand Dialing

You have a few options when you configure ICS. You can enable the on-demand dialing feature, which will cause the ICS computer to automatically dial up the Internet connection whenever an ICS client computer tries to start an Internet-dependent program.

For example, if you have a Windows 2000 Professional computer with a modem that's configured to dial up to your Internet Service Provider, you can install ICS on that computer and configure the others on your LAN to use it as their Internet gateway. Then, when someone opens a Web browser on one of the other computers, or clicks "Send and Receive" in an e-mail program,

Administrative Privileges Required

Note that you will not be able to enable or configure Internet Connection Sharing unless you are logged on with an account that has administrative privileges. This could be a reason to reconsider the common practice of making each user a member of the local administrators group on his/her own workstation. If those workstations have their own modems and phone lines, you could end up with multiple shared connections. Best practice is to designate a computer for the ICS host that is not used by anyone for day-to-day production, or if that is not possible, one that is used only by the office manager or network administrator. Even if you do this, there are many other security-related reasons not to automatically assign local administrative privileges to every user who has a computer.

that will signal the ICS computer, if it is offline, to dial up and connect to the ISP. To the user, all this means is a slight delay while the connection is established; if you have a high-speed digital connection type such as an ISDN dial-up account, the delay is not even noticeable.

Configuring Applications and Services

Another option you have when configuring ICS is to configure certain applications and services to work properly across the Internet. Those applications, and certain services such as the Web server service, must be configured on the ICS computer before the connecting computers will be able to use them. This is done by clicking the "Settings" button on the Internet Connection Sharing tab of the connection's property sheet. We will look at this in the Walk through exercise.

ISP Static IP Addressing

Many Internet Service Providers use DHCP on their servers to assign a new IP address to your connection each time you dial up. By default, Windows 2000 will attempt to get an IP address and other TCP/IP information from a DHCP server when making a dial-up connection.

However, some ISPs give you a static address, which never changes. In this case, you must configure TCP/IP on your dial-up connection to use the static address. To do this, you will need to open the properties sheet for the dial-up connection, double-click TCP/IP (or select it and click the "Properties" button) and then enter the static IP address, subnet mask and default gateway addresses given to you by your ISP. When using static addresses, you will also need to check the "Use the following DNS server addresses" check box and enter the address(es) for your ISP's DNS server(s). See the Walkthrough exercise for an illustration of this.

NOTE
_____

ICS acts as a DNS proxy, passing on the internal computers' requests for name resolution to an Internet DNS server and returning the results. It does not act as a WINS proxy; however, Network Address Translation (see "What is NAT?" below) can perform the WINS proxy function.

_____

What Happens When You Enable ICS

There are several things to be aware of when using ICS. By default, when you enable Internet Connection Sharing, the NIC that you are using to connect to your local network is given a new static IP address, 192.168.0.1, with a subnet mask of 255.255.255.0. Unless this happens to be the address it was already assigned to this system on your internal network, this will cause any already existing TCP/IP connections between the ICS computer and the other computers on the LAN to be lost.

The second thing that occurs when you enable ICS on a computer is that it becomes a DHCP allocator for the other computers connecting to the Internet through it. It will assign those computers IP addresses from its preset range. Using ICS, you cannot disable the DHCP allocator nor modify the address range. You also can't configure inbound mappings. To do any of those things, you will need to use NAT to share your Internet connection.

NOTE

Microsoft's documentation on Windows 2000 Internet Connection Sharing repeatedly warns that it is intended for small peer-to-peer networks only, and that it is not recommended for use on a network running Windows 2000 domain controllers, DNS servers, DHCP servers or other computers that are assigned static IP addresses. In these situations, Network Address Translation should be deployed instead (see the section on NAT below).

Network Address Translation (NAT)

The terminology used in Windows 2000 can be confusing, since both ICS and NAT are translated connections that provide addressing and name resolution for a small LAN to connect to the Internet. Although their function is similar, they differ primarily in terms of simplicity and flexibility. ICS lets you get your small network's Internet connection up and running quickly and with a minimum amount of configuration involved. However, it doesn't allow you to make many changes and is not designed to work on a more sophisticated small network.

How NAT Differs from ICS

NAT, on the other hand, can be thought of as ICS's "big brother." It accomplishes the same end result, but gives administrators the ability to customize the configuration to a much greater degree, including changing the range of allocated addresses assigned to the internal computers, and map them to multiple external, public addresses on the Internet. While ICS supports only one interface to the local network, NAT can support multiple interfaces.

TIP

You can set up either a Windows 2000 Professional computer or a Windows 2000 (non-domain controller) server to be an ICS computer. However, NAT is part of the Routing and Remote Access (RRAS) component that is found only on a Windows 2000 server.

What Is NAT?

While Internet Connection Sharing is perfect for the typical home or simple small business network, Microsoft designed its Windows 2000 Network Address Translation protocol with the more sophisticated small business network in mind. NAT is designed to provide an administrator with the flexibility that ICS lacks, so that you can fine-tune the address translation process depending on your organization's needs.

NOTE

Request for Comments (RFC) 1631, available on the Web at http://www.rfc-editor.org/rfc.html, defines the standards for Network Address Translation.

NAT performs three basic activities, and thus can be divided into three elements:

- Address allocation
- Address translation
- Name resolution

Address allocation: the NAT-enabled computer acts as a DHCP allocator (or a very simplified type of DHCP server) for the other computers on the local network that are configured to use DHCP. The NAT computer can assign not only an IP address and subnet masking information, but can also designate the DNS and WINS server addresses.

Address translation: the main function of the NAT-enabled computer is to translate the private IP addresses with corresponding TCP or UDP port numbers to public addresses, and back again, so that packets can travel between the local network and the Internet.

Name resolution: the NAT-enabled computer acts as a DNS and WINS proxy for the rest of the computers on the network. It is not a name resolution server itself, but forwards name resolution requests from the local network to the DNS and WINS servers for which it is configured, and then relays the responses to the internal computers.

NOTE

You cannot run the DNS, WINS or DHCP services when the NAT addressing and name resolution components are enabled. If you need to use these services, you must disable the corresponding NAT component.

Typically, NAT is used to translate multiple private addresses to a single public IP address provided by the ISP. If your ISP has provided you with a block of addresses, NAT can be configured to translate to multiple public addresses.

Setting up the NAT Computer

Setting up NAT is a bit more complicated than enabling ICS. First, you must manually configure the IP address of the NAT computer's LAN network adapter to 192.168.0.1, with a subnet mask of 255.255.255.0. This is done in the TCP/IP Properties for the NIC, in the same dialog box shown in Figure 8.2 in the "ICS" section earlier in this chapter.

NOTE

This is the recommend IP address to work with the default range of IP addresses to be allocated by NAT. You can change the address range, in which case you would typically set the NAT computer's IP address to be the first address in the range.

The next step is to enable Routing and Remote Access. This is done in the RRAS configuration MMC snap-in, accessed through:

Start | Programs | Administrative Tools | Routing and Remote Access

See Figure 8.3 for an illustration of the RRAS console.

Figure 8.3 The Routing and Remote Access MMC console.

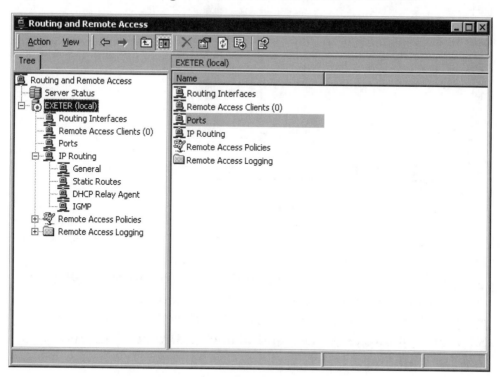

Right-click the name of the server you want to enable with NAT, and click "Configure and Enable Routing and Remote Access" in the context menu. This will open the RRAS wizard, which will guide you through the steps.

Next you must enable routing on your dial-up port. To do this, in the RRAS snap-in, click "Ports" in the console tree, right-click and select Properties, choose the Devices tab, and select the device you want to configure (see Figure 8.4).

Figure 8.4 Configuring the dial-up port for routing.

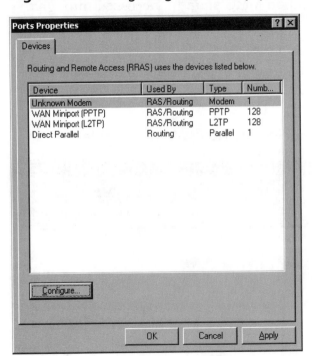

Click "Configure" and select "Demand-dial routing," as shown in Figure 8.5, then click "OK."

Now you have to add a demand-dial interface to your ISP. Once again, go to the RRAS console, and click "Routing Interfaces." Right-click, and choose "New Demand Dial Interface," as shown in Figure 8.6. This will invoke the Demand-dial wizard, which will guide you in setting up the interface.

Figure 8.5 Configuring the device for demand-dial routing connections.

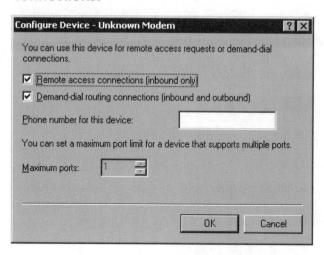

Figure 8.6 Creating a new demand-dial interface.

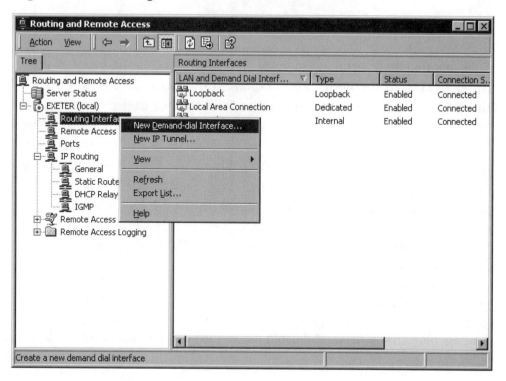

Next you will create a default static route for the interface that connects to the Internet. To do this, in the RRAS console tree, click "Static Routes" and choose "New Static Route." You will see the dialog box shown in Figure 8.7.

Figure 8.7 The New Static Route dialog box.

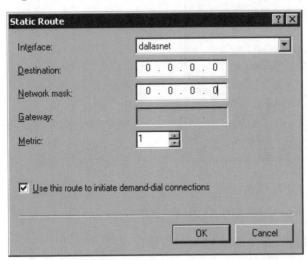

Click on the interface you want to use as the default static route. Enter 0.0.0.0 in the Destination box, and the same in the Network mask box (These settings are used to indicate this is the default route. You may also have other static routes, which will have the IP and subnet information entered. The "Gateway" parameter will be grayed out because this is a demand-dial route). Check the "Use this route to initiate demand-dial connections" check box. Enter 1 for Metric.

Finally, we can add the NAT protocol. In the RRAS console tree, click "General," right-click, and select "New Routing Protocol." Choose "Network Address Translation," as shown in Figure 8.8, and click "OK."

NOTE

If ICS is enabled on this computer, at this point you will see a message box warning that you must disable ICS before you can add NAT.

Figure 8.8 Adding the Network Address Translation routing protocol.

Now it's time to add your Internet connection interface to NAT. In the RRAS console tree, right-click "NAT" and select "New Interface." Click the interface for your Internet connection, and click "OK." On the "General" tab, shown in Figure 8.9, click "Public Interface connected to the Internet," and check the "Translate TCP/UDP headers" check box.

Go through the same process to add your private network interface to NAT, this time selecting "Private interface connected to private network" on the General tab in NAT properties.

In order for the NAT computer to act as a DNS and WINS proxy, you must enable NAT name resolution. To do so, right-click "NAT" in the RRAS console tree, and check both the "WINS" and "DNS" check boxes on the Name Resolution tab, shown in Figure 8-10. For on-demand dialing to occur when one of the internal computers sends a DNS name resolution request, check the "Connect to the public network when a name needs to be resolved" check box

Figure 8.9 Adding your Internet connection interface to NAT.

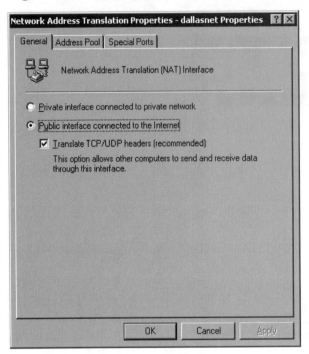

and then select the name of the interface to be used in Demand-dial interfaces.

NOTE

In most cases, you would not want to enable WINS name resolution if the NAT computer is providing address translation for clients to connect to the public Internet. This would be enabled when NAT is used to share a VPN connection to a private network.

The last step is to enable addressing and name resolution. Back in the RRAS console tree, right-click "NAT," and click "Properties." Select the Address Assignment tab, shown in Figure 8.11, and check the "Automatically assign IP addresses by using DHCP" check box.

If you will be using multiple public IP addresses, configure the range (see "Multiple Public Addresses" below).

Figure 8.10 Configuring NAT name resolution.

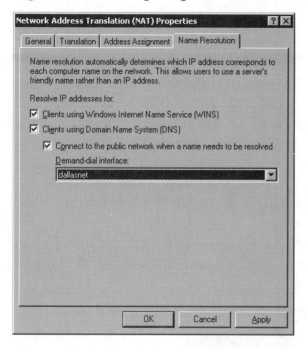

Figure 8.11 Configuring NAT to be a DHCP allocator.

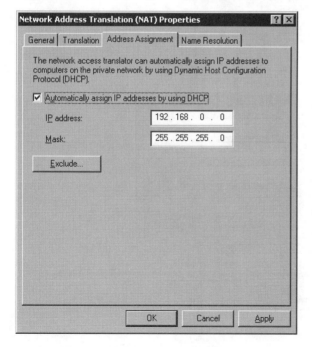

Multiple Public Addresses

Configuring NAT to translate to multiple public addresses requires some knowledge of subnet masking. You must determine whether the range of IP addresses assigned by your ISP can be expressed by an IP address and a mask. For instance: the four public IP addresses 200.100.100.212, 200.100.100.213, 200.100.100.214, and 200.100.100.215 can be expressed as 200.100.100.212 with 255.255.255.252 as the mask. This works when the number of addresses is a power of two.

The alternative method is to enter the starting and ending addresses of the range. This is done in the RRAS configuration MMC snap-in, accessed as noted above.

Double-click "NAT" in the console tree, right-click the interface in the right pane and click "Properties." Choose the Address Pool tab,

Figure 8.12 Entering the range of multiple public IP addresses.

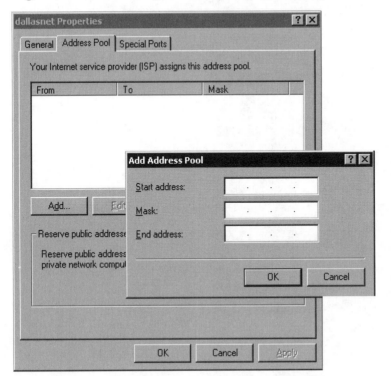

shown in Figure 8.12, click "Add," and enter the range of addresses in the dialog box shown below.

When you have added the address range(s), click OK twice to close the dialog boxes.

Setting up the NAT Client Computers

The other computers on the local network, which will connect to the Internet through the NAT computer, need to have TCP/IP installed and configured to obtain an IP address automatically (as in the "ICS" section above). The NAT computer will also supply them with the subnet mask, default gateway, DNS and WINS server addresses.

An NAT Example

Let's say your small local area network uses the 192.168.0.0 network ID for internal computers, and you purchase a dial-up access account from an ISP, which will assign you one public address when you establish a connection, using DHCP.

The computer on which NAT is enabled has a modem, and connects to the Internet Service Provider. After being authenticated on the network, it is assigned an IP address of 204.215.60.72. This is a legitimate public address, which will be used for the duration of the session by the NAT computer to communicate over the modem with computers on the Internet.

So far, this is the same thing that happens when a stand-alone computer uses a modem to connect to the Internet through an ISP. Here's where NAT comes in, as shown in Figure 8.13.

The NAT computer is also connected to the LAN with a network adapter card, which has been assigned the IP address 192.168.0.1. The other computers on the LAN are using addresses with the same network ID and unique host IDs (192.168.0.x).

A user at the computer whose network card is using the IP 192.168.0.7 wants to connect to a Web site on the Internet, which

Figure 8.13 A small network using NAT to connect to the Internet

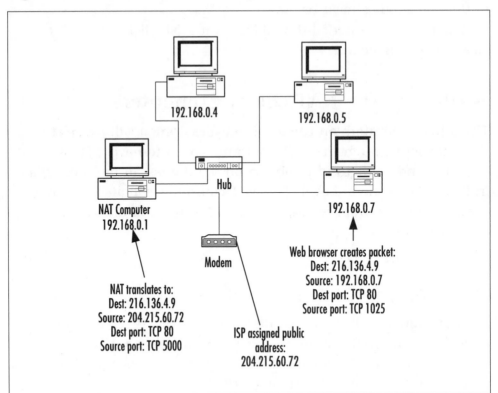

has the IP address 216.136.4.9. He or she opens his or her browser and types in the URL for that Website. Here's what happens:

The user's computer creates a packet with the following header information:

- Destination IP address: 216.136.4.9
- Source IP address: 192.168.0.7 (the originating computer's private address)
- Destination port: TCP port 80
- Source port: TCP port 1025

The packet is sent to NAT, which will translate the addresses of the outgoing packet to:

- Destination IP address: 216.136.4.9
- Source IP address: 204.215.60.72 (the NAT computer's public address)
- Destination port: TCP port 80
- Source port: TCP port 5000

Note that a port is the endpoint in a TCP/IP communication. Because several different applications could be communicating over TCP/IP simultaneously from the same computer (using the same IP address), each application uses a different port number to identify packets sent to and from it. TCP port 80 is the common port used by Web servers, and port 1025 is the port normally used by Web clients to send a request for a Web page to the Web server. NAT maps the internal client's port to port 5000 on the NAT host machine, to identify that particular client's request.

The NAT protocol maintains a mapping table, which in this case will map {192.168.0.7 TCP 1025} to {204.215.60.72 TCP 5000}. Now the translated packet can be sent over the Internet, using the public address, which is "legal" on the global network. When the response is returned with a destination address of 204.215.60.72 TCP 5000, NAT will consult the mapping table and route the response to the computer at 192.168.0.7 on TCP port 1025.

WARNING

NAT works properly only with protocols in which the IP address and port numbers are contained in the headers. Some protocols, such as FTP, store these addresses in the payload instead of the header. Others, such as PPTP, don't use TCP or UDP headers. In these cases, address translation requires additional software, called a NAT editor. Windows 2000 includes NAT editors for the FTP, PPTP and ICMP protocols. Editors for SNMP, LDAP, COM and RPC are not included. (Address translation will not work with IPsec traffic, even with an editor).

What Is a Private Network Address?

We have already mentioned that an advantage of ICS and NAT is the ability to use private IP addresses on your local network. You may be wondering exactly what a private address is for, which addresses are designated as private, and who decides such things. We'll address those questions now.

What Makes an Address "Private?"

We can best answer that question by first taking a look at how IP addresses are assigned. In order for computers to communicate with each other on a TCP/IP network, every computer must have a unique IP address. Duplicate addresses on a TCP/IP network result in the inability of one or both computers to participate on the network. If you set up a small TCP/IP network in your office, it's relatively easy to keep track of the IP addresses you've assigned and make sure each is unique, but the bigger the network, the more difficult it becomes.

Who Assigns IP Addresses?

You can see that, in order for computers all over the world to communicate with each other on a global TCP/IP network (the Internet), there must be some centralized authority to oversee assignment of the addresses and ensure that no two are the same. This duty has been the province of the Internet Network Information Center (InterNIC), an organization charged with handing out IP addresses (or blocks of addresses) to companies and to ISPs for distribution to their customers. These addresses, which are assigned for use on the huge network that is the Internet, are known as "public addresses." Organizations (and individuals) pay a fee to reserve an address or group of addresses when they register a domain name. They may then use those addresses on the Internet, with assurance that no one else will be using the same addresses.

The InterNIC also designated several sets of IP addresses as "reserved for private use." The purpose of this was to provide addresses that organizations could use to assign IP addresses to computers on their isolated networks (not connected to the Internet), without the risk that they were using an address that already "belonged" to another organization. This means you do not have to incur the expense of paying to reserve addresses if they will be used for your internal network only. These are referred to as private addresses.

If you use an IP address that is not designated as private, without registering it with InterNIC (or having it assigned by your ISP, which has registered it), this is called "illegal addressing." The groups of addresses that you may legally use on your private network are shown in Table 8.1.

Table 8.1 Private IP Address Ranges

Network ID	Beginning Address	Subnet Mask
10.0.0.0	10.0.0.1	255.0.0.0
172.15.0.0	172.15.0.1	255.240.0.0
192.168.0.0	192.168.0.1	255.255.255.0

NOTE

RFC (Request for Comments) 1597, available on the Web, contains more information about the allocation of private addresses.

When Should You Use a Private Address or Public Address?

Using private addresses on your LAN has several advantages. You don't have to pay to register a separate public address for every computer on your network; not only does this benefit you, it also leaves more available addresses in the quickly-shrinking pool of unassigned public addresses.

The problem is that private addresses cannot communicate with computers on the Internet — at least, not without some help. If your internal network uses private addresses, the only way they can send to and receive from Internet locations is by using a Network Address Translator, which translates outgoing packets with private addresses into public addresses to be sent over the Internet. Similarly, the public addresses of incoming packets from the Internet are translated into private addresses to be sent over the local network.

When using Network Address Translation, then, you should use private IP addresses from one of the ranges listed above for the computers on your internal network. You must, however, have at least one public address to be used by the NAT-enabled computer. This is the address your private IPs will be translated to when they send packets out onto the Internet. It can be assigned by your ISP, either as a static address, or dynamically each time you make a dial-up connection.

Accessing Other Computers' Printers and Network Drives

The computers on your small TCP/IP network, once configured to share an Internet connection, can also share other resources with one another. The type of access control used will depend on whether your network is set up as a workgroup (peer-to-peer network) or uses a domain controller running server software to authenticate logons. For the Windows 2000 computers on the local network to access one another's files and folders, printers, and other resources, several conditions must be met:

- The server service must be installed and started on each computer that wants to share its resources with other computers.
- The resource must be specifically shared.
- The user accessing the resource must have permission to do so.

NOTE

By default, the server service is installed when the Windows 2000 operating system is installed, and starts automatically when the computer boots up. You can disable the server service to prevent others from accessing your computer.

To share a resource, such as a printer, folder or an entire logical drive, right-click the resource in My Computer or Windows Explorer, and select "Sharing." dialog box shown in Figure 8.14. Here, you can elect to share the resource, give the share a name to identify it on the network, and set access permissions.

Figure 8.14 Sharing a logical drive on a Windows 2000 computer.

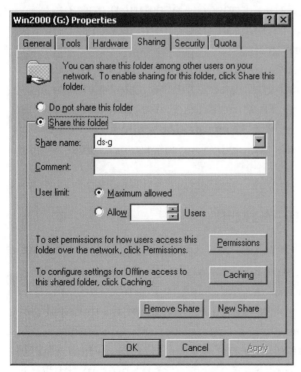

If the computer is a member of a workgroup, share level access control will be used; this means a password must be set on each shared resource. When another user attempts to access the resource across the network, he or she will will be prompted to enter the password. If the computer is part of a Windows 2000 or Windows NT domain, user-level access permissions are assigned. Users will be able to access the resource based on the individual permissions granted to their accounts or the security groups they belong to. If the resource resides on a partition formatted in NTFS, file-level permissions also apply. In a Windows 2000 domain, Active Directory security will also control access to all directory objects.

Accessing Other Computers' Resources over the Internet

When your computer is connected to the Internet, it becomes part of that huge global network of networks. Others can access your resources over the Internet if they know the account name and password of a user who is a member of the administrators, backup operators, or server operators group.

A user who does gain access to your computer's hard drive, whether over the network or the Internet, will be able to view all folders and files on that drive. This includes those that are protected by NTFS permissions, if those NTFS permissions allow access to members of the Administrators, Backup Operators, or Server Operators groups.

Protecting Your Computer from Unauthorized Access

You should always use very strong passwords for the accounts that belong to these groups, and it is a good idea to change the passwords on a regular basis. If you want to ensure that no one will be able to access your computer across the network or the Internet, you may want to consider disabling the server service. When you do this, your computer ceases to share its resources; you can think of the server service as the "sharing service." You will still be able to access other computers' resources from this computer, however.

NOTE

A strong password is one that cannot be easily guessed by someone who does a little research (such as the user's social security number, spouse's name, date of birth, etc), and contains a minimum of eight characters (more is better) consisting of both alpha and numeric characters and a mixture of upper and lowercase letters.

If you wish to be able to share your computer's resources with others on the local network, but do not want anyone from outside to be able to access them when you are connected to your ISP through a dial-up or dedicated connection, you can uninstall File and Print Sharing for Microsoft Networks on the Internet connection only. This is done by right-clicking the connection icon in Network and Dialup Connections, and clicking the "Uninstall" button.

WARNING

Just clearing the File and Printer Sharing for Microsoft Networks check box will not disable sharing; it must be uninstalled.

Comparison of ICS, NAT and Windows Routing

We have seen how both ICS and NAT translate all of your network's private IP addresses to one or more public addresses. However, there is another way to connect your LAN to the Internet if your ISP has provided you with multiple public addresses: IP routing.

You may wonder why Microsoft has given you three different means of accomplishing the same result; ICS, NAT and Windows routing are all used to connect the computers on an internal network to the Internet through one dial-up or dedicated link. Which one is best for your small office depends on your particular situation, as well as performance and security considerations.

A Windows 2000 Routed Connection

If you have a "legal" address for each computer that you want to connect, you can use a Windows 2000 computer with RRAS acting as a software router to connect to the global network, without any address translation required. A routed connection requires manual configuration of IP addresses on all the LAN computers or the use of a full-fledged DHCP server with the proper scope configured. Thus it is more complex to configure than either of the translated connection methods, but it also provides maximum flexibility and allows all IP traffic between Internet and local hosts. The Windows 2000 software router supports both IP and IPX packet filtering, in addition to PPTP and L2TP over IPsec.

Windows 2000 routing requires a machine running a member of the Windows 2000 Server family of operating systems.

Performance Considerations

One common complaint about NAT is the performance hit caused by large address tables in a high-traffic situation. Certainly, the translation process requires resources and time; consequently, NAT will perform best in a smaller, lower-traffic network. In general, NAT will work well with a network in which ten or fewer users simultaneously access the Internet through the NAT computer. However, the number of users NAT can accommodate without unacceptably lowered performance will vary depending on the nature of access, the Internet connection itself (analog modem vs. ISDN, DSL or cable), and the speed of the internal network (for instance, 10Mbs vs. 100Mbs Ethernet).

You will recall that ICS is designed to work in a peer-to-peer situation, where there are only workstation computers and perhaps member servers (non-domain controllers) set up to belong to a workgroup. NAT must be run on a server, but you cannot run the DNS, WINS and DHCP services in conjunction with it.

Windows routing can be used in a Windows 2000 domain, and is the method of choice for the larger network when sufficient public IP addresses are available.

Which connection method will perform best for you depends on what type of network environment you have.

Security

Remember that any time you establish a link from your local network to the Internet, you open your LAN up to possible risks. This is true regardless of which method you use to connect. However, Windows 2000 provides security features that will let you enjoy the benefits of office-wide Internet connectivity with less chance of security-related problems.

How Do NAT and ICS Protect My Network?

Connecting to the Internet through a NAT computer hides the internal IP addresses from "outsiders" on the Internet. External computers communicate only with the NAT computer's public IP address, and none of your internal addresses are exposed.

Additionally, in its typical configuration, NAT allows only outbound connections, traveling from your local network to the Internet. The only inbound packets that are allowed are those sent over a connection that was initiated by an internal computer. For example, when a computer on your local network uses a Web browser to send a request to a Web server on the Internet, the response to that request can come back into the internal network. Otherwise, traffic from the Internet cannot cross the NAT boundary.

NOTE

If you do want to allow access to resources on your local network from the Internet, you can do so by assigning a static IP address to the computer on which the resources are located. Exclude that address from the DHCP allocator's range, and configure a special port to map the inbound Internet connection to the resource server's address on your local network.

Since ICS and NAT are configured to allow only traffic which originated as an outbound connection, this offers you some protection, as does the cloaking of your internal addresses from the rest of the world through the address translation component. On the other hand, NAT prevents the encryption of anything that carries an IP address or information derived from an IP address (such as the TCP-header checksum). Application-level encryption can still be used in most cases, but the TCP header cannot be encrypted.

Security Issues with Routed Connections

A routed connection to the Internet means that communication can occur with any host on the Internet; it also means that the computers on your LAN will be exposed to hackers or others with malicious intent on the Internet. You counteract this is by using packet filtering, which must be configured on the Windows 2000 router to keep undesirable Internet traffic off your internal network. Refer to Chapter 6, "Secure TCP/IP Connections," for more details on securing your network communications.

Comparison of Features

Table 8.2 below shows some of the similarities and differences between Internet Connection Sharing, Network Address Translation and Windows software routing.

Table 8.2 Feature Comparison at a Glance

Feature	ICS	NAT	Routing
NAT	Yes	Yes	Yes
IPX/NetBIOS	No	No	Yes
Configuration	Check box	Manual	Manual
Address range	Fixed	Configurable	Configurable
Proxy	DNS	DNS and WINS	-
LAN interface(s)	Single	Multiple	Multiple

Microsoft cautions that ICS and NAT are not designed for connecting two LANs, but only for establishing a link from an internal network to the Internet. Windows routing, on the other hand, serves a much broader purpose, and can be used to subnet the local network as well as to connect it to the outside network.

Walkthrough

WARNING

Do not perform any of these Walkthrough Exercises on a production network without the express permission of your network administrator. Some of these exercises have the potential to disrupt or disable network communications or stability.

Now comes the fun part — we are going to walk through the steps involved in connecting a simple two-computer network to the Internet, using Windows 2000's Internet Connection Sharing component.

Connecting a Two-computer Network to the Internet

For purposes of this walk-through, we will assume we are using two Windows 2000 computers, which have been networked in a workgroup and are running the TCP/IP protocol.

Before proceeding through this walkthrough, test your Internet connection by dialing up and establishing a connection to your ISP from the computer whose connection you are planning to share. When you have confirmed that the dial-up connection is working properly, enable Internet Connection Sharing on the dial-up connection, by performing the following steps on the computer which has the dial-up Internet connection and will act as the ICS computer:

Figure 8.15 Right-click your dial-up connection and select Properties.

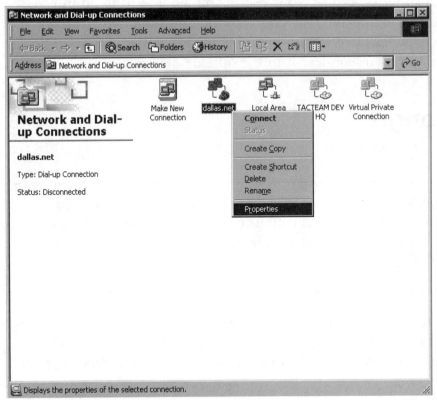

1. Right-click the "My Network Places" icon on the desktop, and select "Properties," to open the window shown in Figure 8.15.

2. You will see the Properties sheet displayed in Figure 8.16.

3. Next, on the Internet Connection Sharing tab (labeled just "Sharing" if the computer is a Windows 2000 server, as shown in Figure 8.17), select the "Enable Internet Connection Sharing" for this connection check box.

If you want this connection to dial automatically when another computer on your home network attempts to access external resources, select the "Enable on-demand dialing" check box, as shown in the figure above.

When you enable Internet Connection Sharing, the ICS computer will be given a new static IP address on the local network. The

Figure 8.16 The dial-up connection's Properties sheet.

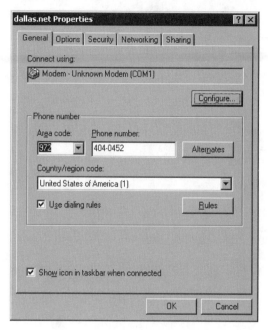

Figure 8.17 Enabling ICS for the dial-up connection.

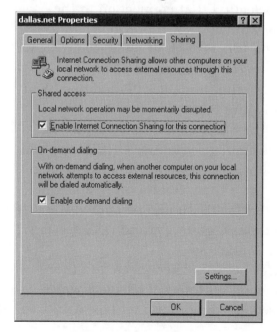

Figure 8.18 Checking for the new static IP address in the Local Area Connection properties.

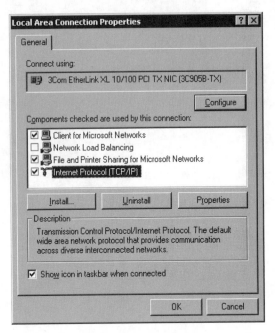

default address is 192.168.0.1. You can check the TCP/IP settings on the local area connection by selecting that connection in the Network and Dialup Connections window shown previously, and clicking "Properties." You will see a Property sheet as shown in Figure 8.18.

Highlight "Internet Protocol (TCP/IP)" and click "Properties." You will see the dialog box shown in Figure 8.19.

The last step is to make sure the other computer that will use the ICS gateway to the Internet is configured to use DHCP to obtain an IP address automatically. Go through the same process to open the TCP/IP properties box and ensure that "Obtain an IP address automatically" is checked. The other fields should be empty; the ICS computer will provide the subnet mask, gateway, and DNS server information when it allocates an IP address.

Congratulations! Your two-user network is connected to the Internet. To test the connection, open an Internet client program, such as a Web browser, on the second computer, and type a URL in

Figure 8.19 The ICS computer will be assigned a new static IP address on the LAN.

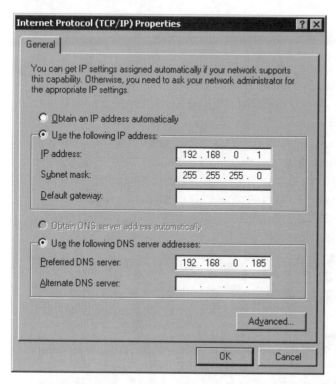

the address field. This should cause the ICS computer to automatically dial and establish an Internet connection. If not, check the "Sharing" tab on the dial-up connection's properties box and be sure "Enable on-demand dialing" is checked.

Summary

In this chapter, we have examined three different ways to connect a small office network to the Internet without the need for multiple modems, phone lines, or ISP accounts. All of these methods are built into the Windows 2000 server operating systems, and ICS is also included in Windows 2000 Professional.

We saw that Internet Connection Sharing (ICS) and Network Address Translation (NAT), although configured differently and

For IT Professionals

The Future of NAT

You will hear Network Address Translation referred to as an "address reuse solution," and indeed the primary purpose of NAT is to conserve IP addresses, which, with the boom in Internet popularity, are now in short supply.

NAT creates a separation between the "reusable" or private addresses on the internal network, and the globally-unique address(es) visible to the Internet. Thus, thousands of different private networks can use the same internal addresses (such as those in the 192.168.0.0 range) without conflicting with one another, even though all their networks have a connection to the Internet.

Most Internet professionals regard NAT as a short-term solution to the problem of depletion of available IP addresses on the Internet. IPv6, when implemented, will solve this problem and make NAT unnecessary. Many IT professionals look forward to the demise of NAT because it creates problems running some applications and does not work with DNS, WINS and DHCP services. However, it seems safe to say that, as long as ISPs charge their customers extra for additional IP addresses, Network Address Translation will remain a viable alternative for organizations that have small networks and small budgets.

intended for different types of networks, both use the same basic technology: translation of private addresses used for communication on the internal network to one or more public addresses used to communicate on the Internet. We also defined private and public addressing, and discussed how the translating computer keeps track of where packets originated and to which computers packets should be returned on the internal network.

We then took a look at how the address translation methods differ from Windows routing, and some of the advantages and disadvantages of each connection type.

Finally, we walked through the process, in a step-by-step manner, of connecting a two-computer network to the Internet using the easy-to-configure Internet Connection Sharing component of Windows 2000's dial-up networking.

The goal of many small businesses is to get everyone in the office online, but most of them have limited in financial resources and technical expertise; they need a simple and inexpensive way to do it. Windows 2000 provides those organizations with not just one, but three ways of doing so, one of which is sure to meet the specific needs of your organization.

FAQs

Q: If I have a small peer-to-peer network with no servers, which type of Internet Connection Sharing is the best choice for my office?

A: Both NAT and Windows routing require a Windows 2000 server with RRAS installed. For a peer-to-peer (workgroup) network, you must use ICS.

Q: If I have DHCP, DNS and WINS servers on my Windows 2000 domain network, and my ISP has assigned me IP addresses for each computer on the local network, which connection solution is best for my office?

A: In this situation, Windows software routing will allow you to use your public IP addresses without the need for translation, and utilize your DHCP, DNS and WINS servers.

Q: I'm confused! I don't understand the difference between ICS and NAT. Are they the same thing?

A: Yes and no. Both ICS and NAT use address translation — ICS is actually a simplified implementation of NAT that is available on both Windows 2000 Professional and Server. ICS can be set up with just a few clicks of the mouse, through the Network and

Dialup Connections properties sheet. To use Windows 2000 NAT, you must first install and configure RRAS on a Windows 2000 server and then proceed through several steps of manual configuration. NAT is more sophisticated and allows for more flexibility.

Q: Why doesn't SNMP work with NAT?

A: Some protocols do not put IP addressing information in the packet headers, and these will not work with NAT unless you use a NAT editor, which is a software component that modifies the IP packet so it will work with NAT. Windows 2000 includes built-in NAT editors for the FTP, ICMP, and PPTP protocols, but does not include an SNMP editor.

Q: If I run a Web server on one of the ICS client computers on my local network, what must I do so that Internet users will be able to access it?

A: You will have to configure the Web server service on the Services tab in the "Internet Connection Sharing Settings" property box for that connection on the ICS computer. To do this, you will need to enter the service port number (in this case, TCP port 80), and the name or IP address of the computer where the service resides.

Q: Does NAT work with the new Windows 2000 IP Security protocol?

A: No. IPSec cannot be translated by NAT, even with a NAT editor.

Chapter 9

Creating a Routable Network Using Windows 2000

Solutions in this chapter:

- **What Is Routing?**

- **Various Types of Routing and Configuration**

- **Using VPNs over the Internet for Companies**

Introduction

Configuring a routed network to provide connectivity over various technologies and to also adapt to changing conditions, such as connectivity failures, can prove to be a daunting task. Many administrators have selected routing and connectivity solutions from networking vendors, which are generally quite expensive and introduce additional configuration and integration issues. Also, most hardware-based solutions do not address the wide range of services that an administrator may wish to incorporate into the enterprise. For small- to medium-sized organization, the costs involved may be beyond their reach.

Windows 2000 Server includes a greatly enhanced version of the Routing and Remote Access add-in from NT 4.0. It has been renamed simply Windows 2000 Router and provides a plethora of functionality, ranging from dial-up solutions and VPN (Virtual Private Networking) to NAT (Network Address Translation) and the capability to provide full-blown router functionality over a variety of interfaces. The advantages of the Windows 2000 Router range from a lower cost when compared to a hardware-based solution to a more seamless integration with your Windows 2000 network, especially when considering that many non-Microsoft dial-up and VPN solutions maintain their own directory. Eliminating the maintenance of an additional user directory reduces administrative costs and minimizes the need for additional training. Windows 2000 Router can also reduce the cost of operating a remote office. If the remote office requires a Windows 2000 Server, the Windows 2000 Router can be utilized to eliminate the need to purchase a dedicated router.

Routing Overview

There are a variety of methods that can be used to perform routing. These range from static routing assignments to the use of routing protocols providing dynamic updates to the routing table. The Windows 2000 Router provides a great deal of flexibility through an adherence to established standards regarding routing and routing protocols. The compliance with standards allows for integration with existing routers in the current network.

What Is Routing?

Routing is the term used to describe the redirection of data from one network segment to another. In the OSI model, this takes place at Layer 3, or the Network Layer. One can also view a router or routing device as a post office. When a letter, or packet, gets delivered to the post office, or router, a decision is made by the desired destination on what is going to be either the most efficient or possibly the only route that this letter, or packet containing data, can follow. If the router cannot send the packet to its destination, the sender is notified. However, if the router has a route to a destination, but the connection is unavailable, the packet may simply be lost. Packet loss can occur for a variety of reasons, ranging from congestion to an undetected link failure to an unresponsive device at the packet's final destination. The destination device can also refuse the packet. Traffic, or groups of packets, will only flow between the source and destination when the route is available.

The main reason that routing is desirable in a local network is an increase in scalability, giving a network the ability to handle more users without sacrificing performance. Additional routing benefits range from security by filtering certain types of traffic or limiting the available destinations for a particular segment, to connecting dissimilar technologies such as Ethernet and Token Ring. An example of connectivity options is shown below in Figure 9.1.

Figure 9.1 Diagram illustrating the diverse connectivity options available to the Windows 2000 Router.

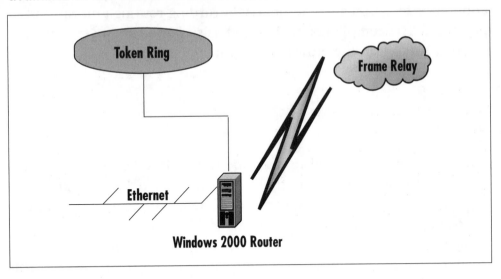

Static versus Dynamic Routing

The two standard methods of creating routes between networks are known as static routing and dynamic routing. Both have advantages and disadvantages, which will greatly influence the type of routing you may choose to deploy in your environment.

Static routing is the method of manually defining the route to a given network. The advantage is that for a remote site or subnet with only one link providing outside connectivity, all non-local traffic can be directed to the next subnet or router. With a remote office, the routing decision is simplified by routing all non-local traffic over the single link, thus eliminating the need for routing updates. The advantages also include reduced network traffic compared to a dynamic routing solution. The traffic reduction is a result of not requiring the routing updates, which typically occur every 60 seconds. On a very small connection, this gain in available bandwidth can prove to be quite valuable. The main disadvantage is that the router will not respond to a change in topology, such as a primary link going down when a secondary is available. This may not apply in the remote office scenario, but definitely applies to a medium to large network where meshing and redundancy are desired.

Dynamic routing is a method by which routing changes occur automatically as network conditions dictate. A routing protocol, such as RIP (Routing Information Protocol), OSPF (Open Shortest Path First), communicates changes and updates between routers. The main advantage to this method is that any connectivity changes, such as a primary link going down when a secondary is available, result in a minimal impact to the users. Typically, the duration of a disruption will be less than three minutes. The amount of route maintenance required in a large organization can be greatly reduced by using a dynamic routing protocol. The greatest disadvantage of dynamic routing is that proper planning must go into the initial design to prevent problems resulting in either a loss of connectivity or even a possible security risk. Another disadvantage is that if the routing protocol fails to perform properly, connectivity could be compromised. Though a failure of a routing protocol is not likely, it could prove to be a severe problem when the sites involved are not local. That is the primary reason that static routing is advisable in remote sites, especially when no support staff is available.

RIP

RIP, or Routing Information Protocol, is a relatively easy-to-use dynamic routing solution. Its feature set is tuned for a small- to medium-sized environment, though it can be used in larger environments where newer routing protocols may not be supported, provided that the maximum number of hops does not exceed 15. As mentioned in the previous section, security risks are possible when using a routing protocol. For example, when broadcasting RIP information, a passive RIP or listen-only RIP device could virtually diagram how each subnet on your network is interconnected. While this typically is not of much concern, certain environments view this type of openness of the network as a security threat. The nuances of securing RIP will be explored later in this chapter. Extensive planning is highly recommended when designing and implementing a dynamically-routed network.

There are two distinct versions of RIP that are not compatible with each other, but the Windows 2000 Router allows for both versions to be supported simultaneously. Both operate in a similar fashion, though version 2 is a bit more efficient.

Version 1 of RIP provides basic routing updates by broadcasting updates at a given interval, whereas version 2 can either broadcast or multicast. The default time between each update is 30 seconds, but the route will remain active for up to 120 seconds before the route is removed from the routing table. The route will expire 180 seconds after the RIP update is received. The default times are generally adequate, but can be tuned for a given environment if the convergence time needs to be lowered, which is done by reducing the removal and expiration times. If a reduction of traffic is the goal, then the update time can be increased along with the removal and expiration times. It is important to make sure all routers in the environment adhere to identical times for each of the three variables; otherwise, a loss in connectivity or looping may occur. For example, when one router expects an update at least once every 120 seconds and another router only sends out updates every 90 seconds, a missed update can result in a routing failure because the route would be removed from the table. The RIP configuration tab from the Windows 2000 Router is shown in Figure 9.2.

Version 2 adds the ability to handle non-standard subnet masks, simple password protection, which is not encrypted, and Classless Inter-Domain Routing (CIDR).

There are several advantages that RIP provides that may prove to be a benefit in a given environment. RIP is by far the most widely used of the routing protocols due to its acceptance by virtually every vendor of not only hardware, but software as well. For example, Windows NT and Windows 2000 provide the ability for the

Figure 9.2 The RIP Interface Advanced configuration tab.

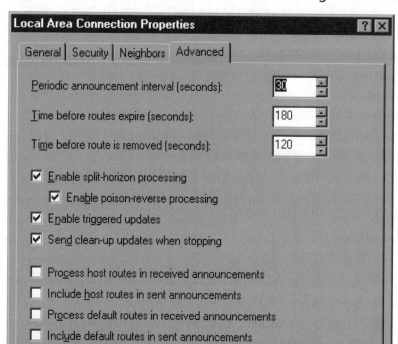

workstation or server to listen to RIP traffic and dynamically adjust their routing tables when a routing device fails. This type of inter-action is considered either silent RIP or passive RIP. An active RIP device, such as a router, would not only receive routing informa-tion, but would also relay its own information. RIP is also the only dynamic routing protocol that can be used with the Windows 2000 Router over temporary or dial-up type connections.

The RIP implementation used by the Windows 2000 Router is very configurable for a variety of situations. There are options available, such as Split-Horizon Processing and Poison-Reverse Processing, that are required in a meshed environment to prevent routing loops and other undesirable scenarios that could potentially wreak havoc on a network. We will explore the intricacies of RIP configuration in the section of this chapter entitled *Implementing RIP.*

RIP has several disadvantages when compared to other dynamic routing solutions. RIP takes a considerable amount of time to converge when network changes occur. Though this convergence typically takes up to three minutes, an outage of that duration is far from acceptable in many organizations. RIP also does not scale well past a medium-sized network, as the routing updates can begin to consume a considerable amount of bandwidth, which could prove to be very disruptive on slower connections in the environment.

NOTE

With the Windows 2000 Router, an interface can support only one routing protocol operating at a time. Enabling multiple routing protocols is not only unsupported, but can generate routing loops and potentially disrupt an entire infrastructure.

OSPF

The Open Shortest Path First, or OSPF, routing protocol was developed to increase the scalability of networks beyond what RIP was able to provide. The fact that OSPF is suited for such large networks is a definite advantage, but the configuration is also much more involved than for RIP. A successful OSPF implementation requires extensive planning and testing due to the complexities involved with using OSPF.

OSPF calculates how to route a given packet via the Shortest Path First algorithm. SPF calculates the distance to each segment of network and updates its routing tables accordingly. SPF maintains a loop-free network, which is a feature that RIP cannot guarantee.

In order to scale to such large networks, OSPF is able to group routers into units called areas. OSPF-enabled routers maintain routes for the areas to which they are connected. This functionality enables the rapid updates to occur in an area or in multiple areas if the changed router is a member of several areas. Routers that connect two areas are called Area Border Routers. Also, these updates occur much more rapidly, allowing for a much faster convergence when compared to RIP.

Additional deployment-related information is available later in this chapter in the section titled *Implementing OSPF*.

Unicast Routing

The standard host-to-destination routing is considered to be unicast routing and would be analogous to two individuals conversing with one another via the telephone. When one person speaks, the phone company routes that information via its network to the single recipient at the other end. This type of communication is not restricted to a single protocol, though the methods by which this communication occurs and is initiated vary from one protocol to the next.

IP Routing

Internet Protocol, or IP, is a component of the protocol suite known as TCP/IP. Routers use the destination address contained in each packet to determine the next hop for a packet. If a router is not sure where to send a packet, it can be configured with a default route. The default route allows the router to forward the packet to another router that may know where the destination device is located. The default route is typically used to indicate a path out of a network, such as to the Internet or other large network. A default route will be listed in a routing table as 0.0.0.0 with a subnet mask of 0.0.0.0. This is shown below in Figure 9.3.

IP routing can be either static or dynamic, as described in the previous section. Dynamic IP routing within the Windows 2000

Figure 9.3 Sample Routing Table showing a default route.

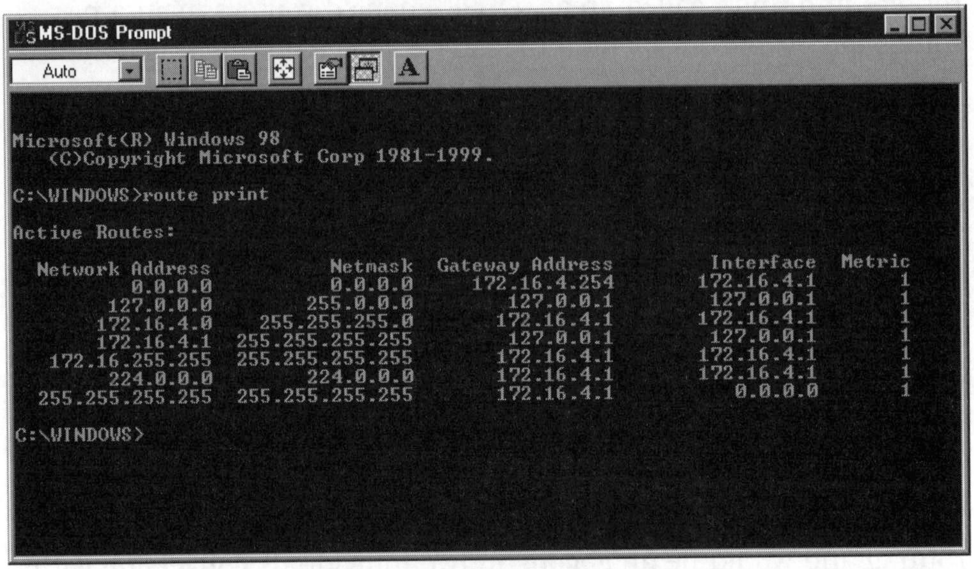

```
MS-DOS Prompt                                                          _ □ ×
Auto     ▼   □ ▣ ▣  ▣  ▣ ▣  A

Microsoft(R) Windows 98
   (C)Copyright Microsoft Corp 1981-1999.

C:\WINDOWS>route print

Active Routes:

   Network Address          Netmask   Gateway Address      Interface   Metric
         0.0.0.0            0.0.0.0      172.16.4.254      172.16.4.1      1
       127.0.0.0          255.0.0.0        127.0.0.1        127.0.0.1      1
      172.16.4.0      255.255.255.0       172.16.4.1       172.16.4.1      1
      172.16.4.1    255.255.255.255        127.0.0.1        127.0.0.1      1
  172.16.255.255    255.255.255.255       172.16.4.1       172.16.4.1      1
       224.0.0.0          224.0.0.0       172.16.4.1       172.16.4.1      1
 255.255.255.255    255.255.255.255       172.16.4.1          0.0.0.0      1

C:\WINDOWS>
```

Router solution is provided by RIP, both versions 1 and 2, and OSPF. Since the architecture of the Windows 2000 Router is extensible, future dynamic routing protocols could become available. Two of the most popular are the Interior Gateway Routing Protocol (IGRP) and the Boarder Gateway Protocol (BGP). IGRP is typically used in a Cisco-based network instead of OSPF.

IPX Routing

The IPX protocol is commonly used in Novell NetWare-based networks. Novell NetWare, version 5 is departing from IPX in favor of IP, so the commonality of the IPX protocol will diminish as the industry moves forward.

IPX uses the term *network* to describe the equivalent of an IP subnet. Each network must have a unique network number, consisting of eight hexadecimal digits. Though IPX can support 2^{32} networks, which is greater than IP is able to sustain, several factors limit the size of IPX networks.

Dynamic routing is almost a necessity for IPX, as Novell servers participate in the network with RIP. RIP for IPX, like RIP for IP-based networks, updates the routing table of participating routers.

IPX also uses another protocol in conjunction with RIP called SAP, or Service Advertising Protocol. The SAP specification defines numbers for various services, such as print servers, file servers, etc. The SAP identifiers are known as IPX Types. The Windows 2000 Router provides the ability to filter networks, but also to filter IPX Types. Since the requirements vary from one network to the next, the nuances of IPX Type filtering are beyond the scope of this book.

AppleTalk Routing

The AppleTalk protocol, also called EtherTalk, is used in Apple Macintosh networks. The AppleTalk protocol is quite inefficient, and considered to be a chatty protocol due to the overhead required for communication. Since the newer versions of the MacOS support IP very well, it is highly recommended that AppleTalk not be routed.

The Windows 2000 Router supports routing AppleTalk and also provides support for the Routing Table Maintenance Protocol, or RTMP.

Routing over a VPN Connection

When connecting offices in two different cities, the practice of utilizing a VPN over the Internet is becoming more common. Chapter 6 went into detail concerning the establishing and securing of data over a VPN connection. The key difference in setting up a VPN to connect offices versus one to connect a single user to a network is merely the addition of a routing protocol.

Since the tunnel or VPN created is a logical subnet, the router hops taken through the Internet do not count towards the hop count performed by a local routing protocol, such as RIP. The VPN created is protocol-independent, so IPX or AppleTalk could be routed over a VPN. This technique is also called IPX over IP or AppleTalk over IP.

When creating a VPN, as shown conceptually in Figure 9.4, several items must be established prior to its creation. The local and remote Internet addresses are very important in establishing the tunnel. To route from a local network to a remote network, proper routing practices must be followed, particularly concerning network addressing. The final piece of the equation is the establishment of a routing protocol. It is not recommended to use static addresses over a VPN, but rather, to use RIP. Since a VPN is established on what is called a demand-dial scenario, OSPF cannot be used. An example of routing over a VPN can be found later in this chapter.

Figure 9.4 The conceptual diagram of a VPN Tunnel.

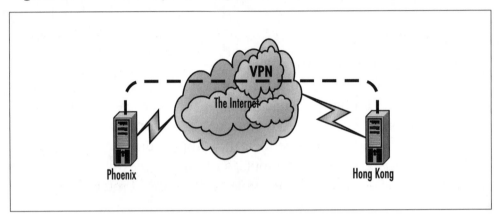

Administration and Management Tools

All management of the Windows 2000 Router should be performed from the Routing and Remote Access application. Though it is possible to manage most features for the Windows 2000 Router from the command line with the *netsh* command, it is far from recommended and is beyond the scope of this book. Further information concerning the *netsh* command can be found within the Routing and Remote Access application help file.

Routing and Remote Access Application

The Routing and Remote Access application is a plug-in to the MMC, or Microsoft Management Console. The Microsoft

Management Console is an extensible interface allowing virtually every aspect of server management to occur through a single interface. There are a few limitations to this approach concerning the updating of information reported by the MMC. As an example, the Routing and Remote Access application asks that it be exited and restarted in order to show changes that were made. These limitations are insignificant when the benefits of a singular interface for management are brought to the table.

To start the Routing and Remote Access application, a link can be found within the Administrative Tools group underneath the Programs heading of your Start menu. Once started, it will attempt to connect to the Windows 2000 Router running on the local machine. Other routers can also be added by right-clicking on the "Routing and Remote Access" or "Server Status" items under the Tree tab. This is shown below in Figure 9.5.

Figure 9.5 The Routing and Remote Access Application Interface.

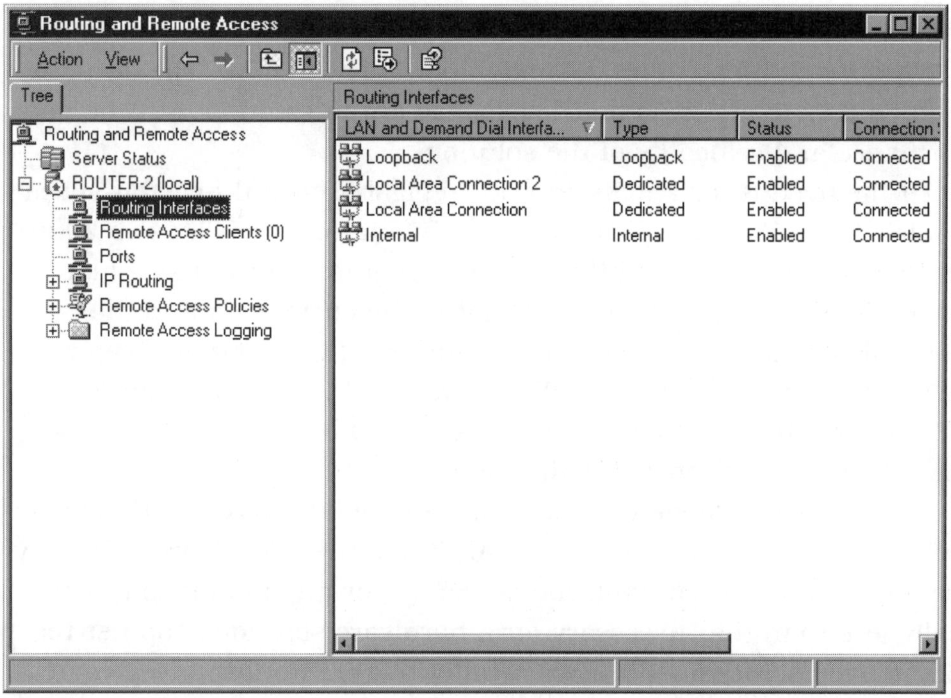

Further functionality of the Routing and Remote Access application will be demonstrated as we perform the Walkthrough exercises later in this chapter.

Role of IP Routing Services in a Network

When a network is configured to use IP, a router becomes a necessity, especially when connectivity to the Internet is desired. A router should be robust, efficient, and well-supported. While those criteria are important, they also encompass virtually every routing solution available. The solution decided upon should be flexible enough to grow with you as well as be cost-effective enough to meet the needs that exist today.

Should You Use Windows 2000 Routing On Your Network?

Once the needs are assessed, the decision on whether or not to use a Windows 2000 solution depends upon a few factors. The deciding elements focus not only on the expense of the solution, but the performance and criticality of the solution.

If the need is for a mission-critical gigabit or multi-gigabit speed router, then Windows 2000 is definitely not for you. Windows 2000 is also not recommended if you have a requirement to route more than IP, IPX, or AppleTalk since that is the current limit to the routable protocols available to the Windows 2000 Router. Keep in mind that out of the box, the Windows 2000 Router only supports OSPF and RIP. Since many networks use IGRP or EIGRP, this may be an influential factor in your decision.

However, if your network is small- to medium-sized, with only a few local subnets or even a few WAN links, then Windows 2000 may be an ideal way to obtain a robust router for an amount that is typically less than that necessary for a hardware solution. Another recommended solution is to use a Windows 2000 Router to segregate a lab environment from a production environment. Since protocol, network, and port filtering can occur on a Windows 2000 Router, it can be tailored for a given scenario. An example would be creating a Windows 2000 test environment with Active Directory Services and DHCP while still allowing HTTP (Port 80) traffic to traverse the router for Internet connectivity.

Another possibility mentioned earlier in the chapter is that of a company with numerous remote offices. If each remote office utilizes a Windows 2000 server, the Windows 2000 Router can be enabled to reduce the initial hardware costs associated with the setup of an office.

Reliability versus Hardware Routers

The reliability of a Windows 2000 Router is definitely debatable. Since the Windows 2000 operating system is typically more complex than that of a hardware router, it opens the Windows 2000 Router up to software instabilities and potential security holes. There are also software instabilities found within even the best Cisco routers. Since both suffer this weakness, there is no decisive winner.

Another point of contention would be the reliability of the hardware platform. Since most middle-of-the-road hardware routers have a single power supply, as do most entry-level servers, there is no clear choice at that performance point. However, a server with multiple PCI slots and redundant power supplies can be obtained for about the price of a fully-loaded Cisco 4700, which has one power supply and only three interfaces. When approaching the upper end of the midrange routers, Windows 2000 starts to really shine in terms of performance and value. It is not a campus router, nor does it address the bargain basement of sub-$1000 routing solutions.

For all of its features, as well as limitations, the Windows 2000 Router does indeed bring value to the Windows 2000 product and does compete very well in the midrange to upper-midrange routing solutions. There isn't a clear winner in general terms, but the solution appropriate for a given environment will shift the preference from one to the other.

Implementing RIP

This section of Chapter 9 delves into the planning phases of a deployment of RIP. There are a few pitfalls that can be avoided by performing proper planning up front.

RIP Environment

As previously mentioned, RIP is tuned for small- to medium-sized networks. A medium-sized network typically has less than 50 networks. The larger the number of networks, the more complex the updates for RIP become, resulting in excessive network traffic that can saturate a slower WAN link.

RIP is also well suited to handle a meshed environment, as there are provisions within the protocol for Poison Reverse and Split Horizon processing. These two features detect the presence of a network loop and prevent a packet from endlessly looping in a network. Without Poison Reverse or Split Horizon processing, creating a reliable network with multiple paths is not possible.

Since RIP is a dynamic routing protocol, it is adaptable to the network changes that may occur. Networks are generally fairly reliable, but are usually very dynamic. These changes that occur, such as the addition of a network or remote site, can be handled in stride and added to the routing table of a RIP- enabled router or other device.

RIP Design Considerations

The Windows 2000 Router implementation of RIP has a limitation of a network diameter of 14 hops, though the RIP standard is 15. The reason that Windows 2000 has this limitation is that all static routes are assigned a hop of two, and since directly connected networks are static, there is a penalty hop added prior to any other calculations that may take place.

Also, RIP hop count metrics can be modified. This flexibility is very handy in a meshed environment with multiple topology speeds.

Figure 9.6 illustrates such a scenario. Network A is a 16Mbs Token Ring, Networks B, C, and D are 100Mbs Fast Ethernet. Without defining an additional hop for the Token Ring network, equal preference is given to Network A and Network D even though they do not perform identically. RIP is not able to determine link speeds and relies solely on hop count metrics to determine the route for a given packet to take.

As mentioned earlier in the chapter, there are two versions of RIP. Most problems do not arise from RIP, version 1, but rather from RIP, version 2. We'll tackle the most common issues for each version.

Figure 9.6 Example of meshed topology.

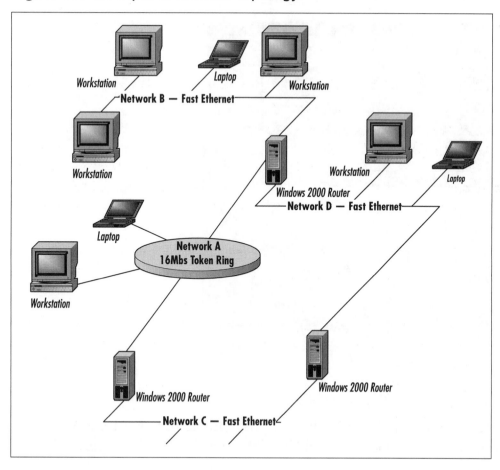

RIP, Version 1

RIP, version 1 is recommended only if there is a previous infrastructure of version 1 equipment. Since RIP, version 1 does not support Variable-Length Subnet Masks (VLSM) or Classless InterDomain Routing (CIDR), this could present a problem in your environment. VLSM is the use of a non-standard Class A, B, or C subnet mask. An example of a non-standard subnet mask is 255.255.252.0.

If you have a mixed environment, it is important that each interface be configured appropriately as shown in Figure 9.7. This screen is accessible by selecting a RIP-enabled interface and selecting properties.

Figure 9.7 RIP Interface Properties.

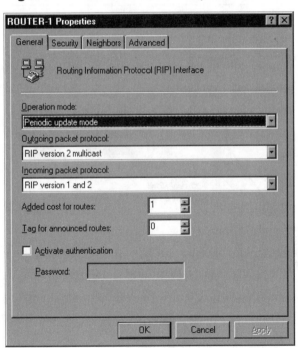

RIP, Version 2

RIP, version 2 adds the ability to use simple password authentication. This cannot be assumed to be secure for the transmission of updates, but adds a level of control to the network when accepting RIP broadcasts. You can use a different password on each network for additional control if desired.

If RIP, version 2 is used over demand-dial connections and auto-static mode is selected, then you must configure each interface of the connection to use multicast announcements as opposed to broadcast announcements. If broadcast is used, the router at the remote end will ignore the RIP updates.

RIP Over Frame Relay

Since Frame Relay is a non-broadcast topology and RIP relies on broadcasts or multicasts to relay updates, certain details must be addressed prior to implementation. The configuration will depend upon the frame relay implementation. If the frame relay adapter appears as a single adapter within Windows 2000 for all virtual circuits, or DLCIs, then the single adapter model will need to be followed. However, if each virtual circuit appears as its own adapter, then the multiple adapter model will apply.

In the single adapter model, the frame relay cloud is treated as an IP network and the connections to the network are each assigned an IP address. In this configuration, unicast RIP is required and each neighbor must be configured. Each remote network router must be listed as a neighbor using the interface available within the frame relay cloud.

In the multiple-adapter model, each DLCI or virtual circuit appears as a point-to-point or dedicated link. Since each link appears as a private network, you can configure RIP to either broadcast or unicast over this connection just as you would a local network.

Passive RIP

When a computer, router, or other device does not send RIP broadcasts, but does receive and process RIP updates, it is considered to be a passive RIP device or silent RIP device. The device uses the announcements to build its routing table. This functionality is used mainly in Unix environments, though it can be implemented even with Windows NT 4.0 to allow the computer to have alternate routes out of an environment in case of link failure or other anomaly. Windows 2000 Professional provides a RIP listener, but is only version 1-compliant.

RIP Security

Following a few common guidelines can enhance the security of the RIP protocol. By addressing the shortcomings of the RIP protocol prior to implementation, denial of service attacks and other problems can be avoided.

Version 2 Authentication

In order to prevent a denial of service attack by a rogue RIP router, you can configure RIP, version 2 to use password authentication. If received announcements contain the incorrect password, or no password at all, the update is discarded. Since the password is sent in clear text format, a network sniffer could easily capture RIP packets, enabling the operator to easily read the password contained therein.

Peer Security

It is also possible to configure both RIP, versions 1 and 2 with a list of valid routers from which to receive updates. If the broadcast source is an unauthorized router, the update is discarded. These valid routers are configurable by adding a peer filter.

Route Filters

By configuring route filters on each RIP-enabled interface, only routes that reflect valid network numbers will be added to the routing table. For instance, if a network relies on 172.16.x.x addresses, it can be defined that all updates must fall within those guidelines and all rogue broadcasts will be ignored.

For IT Professionals

Remember that if Unix or other devices are operating in a passive RIP mode, they also need to be added to the neighbor list.

Defining Neighboring Routers

The default configuration is for RIP to use broadcasts or multicasts (version 2 only). Since using a broadcast is not only insecure, but also inefficient, there is another option for preventing these RIP packets from reaching each and every host on your network. By defining neighboring RIP routers, broadcasts no longer occur and the updates are sent in the form of a unicast packet directly to that router. This is especially secure in a switched environment since an unauthorized sniffer could only detect broadcast traffic.

Implementing OSPF

The Open Shortest Path First (OSPF) routing protocol is designed for large and very large networks, typically those with more than 50 physical networks.

OSPF shares design goals with RIP in terms of support for a meshed, redundant network and that topology updates are handled in stride without extensive enterprise-wide reconfigurations.

OSPF Design Considerations

Designing an OSPF network can be very time-consuming, but well worth the effort. However, failure to plan accordingly prior to implementation, which should include a solid backout plan, will certainly result in either an unscalable network or worse. Therefore, several guidelines must be followed to ensure that problems during deployment are kept at a minimum.

The three levels of OSPF design are:

- Autonomous System Design
- Area Design
- Network Design

Since each level has its own nuances, they will be addressed separately.

Autonomous System Design

Whenever possible, divide your network into logical areas. An area could be considered a remote site or another building. It is also desirable for the areas to adhere to a contiguous set of IP addresses. Though this is not a requirement, it can reduce the headaches of troubleshooting later by associating addresses with an area.

The backbone area of your network should be a single network capable of extremely high speed. This allows for a logical core to be established for router configuration and communication.

It is also advisable to create stub areas, which are extensions to an existing network designed to provide the ability for the network to grow in a controlled manner. When stub areas are not used, the network will not be nearly as scalable and will more than likely not perform as expected.

Virtual links between networks should be avoided as they can create problems when establishing the paths between routed networks. Though virtual links can be added later, it is advisable to use them with extreme care and they should not be in place until the latter stages of deployment.

Area Design

When designing an OSPF area, there are a few guidelines that should be followed. Areas are groups of networks, with a recommended maximum of 100 networks.

Areas should be isolated with controlled points leading to exterior networks. It is also especially important that no unauthorized connections between areas exist and that all area-to-area communication traverses the backbone area.

In an ideal situation, a single route can summarize an area. When this is possible, make the area ID the same as the single route being advertised. Also ensure that multiple area boarder routers for a given area summarize the same routes.

Network Design

When defining a network to an OSPF router, it is advisable to plan for routing out of that network from multiple routers. The least active router should be the designated router as well as the backup designated router, though link costs, speed, and reliability should factor heavily into the decision to designate a primary router. For security purposes, always assign a password.

Since OSPF is designed for very large networks, it is advisable to consult numerous texts on proper OSPF network design prior to finalizing a design and beginning implementation.

OSPF Security

The OSPF security model is very similar to that of RIP. The two types of security available are the use of a password and route filters.

Password Authentication

By default, the Windows 2000 Router implementation of OSPF is configured to send a password of 12345678 in the Hello or announcement messages. This should be changed from the default. Keep in mind that the password, like RIP's password, is sent in clear text and it should be assumed that it is being sniffed. In addition to RIP, it is advised to use other security in addition to the password authentication method.

Route Filters

To minimize the exposure to invalid routes appearing in the routing tables of your routers, it is advisable to configure the Autonomous System Boundary Routers (ASBR) with route filters. These filters are similar to those described with RIP in that they limit the routes that are permitted to appear in the OSPF update. Non-authorized routes will be discarded. Keep in mind that these filters will only affect routes from non-OSPF sources, such as static routes or RIP routes.

What Is Multicast?

Earlier in this chapter, unicast routing was discussed. It is analogous to a phone call between two people with no other participants. Multicast routing is similar to that analogy, but in this case, one end has a single person and the other end includes recipients of a conference call. The caller says a word once, but all parties hear it. Multicast routing is similar, as one packet is sent and many recipients receive it.

Multicasting has several uses and will continue to grow in use, especially with the ever-increasing popularity of the Internet. Since the Internet is evolving into a vehicle for mass communication, functions such as radio and TV are showing up on the Internet. Without multicast technology, the bandwidth requirements and processor requirements for an Internet transmitter would be enormous. Multicasting minimizes the bandwidth used, as one packet can be sent to numerous hosts, thus enabling even a home PC to become an Internet radio or TV station. Essentially, anything that streams data, especially live or real-time data, to numerous hosts can benefit from multicast technology.

There are three methods to transmit data from a single host to multiple destinations. The first method is simply sending unicast packets to each host. This results in excessive network traffic as well as the requirement to maintain the recipient's list.

The second method sends the packet in unicast form to a broad-cast address. While this is somewhat more efficient than unicasting to each station, it results in excessive traffic on a given subnet, which affects each and every device on that subnet. Both the first and second methods of one-to-many communication can cause a loss in productivity due to a potentially sluggish network. Also, routers generally do not forward broadcasts, so the intended recipients may not be reached by this method of distribution.

The final method sends a single packet to a multicast address. The routers then pass the packet to the hosts that are designated to receive the multicast. In a switched environment, this causes only the recipient to receive the packet and other nodes on that particular network to be undisturbed.

Multicast Protocols

The forwarding of multicast traffic can be facilitated through the use of a plethora of protocols, with IGMP being the focus of this writing due to its support within the Windows 2000 Router. However, several third-party companies have developed multicast solutions tailored for their particular network. Interactivity between the Windows 2000 Router and other solutions has not been tested and is beyond the scope of this writing. It is highly recommended that any plans for implementing multicasting within an environment be heavily researched and tested to minimize any unintended results.

Windows 2000 Support

Windows 2000 includes support for the Internet Group Management Protocol, or IGMP. IGMP is not a multicast routing protocol, but can be used to forward multicast packets over one hop. Though a chain of these routers could be created to allow multicasting throughout an environment, it is not recommended and Microsoft does not support it.

The IGMP portion of the Windows 2000 Router was designed to either allow a small intranet to support multicasting or to allow

Intranet-to-Internet or Internet-to-Intranet multicasts to occur. Additional extensions may become available to allow for much more multicast functionality, which will be required for multicast implementations of more than one or two networks.

Demand-Dial Networking

Demand-Dial networking is designed to create a network by using modem connectivity over standard phone lines. Since Windows 2000 has the ability to create multiple connections with multiple modems, also known as multilink, a fair amount of bandwidth can be obtained for very small offices or home offices that cannot obtain, and possibly do not need, a dedicated leased line connection.

It is not recommended to use a Demand Dial approach in place of a dedicated line as several factors weigh heavily against its use. Routing issues are generally not a problem, but connectivity and maintaining that connectivity are the key issues limiting the use of Demand Dial networking. However, it should also be noted that Demand Dial would work very well over ISDN, but such connectivity may prove to be quite expensive in many areas of the United States. Also, long distance phone charges would quickly consume any savings resulting from not using a dedicated connection outside of the local calling area.

For details on the nuances of multilink connectivity and other dial-up networking specific issues, please consult Chapter 7.

Backup Connections for WAN

It has long been an accepted practice to create a backup for a WAN link in case of failure. Typically, the router was configured to dial the remote router over a modem when a link failure occurred. While this may work well for line speeds of 128Kbs or less, T1 speeds (~1.5Mbs) will render this backup link virtually useless. In the case of a remote site linked via a T1, an alternate carrier or secondary T1 or fractional T1 should be used as a backup.

As noted, if the speed of the connection is 128Kbs or less, a demand-dial backup to the primary connection would be a logical step in order to preserve connectivity through the outage of a leased line.

Configuring Demand-Dialing

When configuring a demand-dial interface, several planning steps must occur. First, a bandwidth assessment should be done to ensure that the demand-dial link will be adequate, even if it is only temporary. Secondly, the protocols to be routed over the link should also be decided upon and preferably limited to only IP if possible. Third, since bandwidth is a premium on a demand-dial connection, static routing should be used whenever possible.

The connection can be initiated in a number of ways, varying from on-demand to persistent to one-way or two-way initiated connections.

On-Demand versus Persistent Connectivity

With an on-demand connection, the link will only be established when data needs to be transferred and then disconnected after a timeout period with no activity. This is desirable when the connection is used only a few times a day and the call is not a local one.

A persistent connection is one that is always active and is the dial-up equivalent of a leased line. Persistent connections would be preferred if this was not a backup connection, the call was local, and/or the link was active a large percentage of the time.

One-Way versus Two-Way Initiation

When a connection is of the on-demand variety, two-way initiation would be preferred. The reason is that, since the link can be made active from either location, the result is efficient traffic flow with a minimal wait.

If the connection is to be persistent, one-way initiation is appropriate as if both attempted to dial simultaneously, the line at the other end would be busy, resulting in an inability for the link to become active.

Time Restrictions

A limitation can be placed on the hours of operation for a particular connection. This can help control long distance costs for a remote site to ensure that the link is inactive during non-business hours. The time restriction changes should be made on the initiating router or routers with a secondary set of restrictions added to the receiving or secondary demand dial router.

Demand Dial Filtering

The Demand Dial configuration allows for restriction of the types of traffic that can initiate a demand dial connection. For example, DNS queries or broadcasts could cause the link to stay active even when no business-related traffic is flowing over the link. Fortunately, the response of making the link active can be controlled, as can the traffic that flows over that link, by using the standard IP filters on the Demand Dial interface. These settings will be shown in detail in Exercise 1 of the Walkthrough section of this chapter.

Walkthrough

WARNING

Do not perform any of these Walkthrough Exercises on a production network without the express permission of your network administrator. Some of these exercises have the potential to disrupt or disable network communications or stability.

In this section, we will go step by step through an example of utilizing the Windows 2000 Router as a solution to remote connectivity. The scenario shown is that of connecting two remote offices together via a persistent Demand Dial VPN connection over the Internet.

Connecting Two Small Offices With VPN

Introduction

With the cost of a long-haul dedicated circuit being too expensive for many companies, the alternative of using a VPN is very appealing. The Windows 2000 Router provides a solid platform for a dedicated VPN solution. In this example, we will plan and implement a VPN between two remote offices. This particular example was configured in a lab environment, but the functionality is the same when the Internet is used.

Planning

When connecting two remote offices via the Internet, a few steps should be taken in advance to ensure not only success, but also solid performance over the long term. Since all Internet Service Providers are not created equal, it is recommended that you research those providers that are common to both areas. The advantage of using the same provider is that communications between your two offices generally won't have to go on the Internet, but will stay within your ISP's network. The key advantages to this approach are reliability and speed. Since you minimize the number of hops that would be taken between your offices, you also minimize the number of points of failure, as well as increase performance due to this reduction in hops.

Once an ISP is selected, bandwidth requirements should be assessed. There are no hard and fast rules for what amount of bandwidth is adequate due to the type of traffic that may traverse the connection. In most business settings, a T1 should handle up to around 100 users. Again, your mileage may vary. Also, since higher bandwidth creates a greater expense, size your connection accordingly.

Most ISPs require a router to be installed and maintained by them so that the type of access and traffic levels can be regulated by the ISP. This requirement also gives the ISP the ability to troubleshoot an Internet connectivity issue and take or refuse ownership depending upon the location of the fault. The Ethernet connection from their router will terminate into the Windows 2000 Router's second network card. Your ISP should give you an IP address or addresses that you can use for Internet connectivity. In this scenario, only one IP address will be required at each location, but your needs may vary, so buying a block of four or eight, even if you only use one, is not a bad idea. IP addressing internally should also be planned in advance. It is highly recommended that private addresses be utilized. These addresses can be found in RFC 1918. For our example, we will be using the Class B private address space of 172.16.x.x with a 24-bit (255.255.255.0) mask.

NOTE

Your Windows 2000 Router machine at each location must have two Ethernet adapters. One will be used for the Private or Internal network, while the other will be for the Public or Internet network.

Implementation Prerequisites

Prior to beginning the implementation phase, please ensure that the following items are available as described in the planning section:

- Ethernet-based connection to the Internet router provided by your ISP
- Internet IP address for Windows 2000 Router

The Windows 2000 Router should be connected to the Internet router from your ISP on each end. To verify functionality, you should be able to ping both routers from each location or even from the Internet.

Step 1: Create the Interface

Open up the Routing and Remote Access application from the Administrative Tools group. If this is the first time the application has been started, you may be asked to enable the Routing and Remote Access service. Proceed through the wizard by selecting the manual configuration option.

Once the application has started, the screen should look similar to Figure 9.8.

Figure 9.8 Routing and Remote Access application.

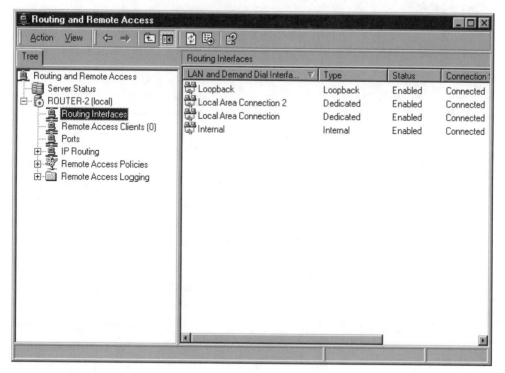

To create the VPN interface, right-click "Routing Interfaces" and select "New Demand Dial Interface." You will then receive the screen shown in Figure 9.9. If you do not and have just enabled the Routing and Remote Access component, you may need to restart your Windows 2000 Router computer.

Figure 9.9 Welcome to the new Demand Dial Interface Wizard.

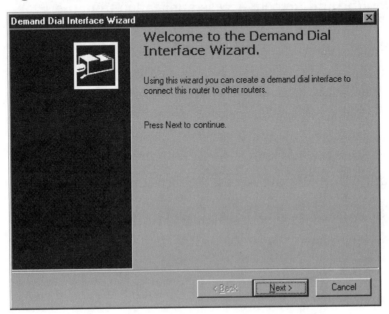

Please select the "Next" button. The next screen that comes up, shown in Figure 9.10, allows for the naming of the VPN connection. It is advisable to name the connection by the router or location at the opposite end of the connection. This way, any logging or troubleshooting that may occur can be easily referenced.

In Figure 9.11, the option is given for connections utilizing modems, ISDN adapters, and other hardware designed for non-dedicated connectivity, or to connect using Virtual Private Networking (VPN). In our example, we will be connecting with VPN.

The next step is to define the type of VPN connectivity desired. The choices are PPTP and L2TP. L2TP requires that security certificates be

Figure 9.10 Naming the Interface.

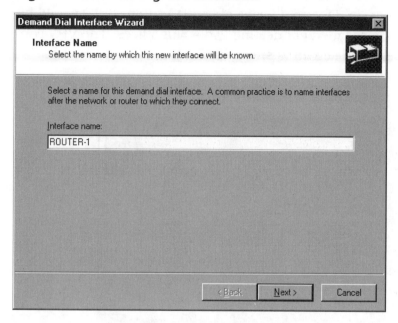

Figure 9.11 Defining the Connection Type.

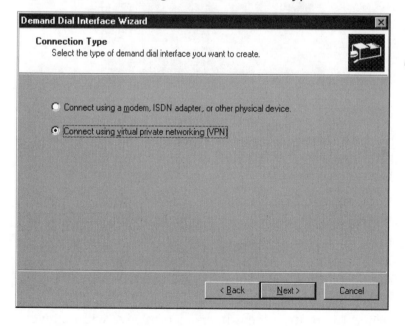

in use prior to the establishment of the connection, whereas PPTP is much easier to set up. Due to its ease of configuration, PPTP would be a much better choice when connecting two small offices. The VPN connectivity type selection screen is shown in Figure 9.12.

Figure 9.12 Choosing the Type of VPN connection.

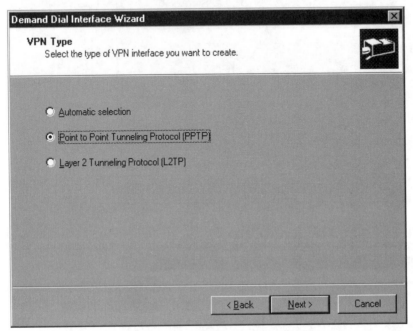

Figure 9.13 shows the next screen in the configuration sequence. At this point, the destination or remote router address is required. This is the Ethernet interface of the remote router that is on the Internet.

Figure 9.14 requires a bit of changing from the default. We will be checking the "Add a user account so a remote router can dial in" selection. If routing for IPX is enabled, please uncheck this protocol, unless you desire to route IPX over the VPN connection. In our example, this functionality is not required and the box remains unchecked.

Since we selected to create a local user account, we will be given the option of selecting a password, as shown in Figure 9.15. Note

Figure 9.13 Assigning the Destination Address.

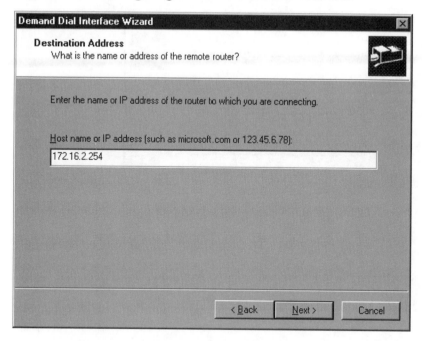

Figure 9.14 Protocols and Security configuration.

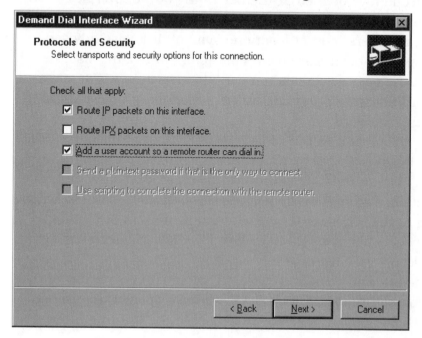

Figure 9.15 Local account creation and password assignment.

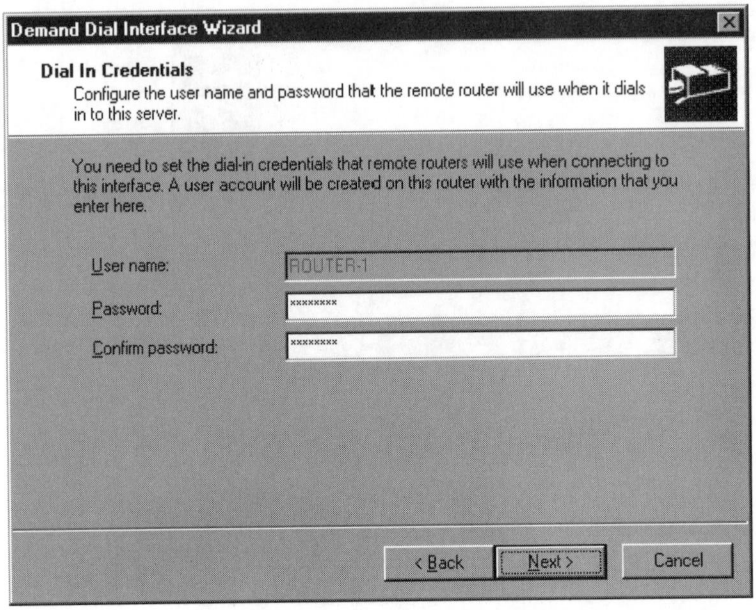

that the username cannot be changed and corresponds to the name of the connection we defined at the beginning of the Interface Wizard. It is highly recommended that the password selected contain letters, numbers, and at least one symbol. It is also advised that the password be at least eight characters in length. Also, be certain that the password does not contain an actual word, since the password cracking programs utilize a dictionary in the attempt to obtain the password.

In order to connect to the remote router, an account must exist for authentication. Since the procedure for interface creation must be done on both routers, accounts will be created at each end of the connection. Figure 9.16 shows the credentials to be used when connecting to the other router. Since both routers in our example are not part of a Windows 2000 or Windows NT domain, that field is left blank.

Once the interface has been created, we must verify a few of the configuration settings. In Figure 9.17, we have opened the properties of the Demand Dial interface underneath the Routing Interfaces

Figure 9.16 Assigning the connection account and password.

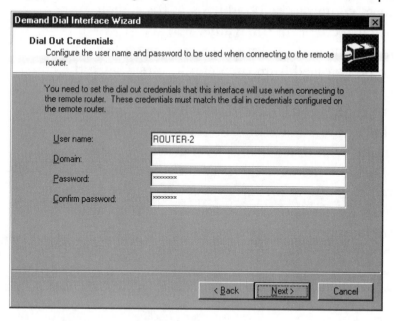

Figure 9.17 Connection properties — General tab.

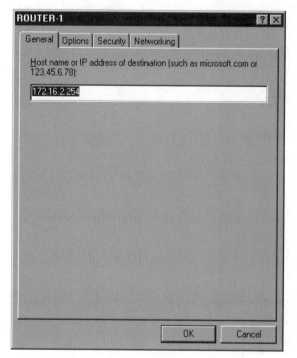

heading within the Routing and Remote Access application. The General tab shown contains the IP address of the remote router. Please verify the correctness of this value.

The Options tab shown in Figure 9.18 contains a few options that will need to be changed from the default. First, since the connection will remain constantly active, the Connection type should be set to "Persistent connection." Also, the Redial attempts should be set at 1000 or greater to ensure that the connection will be retried an acceptable number of times before failing. The "Average redial intervals" could also be increased to accommodate the possibility of connectivity problems due to an Internet or ISP failure. Since we are not using modems for the connection, the selection of "Multiple devices" does not apply.

The Security tab of the Connection Properties page should be left at the default settings, as encryption for both data and passwords is enabled by default. Disabling encryption while operating a VPN over

Figure 9.18 Connection properties — Options tab.

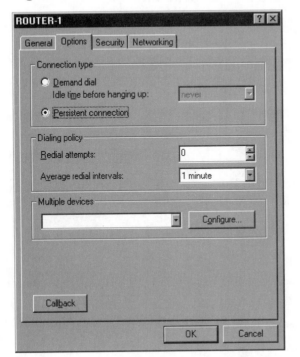

the Internet is not only highly discouraged, but could potentially release private and sensitive information to anyone sniffing Internet data on the many hops taken by the VPN. The default settings are shown in Figure 9.19.

Figure 9.19 Connection properties — Security tab.

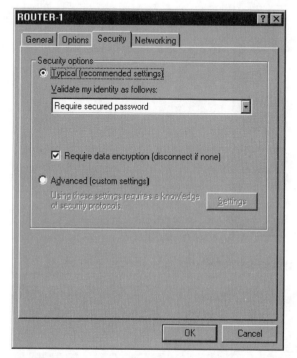

Figure 9.20 shows the Networking tab. The type of VPN being called should be set to PPTP, as L2TP requires additional configuration beyond the scope of this example. Also, the "File and Printer Sharing for Microsoft Networks" is enabled, as administration of the Windows 2000 Router cannot be performed without the binding active.

Once the interface configuration is complete, the listing of the General branch of the IP Routing tree should show the ROUTER-1 interface, such as the listing shown in Figure 9.21. This interface will not show an IP address until active. Remember, the interface creation procedure must be performed on both routers.

Figure 9.20 Connection properties — Networking tab.

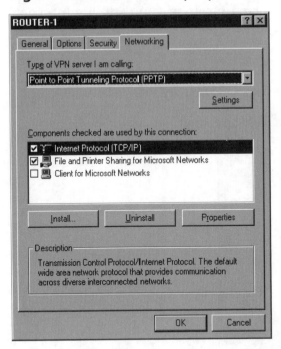

Figure 9.21 Listing of IP-Enabled Interfaces.

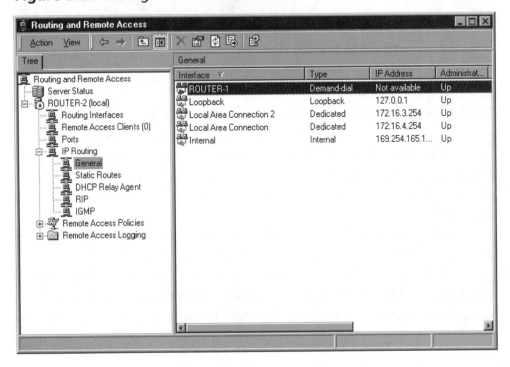

While the interface properties examined above address general settings, the properties of the ROUTER-1 interface within the IP section are much more protocol-specific. Fortunately, we will not need to make any adjustments. If the requirement to add filters to the connection exists, these can easily be added in from this interface. Figure 9.22 shows the General tab of the IP interface properties for ROUTER-1.

Figure 9.22 IP properties for VPN Connection — General tab.

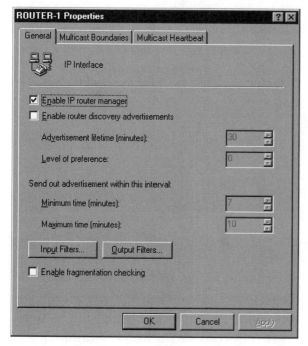

RIP should be added into the configuration. To add RIP, right-click the General branch of the IP tree within the "Routing and Remote Access" application. Select "New Routing Protocol." A window will appear with several choices, but only select RIP.

Once RIP is added, open the new RIP branch of the IP tree. Right-click the right part of the screen, which should be blank. A menu will appear and we want to select "New Interface." A window will list the available IP interfaces and we want to select ROUTER-1.

After the interface is listed, right-click and select its properties. We will see a window, as shown in Figure 9.23. We will want to change

Figure 9.23 RIP Interface properties — General tab.

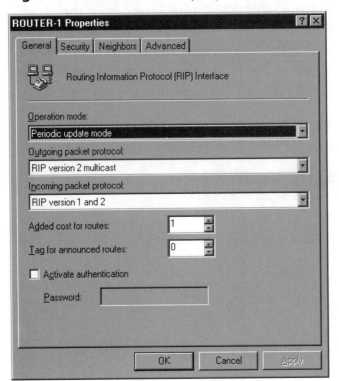

the default of Operation mode from Auto-Static to Periodic Update mode. Since our connection is active at all times, we want to take advantage of this feature and keep the networks in sync with one another by having active routing data exchanged between the routers.

We will need to define a static address range in our example. While a larger network would potentially use DHCP, we will define a pool of addresses to use for the VPN connection. These addresses are used by the VPN and will not be utilized by any users on either network. These addresses create the VPN "hop."

Figure 9.24 shows the Routing and Remote Access application with the properties of the "Routing Interfaces" branch shown. From the "IP" tab, we will want to change the setting for IP address assignment from DHCP to static address pool. We will want to add a new address range as shown below, making sure we add enough to cover any growth.

Figure 9.24 Enabling Static Address Range on VPN server.

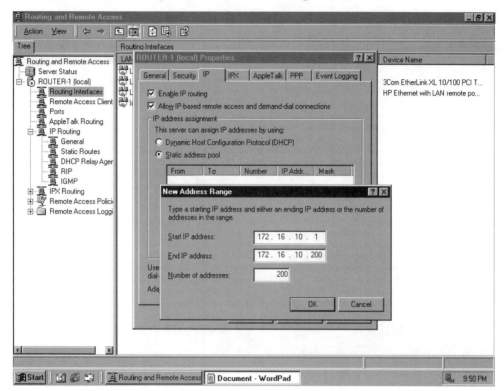

A closer look at the settings after we add the "Static address pool," as shown in Figure 9.25, shows a setting regarding DHCP, DNS, and WINS address references. This should always point to the internal Ethernet interface of your Windows 2000 Router. Setting the wrong interface could result in connectivity problems to servers at the remote location.

The connection, once created and active on each side of the Internet, should work quite well. Since the cost of long-haul bandwidth can be excessive, this lower-cost alternative should enable many companies to increase their communications capabilities and work more effectively.

For additional information on the VPN connectivity within the Windows 2000 product, please consult Chapter 6.

Figure 9.25 Configuring DHCP, DNS, and WINS assignment.

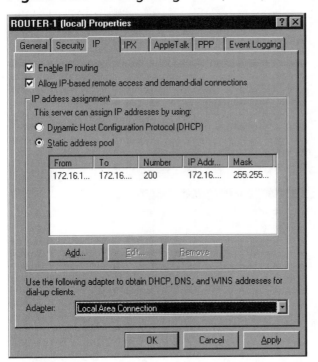

Summary

While the Windows 2000 Router platform is easy to use, we certainly cannot cover its full potential in just a few chapters. There are many resources available on the Internet and within the well-written Microsoft help file that accompanies the Routing and Remote Access application.

The power of the platform extends beyond simple unicast routing to encompass multicast capabilities, routing protocols, and Internet connectivity. Though these functions are there, many will probably go unused in most environments. Since most networks certainly route IP, the focus of the text and examples centered on the IP protocol. IPX is supported, as is AppleTalk. As was mentioned earlier, AppleTalk routing is not a recommended practice, with the MacOS strongly supporting IP.

Routing protocols give the Windows 2000 Router the capability to interact with an already established enterprise class network. Since most networks already support RIP, the focus was applied to it rather than OSPF. RIP is very common and will continue to be so for years to come until another protocol, such as IGRP or EIGRP, becomes more common. OSPF, though powerful, is very complex. Due to its complexity, selecting OSPF over RIP would only be the logical choice when an existing infrastructure using OSPF was available.

Since the Internet is everywhere and access has become less costly, VPN capabilities have proved to be a boon for many companies. In the future, this technology with ever-evolving security features that allow the privacy of a LAN with the low cost of the Internet, will be promoted.

The Windows 2000 Router is an excellent choice for a mid-range routing solution, but simply cannot hold its own when put head-to-head with high-end solutions offering multi-gigabit speeds. When the router is used as a replacement to a WAN router, the platform excels and can easily compete against the big-iron solutions from other vendors. The hardware is developing, as are the drivers, so the solutions will mature over the next year or two, and the Windows 2000 Router should gain the respect it most definitely deserves.

FAQs

Q: I'm connecting the Windows 2000 Router to an existing network running RIP, but I'm not sure which version. How should I configure Windows 2000?

A: It is recommended that all settings be verified ahead of time, but testing by using the passive mode of RIP along with version 1 should allow for the version to be verified.

Q: My Cisco-based network uses EIGRP, but Windows 2000 does not support this routing protocol. How can I have the two work together?

A: Cisco IOS supports the redistribution of routing information over other protocols. It is suggested that RIP be enabled on the Cisco device with a limitation on what networks are valid for RIP updates. Have the Windows 2000-based portion of your network run RIP and occupy IP subnets within the range defined on your Cisco router. The protocol redistribution would only have to occur on one, not all, of your Cisco routers. For additional information, please consult your Cisco documentation as to the configuration of this feature.

Q: I configured a VPN connection to use L2TP and I cannot get it to connect. There is an error showing that a valid certificate is required. How do I obtain this certificate?

A: The addition of L2TP as a VPN connectivity protocol also introduces several configuration issues. The configuration issues center on the use of security by the Windows 2000 Router and the use of security certificates to provide encryption. In most cases, PPTP is adequate except with the most sensitive of information. Due to the security issues generated by L2TP, it is recommended to consult a Windows 2000 security guide, including the numerous white papers located on Microsoft's Web site at www.microsoft.com/windows.

Q: Why can't I route the DLC protocol?

A: DLC is not really a protocol in the truest sense of the word. DLC allows for Layer 2 communications only and protocol routing, such as that with IP, does not take place until Layer 3 of the OSI model. If DLC needs to be available throughout a network, bridging or Layer 2 switching can accomplish this goal, but the scalability of the network as a whole will be severely limited without the capability of segmenting a network into subnets for IP or networks for IPX. Also, since most DLC usage is for SNA, the Microsoft SNA Server, which is part of the BackOffice Family, will provide this functionality while allowing your network to standardize on a single protocol, such as IP. Please consult the

Microsoft Web site for additional information on the SNA Server product.

Q: I have a Windows 2000 Router configured and it appears to be working, but the performance is very sluggish. Each of the two interfaces in the router is 100Mbs Fast Ethernet running full duplex. The memory and CPU utilization were also verified and were shown to be well within acceptable limits. Is the Windows 2000 Router that slow?

A: Actually, testing performed for this book showed that a Pentium II 450 with four 100Mbs Fast Ethernet connections was so fast that the hop was almost unnoticed in terms of throughput! Generally, sluggish performance can be attributed to a duplex mismatch or problems with cabling. The duplex and speed should not be set to automatic, but forced on both your switch and your Windows 2000 Router.

When a duplex mismatch occurs, performance can be terrible at best and potentially result in connection timeouts even over a Fast Ethernet connection. Though auto speed and duplex may work correctly for a workstation in most situations, a duplex mismatch there generally won't be noticed, since sustained throughput is quite low. However, a duplex mismatch for a critical networking component causes an entire segment to operate in a degraded mode. Keep in mind that hubs only operate in half-duplex mode.

Q: Why can't I run NetBEUI over my VPN connection?

A: Similar to DLC, NetBEUI is not a routable protocol. Though NetBEUI is actually very fast in a small workgroup setting, it is not advised for use in a large network, even if IP is also used. The reason is that NetBEUI can generate a considerable amount of broadcast traffic and cause sluggishness to be perceived by the user if NetBEUI is the default protocol and the resource is only available by using IP. The sluggishness would be the timeout period required for NetBEUI's connection attempt to fail.

Chapter 10

Administration and Ease of Use

Solutions in this chapter:

- **Connection Manager**
- **Administering Remote Access with AD**
- **Plug and Play**

Introduction

Windows 2000's networking components are not only much more powerful than those in previous versions of Microsoft operating systems, Windows 95/98 and Windows NT, they are also easier to use and administer.

For example, the poor Plug and Play support in Windows NT 4.0 meant that many users, even very technical ones, had trouble getting their PCMCIA modems to work with their laptops. The Plug and Play support in Windows 2000 is similar in quality to the support in Windows 98 and thus allows the cards to be detected and configured automatically upon insertion.

It doesn't stop there. Once users get their modems, cable modems, or ISDN connections working, they will want to be able to connect to their corporate networks via Point-to-Point Tunneling Protocol (PPTP) over the Internet instead of long-distance dial-up. Users could make PPTP connections using the previous version of Windows, but it required a higher skill level than most users had. In Windows 2000, creating a PPTP connection is a simple matter of selecting a "Make a New Connection" in "Network and Dial-Up Connections" and answering the questions asked by the wizard.

In Windows NT 4.0 Server, controlling access to your network via RAS and PPTP was confusing, as you had to configure settings in two different applets. In Windows 2000, this is all controlled from one centralized location using the "Active Directory Users and Computers" MMC snap-in.

Finally, Windows 2000 gives you a way to provide your users with automated connectivity. With the Connection Manager administration kit, you can create a customized dialer that will get users connected to your service or network with minimal effort or expertise required on their parts.

Both administrators and users benefit from these new features, designed to make networking Windows 2000 as quick and frustration-free as possible. In this chapter, we will look at how these new tools can benefit you and your organization.

Network and Dial-up Connections

Windows 2000's dial-up networking and remote access services are designed to make it easy to connect to a remote network, whether you are connecting to your Internet Service Provider's dial-up server or creating a secure tunnel through the Internet to your company's private Local Area Network (LAN). In this section, we will look at how the Windows 2000 dial-up networking feature works, and examine the processes of dialing up to connect to an ISP or a private network, using the supported tunneling protocols to establish a Virtual Private Network (VPN), and setting up a computer to accept incoming connections as a dial-up server. Then, we will take a look at how the administrator can monitor all these incoming and outgoing connections.

What is a Dial-up Connection?

Before we discuss how to create one, let's define what we mean when we use the term "dial-up connection." There are four basic ways that you can connect a computer to a network:

- Using a Network Interface Card (NIC) and Ethernet or other standard networking cable,

- Using a NIC that works with wireless technology, such as infrared (IR), microwave, or radio signaling,

- Using a device that connects the computer to a dedicated line, usually leased from the telephone company, or

- Using a modem or terminal adapter and analog or digital telephone lines

This last, which normally requires that you establish the connection each time you want to use the network by dialing into a remote access server also equipped with a modem and phone line, is the typical "dial-up connection" to which we will be referring.

Dial-up connections in Windows 2000 can be made using analog telephone lines, Integrated Services Digital Network (ISDN) phone lines, or X.25 technology. We will look at each of these in more detail.

NOTE

You will often hear analog lines referred to as either PSTN (Public Switched Telephone Network) or POTS (Plain Old Telephone Service). Using POTS and a modem is the most common method of making a dial-up connection, although in some geographic areas, digital lines are growing in popularity due to their higher speed and "cleaner" connection.

Dial-up Connections Using Telephone Lines

Analog telephone lines as a means of making a network connection have many disadvantages: they are slow, the line quality is variable, and they were designed to carry voice, not data. But they enjoy one overwhelming advantage that makes them the most popular medium for dial-up networking: almost universal availability. The public telephone network goes everywhere, making it particularly easy for users "on the move" to get connected from most locations when traveling.

Modem equipment to connect computers to analog lines is also readily available and relatively inexpensive. A modem modulates and, at the receiving end, demodulates a signal carrying data, converting it from digital (the form in which your PC communicates) to analog (the form required to travel over the phone lines), and back again.

Windows 2000 supports a large number of common modem brands and models; driver software is included on the Windows 2000 CD for literally hundreds, and for others, the manufacturer may have Windows 2000 drivers on its Web site that can be downloaded at no cost.

The Plug and Play component of Windows 2000 (see the section on Plug and Play later in this chapter) allows the operating system to automatically detect most supported modems. Thus, even if you have none of the documentation or software that came with the modem, in many cases Windows 2000 will still be able to install it with no problem.

TIP

For a list of the modems that have been tested and found to be compatible with Windows 2000, see the Hardware Compatibility List (HCL) on the Microsoft Web site at http://www.microsoft.com/hcl/default.asp.

Dial-up Connections Using ISDN

Integrated Digital Services Network (ISDN) service can be ordered from the telephone companies in many parts of the world, although it is not available in all areas. The advantages of an ISDN connection are:

- Higher data transfer speed than is possible with analog phone lines
- Faster call setup time
- Less noise and interference ("cleaner" connection)

Speed is the primary attraction of ISDN for most users. Analog modems have a top speed of 56Kbs, but rarely achieve that speed; in most cases, line quality limits the connection to a top speed of about 50Kbs (in some areas, it is much lower). Basic Rate ISDN (called BRI by the telephone company) combines two 64Kbs channels, in a process called "channel bonding," to achieve a 128Kbs connection without data compression (BRI also includes a 16Kbs "D" channel that is dedicated to signaling).

To use ISDN, you must have your phone company install an ISDN line, and you must use a device called an ISDN terminal adapter to connect your computer to the ISDN phone line. Not all telephone company central offices (COs) support ISDN, since it requires that they have digital switching equipment. Even if your CO offers ISDN, there are some restrictions. Generally, you must be within a certain distance of the CO (usually 18,000 feet).

ISDN has one more drawback: cost. You generally must pay a higher monthly rate for ISDN lines than for analog lines, and there is often a hefty installation fee and/or the requirement that you sign a one- or two-year contract. Some of the added cost may be offset by the higher transfer speed, however, if you must pay your Internet Service Provider by the minute or hour for the time you are connected.

NOTE

ISDN terminal adapters are sometimes incorrectly referred to as "modems," although they do not modulate and demodulate the signal. However, installation and configuration is very similar to that of a modem, and like modems, they come in both internal and external varieties. Interestingly, the external ISDN adapters show up in Device Manager under "Modems," while the internal adapters are shown under "Network Adapters."

Dial-up Connections Using X.25

X.25 is a packet-switching protocol that was developed in the 1970's, when analog phone lines were considered unreliable for data transfer, and was built with an emphasis on error detection and correction. Its connections are virtually error-free. It is used in such network communications as Automatic Teller Machines (ATM) and credit card approval systems, but its extensive error-checking capabilities cause it to be slower than some other WAN technologies. For this reason, Frame Relay and other high-speed technologies in some areas have replaced it.

Although it is used relatively infrequently for dial-up connections in the U.S. today, it is still popular in many parts of the world. Windows 2000 provides support for X.25 in its dial-up networking.

An X.25 connection requires special hardware, called Data Terminal Equipment (DTE) on the user end, and Data Circuit-terminating Equipment (DCE) on the carrier's end.

A dial-up X.25 connection is called a Switched Virtual Circuit (SVC). The connection is made using an X.121 number, which is a unique address given to each DTE on the network, instead of a telephone number.

Creating a Dial-up Internet Connection in Windows 2000

Those who remember the difficulty involved in configuring Windows 3.x to connect to the Internet or another network over the phone lines will truly appreciate the ease of using Windows 2000's dial-up networking, a refinement of the dial-up component first introduced in Windows 95. Configuring your Windows 2000 computer to use dial-up networking involves a few simple steps: installing your modem or ISDN adapter, setting Telephony Application Programming Interface (TAPI) dialing rules, creating one or more specific dial-up networking connections, and configuring the modem to use the dial-up connection(s).

Installing the Modem or ISDN Adapter

If your modem was in the machine when you installed Windows 2000, there's a good chance that the operating system detected it. However, if you install a new modem after the operating system is in place, or if Windows did not detect the modem properly or at all, you can install it easily by following these steps:

1. Open Start | Settings | Control Panel | Phone and Modem Options.

2. Select the Modems tab, and click "Add."

3. The Install New Modem wizard will guide you through the process of detecting and installing the software for your modem.

Before you are allowed to install the modem, you may see the screen shown in Figure 10.1. If so, enter the location information requested (this will occur only if you have not previously configured the TAPI dialing rules. For more information, see the section on configuring TAPI dialing rules below).

Figure 10.1 You may be required to enter location information before installing a modem.

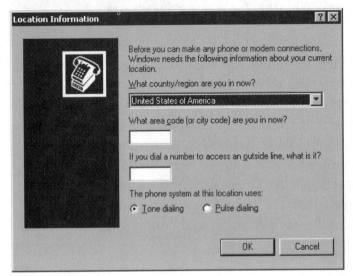

Installation of ISDN adapters will vary depending on the manufacturer. Follow the directions that come with your adapter. The software that comes with the adapter will usually allow you to configure the switch type used by the telephone company (ATT, NT-1 or NTI) and the SPIDs (the identification numbers for each ISDN channel). Your telephone company will provide this information to you when your ISDN line is installed.

Setting TAPI Dialing Rules

If you have a modem physically installed in the computer when you install the Windows 2000 operating system, it will probably be detected and you will be asked to set up dialing rules during that process. This only needs to be done once (unless you wish to make a change), so you may be able to skip this step in creating a dial-up connection. You will be prompted to enter the dialing information, as in Figure 10.1 above, if necessary.

Setting the TAPI rules involves designating a location, which is the name of a set of rules or parameters to be used by TAPI programs in dialing. You can set up more than one location, if you need different sets of rules for different circumstances. The most common scenario is the creation of two different TAPI locations on a laptop computer, one which is the set of rules used to call from home, the other a set of rules to use when dialing from the office. The latter might include a rule to dial "9" before the number to access an outside line, while the former does not. Or you might create different "locations" on a desktop machine that never travels, to be used with different long distance services.

When you create a location, you will need to enter some or all of the following information:

- Name
- Country or region
- Area (or city) code
- Dialing rules
- Area code rules
- Calling card information

To change location information, use the Dialing Rules property sheet, accessed via the Phone and Modem Options applet in Control Panel, as shown in Figure 10.2.

When you click the "Edit" button, you will see a property sheet that includes tabs for entering information about General dialing rules, Area Code Rules and Calling Card Rules. On the General tab, shown in Figure 10.3, you can edit the name of the location, specify the country or region and applicable area code from which you'll be dialing, input a number for accessing an outside line for

Figure 10.2 The Dialing Rules property sheet shows the TAPI locations that have been created on this computer.

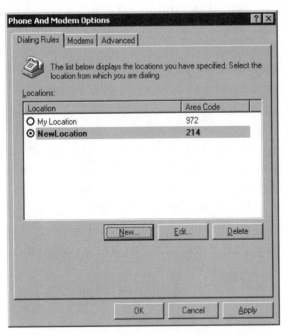

Figure 10.3 Area code and other general dialing information is entered on the first page of the Location properties sheet.

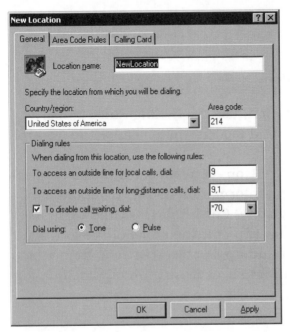

local and/or long distance calls, enter a number code (supplied by your phone company) to disable call waiting if the telephone account has that feature, and choose Tone or Pulse dialing.

The second page, shown in Figure 10.4, allows you to specify whether to dial the area code before the phone number.

Finally, on the third page of the property sheet, as shown in

Figure 10.4 You can specify whether the area code is to be dialed with the phone number.

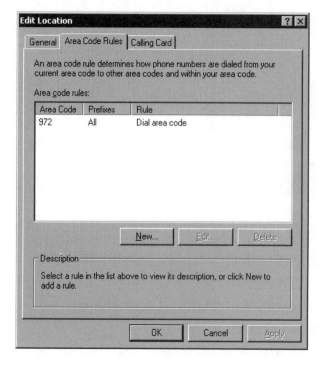

Figure 10.5, you can enter calling card information that will be automatically used when dialing from this location.

Many Windows telephony applications will allow you to select a location to use each time you dial. If you have created more than one location, you will designate one as the default (by selecting its radio button on the Dialing Rules property sheet shown earlier).

Figure 10.5 You can enter information for using a calling card to dial from this location.

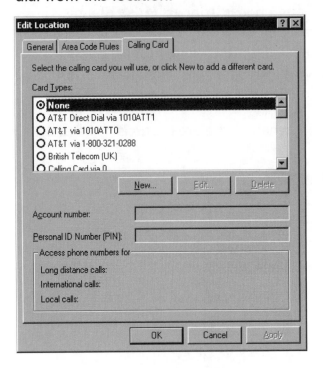

Creating the Dial-up Networking Connection

To create a new dial-up connection, you will start the Network Connection wizard by performing the following:

- Start | Settings | Network and Dial-up Connections.
- Select the "Make New Connection" icon.
- Click "Next" on the wizard's splash screen, and you will see the dialog box shown in Figure 10.6.

As you can see in Figure 10.6, you can choose from several types of network connections. In this example, we are going to create a dial-up connection to an Internet Service Provider, so we have selected the second radio button, "Dial-up to the Internet." Later, we will discuss how to connect directly to a private network, such as your company's LAN, by dialing in to its modem, and how to create a Virtual Private Networking "tunnel" through the Internet to a private network.

Figure 10.6 The Network Connection Wizard guides you through the steps of creating a new dial-up connection.

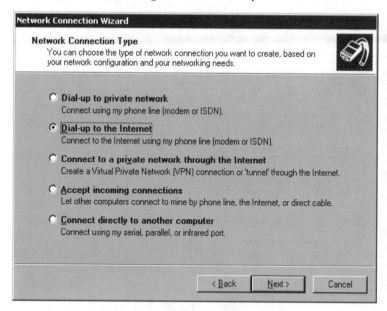

When you choose to create an Internet connection, and click "Next," this starts another wizard, the Internet Connection Wizard shown in Figure 10.7.

In this example, we will show you how to set up the Internet connection manually, so we have selected the third radio button. You should also choose this option if you will be connecting through your local area network, instead of using a modem and phone line. If you already have an ISP account and will connect through a modem, you could choose the second radio button to transfer your existing account information to this computer.

If you choose manual setup, when you click "Next" you will see the dialog box shown in Figure 10.8.

Next, you will need to enter the area code and telephone number of your ISP's modem (provided to you by the ISP), as shown in Figure 10.9, designate the country and region in which the ISP is located, and choose whether to use the area code and dialing rules that are set in the TAPI dialing rules properties.

Figure 10.7 The Internet Connection Wizard helps you create a dial-up connection to your Internet Service Provider.

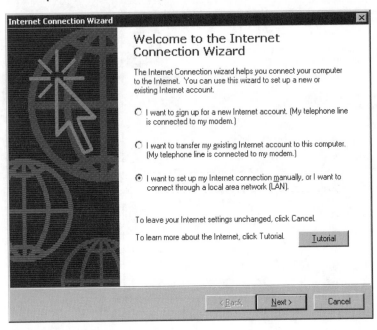

Figure 10.8 The first step in setting up your Internet connection manually is to select the physical method by which you will connect.

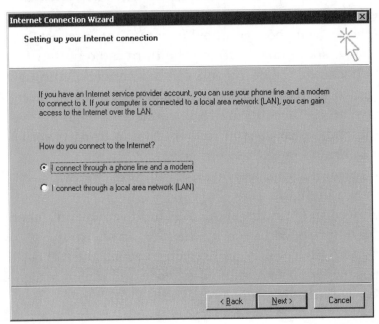

Figure 10.9 Enter the phone number and country/region of your ISP.

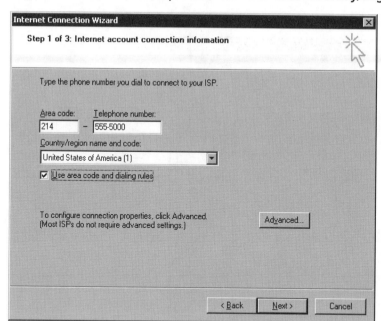

In most cases, you will not have to modify the default Advanced settings, but in some cases, your ISP's setup may require that you do so. Click the "Advanced" button, and you will see the dialog box shown in Figure 10.10.

Serial Line Internet Protocol (SLIP) and Point-to-Point Protocol (PPP) are two WAN link protocols, which can be used to encapsulate the TCP/IP packets for transmission over the phone lines. Most modern Internet Service Providers currently use PPP for the WAN link; however, there are still some ISPs using SLIP or its variant, Compressed SLIP.

NOTE

SLIP has the advantage of lower overhead, but PPP supports advanced features such as data encryption, different authentication methods, and scripted log-ons. SLIP is used by UNIX servers; Windows NT/2000 remote access servers do not support incoming SLIP connections. PPP is the default WAN link protocol.

Figure 10.10 You can modify Advanced settings if your ISP requires that you do so.

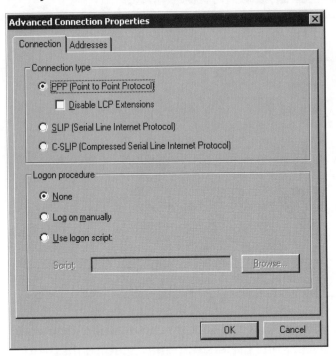

In the second section of the connection properties sheet, you can designate a script to be used at log-on. This might be necessary if the server you are dialing into requires that you enter information other than your username and password in order to log on. Type in the path to the script file or browse for it.

On the second page of the advanced properties sheet, shown in Figure 10.11, you can specify IP addressing and DNS server information.

Many ISPs use Dynamic Host Configuration Protocol (DHCP) to automatically assign you an IP address each time you dial up and establish a connection. However, in some cases, you may be assigned a permanent IP address; SLIP requires a permanent IP address, and there are other instances when you may be able to purchase a permanent, or static address from your ISP — for example, if you wish to host a Web server or FTP server.

Figure 10.11 Enter a static IP address and/or the name of a DNS server in the Addresses section of the Advanced Connection properties sheet.

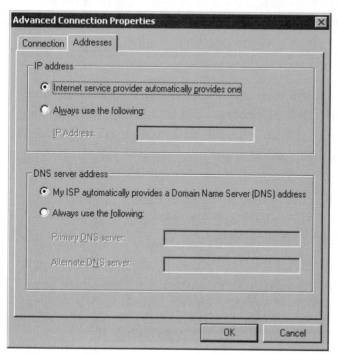

NOTE

See Chapter 3 in this book for more information about the Dynamic Host Configuration Protocol (DHCP).

This property sheet also allows you to the enter the address of a Domain Name Server (DNS), which will be used to resolve Internet names such as www.microsoft.com, to the applicable IP address so communication can be established. Computers running the TCP/IP protocol communicate with one another using IP addresses. TCP/IP is unable to use the "friendly" names that we humans prefer, thus they must be translated into IP addresses to be used. This is the job of a DNS server on your ISP's network or on the Internet.

NOTE

See Chapter 4 in this book for more information about Domain Name Services (DNS).

In most cases, if your ISP automatically assigns your computer an IP address using DHCP, that process will include assigning the address of the DNS server. If not, the ISP will provide a DNS address to you when you sign up for an account.

Once you have completed any necessary modifications to the Advanced settings, click "OK," and then click "Next."

You will be asked to enter the username and password for your ISP account, as shown in Figure 10.12.

Figure 10.12 Enter the username and password assigned by your Internet Service Provider.

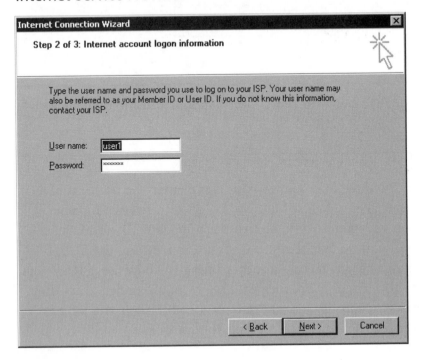

Your ISP will usually allow you to select a username (sometimes called member name or account name) and password of your choice when you sign up for an Internet account. Note that the password is often case-sensitive, but the username usually is not. Click "Next."

In the dialog box shown in Figure 10-13, you will be asked to name this connection. This name will be used to identify the connection icon in your dial-up and networking connections window.

Figure 10.13 The last step in creating a dial-up connection is giving it a name.

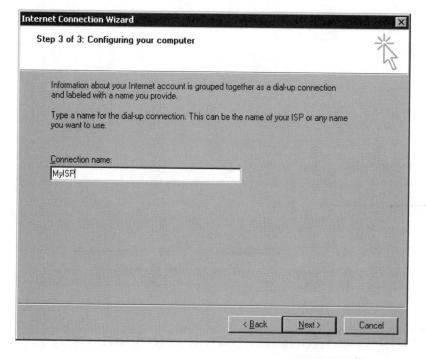

After you have completed the steps necessary to make the dial-up connection, the wizard will ask if you want to set up an e-mail account at this time. If not, you will be informed that the wizard has completed successfully, and the new dial-up connection will appear with your other network and dial-up connections, as shown in Figure 10.14.

The telephone icon indicates that this is a dial-up connection.

Figure 10.14 The newly-created dial-up connection, "MyISP," appears with a telephone icon in your Network and Dial-up Connections folder.

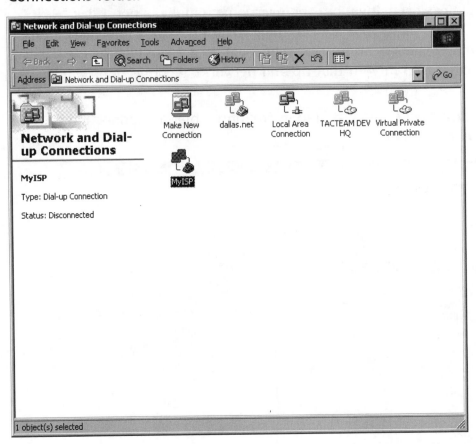

Configuring the Modem to use the Dial-up Connection(s)

To configure a modem to use an existing dial-up networking connection, follow these steps:

1. Open the configuration box: Start | Settings | Network and Dial-up Connections.

2. Right-click the selected dial-up connection and click "Properties."

3. Click the name of the modem you wish to configure, and click "Configure."

4. In the Hardware Features section, check the options you wish to enable.

5. Then under Initialization, check the options you wish to enable.

6. Check "Enable modem speaker" if you wish to hear the modem dial.

7. Click "OK."

This step should be necessary only if you install a new modem after creating your dial-up connection, or if you want to change the modem being used for a connection.

Connecting to a Private Network

In addition to (or instead of) connecting to the public Internet, you may want to configure your Windows 2000 computer to connect to a private network, such as your company's LAN. This is the case when you have employees who need to download files from the company's server when working from home, or when executives or salespeople are on the road and need to access files on their office machines. Or, you may need a low-cost way to temporarily connect the LANs in geographically-separated branch offices.

There are two basic ways to connect to a private network using only the phone lines: by dialing directly into a dial-up server, or by dialing up your ISP and then "tunneling" through the Internet to the private network (which must also be Internet-connected).

Connecting to a Dial-up Server

Creating a dial-up connection to access a private network is similar to creating a dial-up Internet connection as we discussed in the foregoing section. Start the same "Make New Connection" wizard and choose "Dial-up to private network." You will be asked to enter the phone number for the private network. Then you will see the dialog box shown in Figure 10.15, asking whether you wish this connection to be available to all users of this computer, or only to the user whose account is logged-on when the new connection is created.

Figure 10.15 Choose whether to make the connection available to all users or keep it for your use only.

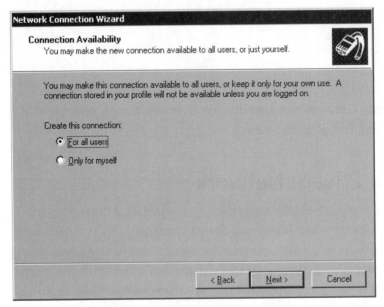

Then you will be given the option, as shown in Figure 10.16, to share the connection with other computers on your network via Internet Connection Sharing. See Chapter 8 for detailed information on using ICS.

In the final dialog box, you will be asked to type a name for the connection, and given the option to place a shortcut to it on your desktop.

Once you've completed the wizard, all you have to do is click on the connection icon, and your modem will dial and connect to the private network. If the dial-in server is an NT or Windows 2000 machine, when the connection is made you will be prompted to enter your username and password. You must have a user account on the dial-in server (or in the domain) in order to be authenticated and logged-on.

Figure 10.16 You can share the connection with other computers on the network via ICS.

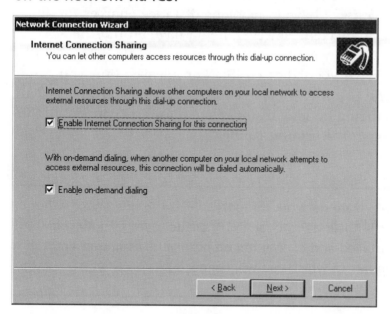

When you connect to a private network in this way (called a Remote Access or RAS connection), your computer becomes a node on the remote network. You can do anything from this computer that you could do from an on-site computer connected to the LAN by cable (so long as the RAS server is set up to allow access to the entire network); the only difference between a RAS connection and a cabled connection is speed (the phone lines are considerably slower.)

Connecting by a Virtual Private Network (VPN)

There may be times when it is advantageous to connect to your company's private network through the Internet, using a "tunneling" protocol to create a Virtual Private Network (see Chapter 6 for details about VPNs) instead of directly dialing into a Remote Access server on the LAN.

One such circumstance is when the private LAN is located in a different calling area. If you use your modem to dial the server's modem directly, you will have to pay long distance charges for all the time you are connected. However, if you have an Internet account with an ISP in your local dialing area, and the LAN is connected to the Internet via dedicated ISDN or a leased line, you can instead create and use a VPN connection. In this case, you can dial up your ISP (incurring no long distance charges) and connect to the private LAN through the secure "tunnel."

NOTE

To connect to the private network through a VPN, you must have either the Point-to-Point Tunneling Protocol (PPTP) or the Layer 2 Tunneling Protocol (L2TP) installed and configured on both your computer and the remote LAN computer to which you will connect.

Chapter 6 explains how to install and configure a VPN connection, and Chapter 8 discusses how you can share the VPN connection with other computers using Internet Connection Sharing (ICS).

Configuring a Computer for Incoming Connections

Your Windows 2000 computer can function not only as a dial-up client, but can also be set up to be a dial-in server; that is, other computers can create dial-up connections to call and log onto it and access its resources. When you configure a computer to be a dial-in server, it will answer the calls, authenticate the user, and transfer data between the dial-in client and the local network.

Configuring a computer to accept incoming connections is another option offered by the Make New Connection wizard. In this case, when you select "Accept incoming connections" as the network connection type, you will be given the option to accept incom-

Figure 10.17 You can specify which users will be allowed to connect to the dial-in server.

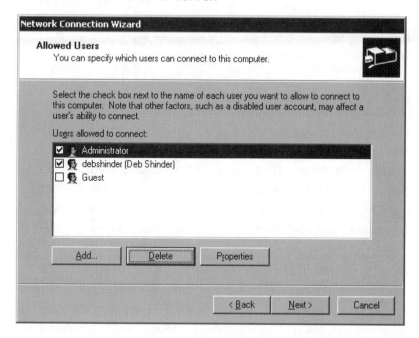

ing VPN connections, and then you will see a dialog box similar to the one shown in Figure 10.17, which allows you to select the users who will be allowed to connect to the dial-in server from a remote computer.

Only a user who has a valid user account, which must also be configured to allow dial-in connections, will be allowed to dial in.

Next, you will be prompted to choose the networking components (such as TCP/IP, NetBEUI, or File and Print Sharing for Microsoft Networks) that you will allow to be used with dial-in connections.

NOTE

If you attempt to set up a Windows 2000 Server computer that belongs to a domain as a dial-in server using the Network Connection Wizard, you will get the message box shown in Figure 10.18. You must use Routing and Remote Access to configure these computers as RAS servers.

Figure 10.18 A Windows 2000 Server must be configured as a RAS server through the RRAS system console.

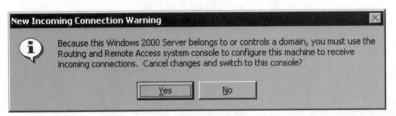

See Chapter 7 for information on configuring a RAS server.

When you have completed the wizard, an incoming connection icon will appear in your Network and Dial-up Connections. You can use it to change the properties settings or to monitor the status of incoming connections (see the section on monitoring, later in this chapter).

To allow users to access the entire network, rather than just the dial-in server computer, through this connection, open the Incoming Connections properties box shown in Figure 10.19 by selecting Start | Settings | Network and Dial-up Connections | Incoming Connections and choosing the "Networking" tab.

Select the protocol to be used for the LAN connection by the remote computers that will dial into this dial-in server. In the Protocol Properties dialog box, shown in Figure 10.20, check the "Allow callers to access my local area network" check box. You must do this for each protocol you will be using for dial-up connections.

In order access network resources, the dial-in user's account must have the appropriate permissions.

WARNING

Enabling a computer that is part of a company network as a dial-in server can present a large security risk, so this should never be done without the knowledge and consent of the network administrator who is monitoring incoming and outgoing connections.

Figure 10.19 Select the protocol to be used for incoming connections by double-clicking it or highlighting it and clicking the "Properties" button.

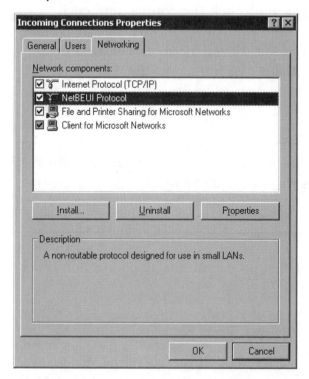

Figure 10.20 Allowing dial-in users to access the entire network through the dial-in server.

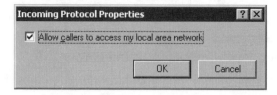

To monitor the activity for a current incoming or outgoing connection, just right-click the icon for that connection in Network and Dial-up Connections, and click on "Status." You will see the connection speed, the duration of the connection, and how many packets have been sent and received.

You can also forcibly disconnect a dial-in connection by selecting "Disconnect" on the right-click menu.

If you want to enable the status monitor automatically every time the connection is active, right-click the connection, click "Properties," and then select the "Show icon in taskbar when connected" check box. Then, you can hover the mouse button over the taskbar icon and you will see a summary of the connection status information.

NOTE

If the computer is a dial-in server, you will see a connection icon with a username assigned to it in the Network and Dial-up Connections folder when a dial-in user connects.

The status monitor is enabled by default for all connection types except local area connections.

Making Dial-up Connectivity Easier

Although Windows 2000's wizards make it relatively easy for an administrator or "power"user to create dial-up connections quickly, many novice users will still have problems configuring all of the settings involved.

If your company needs to provide dial-up access to a group of users who don't have the technical expertise to set up the connections, there is a solution: you can create and distribute a simple dialer interface, using the Connection Manager Administration Kit, discussed in the next section.

Connection Manager Administration Kit

The Connection Manager Administration Kit (CMAK), which comes with Windows 2000 Server, allows you to create a custom dialer with a graphical interface which can be used by your employees, customers or other users to quickly and easily connect to your dial-in server without any technical knowledge about how to create and configure a dial-up connection. Connection Manager is another of Windows 2000's many features, which make the operating system easier to use and administer. The CMAK wizard guides you through the installation process.

What is Connection Manager?

The Connection Manager itself is a user interface that includes a log-on dialog box and a set of property dialog boxes, which users can use to customize their connection settings. You can customize the look of the dialog boxes with your company logo and special icons, and modify the information that will be presented to users.

You can then distribute the executable program created by the Connection Manager wizard to your users, who then install the dialer interface on their Windows 2000, NT or Windows 9x computers.

A typical Connection Manager user interface is shown in Figure 10.21. Users enter their username and password, and can select to have the software remember the password if they wish.

If the "Connect automatically" check box is checked, a user need only double click on the Connection Manager icon (which can be placed on the desktop for added convenience) and the computer will dial up and connect to your network.

Internet Service Providers can use the CMAK to create user interfaces that will make it easier for their non-technical customers to get online.

The CMAK wizard guides you through the process of creating a customized Connection Manager interface to distribute to users of your network. The wizard has an easy-to-use graphical interface that lets you specify custom elements for your service and then builds your customized installation package for you. You can create a self-installing executable file that your users can download or that you can distribute on disk to simplify the distribution process.

Figure 10.21 You can customize the Connection Manager interface with your company name and information, custom graphics and icons.

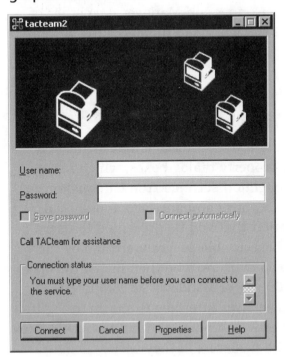

Using Branding to Customize the Dialer

"Branding" refers to customization of the Connection Manager interface to reflect your organization's image. The CMAK wizard makes it easy to insert your own logo, graphics and icons in place of Connection Manager's default bitmaps.

You can also include custom phone book and support information (see the section entitled Custom Phone Book below.)

Although Connection Manager is often used and distributed by ISPs to make it easy for their customers to connect to their services, it also makes a great tool for any company that has multiple access points, including VPNs.

Connect Actions and Auto-applications

Taking the customization process even further, you can designate applications to be included with Connection Manager, which will run automatically at a particular point in the connection process (for instance, when a user logs on or off).

Connect actions can be run at the following times:

- Pre-connect actions: the program runs at the time the user clicks the "Connect" button, prior to dialing and establishing a connection.

- Pre-tunnel actions (for VPN connections only): the program runs after establishing the connection to the Internet, but before establishing the tunnel to your private network.

- Post-connect actions: the program runs immediately after establishing the connection to your network, either through direct dial-in or after the tunnel is established for a VPN.

- Disconnect actions: the program runs just prior to disconnecting the user from your network.

For example, you might set up a disconnect action to run a program that collects status information, such as the total time spent online in this session (if your network has software that tracks this information) and display it so the user will know how long he was connected.

The application specified as a connect action must be a complete program file. You can include one program file per connect action. If the application needs additional (non-executable) files in order to run, you can include them as "additional files" when creating the Connection Manager dialer with the CMAK wizard.

Auto-applications run after the connection to your network is established. They can also be incorporated into a VPN connection, in which case the application will run after the secure tunnel has been established (see Chapter 6 for more information about VPNs). Auto-applications can also be set up to disconnect when the program ends.

There are two primary differences between a connect action and an auto-application:

- A connect action can be a .DLL (dynamic link library), which cannot be run as an auto-application. This is because .DLLs run synchronously, while auto-applications are run asynchronously.

- When the last auto-application is closed, Connection Manager automatically begins the disconnection process. Thus, by designating auto-applications, you can exercise more control over the users' connections.

You could, for example, have a particular e-mail application run as an auto-application after the user connects to your network.

As with connect actions, only complete program files should be designated as auto-applications, and additional files can be included during the CMAK wizard process.

NOTE

Do not include as an auto-application a program that the users already have installed on their computers. This can cause problems on the users' computers.

Multiple Instances of Connection Manager

Users can have multiple instances of Connection Manager on a single computer, configured to connect to different networks, or to connect using different customization features (such as auto-applications). An icon for each Connection Manager Connection will appear in your Network and Dial-up Connections, as shown in Figure 10.22.

In the example, there are two Connection Manager icons, "tacteam" and "tacteam2." One connection includes auto-applications; the other does not.

Figure 10.22 Multiple instances of Connection Manager appear in Network and Dial-up Connections as separate icons.

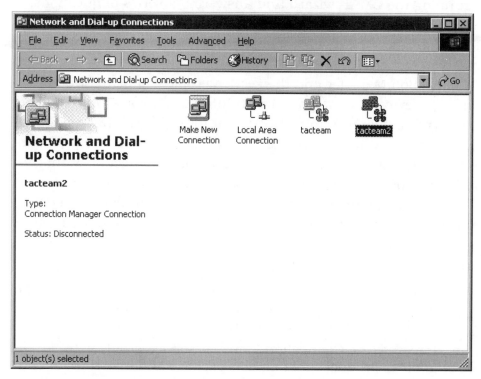

Two service profiles can be configured to run simultaneously. For example, your users could run an Internet Connection at the same time they are running a VPN tunnel to the company network.

Multiple User Support

If two or more users share the same computer, you can create user profiles for each. This allows them to connect using the same service profile, but still maintains authentication credentials based on user account identification information (username and password).

This means that you don't need multiple instances of Connection Manager, one for each user, if the same service profile will be used. Instead, you can save disk space by having only one, and individual users can log on with their own usernames and passwords.

Simplified Distribution

By running the CMAK wizard and answering a series of questions, you can automatically build a service profile. Then when you click on "Finish," the wizard will create a self-extracting executable file, which you can copy to disk or CD.

Connection Manager and the service profile can be distributed alone, or they can be integrated with Internet Explorer. You can use the Internet Explorer Administration Kit (IEAK) to create an installation package, and include the Connection Manager service profile in the package. Then your users can install both Connection Manager and Internet Explorer in a single procedure.

You can use command line parameters to integrate Connection Manager in an installation package and deliver it to your users in one of the following ways:

- Use the Microsoft Systems Management Server (SMS) to distribute and install the Connection Manager service profile over a corporate network and automatically handle the installation process without user intervention.

- Integrate the Connection Manager service profile with another product's installation package and install them both in a single process (an example of this would be integration with the Microsoft Internet Explorer Web browser (MSIE), as mentioned above).

- Post the Connection Manager service profile to a Web site and allow users to download it from there and install the service profile in a standard way.

Custom Phone Book

You can use Connection Point Services (CPS), which consists of the Phone Book Service and the Phone Book Administrator, to create and edit custom phone books that can be downloaded to your users and automatically updated.

The CMAK allows you combine multiple phone books in a service profile, by merging existing profiles. See the section on Connection Point Services later in this chapter for more information about using the Phone Book Service and Phone Book Administrator.

Central Administration of Phone Books

Phone books can be administered either through the Connection Point Services interface (the recommended method), or using command line utilities. This gives administrators the ability to edit multiple phone books from one centralized location, hosting several phone books on a single server.

The Phone Book Service (PBS) must run on a server that has IIS and FTP services installed, but an administrator can use the Phone Book Administrator from a workstation, as well.

You can only have one Phone Book Administrator folder (which is on your primary PBA computer), but you can use one administration tool to post multiple phone books, each to a different PBA server. Figure 10.23 shows PBA with two phone books. The icon indicates which book is currently open.

Figure 10.23 The Phone Book Administrator can be used to manage multiple phone books.

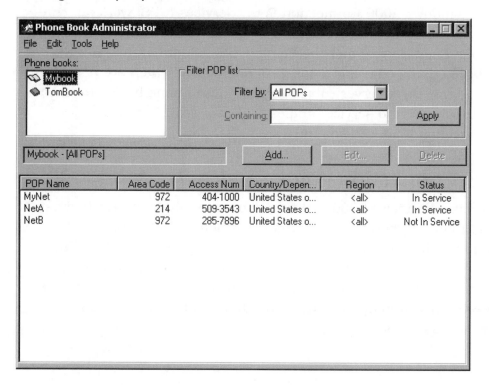

NOTE

After you install Phone Book Administrator on the remote computer (workstation or laptop), you will use it to manage your phone books; you should delete the PBA folder from that computer. This prevents you from accidentally starting Phone Book Administrator from the remote computer, which can cause the data files to become unsynchronized, but leaves the system files intact so you can still use the PBA tool to administer the phone books on the Phone Book Server.

For information on installing and using the Phone Book Administrator and the Phone Book Service, see the next section, Connection Point Services.

Connection Point Services

The Windows 2000 Connection Point Services (CPS) works in conjunction with Connection Manager. CPS has two components: the Phone Book Service and the Phone Book Administrator. You use PBA to create, edit, and publish phone books, which are hosted on the Phone Book server running PBS. These phone books are then incorporated into service profiles that are created with the Connection Manager Administration Kit.

What is Connection Point Services?

CPS is a Windows 2000 tool that allows an administrator to create and manage phone book databases, which include local access numbers for various connectivity points of presence (POPs). With CPS, you can download new access numbers to your users through their Connection Manager software, so you can update the phone books when numbers change, and they will be automatically downloaded to the user.

Phone Book Administrator

If your online service or wide area network has multiple access numbers, perhaps in different localities, these can be organized in a database and distributed to users when they connect using Connection Manager. Phone Book Administrator (PBA) is the administrative tool used to create, manage, and edit these phone books.

What is Phone Book Administrator?

PBA is a GUI (Graphical User Interface) that allows you to create phone books and customize phone book entries (called POPs). For example, you can specify the connection type, such as 56k or ISDN, so users can find an access number that will provide the desired service type. You can associate specific POPs with specific network configurations defined in Connection Manager. You can then use PBA to publish all of the phone book information to PBS, the Phone Book Service that runs on the server.

To install Phone Book Administrator on your Windows 2000 computer, run PBAinst.exe from the Windows 2000 Server CD. You will find it in the VALUEADD\MSFT\MGMT directory. After installation is complete, Phone Book Administrator can be accessed from:

Start | Programs | Administrative Tools | Phone Book Administrator.

NOTE

When you install PBA on a Windows 2000 Professional computer, the Help documentation will not display unless you install the Admin Tools Pack, which is available by launching the adminpak.msi installation package found under the i386 directory of the Windows 2000 Server or Advanced Server CD.

Adding a New Phone Book

To add a new phone book, perform the following steps:

1. Open PBA from the Start menu as indicated above. Then click the "File" menu, and select "New Phone Book."

2. In the Add New Phone Book dialog box, shown in Figure 10.24, type the phone book name, and then click "OK."

Figure 10.24 Type a name for the new phone book in the Add New Phone Book dialog box.

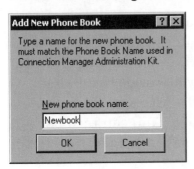

TIP

A phone book name must contain no more than eight characters, cannot consist of all digits, and must not contain a space or any of the following symbols: ! , ; * = / \ : ? ' " < > | . & % {} []. Also, if you created a customized Connection Manager, the name in the Set Up the Phone Book dialog box in the CMAK wizard must match this name.

3. In Phone books, click the new phone book.

4. On the Tools menu, click "Options."

5. In the Options dialog box, shown in Figure 10.25, type the server address, username, and password.

The username and password are used to FTP the phone book to the phone book server when you publish it.

Figure 10.25 Enter the server's Fully Qualified Domain Name and a username and password in the Options dialog box.

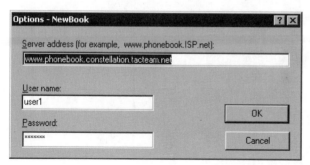

Options - NewBook	? X

Server address (for example, www.phonebook.ISP.net):

`www.phonebook.constellation.tacteam.net`

User name:

`user1`

OK

Password:

`xxxxxxx`

Cancel

NOTE

The entries for server address, username, and password cannot include spaces in the names.

Adding Entries to the Phone Book

To add entries (POPs) to your phone book, open the Phone Book Administrator and perform the following steps:

1. In Phone books, click the name of the phone book to which you want to add POPs.

2. On the Edit menu, click "Add POP."

3. On the Access Information tab, shown in Figure 10.26, enter or edit the information. For countries without area codes, type a space in Area Code field. Choose "In Service" status to include the POP in future updates of the phone book file, and "Not In Service" to exclude it.

4. On the Settings tab, in POP settings, select the options that apply to this POP. See Figure 10.27. Enter a name in the Dial-Up Networking entry field that matches the name specified in the CMAK wizard.

5. You can type additional notes in the Comments section.

6. Click the "Save" button to finish the configuration.

Figure 10.26 Enter the name, country, area code and phone number, and status of the POP.

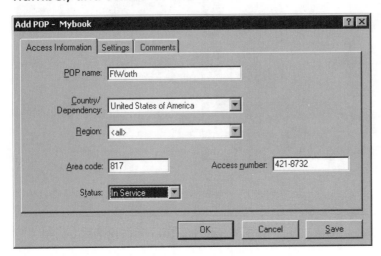

Figure 10.27 Configure optional POP settings on the Settings tab.

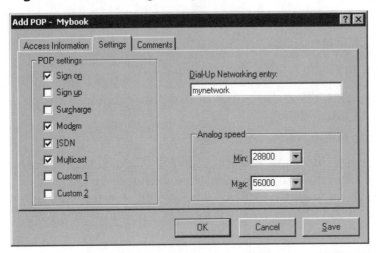

NOTE

You should not clear the Sign on check box. This option must remain selected so that Connection Manager can display the access number.

Publishing a Phone Book

You publish a phone book by posting it to the Phone Book server running Phone Book Services (PBS). To publish your new phone book, open the Phone Book Administrator and perform the following steps:

1. In Phone books, click the phone book you want to post.

2. If you haven't already specified a server address for this phone book, on the Tools menu, click "Options," and then type a server address, username, and password for your Phone Book Service (PBS) host, as shown in Step 5 in the Adding and Configuring a New Phone Book section above.

3. On the "Tools" menu, click "Publish Phone Book."

4. You will see the dialog box shown in Figure 10.28.

Figure 10.28 Browse to the directory in which the phone book file will be stored.

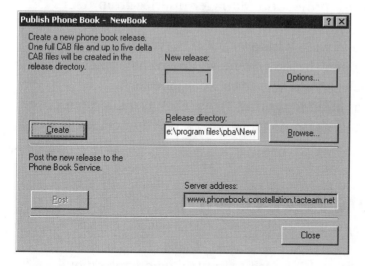

5. In the Release directory, browse to the directory in which you want to keep your files.

6. Click "Create," and then click "Post."

Now, using the CMAK wizard, you can include the phone book in your service profile, with or without automatic updates.

Phone Book Service

The Phone Book Service (PBS) is an extension to Internet Information Services (IIS) 5.0. When your users send a query to your phone book server (which happens automatically via the Connection Manager software if you have configured it for automatic updates), the Phone Book Services will compare their phone book version with the most recent version(s) in your database. If they do not match, PBS will download the appropriate updates to the Connection Manager profile residing on the user's computer.

In order to use PBS on your server, you must be running IIS version 5.0. You must be running both File Transfer Protocol (FTP) and the World Wide Web (WWW) services; however, you can stop the FTP service when you do not wish to update the phone books. The FTP service accepts the updated phone book information, which is transferred from Phone Book Administrator (PBA). The WWW service handles Connection Manager queries from users' computers.

The PBS is included with Windows 2000 Server and Advanced Server. To install it, open the Add/Remove Programs applet in Control Panel and select "Add Windows Components."

Click Management and Monitoring Tools, click Details, then check the "Connection Manager Components" check box and click OK.

Enabling Remote Access with Active Directory

Remote access policies can be used to control who can remotely connect to the network, and set conditions for those connections. Remote access policies can be administered through the Routing and Remote Access console or through an Internet Authentication Service (IAS) server. In a Windows 2000 domain, users are authenticated in the Windows 2000 Active Directory, with support for such Active Directory features as User Principal Names and Universal

Groups (in a native mode Windows 2000 domain, in which all domain controllers are Windows 2000 servers).

What is Remote Access Policy?

A remote access policy is a set of rules that contains specified conditions or attributes, remote access user permissions, and a profile that is applied to the connection.

Conditions

You can specify conditions in the remote access policy. These conditions must match the settings in the attempted connection. Some conditions that can be set include:

- The IP address of the network access server
- The RADIUS service type being requested
- The type of framing for incoming packets (such as PPP or SLIP)
- The phone number of the network access server
- The phone number of the calling computer
- The media type being used (for example, analog phone lines or ISDN)
- Day of week and time of day
- The IP address of the RADIUS client
- The vendor of the network access server (for example, Microsoft Remote Access Server)
- The "friendly" name of the RADIUS client computer
- The security groups to which the user belongs
- The type of tunnel being created if this is a VPN connection (PPTP or L2TP)

NOTE

For more information about RADIUS, see RFC 2138, "Remote Authentication Dial-in User Service (RADIUS)."

Permissions

First, the connection attempt must meet the specified conditions of the policy, as discussed above. Then, remote access permission is granted or denied, both generally and for each user. The user account is configured through the Active Directory Users and Computers administrative tools (see the section on Using the MMC below.)

Profiles

A remote access policy profile is a group of properties to be applied to a connection at the time it is authorized through the user

For Managers

Local vs. Centralized Administration

Remote access policies are stored locally on either a remote access server or an IAS server. If you wish to be able to centrally manage a set of remote access policies for multiple remote access servers, you must install the Internet Authentication Service (IAS) as a Remote Authentication Dial-In User Service (RADIUS) server.

Then you must configure IAS with RADIUS clients that represent each Windows 2000 remote access server, and set up each Windows 2000 remote access server as a RADIUS client to the IAS server. You can then create a central set of policies for all of the Windows 2000 remote access servers on the IAS server.

When you have set up a Windows 2000 remote access server to be a RADIUS client to an IAS server, the local remote access policies that are stored on the remote access server/RADIUS client will no longer be used. The IAS server now provides centralized remote access authentication and must authenticate the user before access will be allowed.

account permission setting or the policy permission setting. The properties included in a profile are:

- Dial-in constraints, such as the amount of idle time allowed before automatic disconnection, or specific days and times when a connection is allowed

- IP properties, such as whether the dial-in client will be automatically allocated an IP address or can request a specific IP address

- Multilink properties, such as whether to allow multilink (the bonding of two lines for greater bandwidth) and how many ports the multilink connection can use

- Authentication properties, specifying what authentication protocols are allowed

- Encryption properties, specifying whether a non-encrypted connection is allowed, or whether Basic, Strong, or Strongest encryption methods should be used

You can also set Advanced properties, specifying the series of RADIUS attributes to be sent back to the RADIUS client by the IAS server.

Using the "Active Directory Users and Computers" MMC

To configure remote access permissions for a user account, open the MMC:

Start | Programs | Administrative Tools | Active Directory Users and Computers.

To grant remote access permission to a user or group, expand the Users folder by double-clicking on it in the left console pane, as shown in Figure 10.29.

In the right pane, you will see a listing of the user and group accounts in this domain that are in the Users container.

Figure 10.29 Open the Active Directory Users and Computers MMC and expand the Users folder.

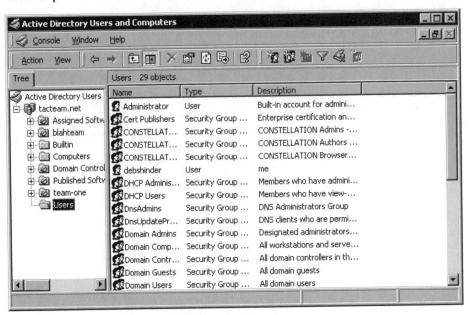

Assigning Access to Individual Users

Highlight and right-click the username in the right pane, to open the user account properties sheet shown in Figure 10.30.

On the Dial-in tab, you can select whether to allow or deny remote access, or if you have established Remote Access policies in IAS, you can select to have this user's remote access governed by that policy.

NOTE

The option to control access through remote access policy option is only available on user accounts in a Windows 2000 native-mode domain or for local accounts on remote access servers running stand-alone Windows 2000. Also, be aware that if remote access policies are established, their conditions can cause a denial of access even if a user account is granted access in the user account properties sheet.

Figure 10.30 Grant remote access through the Dial-in tab on the user account properties sheet.

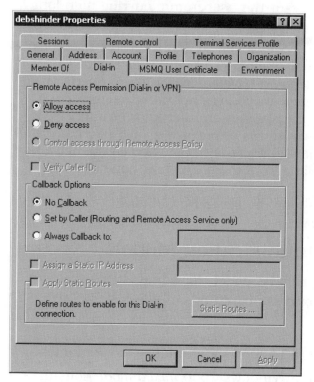

Verification of Caller ID

If the remote access server has Caller ID enabled by the phone company on its incoming line, you can set up the server to use that service to verify that the call is coming from a preset number that you enter here.

Callback Options

When you grant remote access permission to a user, you can also elect to enable callback security for that user. This can be done in one of two ways:

- With Routing and Remote Access Services enabled, you can set callback so that when the user dials in and enters a valid username and password, he or she will be prompted to enter the phone number he or she is calling from. Then, the RAS server will hang up and call him back at that number. This is useful to prevent the user from incurring high long distance charges for the connect time.

■ Alternately, you can set callback so that when the user logs on, the server immediately hangs up and calls back to a preset number (which you have entered in the property sheet shown above). In this way, you restrict users to connecting remotely only from their homes or other known numbers. If an unauthorized user knows or guesses a valid username and password, he or she still won't be able to access the network if he or she is not calling from the preset telephone number.

By default, callback options are set to No Callback.

Remote Access Administration Models

Microsoft suggests three primary models for administering remote access permissions and connection settings in Windows 2000:

■ Access by user

■ Access by policy in a Windows 2000 *native-mode* domain

■ Access by policy in a Windows 2000 *mixed-mode* domain

Access by User

In this model, remote access permissions are determined by the remote access permission on the Dial-in tab of the user account. You can enable or disable the permission on a per-user basis.

The access-by-user model can be used on a stand-alone remote access server, a remote access server that is a member of a Windows 2000 native-mode domain, a remote access server that is a member of a Windows 2000 mixed-mode domain, or a remote access server that is a member of a Windows NT 4.0 domain.

Access by Policy — Windows 2000 Native-Mode Domain

In this model, the remote access permission on all user accounts is set to "Control access through Remote Access Policy." The permissions are defined by the remote access permission setting on the remote access policy.

If you use this administrative model and use the default remote access policy, no users will be allowed to access the RAS server remotely. The default permission on the default remote access policy is set to "Deny remote access permission."

You can use security groups to designate which users have remote access permissions.

Access by Policy — Windows 2000 Mixed-mode Domain

In this model, the remote access permission on all user accounts is set to "Allow access." The policy is deleted, and separate remote access policies are created to define the types of connections that are allowed. The option to control access through Remote Access Policy will be grayed out on the user account properties sheet. If the conditions of a policy (subject to the profile and user account dial-in settings) are met, the connection will be accepted.

If you do not delete the default remote access policy, the effect is the opposite of that in a native-mode domain: all users will be able to establish a remote access connection.

NOTE

If your network has Windows NT 4.0 Routing and Remote Access Service (RRAS) servers, in order to use access-by-policy in a Windows 2000 mixed-mode domain administrative model, the RRAS servers must be configured as RADIUS clients to a Windows 2000 IAS server.

Assigning Access to Groups of Users

In many cases, it will be more convenient to grant or deny remote access to members of a group rather than on a per-user basis. You can use security groups for this purpose.

For example, if you want to deny access to all members of a particular group, you will need to create a remote access policy. Follow these steps:

1. First, set the access permissions on all user accounts to allow remote access.

2. Make sure that the following default policy is in place: Allow access if dial-in permission is enabled.

3. Now we must create a new remote access policy. Access the RRAS console:

    Start | Programs | Administrative Tools | Routing and Remote Access.

4. Double-click on the server name and select "Remote Access Policies" in the right pane, then right-click and select "New Remote Access Policy," as shown in Figure 10.31.

5. You will be asked first to type a "friendly" name for the policy to identify it, such as "DenyBadgroup."

Figure 10.31 Create a new remote access policy using the RRAS MMC.

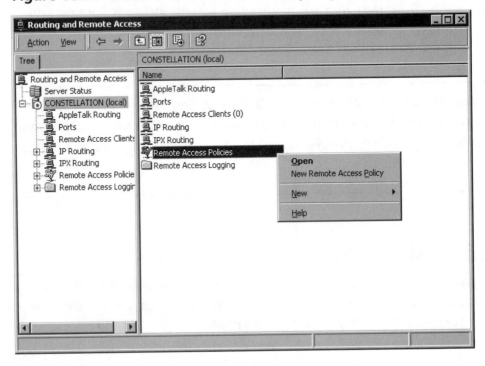

For IT Professionals

RADIUS, or Remote Authentication Dial-in User Service, is a non-vendor-specific security authentication protocol. It is client-server based, and used by many Internet Service Providers to authenticate their users' accounts.

RADIUS allows multiple remote access servers to act as RADIUS clients to a RADIUS server (the IAS server in Windows 2000's implementation). The user information received by these computers is sent to the RADIUS server, which then authenticates the clients' requests.

RADIUS can provide both authentication and accounting, but Windows 2000 allows these to be configured separately. A Windows 2000 remote access server could use a RADIUS server as its accounting provider, while using Windows 2000 as its authentication provider. You can also provide for secondary RADIUS servers that can be used if a primary RADIUS server goes down.

The RADIUS client and the RADIUS server use a shared secret to encrypt messages that are sent between them. You must configure both the RADIUS client and the RADIUS server to use the same shared secret. The RADIUS client sends accounting requests a UDP port. By default, Windows 2000 uses UDP 1813, but with some older RADIUS servers, you must configure the client to use UDP 1646.

6. Add the Windows-Groups condition to the new policy, as shown in Figure 10.32.

7. Click "Add" and add the Badgroup security group, as shown in Figure 10.33.

8. Now verify that the "Deny remote access permission" option is selected on the new policy, as shown in Figure 10.34.

9. Modify the profile on the new policy. On the "Dial-in Constraints" tab, select the "Restrict Dial-in to this number only" check box and type "555-5500," as shown in Figure 10.35.

Figure 10.32 Selecting the Windows groups attribute for setting your new policy.

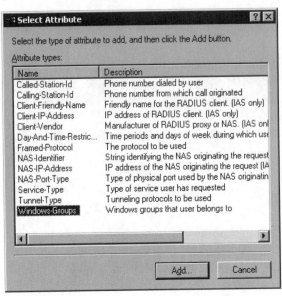

Figure 10.33 Adding a group to the remote access policy.

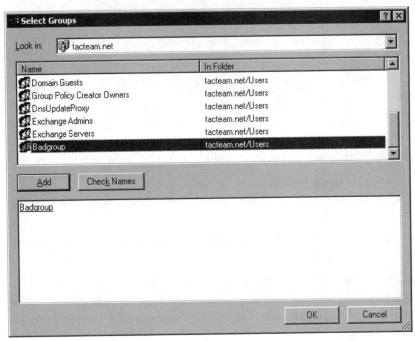

Figure 10.34 Using the remote access policy to deny permission to the group.

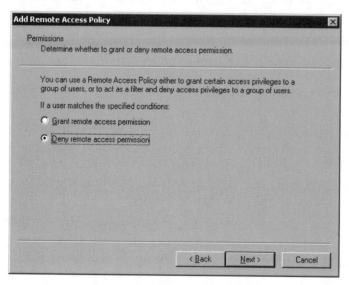

Figure 10.35 Entering a bogus telephone number so that the connection properties will not match the policy settings, thus causing a denial of access.

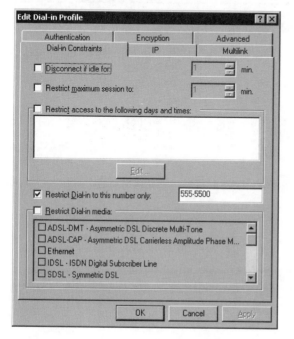

NOTE

This number is not a dial-in number of the remote access server and is deliberately entered here so that the properties of the connection attempt will not match the settings of the remote access policy.

10. After creating the policy, you should move it so that it will be the first policy evaluated. To do so, double-click "Remote Access Policies" in the left pane of the RRAS console, and then select the policy in the right pane. Right-click it and select "Move up," as shown in Figure 10.36.

Figure 10.36 Moving the DenyBadgroup policy up in the remote access policies hierarchy.

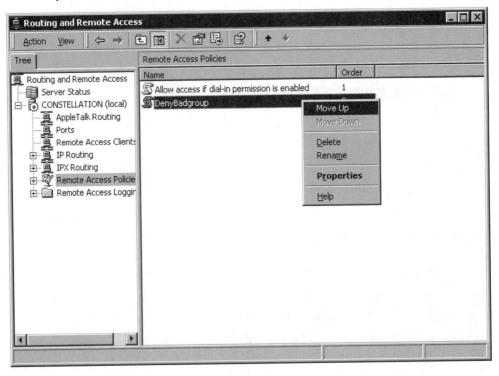

Plug and Play

No discussion of Windows 2000's new ease of use features would be complete without mentioning what NT professionals have long been waiting for: Plug and Play support. Although NT 4.0 did in fact offer limited Plug and Play capabilities, in most cases, hardware had to be configured manually. Most NT users can tell at least one horror story about struggling with IRQ or other device conflicts, and more than one company has based its decision to use Windows 95 or 98 on their network client machines, instead of NT Workstation, primarily or solely because of Windows 9x Plug and Play.

With Windows 2000, we don't have to choose between the advantages of NT-based technology and automatic hardware detection and configuration; now we can have both.

What is Plug and Play?

Plug and Play (PnP) is actually a set of specifications or standards that allows a computer to detect installed devices, locate and install device drivers, and configure the device to work without conflicting with other devices.

With Plug and Play, when you physically install a new network card, modem, CD-ROM drive, or other hardware device in your computer and boot the operating system (or, with USB or PCMCIA devices, insert the card or connector), you will receive a message during startup that Windows has found new hardware, and the operating system will attempt to locate drivers (the software that allows the device to work with the operating system) on your hard drive, a floppy, or CD-ROM. You may be prompted to supply a disk or type in a network path to the driver files. The operating system will then automatically configure the device to use IRQs and memory addresses that are not in use by any already-existing device. You can manually configure device properties and settings instead, but Microsoft recommends that you let Windows 2000 do it. This is because if you manually configure the settings, they become fixed, and Windows 2000 will not be able to automatically change them later, if a conflict occurs with another device.

NOTE

For Plug and Play to work properly, three conditions must be met: you must be running a PnP operating system such as Windows 9x or Windows 2000, you must have a computer with a PnP-compliant BIOS, and the hardware device you install must support PnP.

Even if the device you install is not PnP-compliant, Windows 2000 may still provide some Plug and Play support. The hardware may not be recognized automatically, and you will have to manually load the drivers, but Plug and Play can still allocate resources and record events related to the installation in the Event Log.

Hardware Compatibility List

One way to avoid hardware-related problems during installation of Windows 2000 or later is to ensure that your system and its peripherals have already been tested and found to be compatible with the operating system. You do this by consulting Microsoft's Hardware Compatibility List (HCL), which contains a list of those devices that are known to work properly with Windows 2000.

The HCL is updated regularly by Microsoft, and is available on the Web at http://www.microsoft.com/hcl/default.asp. This site provides compatibility information for Windows 95, 98, NT, and Windows 2000.

NOTE

The fact that a device is not on the HCL does not necessarily mean it won't work with Windows 2000; it may only be that it hasn't been tested. New devices are added to the HCL constantly, and if you have a device that isn't on the HCL, you could set up a test environment and try it. Check the Web site of the manufacturer of the device for Windows 2000 drivers.

Summary

In this chapter, we have discussed a few of the features that make Windows 2000 easy to use and administer.

Since the computer world is becoming more and more network-centric, it is important for any operating system in widespread use to provide the ability to set up dial-up networking connections quickly and simply. Windows 2000 uses wizards to help you create dial-up connections. We examined the process of creating a dial-up connection to the public Internet, as well as how to connect to a private network, either directly or through a VPN tunnel.

Taking the concept of user-friendliness a step further, we looked at a feature that's new in Windows 2000: the Connection Manager Administration Kit. The CMAK allows administrators to create and distribute customized dialer software so that users need no technical expertise to set up their dial-up connections. We also discussed Phone Book administration using Connection Point Services, and saw how the CPS components work with Connection Manager to allow you to automatically update local access number information for your users by running the Phone Books Services on a server and managing your phone books with the Phone Book Administrator.

Then we talked about remote access policies, and how dial-in or VPN access to a Windows 2000 network can be controlled through the Active Directory. We walked through the process of granting remote access permissions to users and groups, and learned how to create, modify, and apply remote access policies using Windows 2000's Routing and Remote Access features.

Finally, we provided a brief overview of Plug and Play, and how the Windows 2000 operating system uses its specifications to simplify the installation of new hardware devices. We discussed the advantages of checking the Microsoft Hardware Compatibility List to ensure that your computers and peripheral devices are supported by Windows 2000.

Increasing ease of use and administration was one of Microsoft's stated major goals in developing the Windows 2000 operating system, and network administrators will welcome many of the features that were improved upon, or included for the first time, in order to accomplish that objective.

FAQs

Q: What if I need to dial the number manually, or have the operator assist in making the connection to the dial-up server's telephone number?

A: You can configure dial-up network to allow manual or operator-assisted calls by opening the Advanced menu in Network and Dial-up Connections, and clicking "Operator-Assisted Dialing." Then you double-click on the connection you want to dial, pick up the telephone handset, and dial the number or request that the operator make the connection for you.

Q: How can I limit remote access to only certain times of the day or certain days of the week?

A: In the RRAS console, open the applicable remote access policy (this can be the default policy, or a policy you have created to apply only to members of certain groups, etc.), by right-clicking and selecting Properties. Then click the "Edit Profile" button and select the "Dial-in Constraints" tab. Check the "Restrict access to the following days and times" check box and select the desired days and/or times.

Q: How can I enable a computer to be a remote access server?

A: In the RRAS console, right-click the name of the server computer, and select "Properties." On the General tab, select the "Remote access server" check box.

Q: What can I do if Plug and Play does not detect my modem or network card when I install it?

A: First, check to ensure that Windows 2000 supports the device by consulting the HCL. Remember that some devices advertised as "Plug and Play" only have drivers for Windows 95 and/or 98. Check the manufacturer's Web site for Windows 2000 drivers. If you have Windows 2000 drivers, you can load the device drivers and configure the device manually, as you did in NT.

Q: Can a computer be both a dial-up client and a dial-up server at the same time?

A: Yes. You would need two modems or other connectivity devices. You can configure one to use dial-up networking to connect to another computer or network as a client, and configure the other to function as a dial-in server so that other computers can connect to it.

Chapter 11

Managing Windows 2000 Network Services Fast Track

Solutions in this chapter:

- **Rapid Review of Chapter Concepts**

What is a Managing Windows 2000 Network Services Fast Track?

This chapter is about giving you the edge. Do you need a quick and succinct rundown on all the Windows 2000 network services? Just check the subject headings in this chapter and jump to the subject of interest. You'll get a high-level view of the subject that will allow you to be conversant with the basic concepts related to that network technology.

Are you about to take the Windows 2000 Designing a Network Infrastructure certification exam (70-221)? Read this entire chapter and test how much you remember. When you encounter a subject that you feel you need to "brush up" on, turn to the chapter that covers that material and read it through. The Fast Track helps you quickly home in on those areas that you need to review.

If you're about to go on a job interview, read this chapter to learn how to "talk the talk." You should be able to read this chapter in about 30 minutes and cover a wide array of Windows 2000 networking technologies. When you're done, you'll have the vocabulary and basic information you need to sound intelligent and informed.

If you're like me, you start reading a magazine or book from the end first. If that's the case, this chapter is definitely for you! Read the material in this chapter to whet your appetite and stoke your curiosity. Then dive into the text. After you've finished all the chapters, come back to this chapter to review and confirm that you know what you need to know. If you have forgotten something or feel fuzzy on a subject, charge back to the chapter and sharpen your focus.

Managing Windows 2000 TCP/IP

TCP/IP is the default and preferred protocol for Windows 2000. All major networks operating now use TCP/IP because of the need to connect to the Internet. Here, we review some of the major components of the Windows 2000 implementation of the TCP/IP protocol stack.

The Role of TCP/IP

In the past, private networks implemented a variety of protocols. These included NetBEUI, IPX/SPX, TCP/IP, Appletalk, and DLC. The era of the stand-alone network has passed. All corporate networks need to be connected to the Internet for a business to remain viable in a competitive marketplace.

TCP/IP has many advantages over other networking protocols. It is a routable protocol, which allows a business to scale to thousands, even tens of thousands of computers. TCP/IP is also a reliable protocol, and much of the network overhead associated with TCP/IP is related to ensuring reliable delivery of messages. TCP/IP is not a broadcast-based protocol. This lessens the amount of "noise" or broadcast traffic on each IP segment.

Many technologies developed for the Internet now find themselves being used in the corporate intranet environment. Previously, Web servers, SMTP servers, news servers, chat servers, and FTP servers were only found on the Internet. Businesses now use these Internet technologies to optimize their own positions, and incorporate them into their private intranet.

The TCP/IP Protocol Suite

The term "TCP/IP" represents an entire group of protocols that use the Transmission Control Protocol as their transport. The name of the protocol itself is derived from the Transport and Network layer protocols that are used by all protocols in the TCP/IP "suite" of protocol: the Transmission Control Protocol and the Internet Protocol. The layer they inhabit in the DoD model can categorize the protocols.

Popular protocols in the TCP/IP Protocol suite include:

APPLICATION LAYER PROTOCOLS

File Transfer Protocol (FTP) An application layer protocol, the File Transfer Protocol is used to transfer files to and from computers over IP networks. FTP uses TCP as its transport layer protocol.

HyperText Transfer Protocol (HTTP) The hypertext transfer protocol provides a mechanism to access "Web pages" created with "hypertext markup language (HTML)." HTML-coded files are transferred from a "Web Server" to a Web client application (Web browser) via HTTP.

Simple Mail Transfer Protocol (SMTP) SMTP is the application level protocol that is used on the Internet to transfer e-mail between servers.

Post Office Protocol 3 (POP3) POP3 is a mail retrieval application level protocol. It is used by client applications (like Outlook Express) to retrieve e-mail from mail servers.

Network News Transfer Protocol (NNTP) The Network News Transfer Protocol allows users with NNTP agent software (newsreaders) to access the content on NNTP servers (news servers). News Servers provide a way for sharing information in a "bulletin board" style.

TRANSPORT LAYER PROTOCOLS

Transmission Control Protocol (TCP) The Transmission Control Protocol provides for connection-oriented, reliable communications between participating hosts. TCP provides mechanisms to ensure reliable delivery of information by using a system of acknowledgements. This reliability also makes TCP relatively slow as a transport protocol. Information encapsulated with a TCP header is often referred to as a "segment."

User Datagram Protocol (UDP) User Datagram Protocol is a connectionless "unreliable" transport protocol. UDP hosts do not establish a session with each other. There is no method to ensure that messages have been delivered. Reliable message transfer is the responsibility of the application using the UDP protocol as its transport.

INTERNET LAYER PROTOCOLS

Internet Protocol (IP) The Internet Protocol conforms with the standards that are part of the Network Layer of the OSI model. IP is responsible for addressing and routing messages so that they arrive at the desired location. One of the primary functions of the Internet Protocol is to assess whether a message is destined for a local or a remote host. It does this via a process of bitwise ANDing. If the ANDed results of the local host and the destination host are different, the packet is sent to the source computer's "Default Gateway." Information encapsulated by the Internet Protocol header is often referred to as an "IP Datagram" or Datagram.

Internet Control Message Protocol (ICMP) The Internet Control Message Protocol is responsible for providing feedback about network conditions, including network errors. Two popular TCP/IP utilities, PING and TRACERT, use the ICMP protocol. ICMP also relays "Source Quench Messages" from an overtaxed router, informing the client to reduce the rate of data transfer.

Internet Group Management Protocol (IGMP) The Internet Group Management Protocol manages host membership in IP multicast groups. An IP multicast group is a collection of hosts listening for IP traffic destined for a specific, Class D, multicast IP address. Multicast IP traffic is sent to a single hardware address, and forwarded to multiple IP hosts. This is much like an Internet Mailing List, where messages are sent to a single mailing list address, but all members of the mailing list receive a copy of the message. A given host listens on a specific IP multicast address and receives packets sent to that IP address.

Address Resolution Protocol (ARP) The Address Resolution Protocol resolves IP addresses to hardware addresses. IP Addresses must be matched up with MAC addresses in order for two computers to participate in direct, unmediated communications. IP host computers sending messages to machines on remote subnets must obtain the hardware address of the default gateway via ARP.

TCP/IP Utilities

One of the major advantages of using the TCP/IP protocol suite is the array of tools available for testing and troubleshooting the network. All versions of Microsoft operating systems that use TCP/IP include some of these troubleshooting tools. Windows 2000 includes all the TCP/IP utilities found in Windows NT 4.0 and some new ones. Some of the more frequently used TCP/IP utilities include:

PING (Packet Internet Grouper) PING uses the Internet Control Message Protocol to send messages to a destination computer. PING is used to test basic TCP/IP connectivity. When a user issues a PING command, an ICMP echo request is sent to the destination, and the destination computer returns an ICMP echo reply. The round trip time is included in the printout of the PING messages.

TRACERT (Trace Route) The TRACERT utility is used to investigate bottlenecks in the path of a TCP/IP communication. The TRACERT utility determines the route taken to a destination host by sending (ICMP) echo requests with varying IP Time-To-Live (TTL) values to the destination. Each router in the path decrements the packet's TTL by at least 1 before forwarding it. When the TTL on a packet reaches 0, the router should send an ICMP Time Exceeded message back to the source computer. Each router's host name is listed in the printout, and the round trip times are included, just as with the PING command. TRACERT is helpful in identifying congested routers and router loops.

IPCONFIG (TCP/IP Configuration) The IPCONFIG utility provides information on a machine's current TCP/IP configuration. In addition, a number of switches are available with this utility that allow the user to renew or release a DHCP-assigned IP address, flush the DNS resolver cache, release and re-register a host record with a DNS server, and more. The IPCONG utility provides functionality similar to that found with the "winipcfg" application used with Windows 95 and 98 computers.

NETSTAT (Network Statistics) The NETSTAT command displays information about the current TCP/IP sessions. Information such as the current TCP and UDP listening ports, per protocol statistics, and the contents of the routing table are available using the NETSTAT command. NETSTAT is useful when doing an IP Security check to assess for open ports that may represent a risk on a secure network.

NSLOOKUP (Name Server Lookup) The NSLOOKUP utility provides the means to troubleshoot DNS-related problems. This command can check DNS records, host aliases, and operating system information. NSLOOKUP provides a wide variety of switches that allow detailed analysis of DNS-related problems.

NEW: Quality of Service (QoS)

A new service available with Windows 2000, the Quality of Service network service, allows the administrator to control the amount of bandwidth allocated to specific resources.

This ability to control network resource allotment is important if you wish to run time-sensitive applications. Examples of time-sensitive applications include voice and video transmissions over an IP network. Without the ability to control bandwidth allotment, these time-sensitive applications will appear "choppy" to the end user. QoS services provide a mechanism to give preferential treatment to these applications.

NEW: IPSec

Internet Protocol Security (IPSec) provides a means for secure Layer 3 encryption, authentication, and message integrity over either a public or a private network. IPSec is an application-independent protocol; therefore, applications do not need to be created with IPSec in mind. Security is applied as application-level information makes its way to the network layer.

Managing Windows 2000 DHCP

As we saw in Chapter 3, the Dynamic Configuration Host Protocol allows the administrator to automatically assign IP addressing information to TCP/IP hosts on the corporate network. Prior to DHCP, each host had to be manually configured. Manual configuration has high liability for human error. DCHP provides the potential for large cost savings when implementing expansive TCP/IP-based networks. The Windows 2000 DHCP server includes many new features, including integration with the Windows 2000 Dynamic DNS server and with the Active Directory.

The Role of DHCP

DHCP is used for a variety of reasons. It allows the administrator to allocate predefined groups of IP addresses to selected DHCP client machines. DHCP is a client/server protocol. The DHCP server contains pools of IP address and IP addressing information, which are delivered to machines configured as DHCP clients. When IP configuration changes need to be made, they can be implemented on a single DHCP server and "pushed" to a large number of DHCP clients. This obviates the need to visit every TCP/IP host on the network.

DHCP Lease Process

The DHCP server doesn't let the DHCP client have an IP address indefinitely. IP addresses are leased to DHCP clients for a period of time defined on the DHCP server. There are four primary communications that take place between a DHCP client and DHCP server:

DHCPDISCOVER The DHCPDISCOVER message is issued by a DHCP client at startup if it has never had an IP address before, or when the DHCP client must obtain a new IP address after it has lost its lease.

DHCPOFFER A DHCP server that receives a DHCPDISCOVER message from the DHCP client will send an IP address to the DHCP client via a DHCPOFFER message.

DHCPREQUEST When the DHCP client receives a DHCPOFFER message, it will return to the DHCP server a DHCPREQUEST message. This confirms that the client received the IP address, and that the client wishes to keep the offered address.

DHCPACK After receiving a DHCPREQUEST message from the DHCP client, the DHCP server returns to the client a DHCPACK message, confirming that the client now owns the IP address delivered to it in the DHCPOFFER message. The DHCP server marks this IP address as used, and will not hand it out to another client.

The DHCP client must renew its lease on a periodic basis. For a Windows 2000 DHCP Service, the default lease period is eight days. At 50% of the lease period, the DHCP client will issue a DHCPRE-QUEST to the DHCP server that offered it the lease. If the DHCP server is available, it returns to the client a DHCPACK, and the client keeps the same IP address. If the DHCP server is not available, the client keeps its lease and tries again at 87.5% of the lease period. If the DHCP server is available at this time, the lease is renewed. If the DHCP server is not available, the client must seek another IP address, and issues a DHCPDISCOVER message.

DHCP Fault Tolerance

DHCP servers do not share information with each other, unlike WINS or DNS servers. Microsoft recommends that multiple DHCP servers be configured with information for each subnet. A DHCP server would contain 80% of the IP addresses for a single subnet, and the remaining 20% of the IP addresses for the subnet would be distributed to other DHCP servers that might be located on other segments. This provides a measure of fault tolerance in the event that the primary DHCP server becomes unavailable. The clients can obtain IP addresses for their subnet from other DHCP servers.

DHCP Scopes and Scope Options

A group or "pool" of IP addresses are maintained in a DHCP scope. Each subnet requires a single DHCP scope. For example, all IP addresses for network ID 192.168.1.0 are contained in a single DHCP scope.

A scope contains more than just IP addresses. Various TCP/IP "options" can be selected and assigned to DHCP client computers. These options are known as "DHCP Options." Examples of such

DHCP Options include DNS server IP address, WINS server IP address, Default Gateway IP address, and NetBIOS node type.

There are three ways to assign DHCP Options. They can be assigned via Server Options, Scope Options, Reserved Client Options or User/Vendor Class Options. Server Options apply to all scopes maintained on a particular DHCP server. Scope Options apply to only the particular scope. Reserved Client Options apply only to the specific client that has a DHCP reservation. User Class Options are apply to members of a defined User Class, and Vendor Class Options are apply to computers identifying themselves to a DHCP server as members of a particular Vendor class.

NEW: Vendor Classes and User Classes

User Classes allow DHCP clients to identify their "class member-ship" to a DHCP server. The DHCP server returns to the client set of options relevant to the "class."

For example, you could classify a group of computers to use a specific IP address, subnet mask and default gateway. You then create a class called "portable." All the clients you want to use these options will identify themselves as members of the portable user class.

Vendor Classes allow hardware and software vendors to add their own options to the DHCP server. If a manufacturer wants custom DHCP options sent to a DHCP client, custom option information can be made available to the DHCP client. A DHCP client sends a vendor class identifier to the DHCP server. The DHCP server recognizes the vendor's class identifiers and forwards vendor-specific options to the client.

NEW: DHCP Integration with DNS, Active Directory and RRAS

The Windows 2000 DHCP Service tightly integrates with DNS, Active Directory and the Routing and Remote Access Server.

The Windows 2000 DHCP can report host name and IP address information to a Dynamic DNS server. Windows 2000 clients register their own "A" Address records with the DDNS server, while the DHCP server creates the Pointer record on the DDNS server. Downlevel clients, such as Windows NT 4.0 or Windows 9x, cannot directly communicate with Windows 2000 DDNS server. The Windows 2000 DHCP Service can create for the downlevel DHCP client both a Host record and a Pointer record in behalf of the downlevel DHCP client.

Windows 2000 DHCP Service can provide IP addresses for RRAS clients. The RRAS server acts as a "proxy" between the RRAS client and the DHCP server. The RRAS server obtains a group of IP addresses from the DHCP server. The RRAS server obtains these addresses during RRAS initialization. RRAS clients do not receive information directly from the DHCP server. When the RRAS server obtains its group of IP addresses, any option information sent from the DHCP server to the RRAS server is ignored. DHCP Option parameters, such as WINS and DNS server IP addresses, are defined by the specific RRAS connection. There is no assigned lease period for the RRAS client. The lease expires when the connection is terminated.

Windows 2000 DHCP Services must be authorized in the Active Directory. If the DHCP server is not authorized, it is considered a "rogue" DHCP server. Rogue DHCP servers can be prevented in an all-Windows 2000 DHCP Service environment. This prevents the unfortunate circumstance of clients receiving bogus IP addresses from someone's "experimental" DHCP server.

DHCP Best Practices

If you have a network that is extremely stable, and especially if it consists of multiple physical LANs connected by routers, it may be beneficial to increase the lease duration. This reduces the amount of DHCP-related broadcast traffic. This solution should be used only if there are plenty of extra IP addresses available.

When the supply of available IP addresses in the DHCP scope is limited, or if your computers often change location, it may be best to decrease the lease duration so that addresses are returned to pool more quickly.

There are also situations in which you can optimize performance by reducing the duration of the lease for selected clients. You may have a segment that sees a lot of laptop computers entering and exciting that segment. Their leases will be released more quickly to be available for assignment to other DHCP clients. You can create a User Class for laptop computers, as discussed above.

Managing Windows 2000 DNS Service

In Chapter 4, we saw that the Windows 2000 implementation of the Domain Name Service includes enhanced features reflecting the elevated role of DNS in the Windows 2000 environment. Windows 2000 domains are now DNS domains. The Windows 2000 DNS Service supports dynamic registration of DNS client host names and IP addresses, giving it functionality similar to that seen in WINS servers. Clients locate Domain Controllers to authenticate against via DNS queries rather than WINS queries. Microsoft's long-term goal is to eliminate NetBIOS from core operating system components and have a pure WinSock environment. Network services will be located via DNS queries.

Host Names

Windows 2000 computers' names are host names. All previous Microsoft operating systems defined a computer name as a NetBIOS name. While the NetBIOS name was limited to 15 user-defined characters, a DNS hostname can use up to 63 characters. The fully qualified domain name may be up to 255 characters in length. The Windows 2000 DDNS Service supports the UTF-8 character set, which allow the use of extended characters in a DNS label. Care must be used when employing extended characters, since they are not available to downlevel DNS servers.

When a host name is combined with its domain name, it is called a Fully Qualified Domain Name. Multiple hosts can share the same host name because of the hierarchical nature of the Domain Name System.

DNS Name Space

The DNS name space is hierarchical in nature, with the top of the hierarchy defined as the Internet "root" domain. Top Level domains, such as com, net, org, and edu lie under the Root domain. Second Level domains define the name of a company or organization, such as Microsoft.com or Syngress.com. Central authorities manage the DNS name space from Root to Second Level domains. Subdomains that lie under the Second Level domains are maintained by the organization owning the Second Level domain.

Host Name Resolution

The destination IP address is required to establish a session with a destination host. A computer name is not required. This is in contrast to NetBIOS-based networks, where the endpoint of communication was the destination computer's NetBIOS name. Computers on a TCP/IP networks are assigned host names to make identification easier for those that have difficulty remembering IP addresses. They are not a requirement.

In order to use host names to identify and connect to a destination computer, that host name must be resolved to an IP address. WinSock applications will use the host name resolution sequence as follows: Localhost, HOSTS file, DNS, NetBIOS name cache, WINS, Broadcast, and LMHOSTS. Once the host name is resolved to an IP address, the WinSock client can establish a session with a destination host.

DNS Zones and Resource Records

Domain information is stored in a zone file. The zone file is a physical file located on the hard drive of the DNS server and takes the format of <domain_name>. dns. One or multiple domains can be stored in a single zone file. Domains may be assigned to different zones based on location of the DNS servers, or upon location of personnel capable of maintaining the information contained in each domain.

The purpose of domains is to track IP-based resources contained within. Resources are entered into the DNS domain database zone file by using Resource Records. The most common resource record is the "host" or "A" Address record that contains the host name and IP address. An MX record contains the name and IP address of a mail server. Windows 2000 includes the recently introduced SRV records. Windows 2000 domain members find authenticating domain controllers by querying the DNS database SRV record information.

DNS Server Types

DNS servers can take different roles depending on need. Standard DNS server roles include the following:

Primary DNS Server A Primary DNS server contains the only read/write copy of the zone database file. This is the server where the zone file was created. The Primary DNS server is authoritative of its zone records, and contains the Start of Authority Resource Record (SOA). The SOA record contains important information including Refresh Interval, Retry Interval, Default TTL, and the zone file serial number.

Secondary DNS Server A Secondary DNS server contains a copy of a zone database file created on a Primary DNS server. Secondary DNS servers are used for fault tolerance and load balancing. They also provide local access to DNS records for remote clients, thus avoiding the need to reach across a WAN to resolve host names to IP addresses. The Secondary DNS servers contain a read-only copy of the zone files.

Caching-Only DNS Server The caching-only DNS server does not contain zone information. This server contains only the cache.dns file, which has the IP addresses of the Internet root DNS servers. Caching-only servers can respond to recursive queries by issuing iterative queries, beginning with the Internet root. Caching-only DNS servers are useful when placed on the far side of a corporate WAN link, and can be used as forwarders on the outside of a firewall.

DNS Forwarders A DNS forwarder accepts DNS queries from another DNS server. The forwarding server is configured to sent DNS queries to the forwarder. Forwarders are useful in certain DNS security configurations.

NEW: Zone Transfer and Active Directory Integration

The Primary DNS server copies the zone database files to Secondary DNS servers via the process of a "zone transfer." A Secondary DNS server will poll a Primary DNS server periodically, based on the value configured as the Refresh Interval. If the serial number of the zone database file on the Primary DNS server is higher than the one on the Secondary, an AXFR query is sent by the Secondary to the Primary DNS server. This initiates a zone transfer, and the entire contents of the zone database are copied to the Secondary DNS server.

Standard zone transfer mechanisms can lead to an excessive use of available bandwidth. The Windows 2000 DNS server can integrate zone information into the Active Directory. When DNS zones are integrated into the Active Directory, the Primary/Secondary relationships between DNS servers no longer apply. All DNS servers are considered Primary, thus creating a "Multi-master" zone replication scheme. The zone information is shared among all Windows 2000 Domain Controllers. When zone information is copied between Domain Controllers, an IXFR query is sent, and incremental zone updates are sent. Incremental updates only send changed records, rather than the entire zone database.

NEW: Integration with DHCP Service

As mentioned earlier, the Windows 2000 DNS Service accepts information from the Windows 2000 DHCP Service. Windows 2000 clients register their own Host "A" Address record, and the DHCP server creates the reverse lookup record, or Pointer record. Downlevel clients cannot communicate directly with a Dynamic DNS server. Downlevel clients that are DHCP clients will have both their Host records and Pointer records updated on the DNS server by the DHCP server. In this way, the Windows 2000 DHCP Service acts as a "Dynamic DNS update Proxy" for these downlevel clients.

NEW: Dynamic Host Record Updates

The Windows 2000 DNS Service can accept information from DNS clients that allows them to update their own records in the DNS database. When changes in host configuration take place, this information is automatically entered into the DNS zone database, in a manner similar to that seen with WINS servers. This is a tremendous timesaver for the DNS administrator, who traditionally had to manually make changes to the zone's data files.

Windows 2000 clients that have static IP addresses dynamically register Host and Pointer records for their host name and IP address. Computers register records based on their full computer name. Dynamic updates are sent when:

- There is a manual change of the host's IP address or computer name.
- An IP address lease changes or renews with the DHCP server.
- The **ipconfig /registerdns** command is issued. This forces a refresh of the client's entry in the DNS zone database.
- The DNS client powers up.

The DHCP Client service (not the DNS Client service) sends updates. This is the case even when the DNS client is not a DHCP client. The DHCP Client service performs this function for all network connections used on the system.

DNS Security Considerations

Setting access permissions on the DNS container object in the Active Directory can securely transfer Active Directory-integrated zones. This level of zone transfer security is not available with standard zone configurations.

Intranets should avoid having their DNS server contact computers on the Internet directly. This includes contact that would take place when the internal DNS server issues iterative query requests to an Internet server in order to obtain Internet host name resolution. The internal DNS server should be set up as a forwarding DNS server, and send all DNS requests to a DNS server on the outside of a firewall. This external DNS server is configured as a forward to the forwarding DNS server. The external server completes recursions and returns the answer to the internal DNS server, which completes its recursion, and sends the answer to the requesting host machine.

DNS Client Setup

The Windows 2000 DNS client setup can be performed at the client machine itself, or can be configured via DHCP. The DNS client setup interface has changed since Windows NT 4.0, and looks somewhat like the Win9x networking setup interface. The clients are config- ured with the IP addresses of the preferred and alternate DNS servers to which DNS queries are sent.

Managing Windows 2000 WINS Service

Microsoft's stated goal is to eliminate the need for NetBIOS from their network operating systems. By doing so, a significant amount of network traffic can be eliminated. However, the vast majority of the network-enabled applications created for the Windows environ- ment are dependent on the NetBIOS interface. For this reason, Windows 2000 includes a NetBIOS name server, known as WINS (Windows Internet Name Server). As we discussed in Chapter 5, the Windows 2000 implementation of WINS includes features enhanced over those seen in previous iterations.

NetBIOS Name Resolution

NetBIOS applications require knowledge of the NetBIOS name of a destination computer in order to establish a session. When a com- puter needs to establish a session with another NetBIOS-based machine, it will issue a NetBIOS Name Query Request. If a machine with the name being sought is on the same segment, it will respond with its MAC address. The source machine with the destination host's MAC address can now establish a connection with the destination computer.

NetBIOS applications only care about NetBIOS names when connected to NetBIOS applications on a destination computer. However, TCP/IP uses IP addresses to connect to destination hosts. The NetBIOS interface accepts calls from NetBIOS applications, and attempts to resolve the NetBIOS name to an IP address before sending the request down the TCP/IP protocol stack. This can be done via broadcasts, LMHOSTS files, or NetBIOS name servers. Microsoft's NetBIOS name server, WINS, is the superior solution in a routed network.

WINS Servers

WINS servers accept NetBIOS Name Registration Requests from WINS clients. WINS clients are configured with the IP addresses of their Primary and Secondary WINS servers. When the WINS server receives the request, it enters the computer's NetBIOS name and IP address into the WINS database. When a WINS client needs to resolve a NetBIOS name to an IP address, it issues a NetBIOS Name Query Request to the WINS server. The WINS server searches the WINS database, and if the NetBIOS name sought is in the database, the IP address of the destination host is sent back to the WINS client. If the NetBIOS name is not found in the server's WINS database, the client will query its secondary WINS servers.

Records are removed from the WINS database when a WINS client shuts down gracefully. During an orderly shutdown, the WINS client sends to the WINS server a NetBIOS Name Release message. The WINS server marks the name released, and other computers that wish to use the same name can do so at this point. If the computer is not shut down gracefully, the name will be released if the machine does not refresh its name in the WINS database before the end of the Renewal Interval. If it fails to refresh its name, the name will be marked as released. WINS records are removed after they have been "tombstoned" for a period of time. The tombstoning process prevents records from being re-replicated to a server that has already removed or "scavenged" the record from its own database.

WINS Server Replication

WINS servers share information with each other unlike DHCP Servers. This is done via a process of WINS replication. There are two types of WINS replication modes: Push and Pull. When WINS servers are configured as Push Partners, a machine will send an update message to its Push partner, telling it that enough records have changed so that it may request the changes. A Pull partner is configured to send a Pull Request on a periodic basis. The Push and Pull parameters are configurable at the WINS server.

In distributed environments where segments are separated by space and slow WAN links, it is good to configure WINS server replication using a Spoke and Hub model. Each site will have multiple WINS servers. A single WINS server at each site should be configured as the Push and Pull partner of all other WINS servers at its site. This allows efficient replication of WINS records among WINS servers at each site. The Hub WINS servers can replicate with each other using a Spoke and Hub arrangement as well.

NEW: Enhanced WINS Features

It is somewhat paradoxical that the Windows 2000 WINS Service contains tremendous enhancements at a time when NetBIOS should be in the process of being decommissioned. The Windows 2000 WINS Service includes the following changes and improvements:

Persistent Connections When previous versions of the WINS server replicated, a session had to be established with each replication cycle. The Windows 2000 WINS replication partners maintain an open connection, which saves process cycles on each machine. Persistent connections find their best use when machines are configured to immediately update replication partners of changes to their WINS database.

Manual Tombstoning In NT 4, there were sometimes cases where it was very hard to remove an old record from WINS. Windows 2000 WINS server allows you to tombstone a record manually, rather than having to wait for the extinction timeout period to be completed.

Multiple Secondary WINS Servers While not a function of the WINS server itself, WINS clients now support up to 12 Secondary WINS servers. Previous Microsoft operating systems WINS clients supported only a Primary and a Secondary WINS server.

Dynamic Update of WINS Client Records Prior to Windows 2000, if you changed the IP address on a WINS client, you would have to restart the computer to have the changed name registered in the WINS database. The "nbtstat" command now allows you to dynamically re-register a WINS client by issuing the "nbtstat –RR" command.

WINS Database Export The Windows 2000 WINS server allows you to export the contents of the WINS database into a delimited format that can be imported into your favorite spreadsheet or database program.

Managing Windows 2000 TCP/IP Security

The elevated level of connectivity among disparate networks leads to an increased concern over security. Stand-alone networks could rely on local machine/operating system security technologies. Interconnected networks that transmit information over private and public networks require methodologies that protect information in transit. The technologies discussed in this section aim to protect data as it is transferred from host to host. Please refer to Chapter 6 for more details.

Secure Sockets Layer (SSL)

The Secure Sockets Layer (SSL) protocol provides a means to secure information between Web clients and Web servers. SSL communications provide authentication of the server's identity and encryption of data between the Web client and server. Authentication of the Web server is accomplished via the use of certificates granted by trusted third parties. It is assumed that a trusted third party has confirmed the identity of the Web server prior to granting it a certificate of authenticity that can be trusted by Web client applications. SSL is frequently used in the transmission of private information such as credit card numbers over the Internet.

Virtual Private Networks (VPN)

Virtual Private Networks (VPNs) allow for secure communications between hosts on either a public or private network, including the Internet. The goal of most VPNs is to provide a way to connect two private networks over a public medium, such as the Internet. By connecting the two networks via an Internet connection we create a "virtual network," and by employing encryption algorithms to the data prior to transmission, which creates a private network. VPNs are popular because they save the cost of having dedicated connections of modem pools for dial-up users. Dial-up users can connect to a local ISP and create a VPN secured "tunnel" between themselves and the corporate network via the Internet.

Point-to-Point Tunneling Protocol (PPTP)

The Point-to-Point Tunnel protocol supports creation of multiprotocol virtual private networks (VPNs). By using PPTP, remote users can create a secure connection via a dial-up ISP account, or by connecting two networks via two PPTP servers. The host or network can run IPX/SPX, NetBEUI, or TCP/IP. The Point-to-Point Tunnel protocol tunnels, or encapsulates, IP, IPX, or NetBEUI traffic inside IP packets. Users can access data on remote networks via the tunnel. The tunneled connection acts just like a local connection, and the difference between a tunneled and local connection is transparent to the user. Data is secured prior to transmission across the wire using the Microsoft Point-to-Point Encryption (MPPE), which can provide either 40- or 128-bit encryption. MPPE-secured data can be transmitted over NAT (Network Translation Table) networks.

NEW: Layer 2 Tunneling Protocol (L2TP) and IP Security (IPSec)

PPTP is implemented only on Microsoft operating systems, making it a proprietary protocol. Layer 2 Tunnel Protocol (L2TP) is based on the Layer 2 Forwarding Protocol developed by Cisco Systems. IPSec is a protocol that allows for data encryption, authentication, and integrity. The combination of L2TP and IPSec allows the creation of secure tunnels over public media such as the Internet.

Security is applied to packets at the network layer, which makes the process entirely transportable to application layer protocols. IPSec communications can only take place between IPSec-enabled hosts. When networks are connected via IPSec tunnels, NAT cannot be used on either end. Both networks and hosts must be using TCP/IP in order to take advantage of L2TP/IPSec secure tunnels.

Managing Windows 2000 External Network Connections

Windows 2000 supports a variety of methods that allow the user to connect to other computers on the same network, or to connect to a Windows 2000 computer over the Internet. See Chapter 7 for more details.

Internet Connection Device Support

Windows 2000 supports connections via analog modems, leased lines, Integrated Digital Services Network (ISDN) terminal adapters, cable modems, Asynchronous Digital Subscriber Line (ADSL), and ATM interfaces.

NEW: RADIUS

RADIUS (Remote Authentication Dial-in User Service) provides accounting, authentication, and authorization services in a distributed dial-up networking environment. RADIUS is often used by Internet service providers, and enables a dial-up server acting as a RADIUS client to receive user authentication and authorization from a RADIUS server. Windows 2000 RAS includes RADIUS client capabilities, enabling deployment in RADIUS environments. RADIUS authentication and accounting is separate, so you can utilize either component or both.

Windows 2000 Internet Authentication Service (IAS) provides the RADIUS server component. IAS will enable you to contract with an ISP that will provide Network Access Servers (NAS) to which your users can connect when they are mobile. Using RADIUS, the NAS will contact your Windows 2000 server to authenticate your users and report accounting information. The advantages are that you are able to control which users are authorized to use the ISP's network, and that data regarding usage of the service is up-to-date on your system

Managing Windows 2000 Internet Access for Small and Home Offices

Windows 2000 includes several new components that allow the Small Office/Home Office (SOHO) worker to become more productive than ever. These features include Automatic Private IP Addressing (APIPA), Network Address Translation (NAT), and the Internet Connection Services (ICA).

NEW: Automatic Private IP Addressing

Windows 2000 incorporates the Automatic Private IP Addressing (APIPA) technology presently available with Windows 98. APIPA allows a user to plug into any network and know little or nothing about how to configure IP addressing information. APIPA is used in conjunction with DHCP servers, to allow a maximum level of flexibility in host IP address configuration options.

When a Windows 2000 computer is configured as a DHCP client, it attempts to contact a DHCP server on startup. If a DHCP server is not located, the Windows 2000 computer will assign itself an IP address from the Class B network ID 169.254.0.0. The DHCP client will continue to probe the network every five minutes in an attempt to find a DHCP server. If a DHCP server does become available, the computer will obtain IP addressing information from the DHCP server.

APIPA is useful for the home network because all the user has to do is configure the computer to be a DHCP client. If the user has multiple Windows 2000 or Windows 98 computers on their single segment LAN, all computers will be assigned IP addresses on the same network ID, and therefore will be able to communicate with each other. The technology is also useful for mobile clients that plug into a corporate network, and then bring the computer home to plug into their home network. APIPA allows the mobile user to participate in both the home and corporate network without having to manually manipulate IP addressing configuration settings.

NEW: Network Address Translation

Network Address Translation (NAT) performs three basic activities. These include Address allocation, Address translation, and Name resolution. The computer on which NAT is enabled acts as a DHCP *allocator* (or a very simplified type of DHCP server). The NAT computer can assign IP addresses, subnet masks, DNS server and WINS server addresses. The main function of the NAT-enabled computer is to translate private IP addresses (with their corresponding TCP or UDP port numbers) to public addresses, and back again. This allows packets to travel between the local network and the Internet. The NAT-enabled computer acts as a DNS and WINS proxy for the rest of the computers on the network. It is not a name resolution server itself, but forwards name resolution requests from the local network to the DNS and WINS servers for which it is configured, and then relays the responses to the internal computers.

NAT allows the home or business user to connect all their computers to the Internet via a single, dial-up or dedicated connection.

The advantage of NAT is that you don't have to pay for a block of public IP addresses, and you don't have to have a modem, phone, and ISP account for every computer on the network.

NEW: Internet Connection Sharing

Internet Connection Sharing (ICS) can be thought of as "NAT-lite." ICS is aimed at the home or small office user (SOHO). The primary difference between ICS and NAT is ICS's lower level of configurability. Microsoft recommends that you do not run ICS on networks that have Domain Controllers, DNS servers, or DHCP servers. ICS will change the IP address of the machines it is installed in, which makes it unfriendly for networks that already have an existing IP addressing scheme.

ICS does perform network address translation in the same way that NAT does. Another important limitation is that you cannot configure static routing entries on an ICS computer. ICS automates many of the procedures that must be manually configured when using NAT, and is the ideal solution of the less sophisticated home or SOHO user that wants their network connected to the Internet via a single connection.

Managing Windows 2000 Routing

Windows 2000 introduces a new era in the ability to connect a Windows computer to any other computer in the world. Microsoft has made significant improvements and enhancements to the Windows family by providing powerful and robust RAS and Routing capabilities in the Windows 2000 Routing and Remote Access Service. Please see Chapter 9 for a complete discussion.

NEW: RRAS Administration Tools

The Routing and Remote Access services are now brought together in the RRAS Management Console, that allows the administrator to configure both RAS and Routing parameters from a single location. This is a major improvement over the interfaces for these services seen in Windows NT 4.0. Static routes can now be configured via a GUI, rather than from the command line, as was the case with NT. New ports can be added, the DHCP Relay Agent can be configured, and Remote Access Clients can be monitored, all from the RRAS Management Console.

The RRAS services are controlled via local RRAS policies that are created in the RRAS Console. RRAS logging is defined in this location too.

Unicast Routing

Unicast communication occurs when two computers address or communicate with each other directly. A source computer establishes a session with a destination computer. Unicast routing involves defining routing table entries that allow routing of packets to a destination network ID in order to access a selected destination host. This is the type of routing table configuration most network administrators are accustomed to configuring.

Multicast Routing

Multicast routing allows a communication to be sent to a group of computers that are members of a defined multicast group. Multicast groups are similar to Internet e-mail lists (which most network administrators know all too well). When you join an Internet mailing list, you become a member of an e-mail "group." When a message is sent to the e-mail address for the mailing list, all members of the "group" receive a copy of the message. In a similar fashion, when computers identify themselves as members of a multicast group, any messages sent to that group IP address are received by all group member computers.

Multicasting minimizes the bandwidth used since one packet can be sent to numerous hosts. This enables even a home PC to become an Internet radio or TV station. Any application that requires data streaming to numerous hosts, especially live or real-time data, can benefit from multicast technology.

Windows 2000 supports the Internet Group Management Protocol, or IGMP. IGMP is not a multicast routing protocol, but can be used to forward multicast packets over one hop. Although a chain of these routers could be created to allow multicasting throughout an environment, it is not recommended nor does Microsoft support it. The IGMP portion of the Windows 2000 Router was designed to allow a small intranet to support multicasting or to allow Intranet-to-Internet or Internet-to-intranet multicasts to occur.

NEW: OSPF

The Open Shortest Path First, or OSPF, was first made available with the RRAS add-on for Windows NT 4.0. OSPF provides more robust and fault-tolerant routing that RIP, the other routing protocol supported by Windows 2000. OSPF calculates how to route a given packet via the Shortest Path First (SPF) algorithm. SPF calculates the distance to each segment of a network and updates its routing tables accordingly. SPF maintains a loop-free network. The RIP routing protocol's major weakness is routing loops, which are avoided with OSPF.

In order to scale large networks, OSPF groups routers into units called *areas*. OSPF-enabled routers maintain routing information for areas to which they are connected. This allows rapid updates to occur within an area or between multiple areas. Routers that connect two areas are called Area Border Routers. These updates occur much more rapidly, allowing a much faster convergence compared to RIP. OSPF fits into the family of "Interior Gateway Protocols."

Demand-Dial Networking

Demand-Dial Networking allows you to create on-demand connections to another network or the Internet. Demand dial is often used with NAT or ICS for offices that do not have dedicated connections to the Internet, and use dial-up accounts to access their Internet Service Provider. Demand dial also allows packets destined for foreign networks to be routed via a temporary connection, such as a VPN connection.

It is not recommended to use a demand-dial approach in place of a dedicated line. Connectivity and maintaining connectivity are limiting issues. However, it should also be noted that demand-dial works very well over ISDN. This is because of the more stable connection and lower call setup latency seen with ISDN connections.

Managing Windows 2000 Administrative Tools

In Chapter 10, we discussed how Windows 2000 includes a generous helping of add-ons that simplify and enhance the connection capabilities for Windows networking. These utilities include the Connection Manager Administration Kit (CMAK), the Phone Book Administrator (PBA), Remote Access Permissions via the Active Directory, and new Plug and Play capabilities found in Windows 2000.

NEW: Connection Manager Administration Kit

The Connection Manager Administration Kit (CMAK) allows you to create a custom dialer with a graphical interface that can be used by your employees, customers, or other users to easily connect to your dial-in server. This interface provides a "no-brainer" dial-up interface akin to the AOL dial-up interface.

The Connection Manager itself is a user interface that includes a log-on dialog box and a set of property dialog boxes, which users can use to customize their connection settings. You can customize the look of the dialog boxes with your company logo and special icons, and modify the information that will be presented to users. The process of creating a custom dialer is entirely wizard-driven. This greatly simplifies the task of providing dial-up access to employees and circumvents the need for the administrator to spend countless hours educating otherwise clueless users on how to "use the computer."

NEW: Phone Book Administrator

If your online service or WAN has multiple access numbers, these can be organized in a database and distributed to users when they connect using Connection Manager. The Phone Book Administrator (PBA) is the administrative tool used to create, manage, and edit these phone books.

The PBA provides a GUI that allows you to create phone books and customize phone book entries (called Points of Presence or POPs). For example, you can specify the connection type, such as 56k or ISDN, so users can find an access number that provides the desired service type. You can associate specific POPs with specific network configurations defined in Connection Manager. You use PBA to publish all phone book information to a Phone Book Service (PBS) that runs on the server. After this information is published to the Phone Book Service, it can be downloaded automatically to the client's machines. This allows them to have an up-to-date list of POPs and allows phone number changes to be virtually transparent to the user.

NEW: Assigning Remote Access Using the Active Directory

Remote access policies can be used to control remote access to the network, and set conditions for those connections. Remote access policies can be administered through the Routing and Remote Access console or through an Internet Authentication Service (IAS) server, such as the Windows 2000 RADIUS server. Users are authenticated in the Windows 2000 Active Directory. A remote access policy is a set of rules that contains specified conditions or attributes, remote access user permissions, and a profile that is applied to the connection. Remote Access Policies are configured both on the RRAS server and in the Active Directory.

A connection attempt must meet the specified conditions of the policy. Remote access permission is granted or denied, both generally (for all users), or for individual users. The user account is configured through the Active Directory Users and Computers administrative tools (see the section on Using the MMC below). A remote access policy profile is a group of properties to be applied to a connection at the time it is authorized through the user account permission setting or the policy permission setting. Settings are configured in the Active Directory for individual user accounts; settings that apply to all users are configured at the RRAS server console at the RRAS server itself.

Much Improved: Plug and Play

Windows 2000 now supports Plug and Play hardware. This capability was formerly available only with Windows 9x computers, and to a limited extent, for Windows NT 4.0 computers. Plug and Play makes it much easier to configure Plug and Play compliant network access devices, from modems to network cards.

Summary

In this chapter we have taken a high-level view of some of the most important topics included in this book. After reading this Fast Track chapter, you should now go to the chapter that covers the material of interest to get a more thorough account of the subject. Each chapter contains helpful figures, charts, tables, and screen shots from Windows 2000 that will aid you in understanding and implementing each of these technologies.

Secrets

Solutions in this appendix:

- Lesser Known Functions
- Under-documented Functions and Procedures
- Undocumented Features
- For Experts Only
- Troubleshooting Tips
- Optimization Tips

Lesser Known Functions

Windows 2000 and CD-RW Media

Most users that own CD-Rewritable drives have found that the CD-RW media, due to the use of the UDF file format, does not work on most machines. The workaround was to load the CD-RW software on each and every machine that needed to read the CD-RW discs, thus limiting the distribution capability of this wonderful medium.

Microsoft has come to the rescue of the CD-RW users; reading the UDF file system is now fully supported without the addition of a third-party utility. This quiet addition to the Windows 2000 operating system allows the same acceptance of the CD-RW media that has previously only been given to the CD-R. It should be noted that the CD-ROM or DVD-ROM device must be capable of reading the discs, as some drives are not compatible with certain CD-R discs and/or formats.

The New IPCONFIG Switches

Windows NT 4.0 administrators are aware of the IPCONFIG's ability to provide IP addressing information. The Windows NT 4.0 version contained three switches: /all, /renew, and /release. Windows 2000's IPCONFIG utility contains many new features and switches.

If you are a Windows 95/98 administrator you will note that this feature replaces *winipcfg.exe.*

The Windows 2000 IPCONFIG command can be used with the following switches:

/?

This switch diplays the help information for IPCONFIG.

/all

The all switch works the same way as it did in Windows NT 4.0. It provides full IP addressing information for the computer the command is executed on.

/release

The release switch causes a DHCPRELEASE message to be sent to the DHCP server.

/renew

The renew switch causes the machine to issue a DHCPREQUEST message to the DHCP server that issued the machine its IP addressing information. The machine will request to renew the IP address it already has a lease for.

/flushdns

The flushdns switch causes the machine to empty its cached DNS information. This is particularly helpful if you are connecting to machines that dynamically register their fully qualified domain names. If the machine changes its IP address between sessions, you can issue the ipconfig /flushdns command to clear your cache and connect to the destination host by re-querying the dynamic DNS server

/registerdns

The registerdns switch actually accomplishes two things. First, it causes a DHCPREQUEST message to be sent to the DHCP server that issues the machines its IP address, and then it updates its record at the Dynamic DNS server.

/displaydns

The displaydns switch shows the entire contents of the DNS resolver cache.

/showclassid

The showclssid switch displays which DHCP user or vendor classes the computer belongs to. This command applies to each adapter installed on the computer. If you have difficulty identifying which adapter you have on your computer, or how to identify it to the /showclassid command, type the following command:

ipconfig /showclassid *

This will get around some of the difficulty you might have with NICs that identify themselves as a long text string.

/setclassid

The setclassid switch allows you to assign the computer to a specific user or vendor class. This information is sent to the DHCP server when the DHCP client communicates with the DHCP server to obtain IP addressing information.

Using TCP Sliding Windows

One of the more mysterious concepts related to the TCP protocol, for networking students and practicing administrators alike, is the idea of "sliding windows." What and where are these "windows," how and why do they slide, and is there any benefit to you (other than the prospect of winning the next game of Networking Trivia) in taking the time to understand them?

The Transport Layer of the OSI model, where TCP operates, is responsible for — among other things — flow control. The sliding window algorithm is TCP's way of controlling the flow of data. The "window" refers to the number of packets of data that can be received before waiting for an ACK, or acknowledgment, to be sent.

The size of the TCP window can have a significant impact on performance, and Microsoft has made changes to the TCP/IP protocol stack in Windows 2000 to allow for larger window sizes. When there is a large amount of data being transferred, especially when the high-bandwidth network also experiences a high latency, large window size will make for faster TCP/IP performance. In Windows NT, the TCP window size was limited to 64KB, but Windows 2000, in accordance with RFC 1323, supports larger windows.

To change the TCP window size, it is necessary to edit the Registry. At the "Run" command, type Regedt32 and in the Registry Editor, open the following key:

```
HKEY_LOCAL_MACHINE\System\CurrentControlSet\Services\Tcpip\Parameters
```

Now add a registry key: TcpWindowSize of the type REG_DWORD. Set the value to the desired number of bytes. This will be the window size in the receive window that will be announced to clients that establish a TCP/IP connection with the computer. Only TCP/IP communications in which this computer acts as the server will be affected, since it is the server's value that determines the connection window size.

Under-documented Functions and Procedures

Internet Connection Sharing versus Network Address Translation

Most server administrators may wonder if there is a significant difference between the Internet Connection Sharing, found in both Windows 98SE and Windows 2000 Professional, and the Network Address Translation routing protocol found within the Routing and Remote Access service of the Windows 2000 Service. Since both perform NAT, or Network Address Translation, their functionality from a pure networking standpoint is identical. The differences lie within the configuration options available to each platform.

The Windows 98SE and Windows 2000 Professional implementation of NAT has a few drawbacks. The first is that you are unable to run the Microsoft DHCP or DNS server on either platform, which could be desirable for a few administrators. The second shortcoming is the inability of either platform to route between two local subnets. The lack of routing ability could be significant to some, since, like Windows 98SE and Windows 2000 Professional, there is one connection to the Internet and one connection to the Local Area Network (LAN).

The Windows 2000 Server Network Address Translation routing protocol is built for the extensible Windows 2000 Router, thus providing a much more robust and plentiful feature set. The ability of the Windows 2000 Router to control multiple LAN segments and utilize NAT for Internet connectivity for all connected subnets is a real boon. The strongest case for the Windows 2000 Service platform lies in the fact that additional services can operate on the platform concurrently with the router.

It should be noted that the WINS server service was not successfully tested on a server running NAT under Windows 2000 Service at the time of this writing. The non-functionality is related to the lack of adapter preferences available to the WINS service. Since DHCP and DNS are able to specify adapter preferences, in terms of IP addresses, they are fully functional.

New TCP/IP Utility: Pathping

If you ever thought it would be useful to have a tool that combines the features of PING with those of TRACERT, you'll find PATHPING to be the "best of both worlds." It is a tracing tool that gives you the functions of those two utilities, and more.

You can use the PATHPING command to determine the amount of packet loss at each router along the way to a final destination address, which is helpful in troubleshooting router malfunctions.

PATHPING Syntax

The syntax for the PATHPING command is as follows:

```
pathping [-n] [-h maximum_hops] [-g host-list] [-p period]
[-q num_queries] [-w timeout] [-t] [-R] [-r] target_name
```

PATHPING Switches

The following switches can be used with the PATHPING command:

- -n: instructs that addresses are not to be resolved to hostnames.
- -h: maximum_hops: indicates the maximum number of hops (router links) should be searched for the target, or destination address.
- -g host-list: indicates loose source route along host-list.
- -p period: indicates the wait period between pings in milliseconds.
- -q num_queries: indicates the number of queries per hop.

- -w timeout: indicates the amount of time, in milliseconds, to wait for a reply before timing out.

- -R: tests each hop for RSVP awareness

- -t: tests connectivity to each hop with Layer-2 priority tags.

Using PATHPING

When you issue the PATHPING command, it first returns the same path information that is returned by TRACERT, but it doesn't stop there. You'll see a message that says, "Computing statistics for 125 seconds" (the actual period of time, however, depends on the number of hops, or router links, it takes to get to the destination address). When PATHPING is finished gathering information from all the routers, it will display the results in the following format:

- Hop number: This is the number of the router in the sequence passed through.

- RTT: This is the Roundtrip Time, or the amount of time required for a full roundtrip communication between a sender and a receiver. The time for each route is shown in milliseconds.

NOTE

Windows 2000 supports the use of the TCP Round Trip Time Measurement option to improve how RTT is estimated.

- Source to Here Lost/Sent Pct: This is the percentage of packets lost between the source host and the link.

- This Node/Link Lost/Sent Pct: This is the percentage of lost packets for the particular node or link.

- Address: the IP address of the node.

Figure A.1 on the next page shows the results of a typical PATHPING command.

Figure A.1 The results of using the PATHPING route tracing command.

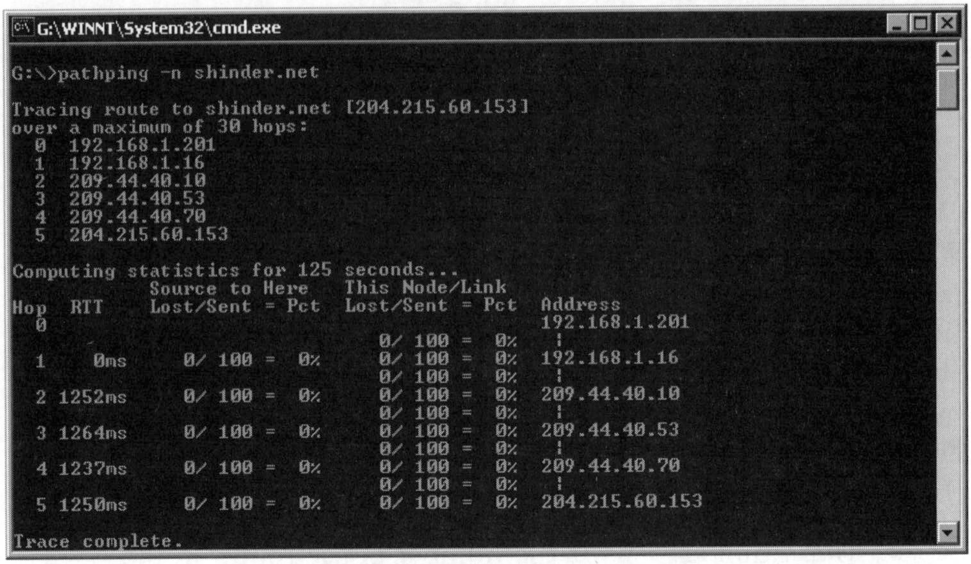

```
G:\WINNT\System32\cmd.exe

G:\>pathping -n shinder.net

Tracing route to shinder.net [204.215.60.153]
over a maximum of 30 hops:
  0  192.168.1.201
  1  192.168.1.16
  2  209.44.40.10
  3  209.44.40.53
  4  209.44.40.70
  5  204.215.60.153

Computing statistics for 125 seconds...
            Source to Here   This Node/Link
Hop  RTT    Lost/Sent = Pct  Lost/Sent = Pct  Address
  0                                           192.168.1.201
                                0/ 100 =  0%   |
  1    0ms     0/ 100 =  0%     0/ 100 =  0%  192.168.1.16
                                0/ 100 =  0%   |
  2 1252ms     0/ 100 =  0%     0/ 100 =  0%  209.44.40.10
                                0/ 100 =  0%   |
  3 1264ms     0/ 100 =  0%     0/ 100 =  0%  209.44.40.53
                                0/ 100 =  0%   |
  4 1237ms     0/ 100 =  0%     0/ 100 =  0%  209.44.40.70
                                0/ 100 =  0%   |
  5 1250ms     0/ 100 =  0%     0/ 100 =  0%  204.215.60.153

Trace complete.
```

The loss rates shown for each router link indicate any losses of packets being forwarded along the path. In the example shown, all routers are working properly, as indicated by the fact that 100 percent of the packets were sent, and zero were lost.

If a significant percentage of packets were shown as lost from a particular router or routers, this might mean that those routers' CPUs are overloaded. These congested routers could be the cause of network communication problems between the source and destination hosts.

Taking Advantage of WINS Automatic Partner Configuration

WINS server can be configured to find replication partners automatically. They do this by sending out a multicast packet to 224.0.1.24, and WINS servers that are configured for Automatic Partner Configuration will respond to the request.

When a computer is configured to enable automatic partner configuration, it will automatically add the IP address of the computers it finds to its list of replications partners. It configures the machines as Push and Pull partners, and the Pull interval is automatically set for 120 minutes (two hours).

The default multicast interval is 40 minutes. Each WINS server will send out a multicast message every 40 minutes by default. You can have WINS servers find remote WINS replication partners if you open up routers to the WINS multicast address. This might not be a good idea, since an organization with seven WINS servers multicasting every 40 minutes is going to see 144 multicast messages a day. However, this may not be a problem for fast LAN connections.

If you have segments that have multiple WINS servers (not recommended), you should have each segment's WINS servers configured for automatic partner discovery. Then dedicate one of the WINS servers as a "hub" for that segment. Have the segment "hub" WINS server set up as a Push and Pull partner for a site's hub WINS server. In this way, you can take advantage of the Hub and Spoke model on a segment and site level. (See Figure A.2 below).

Figure A.2 WINS Replication Partners

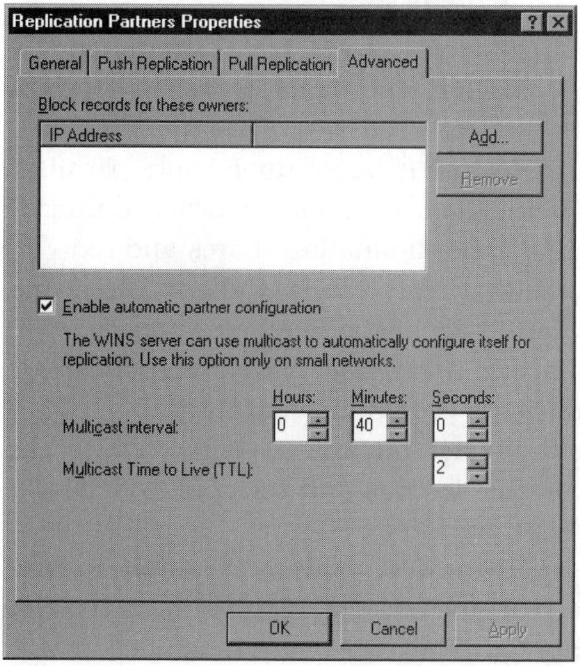

Undocumented Features

Deep Drive Mappings

Windows 2000 includes a new feature, deep drive mapping, that can greatly reduce the number of shares you need to create and manage on servers. Before Windows 2000, Microsoft network clients were only able to map network drives to shares on a server. If an administrator wanted to provide a private network drive for a user, a separate share for each user had to be created. In enterprise environments, this meant that a server could have hundreds of shares. This architecture, although manageable, was certainly not optimal.

With Windows 2000, network drives can be mapped to any directory below a share. For example, a user can map a network drive to his or her home directory found under a share named USERS (e.g., net use H: \\LDN001\USERS\BSMITH). This eliminates the need to create a share for each user, saving both administration time and system resources.

Windows 2000 computers can create deep drive mappings to any Windows NT or Windows 2000 computer. If you have experience with NetWare, you are already familiar with how this works, since NetWare client software has always allowed deep drive mapping.

If your current security architecture is based upon share permissions, you will need to begin using file permissions in order to utilize deep drive mapping. Since you will be eliminating shares and redirecting users through one share that replaces many shares, the same security on the many shares cannot be applied to the one share, so file permissions must be in place so that a user cannot map a drive directly to the new share and access everything beneath it.

To map a drive to a directory beneath a share, simply right click the My Network Places icon on the desktop and select Map Network Drive. In the Map Network Drive dialog box (Figure A.3), select the drive letter you wish to use, enter the UNC path to the folder in the Folder field, and click Finish. The Folder field is limited to 260 characters, which should be plenty for almost every circumstance.

Figure A.3 Mapping a drive.

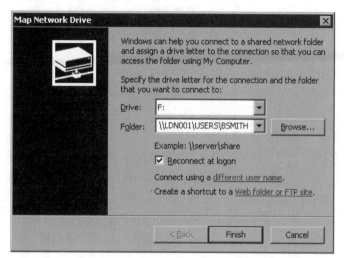

The NET USE command can also be used to map a drive to a directory below a share. To connect the G: drive to the BSMITH directory in the USERS share on the LDN001 server, enter NET USE G: \\LDN001\USERS\BSMITH at a command prompt.

For Experts Only

Editing the Registry to Remove Corrupted Network Connections

Normally, you can remove a dialup or local area network connection simply by going to Start | Settings | Network and Dialup Connections, choosing the connection you wish to remove, right-clicking and selecting "Delete."

However, sometimes if the connection's configuration has become corrupted, this may not remove all traces of it from the Registry. If this happens, even though the connection icon no longer shows up in the "Network and Dialup Connections" window, you may have problems if you try to create a new connection with the same name as the old one.

In the Windows 2000 Registry, you can edit the Registry to remove entries for network or remote connections. The settings are contained in HKEY_LOCAL_MACHINE\SYSTEM\ CurrentControlSet\ Control\Network\Connection\GUID.

The GUID is the Globally Unique Identifier for the connection, which is shown in the Registry key value as a hexadecimal number.

Telnet Server

One of the most overlooked security holes on Windows 2000 can be the telnet server. The telnet server component can be very useful in remote administration, such as restarting services. Since the telnet server can be configured to use clear text names and passwords during logon, these can be captured during a sniffer trace. While that is not generally a concern in a LAN environment, it is something that cannot be overlooked on a server placed on the Internet. In order to minimize access to a machine, it is recommended that you disable the telnet server. If it must be enabled, it is recommended that you only use the NTLM authentication, which is only available to Windows 2000 clients, as Windows 9x and NT do not use NTLM authentication within the telnet application.

Terminal Services for Remote Administration

Most administrators have placed Symantec's PC Anywhere on their servers as a method of remote administration. While PC Anywhere is a stable application, it is generally not robust enough to use on all servers. This is especially true with Windows 2000 servers as older versions of PC Anywhere do not work. The caveats of PC Anywhere with Windows 2000 are expanded upon in the Troubleshooting Tips section of this Appendix.

Microsoft provides the Terminal Services as a way to manage applications centrally, but there is also the option to install the service specifically for remote administration of the server. In that mode, no additional licenses need to be purchased. Since Terminal Services are able to use encryption, and authentication is based off NTLM, the connection is far more secure than that provided by PC Anywhere.

It is highly recommended to remove PC Anywhere prior to installing Windows 2000, regardless of the version installed. If PC Anywhere prior to version 9.01 is installed under Windows 2000, the system will not reboot. Recovery is difficult at best, so proper testing a research of this product prior to installation is a must. The latest information can be found at the Symantec Web-site.

Troubleshooting Tips

How to Rid Yourself of the "Cannot Find Server for [IP Address]" Message When Doing NSLOOKUP

If you've worked with DNS for awhile, you've probably run into the situation where you are trying to do an NSLOOKUP for a computer your know is in the domain, but when you do an NSLOOKUP for that computer, you get a message that says, "Can't find server name for address 192.168.1.xxx: Non-existent domain." Then, after giving some timeout messages, it finally resolves the IP address of the computer that you're searching for.

These types of errors occur when you create a new domain on the DNS server and don't yet have a reverse lookup domain configured. When you create a new domain, and there is no reverse lookup domain configured, a Pointer record for the DNS server is not created. It's not created because it can't be created, because there isn't a reverse lookup domain.

Microsoft documentation states that you are not required to create a reverse lookup domain. However, you will see these errors if you do not create one. Note that the host names will be successfully resolved even if no reverse lookup domain is created. It's just that it might take a little longer to accomplish the task.

If you do choose to create a reverse lookup domain, be sure to add the Pointer record manually. The DNS server will not automatically include its Pointer record when you create the reverse lookup zone.

DVD Playback

Windows 2000 supports the latest multimedia hardware available, including several DVD playback solutions. It is important to obtain the latest drivers for your DVD solution, including graphics drivers, DVD-ROM drive firmware, and playback software.

It is also important to verify that the DMA transfer mode is enabled for the drive to minimize any possible problems during playback, including a complete system lockup.

The decoding solution installed should be compliant with Windows 2000, as most Windows 98 and NT 4.0 solutions will not work properly under Windows 2000. The problems could be as minimal as non-functionality or as catastrophic as inducing a reboot upon playing a DVD movie. It is advisable to consult the manufacturer of your computer, if the DVD solution was supplied as original equipment, or the manufacturer of your DVD upgrade kit.

Optimization Tips

Optimizing Dial-up Connections

It is impossible to get the kind of performance from a dial-up connection, using analog phone lines, that you can attain with a digital connection such as DSL or ISDN. Although it might appear, based on the numbers alone, that by combining two 56K modem connections with Multilink PPP, you would have a speed (112K) close to that of a BRI ISDN connection, the throughput would still fall far short of that achieved with the digital line. This is because a so-called 56K analog modem achieves (or more often, doesn't achieve) perceived speeds of up to 53K (the limit imposed by the federal government in the U.S.) by using compression, whereas the 128K of an ISDN line is uncompressed. With compression, the ISDN circuit can outdo the analog line by at least a factor of five.

However, many modem users are not getting as much throughput as their equipment has the potential to deliver. There are a few optimization tips and tricks that will help you squeeze all the bandwidth possible out of that dial-up connection.

Compatibility

Be sure the modem you use is compatible with your ISP's equipment. In order to get high speeds from a 56K modem, both ends of the connection must support the same protocol. Unfortunately, in the early days of 56K, there were two different standards, K56flex and X2. Some modem manufacturers, such as Motorola, built to the K56flex specifications and others, like U.S. Robotics, supported X2. A new standard, V.90, has been adopted by most manufacturers, but if you have one of the older modems (or if your ISP does), incompatible standards could cause you to connect at low speeds.

In this case, the modem connection would "fall back" to a standard supported on both ends, meaning that the V.34, which is limited to 33.6K, would be used.

Telephone Lines and Devices

Some devices designed to improve transmission of voice communications can interfere with modem performance. Load coils, digital pads, and analog pads will not usually prevent the modem from connecting but may reduce its attainable speed. The solution may be to obtain another phone line dedicated to data transfer only, or to make a choice to sacrifice either voice quality or data speed for the sake of the other.

In some cases, the telephone line itself may be the bottleneck. The lines in some areas are "dirty," that is, there is a great deal of noise or interference on the line. This could be a result of physical or environmental factors. In some cases, the telephone company may be able to "condition" the line and improve its quality. Sometimes, there will be a significant difference in modem performance between two different telephone lines coming into the same office or home. In this case, it may be possible to use the low performance line for your voice communications and do data transfer over the other. If not, with diligence, you may be able to track down and fix the problem by noting physical differences between the good line and the bad one.

Careless wiring, poor connections, connecting cables that are too long and other related factors can impact phone line/modem performance. Additional extension phones on the line, especially portable phones, or fax machines and other devices can also degrade the transmission quality. Even a surge protector that the phone line plugs into may affect performance.

Updated Modem Drivers

An often-overlooked way of (sometimes) improving your modem's throughput is to ensure you're using the latest drivers from the manufacturer. It is easy to install the drivers that were available at the time you installed the modem, and then forget about driver issues as long as you are able to establish a connection. New drivers can occasionally make a dramatic difference.

Port Speed Setting

It's not uncommon for poor modem performance to be caused by a com port setting that limits the maximum port speed to a speed that is lower than the modem's rated speed. To check or change the port speed, go to Settings | Control Panel | Phone and Modem Options. Select the Modems tab, click the modem, and choose "Properties." Then on the General tab, click the appropriate speed for your modem in the "Maximum Port Speed" list. For a 56K modem, this setting should be 115,200.

Optimize Subnetting Flexibility with RFC 1219

When planning out your IP addressing scheme, be sure to use the rightmost digits for the host ID's first. In this way, you leave the leftmost digits of the Host ID portion of the IP address as zero, which makes them available to use for subnetting if you need to subnet, or to further subnet your network in the future.

RFC 1219, "On the Assignment of Subnet Numbers," provides recommendations on how to assign IP addresses by assigning Host IDs only by using the rightmost portions of the IP address. This provides the administrator the most flexibility when planning for future growth of the organization.

Let's look at a simple example. You are using network ID 192.168.1.0 and at the time, you have not subnetted the network, because there are only 12 computers on the network. However, you do imagine that the time will come when you will need to subnet because the company is a dynamic one, and you don't want all 254 computers on the same segment.

When numbering the computers, do not use the three leftmost bits. In this way, you can number computers using the rightmost five bits without worrying about subnetting. When you get to Host ID 31 (which will require six bits) you come to a decision point: Should you start subnetting your network now? If you decide to subnet the network, you can use those three bits to create a subnet mask of 255.255.255.224, which will allow you to keep the IP addresses you already have in use and not need to change any of them. This arrangement allows you to create six subnets with 30 hosts each.

If you decide that you don't want to subnet at the time, you can continue using the rightmost six bits to number the clients. When you reach Host ID 62 you will have used up all six bits, and you reach another decision point. You have the two leftmost bits free to use for a subnet mask of 255.255.255.192 that allows for two subnets with 62 hosts each. If you don't choose to subnet at this point, then you could just go ahead and use all the bits in the last octet for host IDs.

The point is that you are able to keep your options open when you number your clients by using the rightmost bits first when assigning host IDs to the computers on your network. Many administrators without a good understanding of TCP/IP will just "randomly" assign host IDs to the computers on their network, and in the process, lock themselves into a situation where they may need to completely renumber all the clients on the network in order to subnet. By using the recommended procedure here, you never have to renumber the clients!

Correct Settings for IDE DMA

The introduction of the Intel 430FX Pentium chipset a few years ago added the capability of DMA hard drive data transfers. DMA, or Direct Memory Access, is able to increase the overall responsiveness of a system by limiting the involvement of the CPU in the data transfer. Though CPU efficiency is a desired trait, there are instances in which it is not desirable.

When using a hard drive, it is recommended that the DMA feature be enabled. The setting is found by right-clicking on "My Computer" and selecting "Properties." Once the "System Properties" sheet appears, select the "Hardware" tab. On the "Hardware" tab, click the "Device Manager" button. The device manager is a configuration tool that most administrators should be very familiar with. The settings that we will focus on are located within the IDE ATA/ATAPI Controllers branch of the tree shown in the figure below. Each channel will be shown separately, and the two devices on the channel are controllable independently of one another. Though having disparity of speeds on a given IDE channel is possible, it is not recommended. Several timeout issues and transfer problems result from devices operating under different parameters on the same bus, or channel (See Figure A.4).

In order to achieve the best performance, ensure that DMA is enabled on all hard drives. The exception would be if a non-hard drive device were on the same bus. Since the configurations are numerous, consult the secondary device's documentation.

Most CD-ROM and DVD-ROM drives support DMA to assist data transfer from the device to memory. DVD-ROM drives will definitely want DMA enabled, as the data transfer rate for DVD-ROM drives is

Figure A.4 Settings under IDE ATA/ATAPI controllers.

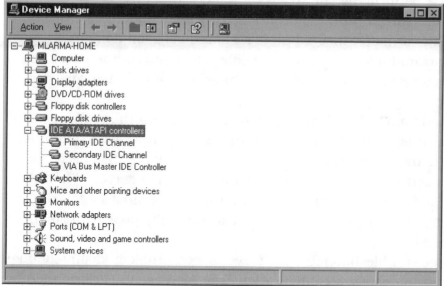

considerably higher than that of a typical CD. Another reason for DMA on the DVD-ROM drive is that when a DVD movie or other video is played, data must flow very quickly and efficiently due to the great involvement of the CPU in the decoding process on most computers.

The exception to the rule is the CD-R or CD-recordable device. The CPU must be very involved in the writing process, including the flow of data. When DMA is enabled on a CD-R device, the recording may fail, with an error related to the buffer on the CD-R drive becoming empty during the writing phase. The empty buffer results in blank data being written, as the laser does not turn off during the writing of a given track. Unless your documentation specifies a different setting, please verify that DMA is disabled and PIO mode is selected for the CD recording device.

Network Speed and Duplex Settings

Most users have seen the options on a network card to configure speed and duplex, but most are unaware of the effects of a duplex mismatch. Even if the speed is correct, a duplex mismatch can decrease performance in excess of 50 percent.

When using a hub, the duplex setting used should be either automatic or half. Since a hub is a shared collision domain, full duplex communication is not possible. The result of the mismatch will appear as excessive collisions either on the hub, network card, or both.

When your network connection is to a switch that supports full duplex, it is recommended to consult with your network administrator to determine the proper setting. Many force the speed and duplex settings, especially when connecting to a server. When the speed and duplex are forced, the network card must match the settings, or a failure to connect or exceptionally poor performance will result.

When troubleshooting a file server speed problem, definitely take a look at the network configuration. The increase in performance can be very dramatic if a mismatch is present and could even prevent the unnecessary expenditure on networking equipment or a server upgrade.

Index

The Global Knowledge Advantage

Global Knowledge has a global delivery system for its products and services. The company has 28 subsidiaries, and offers its programs through a total of 60+ locations. No other vendor can provide consistent services across a geographic area this large. Global Knowledge is the largest independent information technology education provider, offering programs on a variety of platforms. This enables our multi-platform and multi-national customers to obtain all of their programs from a single vendor. The company has developed the unique CompetusTM Framework software tool and methodology which can quickly reconfigure courseware to the proficiency level of a student on an interactive basis. Combined with self-paced and on-line programs, this technology can reduce the time required for training by prescribing content in only the deficient skills areas. The company has fully automated every aspect of the education process, from registration and follow-up, to "just-in-time" production of courseware. Global Knowledge through its Enterprise Services Consultancy, can customize programs and products to suit the needs of an individual customer.

Global Knowledge Classroom Education Programs

The backbone of our delivery options is classroom-based education. Our modern, well-equipped facilities staffed with the finest instructors offer programs in a wide variety of information technology topics, many of which lead to professional certifications.

Custom Learning Solutions

This delivery option has been created for companies and governments that value customized learning solutions. For them, our consultancy-based approach of developing targeted education solutions is most effective at helping them meet specific objectives.

Self-Paced and Multimedia Products

This delivery option offers self-paced program titles in interactive CD-ROM, videotape and audio tape programs. In addition, we offer custom development of interactive multimedia courseware to customers and partners. Call us at 1-888-427-4228.

Electronic Delivery of Training

Our network-based training service delivers efficient competency-based, interactive training via the World Wide Web and organizational intranets. This leading-edge delivery option provides a custom learning path and "just-in-time" training for maximum convenience to students.

Global Knowledge Courses Available

Microsoft
- Windows 2000 Deployment Strategies
- Introduction to Directory Services
- Windows 2000 Client Administration
- Windows 2000 Server
- Windows 2000 Update
- MCSE Bootcamp
- Microsoft Networking Essentials
- Windows NT 4.0 Workstation
- Windows NT 4.0 Server
- Windows NT Troubleshooting
- Windows NT 4.0 Security
- Windows 2000 Security
- Introduction to Microsoft Web Tools

Management Skills
- Project Management for IT Professionals
- Microsoft Project Workshop
- Management Skills for IT Professionals

Network Fundamentals
- Understanding Computer Networks
- Telecommunications Fundamentals I
- Telecommunications Fundamentals II
- Understanding Networking Fundamentals
- Upgrading and Repairing PCs
- DOS/Windows A+ Preparation
- Network Cabling Systems

WAN Networking and Telephony
- Building Broadband Networks
- Frame Relay Internetworking
- Converging Voice and Data Networks
- Introduction to Voice Over IP
- Understanding Digital Subscriber Line (xDSL)

Internetworking
- ATM Essentials
- ATM Internetworking
- ATM Troubleshooting
- Understanding Networking Protocols
- Internetworking Routers and Switches
- Network Troubleshooting
- Internetworking with TCP/IP
- Troubleshooting TCP/IP Networks
- Network Management
- Network Security Administration
- Virtual Private Networks
- Storage Area Networks
- Cisco OSPF Design and Configuration
- Cisco Border Gateway Protocol (BGP) Configuration

Web Site Management and Development
- Advanced Web Site Design
- Introduction to XML
- Building a Web Site
- Introduction to JavaScript
- Web Development Fundamentals
- Introduction to Web Databases

PERL, UNIX, and Linux
- PERL Scripting
- PERL with CGI for the Web
- UNIX Level I
- UNIX Level II
- Introduction to Linux for New Users
- Linux Installation, Configuration, and Maintenance

Authorized Vendor Training
Red Hat
- Introduction to Red Hat Linux
- Red Hat Linux Systems Administration
- Red Hat Linux Network and Security Administration
- RHCE Rapid Track Certification

Cisco Systems
- Interconnecting Cisco Network Devices
- Advanced Cisco Router Configuration
- Installation and Maintenance of Cisco Routers
- Cisco Internetwork Troubleshooting
- Designing Cisco Networks
- Cisco Internetwork Design
- Configuring Cisco Catalyst Switches
- Cisco Campus ATM Solutions
- Cisco Voice Over Frame Relay, ATM, and IP
- Configuring for Selsius IP Phones
- Building Cisco Remote Access Networks
- Managing Cisco Network Security
- Cisco Enterprise Management Solutions

Nortel Networks
- Nortel Networks Accelerated Router Configuration
- Nortel Networks Advanced IP Routing
- Nortel Networks WAN Protocols
- Nortel Networks Frame Switching
- Nortel Networks Accelar 1000
- Comprehensive Configuration
- Nortel Networks Centillion Switching
- Network Management with Optivity for Windows

Oracle Training
- Introduction to Oracle8 and PL/SQL
- Oracle8 Database Administration

Custom Corporate Network Training

Train on Cutting Edge Technology

We can bring the best in skill-based training to your facility to create a real-world hands-on training experience. Global Knowledge has invested millions of dollars in network hardware and software to train our students on the same equipment they will work with on the job. Our relationships with vendors allow us to incorporate the latest equipment and platforms into your on-site labs.

Maximize Your Training Budget

Global Knowledge provides experienced instructors, comprehensive course materials, and all the networking equipment needed to deliver high quality training. You provide the students; we provide the knowledge.

Avoid Travel Expenses

On-site courses allow you to schedule technical training at your convenience, saving time, expense, and the opportunity cost of travel away from the workplace.

Discuss Confidential Topics

Private on-site training permits the open discussion of sensitive issues such as security, access, and network design. We can work with your existing network's proprietary files while demonstrating the latest technologies.

Customize Course Content

Global Knowledge can tailor your courses to include the technologies and the topics which have the greatest impact on your business. We can complement your internal training efforts or provide a total solution to your training needs.

Corporate Pass

The Corporate Pass Discount Program rewards our best network training customers with preferred pricing on public courses, discounts on multimedia training packages, and an array of career planning services.

Global Knowledge Training Lifecycle

Supporting the Dynamic and Specialized Training Requirements of Information Technology Professionals

- Define Profile
- Assess Skills
- Design Training
- Deliver Training
- Test Knowledge
- Update Profile
- Use New Skills

Global Knowledge

Global Knowledge programs are developed and presented by industry professionals with "real-world" experience. Designed to help professionals meet today's interconnectivity and interoperability challenges, most of our programs feature hands-on labs that incorporate state-of-the-art communication components and equipment.

ON-SITE TEAM TRAINING

Bring Global Knowledge's powerful training programs to your company. At Global Knowledge, we will custom design courses to meet your specific network requirements. Call (919)-461-8686 for more information.

YOUR GUARANTEE

Global Knowledge believes its courses offer the best possible training in this field. If during the first day you are not satisfied and wish to withdraw from the course, simply notify the instructor, return all course materials and receive a 100% refund.

REGISTRATION INFORMATION

In the US:
call: (888) 762–4442
fax: (919) 469–7070
visit our website:
www.globalknowledge.com